NORTHUMBERLAND COUNTY LIBRARY

Please return this book on or before the last date stamped below unless an extension of the loan period is granted.

Application for renewal may be made by letter or telephone.

Fines at the approved rate will be charged when a book is overdue.

Books are to be returned on or before the last date below.

THE
DOG'S
HEALTH
FROM A TO Z
A CANINE VETERINARY DICTIONARY

**John Bleby
& Gerald Bishop**

David & Charles

To all our canine friends

A DAVID & CHARLES BOOK

Illustrations by G. Ronald Smith

First published in the UK in 1986

Revised paperback edition published 2003

Text and illustrations copyright © John Bleby and Gerald Bishop 1986, 2003

Distributed in North America by F&W Publications, Inc.
4700 E. Galbraith Rd. Cincinnati, OH 45236
1-800-289-0963

A catalogue record for this book is available from the British Library

ISBN 0 7153 1591 9

Typeset by Westkey Limited, Falmouth, Cornwall

Printed in Great Britain
by Antony Rowe Limited, Wiltshire
for David & Charles Publishers plc
Brunel House, Newton Abbot, Devon

CONTENTS

Acknowledgements   4

Introduction   5

THE DICTIONARY   7

Useful Addresses   287

Further Reading   288

ACKNOWLEDGEMENTS

We would like to thank all who have helped and encouraged us in the production of this book – including our families. During the writing of the first edition we were especially grateful to Dr A O Betts, MA, PhD, BSc, MRCVS, Principal and Dean of the Royal Veterinary College, University of London, for allowing use of the library and for other assistance.

We would also like to thank Dr Andrew Edney, MA, DVetMed, MRCVS for further reading suggestions on canine nutrition, Jo Fairley BSc of the Rowe Veterinary Group, Gloucestershire, for assistance with information on veterinary nursing and other details, and Clarissa Baldwin of NCDL for her help with information on aspects of dog welfare.

To G Roland Smith we offer our gratitude for tireless enthusiasm and thorough detail to the point of perfection in the production of drawings for this and the earlier edition.

Although every effort has been made to eliminate and correct errors any that have slipped through are entirely the responsibility of the authors.

Finally our sincere thanks to Judy, Bruce, Chloe, Khan, Gipsy, Joanna, Claret, Bramble, Megan, Suzi, Abi and all other canine contributors living and departed who, knowingly or unwittingly, provided knowledge to be used in this book, which we hope will benefit many others of their kind – and their human companions – in the years to come.

INTRODUCTION

Good health is the most desirable condition of life. Healthy dogs are happier and more active; they are less worry to their owners, and they make the very best companions or working animals. It should, therefore, be the most sensible and altruistic aim of all dog owners and breeders alike to ensure optimum health for dogs in their care.

While illness sometimes strikes the unwary and disease may attack when it is difficult to find a reason, there are very many cases of ill health which can be cured, avoided or entirely prevented. Often a cure can only be effected if the disease is detected early; frequently an unhealthy condition can be prevented from worsening by timely treatment, and, more frequently still, illness or accident can be prevented from happening. Correct care and a continuing watchfulness for the first signs of ill-health in all its forms, coupled with an understanding of the dog itself, will usually save it from unnecessary suffering and will provide it with the best chances of survival in serious situations.

In writing this book we have been aware of the shortcomings in terms of general knowledge about the dog and its health. While many owners realise that a sick dog requires treatment, not much is at hand on how to *prevent* ill-health, accidents, injuries, mental discomfort and general unhappiness due to the dog being 'out of condition'. Secondly, there is a shortage of useful information on the basic anatomy and physiology of the dog (for both owner and breeder) in comprehensive but concise form, and in everyday language; there is little to tell the owner just 'how the dog works'. Nor is there much literature available on actual treatments in terms of the *combined* actions of veterinarian and dog owner and/or breeder. A sick dog may be taken to a veterinarian and treated by the veterinarian – in some cases without the owner really knowing what is wrong with the dog or how best to cope with its sickness either on a long- or short-term basis.

We have done our best not only to bridge the gap between dog owner (and/or breeder) and veterinarian, but also to include useful information about canine health care in general. We have tried to produce a work which is specifically designed for the dog owner and breeder, and we hope it will give a detailed insight into the dog and its needs in order to ensure as far as possible that its life from conception to the autumn of its days is as happy and as healthy as it can be.

Sadly, millions of dogs are destroyed by one or another means each year. While some are old and incurable, the vast majority are young, fit and eagerly awaiting the happy life they will never have. Many are destined to be destroyed because their owners have taken them on without sufficient knowledge and understanding to fully accept their own responsibilities. Frequently, through intolerance, ignorance, careless neglect or merely 'waiting to see if it will get better', a dog will die or become seriously ill. More often still, an owner will be surprised by the demanding nature of the dog which, like a child, is constantly in need of care. Some people may aptly be described as temporary owners, having taken a dog into their family with little regard for its future, regarding it as an interesting 'toy'. The dogs of such owners are condemned to suffering of one sort or another, although the owner may not intend this, and at best the quality of their lives will be far less than they deserve. It is hoped that this book will also help to remedy these shortcomings.

We have laid emphasis not only on how the dog 'works', but also on how it behaves (and how that behaviour may be significant in health matters); on how to prevent ill-health, accident and disease wherever possible; how to set about restoring a dog safely to optimum health should sickness overtake it; how to speed its recovery; how to maintain it in good health and how to provide the requirements (many of which are unique to the dog) for a happy, healthy, full and long life.

The saying 'prevention is better than cure' is a wise one and preventive medicine is a subject which requires careful attention. While disease itself can often be prevented from attacking, accidents and injuries can also be forestalled if those who carry the responsibility for the dog are aware of potential dangers and how to circumvent them. We have therefore included guidance on preventive medicine in large doses where applicable while, hopefully, not neglecting cures and treatments.

Before a dog owner or breeder can hope to maintain a dog in the best of health there must be an adequate understanding of diet and nutrition, exercise and grooming, training and play. If a sick dog is to recover effectively with the absolute minimum of suffering, a knowledge of symptoms and diagnosis is important and, if recovery is to be given the best chance, a sound approach to nursing is needed. If breeding is to be undertaken, details must be absorbed on all aspects from mating to whelping and puppy care. Such information is to be found among these pages. It is our hope that this book will be thoroughly read as well as used as a reference dictionary. We have cross-referenced wherever possible, and an unexplained word in an entry can usually be found in the main sequence of entries so that the reader can build up a comprehensive picture of any one or more subjects and link them with other aspects of health.

The dog, *Canis familiaris*, is the only animal to submit itself willingly to domestication by man. It has been 'man's best friend' for over 10,000 years and in that time a plethora of breeds and mongrel mutations have emerged, changed and re-formed. The dog's loyalty, dependence, affection and total trust in man, however, has never changed. The very least we owe these faithful creatures is the best of health care during their lives with us.

This book is intended for the benefit of the dog. While we are blessed with the ability to read and fend for ourselves in a rather harsh environment, our canine friends have no literary capabilities and by and large have lost their ability to survive in the environment man has built for himself. They must, therefore, rely upon us to interpret their needs and act upon knowledge, advice and information concerning their welfare. While we stress the vital role played by the owner in preventing disease, combating illness and maintaining good health, there should never be a delay in seeking veterinary advice. It is best for the dog – and frequently cheaper – to obtain this advice as early as possible.

It is our sincere hope that the readers who accept responsibility for a dog will also safeguard its health and welfare throughout its lifetime. We hope that this book will be of help, but ultimately it is you, the reader, who will decide.

GERALD BISHOP
JOHN BLEBY

THE DICTIONARY

abdomen

The area extending from the diaphragm at the lower portion of the chest or thorax down to the pelvis or hips. It contains the stomach, liver, spleen, pancreas, kidneys, adrenal glands, bladder, omentum and intestine.

The exact positioning of the abdominal organs in the abdominal cavity varies slightly with the different breeds but the stomach is situated behind the liver at the top of the cavity, with the spleen on the left side above the left kidney and the pancreas high up on the right side. On the right of the spleen the intestines begin, coiled in and across the cavity and ending at the rectum. The positioning of the organs also varies a little depending upon whether the stomach is full or empty.

The abdominal cavity contains varying amounts of fat related to the dog's state of health and degree of obesity. In the bitch the abdominal cavity also contains the uterus and ovaries. It should be noted that the commonest cause of abdominal swelling in the bitch is pregnancy.

abdomen, injuries of

These are most commonly caused by accidents such as collision with a vehicle on the road, by jumping over railings or barbed-wire fences, dog fights or a kick by a human or horse. In all cases examination by a veterinarian, for obvious injuries or for the detection of obscured internal complications, should be made so that appropriate treatment can be prescribed without delay.

If there is protrusion of abdominal contents the dog should be restrained on its back if possible and warm clean cloths, soaked in a saline solution (see entry) and wrung out, applied and bound firmly in place prior to the arrival of the veterinarian. The dog should also be treated for shock. (See also wounds.)

abortion

A miscarriage during pregnancy. Natural abortions are uncommon in healthy bitches. A sound diet and steady exercise are the best safeguards. Brucellosis, herpes virus and toxoplasmosis infections are likely to cause abortion. Violence is another possible cause.

A bitch may be aborted deliberately if a misalliance has occurred and this can be carried out by a veterinary surgeon, if possible within about forty-eight hours of mating – it is preferable to a litter of unwanted puppies and should be done if the bitch is not in good health or recovering from surgery. (See also breeding.)

abrasion

A graze caused by scraping or rubbing against a hard surface or by a glancing blow – a superficial wound with the loss of upper skin layers only. It is none the less painful and can become contaminated or infected it left untreated.

Generally, abrasions should be left uncovered after first being cleansed thoroughly with a warm saline solution (see entry) or acriflavine in weak solution. The dog may thereafter lick the site and keep it clean, though continual licking slows the healing process. Inspect the wound two or three times a day to ensure that there is no increasing inflammation or tenderness and keep it clean and dry while the new layers of skin are regenerated. (See also wounds.)

abrasion

An abscess is an enclosed collection of pus. It may be internal, external, acute or chronic. It is accompanied by a throbbing pain, inflammation and swelling and sometimes a slight fever. It is caused in the acute state by an irritant in the tissues or, more frequently, by a bacterial infection. Chronic abscesses are less painful generally and can be caused by bacterial infection or by a subsiding acute abscess.

abscess

Veterinary treatment consists mainly of the prescription of antibiotics to combat infection and the application of fairly hot fomentations such as salt water to relieve pain. Surgery is sometimes necessary but this will depend on the response to antibiotic treatment and the site of the abscess.

Maximum vigilance and an understanding of your dog's reactions in certain situations will help to minimise accidents. The home, the road and exercise areas are all potentially hazardous sites.

accidents

In the home, all sensible precautions should be taken. Keep harmful solutions, poisons, cleaning fluids, matches, for example, well out of a dog's reach – and especially away from puppies which, of course, are much more accident-prone than the average adult dog. Keep your dog out of the way in the kitchen when serving hot foods, boiling water or opening the oven. Keep children's toys away from puppies, and keep small objects which may be dangerous playthings away from dogs of all ages. Bones, such as chop or chicken, should not be left where a dog will steal them, risking potential choking, and household rubbish should be safely shut away in a dustbin.

On the road, a dog, however well trained, should always be on a lead if traffic is likely to be around. A sudden distraction, like a cat or a bird flitting across a dog's vision may well cause it to forget its training for a fraction of a second – just long enough to send it under the wheels of a fast-moving car. Even a well-trained dog will not always respond ideally in a dangerous situation; it may panic and charge into the road.

Dog fights can also occur – always keep an eye on your dog and call it to heel if it is either nervous or aggressive towards other dogs. Even if it is neither, it could become the victim of an aggressor on a walk. Dogs rarely fight with bitches (though it has been known) but two dogs or two bitches in an encounter just may not hit it off. Bitches in season should not be walked along streets if possible as their scent attracts roaming dogs which can cause accidents.

A grim and ever-present hazard in almost any area, but particularly in urban districts, is broken glass. Glass shards can cripple or even kill a dog. If your dog is unfortunate enough to be cut, the wound should be carefully bathed in a warm saline solution (see entry), or weak antiseptic solution and the dog taken to the veterinarian as soon as possible.

accidents | Frozen ponds and lakes can be potentially dangerous. A dog may catch sight of a duck or coot sitting on the edge of the water and take off after it. The thinner ice in the centre of the pond may take the weight of the bird but is unlikely to bear a pursuing dog. If the dog falls into the freezing water and is not rescued somehow within minutes, or even seconds, it may slip under the ice and drown very quickly.

The number and variety of accidents that can happen are legion but a little care, understanding of your dog and its reactions, awareness and thinking ahead will do much to prevent most of them. Treatment for non-fatal accidents is described under various headings throughout this book. (See especially artificial respiration; burns and scalds; choking; concussion; drowning; first aid; fractures; poisoning; shock; wounds.)

acetylcholine | A naturally-occurring link in the transmission of nerve impulses to muscles. It is produced around the nerve endings and, when shock or severe pain occurs through injury, production may cease, resulting in paralysis. In such situations, administration of acetylcholine by injection will help restore the transmission.

acid poisoning | See poisoning.

acriflavine | An orange or red crystalline powder which, when diluted one part in one thousand in distilled or boiled water, serves as an effective antiseptic for bathing wounds, cuts and abrasions.

actinomycosis | A rare disease in dogs but found more often in cattle. Symptomised by a swelling in bones, such as the jaw, and other tissue, such as that of the pharynx or cheek. Infection, by the so-called 'ray fungus' (bacterium *Actinomyces bovis*) is through injury and can be transmitted to man. It is treated by antibiotics, including penicillin and streptomycin.

acupuncture | Originating in China, where it has been used for centuries, this method of treatment to relieve pain involves the insertion of needles at precisely-determined points. It can also be used for anaesthesia. Acupuncture is an exact skill and can only be carried out by fully trained people. Veterinarians in the West are showing increased interest in acupuncture as an alternative method of treating certain clinical conditions in the dog.

acute | Sharp, severe; in disease, meaning 'of sudden onset'.

adenoma | A tumour which, microscopically, appears to be glandular tissue. It may originally be benign and subsequently become malignant. (See also tumour.)

adhesion | An abnormal sticking together of membranes or organs, usually following inflammation. The fluid which arises from inflammation originates in blood and contains fibrin which forms a fibrous or connective tissue. Adhesions can form, for example, in joints, lungs, vagina, or in the abdominal cavity. Surgery is often performed to correct the condition. Administration of antibiotics and anti-inflammatory agents to reduce the original inflammation and attack the problem at its source may help to prevent adhesions although they can still form following acute as well as chronic inflammation.

adhesion

This is a fatty tissue consisting of fat globules formed in expanding cells within a network of fibrous or connective tissue. It collects and is stored between muscles when food intake is surplus to the body's requirements. While it serves both as a food store and an insulator it also contributes towards making a dog fat. It is used up during energetic muscular exercise, if and when food intake drops below normal needs, and sometimes during a disease which saps the patient's strength. The fat content of the cells is then absorbed into the blood. (See also obesity.)

adipose tissue

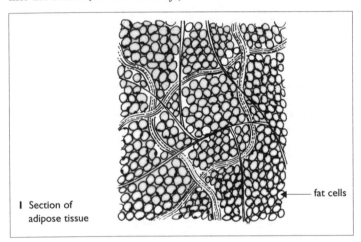

fat cells

I Section of
adipose tissue

Surgical removal of the adrenal glands, such as in the treatment of Cushing's disease. Without the administration of hormones following the operation, the dog's life could be in danger, particularly from stress and infection.

adrenalectomy

The adrenals are also known as the suprarenal glands, meaning 'above the kidney', one being situated over each kidney. Each adrenal has an inner, or medullary, region and an outer cortex; these are structurally and functionally different, though both secrete important hormones. The medulla secretes adrenaline and noradrenaline, and the cortex releases steroids or corticosteroids. An increased or decreased medullary activity can produce stress. (See also endocrine system; glands.)

adrenal glands

The release of the hormone adrenaline, secreted by the medullary region of the adrenal glands, prepares the dog's organs for physical effort such as may be expected in fear-produced flight, defence or

adrenaline

adrenaline

attack mechanisms, or boisterous play. The release is stimulated by sympathetic nerves and results in the temporary diversion of blood from the skin and digestive areas to the muscles. It also increases the action of the heart, raises blood pressure and releases glucose for energy from the liver into the bloodstream.

Adrenaline can be administered in cases of shock or collapse, for example, as a means of raising dangerously low blood pressure. (See also nervous system.)

aerosol

A solution dispersed as a mist or fog, usually from a canister. Home aerosols such as hair sprays, air fresheners, oven cleaners, clothing and deodorant sprays, insecticides, furniture polish, etc, can be harmful to dogs when dispersed in the air, and are certainly dangerous when discharged directly at or near the animal.

When breathed in, the fine mist and the chemicals it contains can produce harmful effects on the dog's respiratory system. It will also adversely affect the coat and damage the eyes.

Viruses can sometimes be transmitted from one dog to another by aerosols created, for example, by sneezing.

afterbirth

See placenta.

age

Approximate canine/human age equivalents

Canine age (years)	Human age (years)	Canine age (years)	Human age (years)
1	13	11	61
2	21	12	66
3	25	13	70
4	28	14	76
5	34	15	80
6	38	16	84
7	41	17	91
8	46	18	94
9	51	19	99
10	56	20	103

aged dogs

A dog is generally considered to be aged from about ten years old, although some may live for seventeen or even nineteen years. There is no reason why a dog should not be kept alive as long as it is in good mental and physical health. However, if it is very ill and in pain then the question of euthanasia should sensibly be considered. Extra care of the old, or geriatric, dog should prolong its life happily, and is important.

Diet needs to be adjusted gradually as the dog becomes older, with two or even three small meals fed in a day rather than one large one. This helps the digestive system as it becomes more sluggish. However, most dogs have established dietary preferences and their favourite foods offered regularly make them more likely to retain a good appetite and an interest in their meals in old age. Honey, egg custard, and milk in small quantities, together with a vitamin supplement, make useful additives. Small doses of cod-liver oil in winter are an effective insulator against the cold.

Hypothermia, a common enough problem with humans in old age, also affects aged dogs and extra warmth may be needed on cold days in the form of an additional blanket or a warm, well-covered hot-water bottle in the dog basket. Thorough drying when an old dog gets wet is essential, and so are dry, draught-free quarters. Damp exacerbates arthritis, a fairly common complaint of elderly dogs, and kidney disorders. Special care must be taken during grooming (which should not be neglected) since skin is more tender and joints and muscles stiffer than in the younger dog. Check teeth regularly, having them scaled if and when necessary, and see the veterinarian if any are bad or painful and may require extraction.

Exercise should not be neglected so long as the dog can cope with it, but the dog should be allowed to make its own pace with interesting, if slower, walks on a regular basis.

Elderly bitches may be prone to gynaecological problems and should be examined often for any tenderness or small lumps in the abdominal region and around the nipples.

Deafness and impaired eyesight, which may occur in old age, should be recognised by the owner and allowances made, especially with safety in mind.

Occasionally old dogs suffer from urinary incontinence during the night; they cannot manage for long periods without passing urine. A few old newspapers placed near the door at bedtime assist, and ease the mind of a dog – which cannot help the lapses in its house training. A scolding in such cases is inappropriate and only makes the animal miserable.

In summary, make sure that an old dog has extra attention and is kept interested; make sure it is made to feel wanted, even if there is a younger dog in the house. These actions, together with those outlined above and regular veterinary checks, will help to keep a dog in good shape both mentally and physically through old age.

agglutination

The clumping together of red blood cells, bacteria, etc. This takes place when plasma of one animal incompatibly mixes with the red cells of another. The effect is caused by an antibody substance – agglutinin – present in the blood. Bacteria will agglutinate when an appropriate antiserum is added.

Tests based on the principle of agglutination are performed in the laboratory either to help in the identification of certain bacteria or as a safeguard in blood transfusions. In the latter case, a 'cross-match' is carried out to ensure that the donor's blood will not cause a reaction when transfused to that of the recipient.

aggressiveness

There are many root causes. It may be the result of fear: if a dog is often ill-treated, for example, it may show aggression as a form of self-defence. If it is tied or shut up in a house or shed for a long time on its own, it may become aggressive through boredom or anxiety. A tethered dog attacked by another dog responds very differently from a free animal and becomes increasingly belligerent.

aggressiveness

Protectiveness is another reason for aggression, though this is of a temporary nature; a bitch may be aggressively protective over her puppies, or a dog or bitch may be protective in the same manner over its owner, property or food. A certain amount of aggression can be of value, if for example an intruder enters your house, but it must not be allowed to get out of hand.

Jealousy can make even a mild-tempered dog aggressive. If a new baby or another dog is introduced into the household, handle the dog carefully to make sure that it does not feel its status has been reduced or your affection turned elsewhere.

Pain will naturally make a dog aggressive: take care in approaching and handling an injured animal, especially as it will almost certainly be frightened as well. Occasionally two dogs that have lived together for some time suddenly show resentment towards each other; this may be stronger in one than the other, with the less dominant becoming aggressive to the other in self-defence. This can be caused by over-possessiveness of owner or territory and is often cured by providing both dogs with more room to move around and more regular exercise.

Some breeds, such as dobermanns, rottweilers, German shepherds, etc, are of course by nature more aggressive than others – especially those most often used as guard dogs. They must be kept under strict control.

Provided aggression is not the result of heredity (dogs or bitches showing too much aggression should not be used for breeding), or does not suddenly appear as a change in temperament due to disease such as encephalitis or brain tumour, it can generally be prevented by sensible care and training.

A dog showing sudden aggression for no apparent reason should be examined by a veterinarian.

agranulocytosis

A lack of white cells or leucocytes in the blood. It may be found in dogs following treatment with a drug that depresses the activity of the bone marrow.

albino

A creature with congenital lack of pigment in hair, skin and eyes. A true albino has pink skin, white hair and pink irises in the eyes. This is often associated with weakness, sensitivity to sunlight, inferior vision and a lower resistance to infection. In dogs the condition is relatively rare.

albumin

A protein found in animal tissue which maintains the fluid content of the blood at its normal level. It also assists in the transportation of bilirubin, calcium and fats. It occurs in foods such as milk and eggs. Its presence in urine can be indicative of disease.

albuminuria

The presence of albumin in urine, indicative of early kidney inflammation and cystitis. A laboratory test will confirm.

alcohol

Ethyl and isopropyl alcohols are sometimes utilised as antiseptics in veterinary practice but are of more use as fat solvents in instrument cleaning, bench swabbing, etc, since their bactericidal activity is too slow and spores remain unaffected. As a stimulant, alcohol cannot be recommended either since its administration is usually followed by depression and dehydration.

alcohol

See poisoning.

alcohol poisoning

The digestive tract which runs from mouth to anus. From the mouth the alimentary tract or canal consists of pharynx, oesophagus, stomach, small intestine and large intestine (which, in order, comprises caecum, large colon, small colon and rectum). (See also digestion; intestines.)

alimentary tract

An acid neutraliser. Some alkalis are corrosive and poisonous, such as ammonia, caustic soda and caustic potash – floor cleaners, drain cleaners, soil treatments, etc. Others, such as sodium bicarbonate, are used as antacid treatments to neutralise acidity. (See also poisoning.)

alkali

Organic substance derived from plants. Alkaloids named as drugs usually have the suffix 'me' or 'in' – such as morphine, atropine, digitalin, quinine, strychnine, codeine, etc. All alkaloids have a strong physiological action; some are medicinal, others poisonous.

alkaloid

Component of the foetal membrane, partly extending through the foetal abdomen via the umbilicus and partly remaining in the foetal abdomen to form the urinary bladder. (See also foetus; placenta.)

allantois

Also known as allelomorphs, these are genes which influence the inherited character of the body such as size, coat colour, etc.

alleles

The causative substance of an allergy.

allergen

Eczema (inflammation of the skin) produced as an allergic reaction.

allergic dermatitis

A specific sensitivity by the body to an allergen. The substance which causes the allergic reaction may be in contact with the dog, inhaled, drunk or eaten. An allergy is a misapplication of the body's immunity system, ie a provocation of the infection defence mechanism when there is no hazard to fight.

allergy

Some dogs are allergic to fleas and other parasites, or to such foodstuffs as cow's milk, eggs, pork and some fish; others to pollens, certain antibiotics, hormone treatments or stings from insects such as wasps or bees. They can also be allergic to contact with bedding or carpet materials, rubber products, household sprays and cleaning fluids in the air.

Some breeds, such as West Highlands, retrievers, smooth-haired fox terriers and pointers, appear to be more liable to allergic reactions than others and symptoms include a rash, itching, redness and sometimes swelling and eczema, producing a local reaction which the dog worries and chews causing an exacerbation of the *allergy*   problem. Sneezing and weeping eyes are other signs usually associated with pollen allergies.

Treatment consists of first attempting to track down the cause of the allergy and if possible removing it from contact with the dog. This can sometimes be a lengthy procedure and meanwhile the dog requires remedial treatment which usually consists of antihistamines and preparations containing various mixtures of calamine, coal tar and sulphur applied locally. Since a vitamin deficiency can also be contributory to weakness in a dog with an allergy, a vitamin food supplement often helps. Fitting an 'Elizabethan' collar (see entry) or plastic bucket sometimes helps the local areas to heal during treatment without the dog continually licking and worrying them. (See also eczema.)

alopecia   Baldness, loss of hair due to a nutritional deficiency, selenium poisoning or, more frequently, a hormone imbalance such as a reduced level of iodine or of thyroxine from the thyroid gland. It also appears in Cushing's disease, tumour of the testis and, again due to hormone imbalance, in some male dogs older than five years which become attracted to other males. In this latter condition castration is sometimes an effective remedy, though in most other cases hormone therapy to correct the imbalance of hormones is the treatment.

alum   A white powder or colourless crystals used in dilute form (about a teaspoonful in 300ml (½pt) of boiled water) as an astringent.

alveoli   Small cavities – air sacs in lungs where oxygen enters and carbon dioxide leaves the blood. The term is also used for tooth sockets.

amino acids   There are about twenty amino acids which act as 'building blocks' to compose proteins needed in tissue production. Dogs need dietary protein in variety to ensure a healthy life. Most high-class dog foods commercially available contain a balanced protein content.

Whole eggs are a good source of the amino acids needed by the dog (histidine, isoleucine, leucine, lysine, methionine, phenylalanine, threonine, tryptophan and valine). (See also diet; feeding; nutrition.)

amnion   An 'envelope' or foetal membrane which contains the amniotic fluid in which the foetus floats. It helps to dilate the cervix during whelping and forms part of the 'bag of water' which breaks just before birth to release the fluid which helps to lubricate the birth canal or passage the pups take into the outside world. (See also whelping.)

ampicillin   Active synthetic penicillin which can be administered orally or by injection and is effective against a wider range of infections than penicillin, though resistance is common. Useful in treatment of pneumonia and some skin diseases. (See also antibiotics.)

The surgical or accidental removal of a limb. Nowadays canine amputations are relatively rare. Although a dog can manage on three legs, it is still important that the effects of violent accidents should be treated quickly by a veterinarian to prevent the need for subsequent amputations due to gangrene arising from compound fractures or other wounds which become infected. (See also prosthesis.)

amputation

A deficiency of red blood cells or of haemoglobin. The condition can become serious if not treated. It may be due to a defect in the production of blood cells and/or haemoglobin from a dietary deficiency, eg lack of iron, copper, cobalt (a component of vitamin B_{12}) or vitamin B_6. It can also arise due to haemorrhage or chronic blood losses, perhaps due to tumours or gradual internal bleeding. Stress, which inhibits the production of blood cells, and parasites are also causes of anaemia.

anaemia

Symptoms of anaemia include weakness and fatigue, pale visible mucous membranes such as eyelids, gums etc, a pounding heart when excited, staring coat, reduced appetite and, later, emaciation.

Treatment consists of first tracing the cause of the condition and effecting the appropriate remedy. Good, nutritional food is a prevention as well as a cure, with plenty of fresh air. Liver extract or vitamin B_{12} also help and, if there is a deficiency of other dietary components, these can be administered. It is worth noting, however, that an excess of iron or copper – or of vitamin K in young dogs – can also cause illness, so careful monitoring is needed in dosing dogs in this way. Early attention by a veterinarian to any internal bleeding is essential and, if the cause is either internal or external parasites, steps should be taken to eliminate these without delay. (See also blood; diet; feeding; nutrition; parasites.)

Loss of sensation. Chloroform and ether were first used as anaesthetics in veterinary surgery in 1847. Chloroform causes toxicity in the dog, however, which makes it obsolete today, and ether, mixed with oxygen, is rarely used because it is highly explosive. Pentobarbitone and thiopentone are the most common injectable anaesthetic agents, whilst isoflurane is now the most popular gaseous anaesthetic agent for inducing general anaesthesia. Cocaine, procaine and lignocaine are amongst the most frequently used local anaesthetics.

anaesthesia

Anaesthetics work by limiting the supply of oxygen to the tissues. A *general* anaesthetic first affects nervous tissue, which requires the highest levels of oxygen, and causes total loss of consciousness; it is given in major operations. *Local* anaesthetics cause a loss of sensation in a localised area and are used in minor work such as wound suturing or removal of a small external tumour. Some eye and ear drops and lotions may contain some local anaesthetic to prevent pain or irritation. Prolonged use, however, can cause poisoning, symptomised by convulsions, collapse or vomiting.

A *regional* anaesthetic is sometimes administered to a nerve trunk in a fairly localised region of the body to provide a loss of sensation during examination of, for example, the uterus or rectum.

anaesthesia	*Surface* anaesthetics are also sometimes used to produce a localised 'freezing' sensation. These are in the form of highly volatile substances which are sprayed on to the selected area.
analgesic	A drug, such as aspirin or phenylbutazone, which removes or reduces pain levels without the patient losing consciousness. Although useful in such conditions as arthritis, analgesics do not effect a cure.
anal glands	Two glands, situated just below and one to each side of the anus, used for scentmarking and perhaps to provide lubrication for the passage of faeces through the anus. The duct openings can sometimes become obstructed by non-escaping secretions and become inflamed. The waste matter which collects causes irritation and often pain. The dog can be seen chasing its tail, often yelping when sitting down and dragging its tail end along the ground. This is often referred to as 'sledging'. The condition may be relieved by pressing a pad of lint or cotton wool against the anus and, by pressure of finger and thumb on either side of the anus, squeezing the matter out. Before attempting to express anal glands, owners should be shown how to do it by their veterinarian or a veterinary nurse, otherwise the glands could be damaged and the dog unnecessarily injured. If there is obvious pain, an abscess may have formed, in which case a visit to the veterinarian is essential so that the area can be drained and cleansed, and antibiotics administered.
anaphylaxis	A shock-producing sensitisation to a foreign protein administered through an injection or perhaps a sting, which can be fatal. While there may be no reaction on the first injection, a second injection may produce shock. Antihistamines are usually administered to counteract the shock and the reaction is noted so that, wherever possible, the situation can be avoided in the future.
anatomy	The study of form and structure of an animal. It includes the study of the minute structures of tissue and organs (histology). Surgery is applied anatomy, and medicine is applied physiology, which is an extension of anatomy. Knowledge of anatomy is based on dissection.
androgen	A male hormone influencing the growth and development of the male sex organs.
aneurysm	A bulge in the wall of an artery due to a weakness. It can be a hereditary defect, or caused by injury, violent muscular effort or disease, and is dangerous in that a rupture of the wall can occur, giving rise to serious internal bleeding and often death. Aneurysms can be present in the brain – sometimes causing a stroke – chest or abdomen. Surgery is usually necessary if the aneurysm is found and if the site allows it, when the blood flow may be diverted through other vessels to by-pass the defect if it cannot be repaired.

A tumour consisting of a collection of blood vessels, usually harmless and often a congenital malformation.

angioma

Vessel inflammation, eg of a blood vessel, bile duct, etc.

angitis

A term used to describe the presence of red blood cells of varying sizes and shapes. It is sometimes a symptom, with others, of anaemia or other blood disorders.

anisocytosis

A drug which relieves pain. (See also analgesic.)

anodyne

Loss of appetite

anorexia

A substance, such as sodium bicarbonate, which counteracts and neutralises the effects of excessive acid in the alimentary tract.

antacid

A forward position; in front of. The opposite of posterior.

anterior

Medicinal substance administered to destroy intestinal parasitic worms. It should be effective against worm eggs, immature and adult worms. Anthelmintics are usually given in tablet form; they are not unpalatable and can be ground up in the dog's food. Dosing every few months, especially where several dogs are kept together, is usually advisable and bitches should be 'wormed' after whelping. (See also parasites; worming procedures.)

anthelmintic

Diseases which can be transmitted from man to other animals. Those that can be passed on to the dog include tuberculosis, mumps, scarlet fever infection and tonsillitis.

anthroponoses

Powerful drugs either derived from living organisms or synthesised. Antibiotics have been available to human and veterinary medicine since 1941 and are used effectively to combat infection. They act by inhibiting an enzyme and obstructing a chemical reaction vital to the growth of the bacteria which forms the infection. Their use in veterinary medicine has been especially advantageous, for example, in treating septicaemia of wounds, abscesses and peritonitis where infection is strong and often deadly. Surgery, too, has been made safer by the development of antibiotics.

antibiotics

Penicillin, chloramphenicol and tetracycline are examples of frequently used antibiotics, all of which work in slightly different ways. Penicillin, for example, prevents formation of the bacterial cell wall while streptomycin stops the inner lining of the cell wall forming. Chloramphenicol and tetracycline disturb the protein manufacture within the bacteria. While there is increasing resistance to many antibiotics, there is still an effective range available to the veterinarian.

Selection of the antibiotic likely to be most effective against a specific infection is best done by laboratory sensitivity tests in which a specimen taken from the site of infection is matched against a range of antibiotics to detect the degree of sensitivity to each.

antibodies	Part of the body's system of immunity. They are formed in the lymphatic system and spleen, and distributed throughout the body in the serum and other body fluids. Antibodies, which take several days to form, are produced in response to infection, being released by the presence of an antigen, foreign protein, harmful bacteria or their toxins. They react with part of the infecting micro-organisms, rendering them inactive. Often an immunity to a second infection by the same micro-organism is produced in this way.
anticoagulant	An inhibitor of the blood-clotting mechanism which may be used, for example, in the treatment of coronary thrombosis, although over-dosing can cause internal bleeding. Heparin and sodium-citrate solutions are often used in laboratory tests to prevent blood samples from coagulating, and both heparin and dicoumarol are given for thrombosis treatment in humans.
anticonvulsant	A drug that relaxes muscular tissue and the nerves controlling the muscles. Anticonvulsants are used in the treatment of epilepsy and cramp and occasionally in premedication prior to the administration of an anaesthetic. Examples of anticonvulsants, or antispasmodics, are chlorpromazine, phenytoin, mysoline and phenobarbitone.
antidiarrhoeal	A medicine used to treat diarrhoea. Some forms combine an anti-biotic with kaolin, which can be given in tablet or liquid form.
antidote	A poison neutraliser. Administered in time, the appropriate anti-dote to a poison may save the dog's life – either by rendering the poison harmless by chemical action, or by stimulating the body's own reaction to it. (See also poisoning.)
antigen	A substance which stimulates the production of antibodies by its presence in various forms. Antigens are foreign to the host and usually protein in nature. (See also antibodies.)
antihaemorrhagic	An agent which is used to stop haemorrhage, particularly in cases of haemophilia.
antihistamine	A drug which is used to inhibit the action of histamine when an excess of it is being released by the tissues. It may, for example, be used for the treatment of shock in burns and scalds, and in allergy and urticaria. Antihistamine is also found in eosinophils in blood. Examples of such drugs prescribed by a veterinarian include corticosteriods and mepyramine maleate.
anti-inflammatory	Reducing inflammation. Agents include ice and cold water applied locally, and certain drugs. Inflammation, however, is a symptom of a more serious condition and it is the source of the problem which should be treated. (See also inflammation.)
antipruritic	An anti-itching agent, usually prescribed as an ointment or lotion to be applied at the site of the problem. (See also pruritis.)

A drug which reduces fever by lowering raised body temperature. Aspirin and quinine are two examples.   **antipyretic**

An agent that thwarts the growth of micro-organisms – a disinfectant actually kills them. Many solutions and proprietary products perform both functions, depending on their concentration or dilution. Antiseptics used for the cleansing of wounds should be particularly weak to prevent any tissue damage that will arrest the healing process.   **antiseptic**

Acriflavine is a commonly used antiseptic and very effective without causing tissue damage. Two generally available proprietaries are TCP (a chlorine compound) and Dettol (chloroxylenol) which, according to strength, can be used for both antiseptic and disinfecting purposes. Crystal violet and gentian violet are useful for fungal infections of the skin and sulphonamides are often prescribed for infected wounds.

One of the most useful antiseptics is the simplest – a solution of common salt in distilled water (about 0.85–0.9 per cent, or a teaspoonful of salt to half a pint of water). This saline solution is ideal for wound irrigation and bathing sore eyes, gums, etc. Never use iodine as it delays healing. (See also wounds.)

Produced by stimulating antibody production in a 'donor' animal by injecting harmless concentrations of the specific antigen. The resulting 'antiserum' containing suitable 'ready-made' antibodies is then transferred to another animal which requires temporary immunity or help in fighting a disease. Antisera are used both for treating a disease and for temporary protection against it. Diseases which may be treated in this way include tetanus and leptospirosis.   **antiserum**

See anticonvulsant.   **antispasmodic**

A substance that neutralises the action of bacterial poisons or toxins. Antitoxins are produced naturally in the body and can also be formed in antiserum.   **antitoxin**

A drug utilised against the action of viruses. For many years attempts to develop antiviral agents were unsuccessful but recently acyclovir and bromodioxyuridine have proved effective against the herpes simplex virus. Interferon has so far been disappointing as an antiviral agent.   **antiviral agent**

Absence or negligible passing of urine. The condition may be due to a kidney stone or other obstruction, or to a low fluid intake by the dog. It can also be caused by bladder or ureter damage.   **anuria**

End of the intestines and alimentary tract. It is normally closed by a sphincter muscle which opens when faeces are expelled. There are two anal glands situated just below and one to each side of the anus; these sometimes become impacted and infected. For anal fistula see fistula.   **anus**

aorta	The main artery of the body which commences at the bottom of the left ventricle of the heart and supplies oxygenated blood to the body. (See also artery; vascular system.)
apathy	A general loss of interest which accompanies a variety of disorders, including fever, foreign-body retention and many others. It is also sometimes evident in aged dogs and in dogs whose interest is not stimulated by owners, interesting walks and companionship.
apnoea	A stoppage of breathing which may be caused by an excess of administered oxygen or asphyxiation of puppies during birth. (See also asphyxia; whelping.)
appeasement	Behaviour which reduces or stops aggression by another. It happens between dogs when the possibilities of fight are limited and probably serves as a form of species protection. One dog, threatened by another, may roll over to expose its belly, or stand, head turned away, presenting its neck in what may indicate an expression of trust as well as submission. Some dogs are more submissive than others and are often threatened. Appeasement gestures can also be seen as greeting takes place when dogs allow themselves to be sniffed without reacting aggressively. (See also aggressiveness.)
appetite	A dog's appetite can tell an observant owner much about its state of health. Appetite, unlike hunger, is a pleasurable, conditioned response to thoughts or sight of food and a healthy dog normally has a healthy appetite. Some dogs, however, occasionally 'go off their food' for a day or two – which may not necessarily point to ailments. A good varied diet generally helps to keep a healthy dog interested in its food.
	Loss of appetite or inappetence accompanies the presence of foreign bodies in the alimentary tract, gastritis, gastroenteritis, colitis, dyspepsia and other ailments (including cancer, depression, stress, fevers, throat and mouth infections, and tuberculosis, to name but a few). Inappetence lasting more than two days or so is a 'barometer' indicating that something is wrong with a dog.
	Increase in appetite may indicate diabetes, internal parasites or early tumours. In puppies, excessive appetite is not unusual (but should be curbed by feeding only correct amounts of food related to age and weight) and not necessarily indicative of ill-health.
	A depraved appetite, ie one where the dog eats coal, rubbish or even faeces (coprophagia) may be due to a vitamin or mineral deficiency, boredom or hysteria. (See also coprophagia; diet; feeding; nutrition.)
aqueous humour	A watery fluid which fills the space in the eye between the lens and cornea. It bends light rays and helps to focus them on the retina. (See also eye; vitreous humour.)

A class of Arthropods of which the spider is probably the most well-known member. Also included in the class, however, are mites, causing mange, and ticks. (See also parasites.)

arachnida

A salt of an alkaloid (arecoline) found in the areca nut, seed of the betel-nut tree, which was used in the last century in powder form to expel tapeworms from dogs. Arecoline hydrobromide is used now to stimulate peristalsis and faeces evacuation. It should not be administered to a dog with a weak heart or where intestinal obstruction is suspected and should only be given under the supervision of a veterinarian.

arecoline hydrobromide

A term applied to an irregular heartbeat. Some dogs have this condition without any serious results but it may be an indication of heart disease. It can take the form of a fluttering movement, a missed beat or a quivering fibrillation. (See also tachycardia.)

arrhythmia

An irritant poison contained in weed-killers, rat bait, flypapers, some wallpaper, lead shot and sheep dip. Care should be taken to ensure that dogs – and especially puppies – cannot accidentally swallow it. (See also poisoning.)

arsenic

A small artery leading from a main artery to capillaries.

arteriole

A chronic inflammation of the arterial wall which leads to a thickening of the wall and consequent restricted passage for the blood through the arteries. It occurs sometimes in aged dogs when the arteries have lost their elasticity. If the walls are roughened as well as hardened, a blood clot may form causing thrombosis. Atheroma and atherosclerosis are associated conditions, referring to degenerative changes on the coats and linings of the arteries, which in turn lead to arteriosclerosis. Dogs with arteriosclerosis should not be subjected to sudden effort or undue stress. A quiet life with exercise at their own pace assists the condition. Prevention lies chiefly in giving a balanced diet, preserving a slim dog, and giving regular exercise throughout the animal's life.

arteriosclerosis

A blood vessel carrying oxygenated blood (an exception is the pulmonary artery which carries de-oxygenated blood) from the heart and lungs to the rest of the body. (See also vascular system.)

artery

Inflammation of a joint accompanied usually by some pain which may vary from a minor ache to more noticeable discomfort. Restricted movement is another symptom. Rheumatoid arthritis is chronic, of unknown cause, causing inflammation of the connective tissue around the joints. Osteoarthritis is a degenerative condition with little inflammation but rough deposits of bone laid down in the joints causing restricted activity. It occurs sometimes in aged dogs but is not necessarily a serious ailment if special care is taken to enhance the dog's comfort. Arthritis often attacks heavier, fatter dogs with more severity, as the additional weight gives added discomfort and pain.

arthritis

arthritis   Infection can be the cause of the inflammation associated with arthritis; trauma can be another cause.

Treatment consists largely of keeping the dog warm and dry and providing draught-free sleeping quarters, taking extra care in thoroughly drying the dog after a walk in the rain, and being patient with slowness associated with stiffness of the limbs. Aspirin is a suitable analgesic if needed and sometimes a veterinarian will prescribe phenylbutazone or cortisone in extreme cases. (See also aged dogs; obesity.)

arthrochondritis   Inflamed joint cartilage.

artificial insemination   The practice of inserting semen into the female reproductive tract without the act of mating. In the dog-breeding world, artificial insemination dates back to the eighteenth century. With modern methods, semen from the best strains of dog can be stored and transported to inseminate bitches in other parts of the world. (See also breeding; reproduction.)

artificial respiration   Stimulation of breathing by manual methods should be attempted in cases of drowning, electric shock, asphyxia from fumes or gas, some forms of poisoning or at any time when the respiration stops completely. The dog should be laid on its side with its tail end higher than its head. Place one hand over the rib-cage and the other over the upper side of the abdomen. Apply heavy pressure with both hands and release in about two seconds. Keep up this action rhythmically with a momentary pause between each application of pressure. If a veterinarian is at hand a respiratory stimulant can be administered but in most cases artificial respiration by the above method may be the only means of saving the dog's life and speed is paramount. (See also accidents.)

ascaridae   A class of worms (internal parasites) commonly known as round-worms and found in the intestines. (See also parasites.)

ascites   Fluid in the abdomen which often causes swelling. It is a symp-tom of various diseases including tuberculosis. It may also be indicative of heart, kidney and liver disease (including hepatitis), internal parasites and diabetes. In some cases the administration of diuretics helps but diagnosis of the cause for treatment is important. This condition should be discussed urgently with a veterinarian.

ascorbic acid   Synthetic vitamin C. Dogs, unlike man, do not need a dietary supply of vitamin C as they can synthesise it themselves.

asepsis   The exclusion of micro-organisms from an operating site, a wound, dressings, etc to prevent infection. This ideal situation can be achieved for operative conditions but not always post-operatively, due to the movements of the dog. Maximum care, therefore, should always be taken by owners to ensure that a dog's wounds are kept clean and that the area in which a dog may move about post-operatively is also hygienic. Dressings and instruments should be handled aseptically, and hands should be washed in antiseptic before any attention is given to a wound.

asepsis

A fungus-related disease common in birds and mammals. The fungus *Aspergillus* grows in the tissues causing the cells to die and minute abscesses to form in their place. The spores of the fungus, present in hay, grain, etc, are inhaled and multiply chiefly in the nasal passages, producing a cheesy exudate which clogs the breathing organs and allows reproduction of the fungus itself.

aspergillosis

Dogs sometimes catch the disease from poultry. Convulsions may occur together with rubbing of the muzzle, distress and a bloody nasal discharge. Fresh air and good food will assist recovery and thiabendazole, administered by a veterinarian, is reported to be of use. Aspergillosis is, luckily, relatively rare in dogs as it is difficult to treat and may result in deformation of the nasal bones as it spreads.

Suffocation, or insufficient oxygen being supplied to the body. The dog gasps for breath in order to increase oxygen uptake. If the cause of its distress is not immediately eliminated it will die. If the dog is being overcome by fumes, smoke, gas, etc, it should be taken quickly into the open air and laid down so that it can take in air easily. As long as the heart continues to beat there is a hope of recovery. Artificial respiration may be attempted.

asphyxia

Other causes of asphyxia include obstruction of the air passages by foreign bodies, a crushing pressure on the chest or neck which may be caused during an accident, chest wounds, respiratory paralysis, electric shock, drowning, or complications from accidents or ailments. (See also artificial respiration; foreign bodies.)

An instrument used in surgery which sucks liquid or air from an internal cavity such as the chest or abdomen.

aspirator

Disorder causing heavy or difficult breathing due to spasmodic contraction of the bronchi. It is considered to be of a nervous origin although the symptoms of chronic bronchitis and asthma in the dog are often confused due to similarity. Asthma, however, is usually irregular in its occurrence and accompanied by sudden distress with difficult, spasmodic breathing lasting for several minutes. Some breeds (eg the Maltese terrier) seem more vulnerable to asthma than others and it may be a hereditary condition in such instances. Allergy and stress may be other causes. While bronchodilators relieve the condition in man, these drugs are difficult to administer in dogs since it is almost impossible to get a dog to inhale to order. Asthma often improves with time, a good diet, regular exercise, removal of stress and sometimes the use of amyl nitrite during an attack.

asthma

Chemical substance, usually in solution, which causes a contraction of blood vessels, mucous membranes or tissues, and is used to

astringent

astringent	dry surfaces in order to stop discharges or secretions. Witch hazel is one example; others include alum, copper sulphate, tannin and zinc sulphate. Astringents are useful for bathing discharging eyes, nose, etc.
asymptomatic	Not showing symptoms.
atavism	Inheriting characteristics from far back in ancestry, due to a chance genetic alliance.
ataxia	Defective muscle control or co-ordination. It is one of the symptoms of nervous disorders such as encephalitis, meningitis and brain tumours. Ataxia can also be inherited and can appear in two to four month old fox terriers and Jack Russells.
atlas	The first cervical vertebra at the base of the skull. It is part of a joint which allows the head to pivot.
atrial fibrillation	Irregular heartbeat in the form of a fluttering. (See also arrhythmia.)
atrium	See auricle.
atrophy	Wasting of the tissues. It can occur through inadequate use, old age, a severe emaciating disease, starvation or partial paralysis. The paralysis of nerves may cause atrophy of a local area of tissue. Inactivity following a fracture setting is sometimes a temporary cause. Gentle and gradual exercise after healing is complete is needed to restore the limb to its normal state – a therapy which is advisable for atrophy in all young dogs following treatment of the main cause.
atropine	An alkaloid found in the root and leaves of the deadly nightshade. It is both a poison, paralysing nerves, and an antidote to poisons – such as morphine and some soil-dressing poisons. It can also be used for pupil dilation during examination of the eye. (See also poisoning.)
Aujeszky's disease	A virus-related disease, a symptom of which is intense itching. It is fortunately rare among dogs and is likely to be encountered only where dogs have eaten infected meat from cow, pig or rat. Cooked meat is unlikely to harbour the virus. It was first discovered in 1902 by Aujeszky in Hungary and, although uncommon in the UK, has been diagnosed in parts of the USA, Australia and South America.
aural resection	Removal of part of the external ear canal due to disease such as canker which may become chronic, especially in flap-eared dogs such as spaniels.
auricle	There are two auricles (or atria) in the heart – right and left. They are reception chambers for the blood which is to be pumped into the heart's ventricles. The right auricle (or atrium) receives

de-oxygenated (venous) blood which has returned from the chest, abdomen, head and neck and which is pumped into the right ventricle through the tricuspid valve. The left auricle accepts oxygenated (arterial) blood from the lungs and, by contraction, forces it into the left ventricle via the mitral valve.

auricle

   Auricle is also a name used for the pinna or external ear. (See also heart; vascular system; ventricle.)

Apparatus which operates using steam under pressure for the sterilisation of surgical instruments, cloths, gowns, gloves, dressings, etc. (See also sterilisation of equipment.)

autoclave

The breakdown on self-digestion of cells by enzymes within the cells – an action which takes place after death.

autolysis

Also known as a post-mortem or necropsy, it is an examination of an animal after death. It sometimes helps to provide additional knowledge about a disease or to determine the actual cause of death.

autopsy

A condition caused by lack of vitamins. (See also vitamin deficiency.)

avitaminosis

The area between the humerus and chest wall (corresponding to the human armpit) in which vital arteries (including the axillary artery), lymph glands and nerves run.

axilla

bacillus A type of bacteria recognisable under the microscope by its rod-shaped appearance.

backache Usually a symptom of a condition which requires veterinary examination and treatment. While it can be of muscular origin, it can also be due to disease or injury of the spine, hip dysplasia or other skeletal disorder. It can reflect disease of an internal organ such as the kidney or, in the bitch, a uterine or other gynaecological problem. Whatever the cause, it will generally be worsened, especially if it is associated with the spine, if the dog is suffering from obesity.

bacteria Microbes, germs, or small micro-organisms which can only be seen under a microscope. They are found almost everywhere – in the air, soil, healthy skin and throughout the body, especially in the intestines. They are of various shapes, eg rod-like bacilli, round cocci. The majority of bacteria are harmless and are essential, for example, for proper digestion of food in the gut.

Only a few of the many species of bacteria are pathogens causing disease, such as diarrhoea, abscesses, eczema, or tonsillitis. Some, such as salmonella infections, anthrax and tetanus, are also communicable to man. Such diseases are treated by antibiotics and anti-toxins.

Bacteria are identified microscopically and by culturing in the laboratory in a specialised medium.

bactericidal Drug, solution or substance which kills bacteria, eg antibiotics, disinfectant, antiseptic, etc.

bacteriolysis The process of breaking up or digestion of bacterial cells by an antibody.

bacteriophage A virus which invades and destroys bacteria.

bacteriostatic Substance which inhibits the growth of bacteria without killing them.

balanitis Inflammation of the end of the penis, a fairly common complaint in male dogs. It is usually temporary and not often serious. No treatment is needed unless the inflammation continues, causes obvious pain or distress, or worsens – in which case a visit to the veterinary surgery is necessary. Occasionally a grass seed or other foreign body is the cause and this can be detected if the penis is examined by withdrawing it carefully from its sheath or prepuce and bathing with a warm saline solution (see entry).

ball A useful toy for a dog, stimulating play and assisting in training. However, it is important to remember that some balls can be a potential hazard to health and life; a dog should never be allowed to pick up any ball smaller than a tennis ball. Golf, squash and other small balls can be partially swallowed, blocking the throat or trachea, causing asphyxia and probable death unless removed quickly – an extremely difficult task. Sponge balls are another hazard, as are any small round objects left around the house or garden, such as marbles and pebbles, which can become lodged in the intestines causing a blockage. Usually, surgical removal by a veterinarian is the only remedy. (See also foreign bodies; play; toys.)

ball

A bandage may be used to protect a wound, although wounds are better left uncovered where possible to allow the air and therefore oxygen to promote healing. Bandages are more frequently useful to hold dressings in place, or as a means of support in cases of oedema, fractures, hernia and dislocations. They can also be applied to prevent the dog worrying a wound or site of infection – eg wrapped round a foot to prevent scratching or clawing at an injured ear – and to stop haemorrhage or to correct a deformity.

bandaging

Where needed, bandages should be fixed so that they are comfortable and firm without impeding the circulation of the blood through being too tight; they should be secured with adhesive surgical tape (supplied in rolls), or else tied in place – never pinned, as pins can be loosened or, more dangerously, swallowed. When rolling a bandage, each new turn should overlap the previous one by two-thirds to allow an even application, and only a short length should be unrolled at a time, the roll being kept close to the dog's body.

Bandages are available generally in various forms: the roll or ribbon bandage in widths of 13mm (½in) to about 100mm (4in); a tubular gauze bandage for head, legs or feet; and a 'multi-tailed' type for use on chest and abdomen. (See also dressing; first aid; wounds.)

A class of drugs used in veterinary practice as anaesthetics, sedatives or hypnotics. These include pentobarbitone, phenobarbitone and thiopentone. Dogs can be poisoned by barbiturates, usually by swallowing human medicines which should be kept locked away. (See also poisoning.)

barbiturate

Dogs bark when excited, in reply, or when trying to draw attention to something. They may also bark as a warning to others. Tone changes to a high-pitched yelp from a normal deep-throated sound may denote a form of hysteria or over-excitement. There is also a change of voice in a dog suffering from rabies. Owners can soon learn to interpret the reasons for their dogs' barking. (See also voice.)

bark

A bitch is said to be barren or infertile when she is unable to conceive. (See also infertility.)

barren

See beds and bedding.

basket

A type of white blood cell which is rarely seen in the microscopic blood examination of the dog. It has blue-staining granules in the

basophil

basophil   cytoplasm. It also contains histamine which may be released during an allergy. Basophils sometimes appear pathologically in adenomas.

bathing

A dog should be bathed if the coat becomes contaminated or smelly and dirty, for instance after the animal has rolled in rotting or oily substances. Regular brushing and grooming, however, will remove the need for frequent bathing. Show dogs are bathed before a show to put their coats in tip-top condition, but two or three baths a year are probably enough for most other dogs.

Eucalyptus oil rubbed into the affected part before bathing will rid the coat of oil-based contaminants. Use a good dog shampoo – not a human one – so that the natural oils of the dog's coat will be preserved rather than destroyed. Use an insecticidal shampoo if there are external parasites to be eliminated.

Stand the dog in the bath on a rubber mat to prevent it being frightened by its feet slipping. Have two non-fluffy towels close at hand throughout the procedures so that you do not have to leave the dog in order to get one. Rinse the coat with warm (not hot or cold) water first (if you have a shower, so much the better), and then rub in the dog shampoo to a fine lather, keeping it away from eyes and the insides of ears. Then rinse again with more warm water until all traces of shampoo have vanished. Dry the dog thoroughly all over, including under the tail, around the genitals, in the creases under thighs and 'armpits' and between toes. Use the second towel to dry the head, eyes and ears. Ideally, finish off the process with a clean, soft chamois leather. Some dogs enjoy the warm air from a hair dryer, but keep it away from eyes and the insides of ears, under the tail etc.

A dog may be bathed before a meal but not for three hours after one. Do not bath outside in cold weather and never bath a bitch in season or close to whelping, or a sick or recuperating dog. Extra care throughout, including very careful drying, is needed when bathing an aged dog. (See also grooming; shampoo.)

Battersea Dogs' Home

An animal rescue centre in south-west London with two satellite kennels in Berkshire and Kent operating identically to the main centre but on a smaller scale. The centre provides a shelter and rehoming service for lost, stray and unwanted dogs and cats. The chief objectives of this registered charity (which depends on donations and legacies for its survival) are to rescue, reunite, rehabilitate and rehome the lost and abandoned dogs and cats that come into its care. The Home provides temporary shelter and care to the thousands of stray dogs and cats in the London area, restores lost dogs to their owners, works on the behavioural issues facing many of its charges and endeavours to find good homes for unclaimed or unwanted dogs and cats. There is no time limit on how long a dog or cat can spend at Battersea and the Home never refuses a dog.

Some 10,000 dogs and 3,500 cats pass through the Home in a year and over three million have been cared for since the organisation was founded in 1860 by an elderly lady who was distressed by the

Battersea Dogs' Home

large numbers of stray, diseased and crippled dogs roaming London's streets. Some dogs are brought to the home by London's animal wardens, or collected from police stations by Battersea's fleet of animal ambulances; others arrive from people who can no longer care for them, while many are simply abandoned. A wide variety of dog breeds, particularly the Staffordshire Bull Terrier and the German Shepherd, come to the centre as well as many cross-breeds and mongrels.

The Home has four resident veterinarians, trained nurses and a team of behaviour, rehoming and kennel staff. The modern kennel accommodation was rebuilt in 1997. All animals entering Battersea Dogs' Home are vaccinated and microchipped before going to a new household. Every dog is given a thorough temperament and behaviour assessment to establish each individual's requirements and the type of environment that will be suitable for it. The Home's rehabilitation team works with dogs that need help with their temperament or behaviour before they are put forward for rehoming.

Such a service is not only valuable in finding suitable homes for stray dogs but helps prevent the spread of disease and improve the health of canine society as a whole. Moreover it lowers the incidence of traffic accidents due to stray dogs running across the road, and reduces the number of unwanted puppies that would inevitably be born. In countries where such facilities are rare or absent, disease among dogs is much more widespread. (See also microchipping, NCDL, unwanted dogs; and useful addresses,)

beds and bedding

Unless a dog is to be kept permanently outside where it may sleep in a kennel or barn (for example, in the case of a gundog or farm dog), it should always have its own bed in the house. It can retreat to it in safety when it wishes and rest on it at night. In outside kennels a bed can still be made up with blankets or other soft material as in the house; or soft oat-straw, removed and burnt each week, can be used. If making a bed with old clothing, remove all buttons and fastenings. A lining of clean newspaper acts as a useful insulator during the winter if needed. Never use wood shavings and sawdust as bedding material; the latter is often harmful to respiration and both can be poisonous to the dog. Some woods are themselves poisonous and others used as timber are often treated with a poisonous fungicide. In kennels, wooden beds are often provided. Whatever the bed, it must be raised off the floor to avoid draughts.

One of the best forms of dog bed is the basket and so-called designer beds that are usually made of washable, padded material with a removable floor cushion. These are usually circular with a small cut-out section on the upper half of the rim. Modern pet-accessory suppliers often offer shapeless creations known as 'bean bags', made in various sizes and filled with polystyrene 'beans'; these can be comfortable beds for dogs of most breeds – as long as the beans cannot escape and the bags are large enough for the breed. For this former reason, and for cleanliness, it is useful to have a zip-cover made for the bean bag so that it can be regularly washed

beds and bedding

and brushed; also it will give added strength should the dog feel the need to drag the bag around the room. Other forms of bed are available from pet shops in a wide variety of shapes and sizes.

A dog's bed should be comfortable, of the right size to accommodate the dog when it is fully grown, contain bedding material which can be removed and washed or replaced periodically (and disinfected and allowed to dry in the sun if parasites are detected), be both warm and dry and positioned in a place free from draughts and constant noise but airy. Always have a change of clean bedding ready. (See also kennel.)

behaviour

Since the 1960s it has become increasingly recognised that health and behaviour in dogs are closely connected. Most veterinary schools in the UK and USA now include courses on ethology – animal behaviour – though much research is still needed.

An observant owner gets to know a dog and begins to interpret its behaviour signals and patterns correctly, responding accordingly. Behavioural changes often indicate a change in health status and such signs, combined with other symptoms of a bodily, or physiological, nature help to produce an exact diagnosis.

Behaviour patterns – including speed of eating, response to training, learning, etc – vary between breeds, but most dogs evidently enjoy praise from a respected and beloved owner, and this is one of the greatest stimuli to learning and training and, indeed, to companionship. Some breeds, too, are more companionable (and consequently more anxious to please) than others, such qualities being bred into particular breeds for specific purposes, eg in spaniels, border collies and labradors.

Normal behaviour characteristics, as in man, generally fall into broad, recognisable patterns in, for example, communication (facial expressions, tail wagging, body posturing, ear and eye movements, etc), fear, frustration, aggression, imitation, intelligence, learning, memory, play, problem solving, sexual activity and stimulation, emotion and social interactions. There are also many aspects to each pattern – barking, for example, is just one associated with communication; the Basenji does not have a true bark but still communicates well. Urine marking is another form of communication between dogs, used to delineate a territory.

Early social experiences can influence a dog's later behaviour – whether it will be nervous, aggressive, extrovert or introvert. Up to twelve weeks old is a sensitive time for a puppy but the weeks, months and years that follow are also important in moulding a dog's behaviour beyond that which is hereditary.

Because a dog has patterned behaviour, abnormalities can be produced in those patterns by frequent over-indulgence, such as treating the dog as a child substitute or as an equal in human terms. The abnormalities may be reflected in aggression, hysteria, depression, anorexia, convulsions, vomiting, asthma, skin ailments or stomach and intestinal problems. As in some human response to stress, dogs may exhibit lameness, for example, as a way of attracting sympathy when the owner's attention is diverted by, say, the arrival of a new baby or new pet in the household or when people come to stay.

behaviour

For these reasons dogs should not be over-pampered. Though their physical and emotional needs, in general terms, resemble those of other mammals, including human beings, in specific terms these are in some cases different. Over-dependence on humans can cause a dog stress.

Kindness, affection, companionship and care in canine terms specific to the dog should be offered by the considerate owner. Changing the dog's behaviour patterns to match those of the owner may result in behaviour abnormalities which affect the dog's health. (See also communication; imprinting; social interaction; training.)

belching

Passing wind from the stomach through the mouth. A dog often belches at the end of a meal, indicating that it has eaten sufficient. Constant belching at other times may point to a stomach disorder such as dyspepsia.

belladonna

Flower of the deadly nightshade. (See also atropine.)

benign

A medical term used to describe a cell disorder which is unlikely to spread to other tissues, eg a tumour which will not recur once removed.

benzalkonium chloride

A solution used for cleansing. Hands and arms can be washed in it (diluted 1 part to 50 parts distilled or boiled water or 1 in 500 with alcohol). Metal instruments can be stored in a 1 in 2,000 dilution. (See also cetrimide.)

benzyl benzoate

A chemical treatment for mange used as an emulsion.

betamethasone

A corticosteroid which, as betamethasone sodium phosphate, is a useful anti-inflammatory drug.

biceps

A double-headed muscle.

bile (gall)

A greenish-yellow or golden-brown fluid secreted by the liver and stored in the gall-bladder. It contains water, mucus, excess cholesterol, glycocholic and taurocholic acid salts, and colour pigments which are waste products from the destruction of old red blood cells in the liver. It passes from the gall-bladder into the bile-duct.

Bile combines with other juices in the small intestine. It helps to emulsify fats during digestion and to absorb fats and fat-soluble vitamins A, D and K.

Deficiency in bile means that fat digestion is impeded and fats can sometimes pass unchanged into the faeces as a result. Colour of the faeces is also influenced by the colour pigments in bile.

bile-duct

The union of the common hepatic duct from the liver and the cystic duct of the gall-bladder. It carries the bile into the duodenum.

bile-duct	Obstruction of the bile-duct can, like liver damage, result in jaundice. (See also liver.)
bilirubin	A bile pigment which is the result of old red blood cells being broken down in the liver. It is significant if found in urine and blood in cases of jaundice and can therefore be useful in diagnosis.
biopsy	A minor operation where a small piece of living tissue, eg from a tumour, is removed for examination microscopically, usually for evidence of malignancy. (See also histology.)
birth	See whelping.
biscuit	Often given to a dog mixed with meat as a source of carbohydrate. There are various proprietary brands of biscuit and biscuit meal available and some are fortified with vitamins and calcium. (See also diet; feeding; nutrition.)
bitch	The female dog.
bite	A dog-bite can often result in a nasty wound. A dog bitten in a fight should always be examined by a veterinarian. Antibiotics will almost certainly be needed and wounds should be washed gently in a warm saline solution (see entry) or other weak antiseptic; the surrounding hair must be clipped away (the wound covered temporarily with a piece of clean gauze so that the cut hair does not fall into it) and the wound left open wherever possible.
	A bite does not necessarily need to be large or extensive to be dangerous; a small puncture can be equally troublesome as infection, usually bacteria, gains entry leading to abscesses. (See also wounds.)
'black tongue'	A disease symptomised by a dark discoloration of the tongue, and inflammation and ulceration of the mouth, accompanied by foul breath and blood-stained drooling saliva. It is caused by a diet deficient in nicotinic acid (niacin), and large doses of this may produce a flushing effect. A good diet which includes meat will prevent the condition, which is fatal if not treated.
bladder	A storage reservoir in the body for fluids. The urinary bladder is contained in the abdomen and is connected to the kidneys by two tubes – the ureters. The urethra is the tube which leads from the neck of this pear-shaped bladder to the exterior where urine is passed.
	The bladder has a mucous membrane lining and a muscular outer wall, and folds when empty. When distended, nerves pass information to the brain, muscles contract by motor impulses and an outer sphincter relaxes when the dog is ready to urinate. (See also cystitis; gall-bladder.)
bleeding	See haemorrhage.

Inflammation of the eyelids which can be due to infection or allergy. It can also be caused by flies and often accompanies conjunctivitis. Bathe gently with warm water and, if it does not improve, seek advice from a veterinarian who will probably prescribe eye drops or ointments.

blepharitis

Unless hereditary, it is caused by disease or injury. It is not necessarily a reason for euthanasia as, with some extra care, a blind dog can still be a happy and otherwise healthy one. In the house, positioning the furniture permanently so that the dog can learn where each piece is situated will help; sometimes a 'crash helmet' can be made, for example by adapting a leather muzzle, which the dog can wear when in danger of colliding with unfamiliar objects. Training a blind dog to respond instantly to command is important, as it must rely on its owner completely when out for a walk, in the home or garden. There is some evidence that the senses of smell and hearing are more acute in a blind dog, which helps to compensate for loss of sight. (See also cataract; glaucoma.)

blindness

Rarely seen in animals. (See also burns and scalds.)

blister

The essential body fluid in which red blood cells or erythrocytes, white blood cells or leucocytes, and platelets or thrombocytes, are suspended and various chemical substances are dissolved. The blood is a highly efficient transport system, carrying oxygen from the lungs around the body, nutritional substances from parts of the digestive system to the tissues, hormones from the endocrine system, and waste products, such as urea, to the kidneys. It is pumped around by the heart through an intricate network of arteries, veins and capillaries.

blood

Blood brings defence weapons to combat infection and, by its own clotting mechanisms, defends itself against excessive loss through vessel injury. It also assists in temperature control of the body and balance of water.

The fluid part of the blood is the plasma which carries three proteins: serum albumin, serum globulin and fibrinogen. When blood coagulates outside the body, plasma separates from the blood clot and becomes serum. It also contains trace elements such as sodium, potassium, calcium, etc, and amino acids.

Red blood cells, or erythrocytes, represent just over 30 per cent of the blood and have lost their nuclei by the time they enter the bloodstream from the bone marrow where they are manufactured. An early red cell, when complete with nucleus, is called an erythroblast. Haemoglobin, which absorbs oxygen, is contained in each red blood cell and gives the cell its colouring. Under the microscope the red cells appear as circular, biconcave objects. In disease, the red cells, microscopically viewed, may variously be reduced in numbers, battered or shapeless, weak in colour or nucleated (due to early release into the circulation).

The normal blood values of the dog (see table below) are fairly consistent in good health. In ill health, however, there are often *blood*

very noticeable changes in levels and concentrations, varying with the severity of the disease or disorder, recognisable under laboratory studies. This also applies to the numbers and proportions of white blood cells, or leucocytes, of which there are five types: neutrophils, lymphocytes, monocytes, basophils and eosinophils. These cells play various roles in fighting infection. In the laboratory, the white blood cells are treated with a special stain to differentiate them prior to microscopical examination and counting. There are fewer white cells than red cells and each possesses a nucleus and cytoplasm. (See also vascular system.)

Normal blood values of the dog

Total blood quantity:	calculate 5.5 to 9.1 per cent of body weight
Total red blood cell count:	5.5 to 8.5 million per microlitre of blood*
Total white blood cell count:	6 to 18 thousand per microlitre of blood*
Haemoglobin:	12 to 18g per 100ml of blood*
Lifespan of red blood cells:	approx 100 to 120 days
Differential white cell count*:	neutrophils: 60 to 77%
	eosinophils: 2 to 10%
	basophils: rare
	lymphocytes: 12 to 30%
	monocytes: 3 to 10%
Blood calcium:phosphorus ratio:	from 1.2 to 1.4:1

* Note: Average adult dog. Variations occur according to age.

blood group

There are generally considered to be seven canine blood groups, designated A to G, and each of these can be termed positive or negative. Group A negative is usually recognised as the universal donor, since blood from this group given in a transfusion to a dog with blood of any other group does not often cause a reaction. If A-positive blood, however, is given to an A-negative dog more than once, the second transfusion may produce a reaction, as anti-A antibodies will then have been built up in the recipient's body.

Apart from this, it is seemingly rare for dogs to exhibit a reaction to incompatible blood, particularly on the first transfusion. If a transfusion is likely to be harmful a cross-match test should be performed in the laboratory to match a drop of the donor's blood cells with a drop of the recipient's serum. It is later examined for evidence of agglutination which denotes incompatible blood. This test, coupled to blood grouping tests to determine the group of each dog, will help to prevent possibilities of reaction.

blood transfusion

See transfusions and infusions.

boarding kennels

In the UK, boarding kennels are governed by the Animal Boarding Establishments Act, 1963. This states that they must be licensed annually by the local authority, which must ensure they have suitable accommodation in terms of size, construction, number of occupants, heating, lighting and ventilation, cleanliness and exercising facilities. It also states that animal occupants must be 'adequately supplied with suitable food, drink and bedding material, and adequately exercised'. Fire precautions and isolation facilities are also controlled. This form of licensing means that the establishment can be inspected regularly to make sure that it continues to conform to the Act's requirements.

When selecting a boarding kennel for your dog, a recommendation from another dog owner is a useful starting point. Visit the place before deciding, and check that the dogs there are clean, well-housed and looking fit. They should have clean water at all times, clean and adequate bedding and a place where they can exercise. It is quite easy to see whether this is a pleasant place for your dog to spend his time while you are away.

A dog should not be accepted by a boarding kennel unless its inoculations are up to date, especially those against distemper, parvo virus and leptospirosis, and you will need to produce the relevant certificates signed by the inoculating veterinarian. Leave one or two familiar objects with the dog; if you have more than one dog and they are used to being together, ask for them to be housed together in the kennels. Always discuss the dog's food with the kennel owner, and leave an address where you or someone acting on your behalf can be contacted while you are away.

bone marrow

Connective tissue. Some is very fatty and called yellow marrow and the remainder is red marrow which is a 'factory' for the production of red blood cells and granular white cells.

In puppies all marrow is red and as the dog grows the fat cells of yellow marrow replace some of it. Blood vessels are linked to the marrow and fine nerves run through it.

The bone marrow of beef bones is quite nutritious for dogs and usually very much enjoyed. Large marrow bones can be purchased from a butcher and given raw to the dog. If the marrow bone is sawn in two the dog will extract some with its tongue; the rest can be spooned out and mixed with the dog's dinner. (See also diet.)

bones

See skeleton.

bones, feeding of

It is often said that 'dogs in the wild manage all sorts of bones'. Dogs do, indeed, cope with bones of all shapes and sizes but there are no statistics available of the numbers which die as a result of bones becoming lodged in places where they cause stoppage of breath, obstruction of the intestines and many other lethal conditions. The domesticated dog should *never* be fed small, sharp bones (such as chop, rabbit, fish or fowl bones). The risks are considerable and should not be taken. A dog will enjoy (and be safe with) a large beef thigh bone which contains marrow; let the dog chew it for as long as it wants — it is a useful dental cleaner and polisher — and then saw off one end and extract the marrow, which the dog will doubly

bones, feeding of	enjoy. Give the bone raw; cooked bones are less interesting. (See also foreign bodies.)
booster	A booster is the second or subsequent dose of vaccine, usually to boost the effect of an earlier inoculation. (See also immunisation.)
boredom	A dog can be affected mentally and physically by boredom and reasons for it should be carefully avoided. A dog (and especially a puppy) which lacks companionship, perhaps being left alone in the house all day, will inevitably become bored. As a result it will become mischievous (in order to amuse itself), aggressive (through frustration) or withdrawn and eventually physically ill. The more intelligent the dog, the more easily it can become bored without company, regular exercise and its owner's sustained interest in it.
boric acid (boracic acid) powder	Often used as an antiseptic in solution, especially on mucous membranes, and as a mouthwash. It is not very efficient and may, indeed, be harmful in quantity.
botulism	One of the most dangerous forms of food poisoning which is generally caused by the consumption of infected meat. Paralysis is a symptom. It is rare in dogs but can be extremely serious and is usually fatal.
bowel	See intestines.
bowls, drinking and feeding	See feeding.
brachycephalic	Short-faced with a broad head. Breeds of this description include the Boston terrier, bulldog, Pekinese and pug.
bradycardia	An abnormally slow heart- and pulse-rate.
brain	The brain is the control centre for the nervous system. The fore-brain or cerebrum consists of two cerebral hemispheres and is concerned with intelligence, memory and initiative. Messages are received in the cerebrum from the sensory organs of sight, touch, taste, hearing and smell, and relayed from the thalamus. It is also the origination area for emotion and sends instructions to the muscles of the skeleton for voluntary action. Feeling and muscle control on the left side of the body are directed by the right cerebral hemisphere and vice versa. Nerve tissue is situated in the middle of the brain with the medulla oblongata, which reaches under the cerebellum and joins with the spinal cord, the thalamus, hypothalamus and basal ganglia. The medulla oblongata controls reflex and voluntary actions such as respiration, heartbeat, vomiting, the automatic operation of swallowing, coughing, etc. The cerebellum is the centre for unconscious control of such factors as balance and co-ordinates complex muscular movements. The hypothalamus

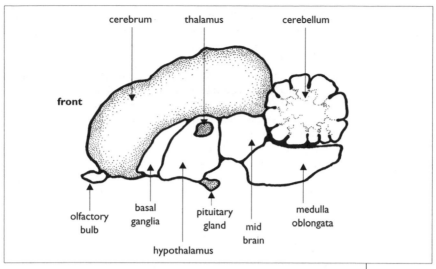

2 Schematic diagram of the brain

brain

affects appetite, urination, vascular system, circulation and body temperature. The basal ganglia direct posture and associated movement. (See also nervous system.)

breath

Malodorous breath from a dog can be a symptom of dental or intestinal disorders and is often present in bronchitis and nasal inflammation.

breathing

See respiration.

breech presentation

A birth where the puppy is presented tail first or upside down rather than head first. Manipulation will often assist but sometimes a Caesarean section is necessary. If the bitch is in difficulty veterinary assistance should be sought as any delay will endanger the puppy's life and subsequently the bitch's also. (See also dystokia, whelping.)

breeding

Taking the decision for your dog to breed should not be made lightly; certainly not until the following criteria have been met: the bitch must be healthy enough to run no risks during pregnancy (ask your veterinarian to check her over before she is mated); there must be adequate space and facilities to keep the bitch and growing, agile, untrained puppies when the litter is born and for about two months after at least; every member of the litter must be assured of a good, permanent, caring home; the dog chosen to sire the litter must not be related to the bitch. Neither bitch nor dog should be mentally or physically defective in any way.

Breeders bear a heavy responsibility not only to ensure a safe and happy future for all resulting puppies, but also that those puppies have every chance of being kept healthy if they are to perpetuate their line. Only the strongest (healthiest) points of the canine race *breeding* should be bred on and the weakest bred out. Weak, nervous, aggressive, unhealthy or otherwise defective dogs should not be mated, however attractive their appearance.

Theoretically a bitch can be mated after she has had her first season but in practice she should be at least fifteen months old. A bitch over six years would be considered too old for her first litter. A suitable stud dog can be found by contacting a professional breeder, the Kennel Club or local breed association.

A bitch is most likely to accept a dog for mating in the second stage of her season, between the tenth and fifteenth day. After mating, confirmation of the pregnancy cannot be made until about the fortieth day by a veterinarian with whom the owner should thereafter keep in touch. A whelping calendar (given in whelping entry) is a useful way of keeping a check on the progress of the pregnancy. False pregnancies sometimes occur and the bitch can then be remated when they are over. The gestation period is usually sixty-three days, within a day or so.

After the fortieth day, attention to diet is important: extra milk and vitamins (especially A and D) will be needed without increasing the quantity of the food intake. Exercise should not be too strenuous and preparations should be made well in advance of the arrival of the litter for accommodation, feeding, veterinary attention – and time!

After whelping the bitch will need peace and quiet with her puppies and without noisy strangers or animals around her for at least forty-eight hours. During the first twenty-four hours she will need a liquid diet of milk, water and honey or glucose fed to her about five times. Her temperature, which will probably have dropped to below 38°C (100.4°F) before whelping, should have returned to normal and the liquid diet can, after the first day, be alternated with a light nourishing diet such as scrambled egg, boiled fish or cooked minced beef as well as fresh, clean, cool water constantly at hand.

The puppies will open their eyes at about two weeks and be weaned at about three to four weeks when they, too, need to be fed a special diet every four hours during the day for the next three months. At weaning the bitch's fluid intake can be reduced and solid, nutritious food substituted to help build her up to normal health and strength. Puppies should be removed to their new homes at intervals so that the bitch does not experience a sudden loss. The litter will need to be registered at the Kennel Club if a pure breed, and a pedigree supplied to the new owner with a puppy diet sheet and care instructions to cover the next three months of its life. The puppies should also be wormed.

The bitch should be carefully observed for any health complications, eg eclampsia, mastitis, metritis, up to, during and after whelping. Breeding accommodation, food, utensils and containers should be kept scrupulously clean at all times to prevent any form of infection.

Breeding dogs on a commercial scale needs careful consideration and planning. Dog-breeding establishments have to conform to strict regulations and in the UK are licensed by the local authority and governed by the Breeding of Dogs Act, 1999. Adequate facilities are as essential as sound breeding stock. Accommodation requires proper lighting, ventilation and cleansing facilities, winter heating and plenty of room. It must be draught-free and comfortable, cool in the summer and warm in the winter. There must also be kennelling and facilities to keep and exercise stud dogs well away from bitches in season. Only happy, healthy dogs should be used for breeding and they, and their offspring, need constant care every day (and often during the night) all the year round. If the business is run with proper care and attention there are no huge profits to be made.

breeding

Successful dog breeders probably need to spend time and money on showing their best dogs and bear responsibility for improving and perpetuating the best, not only physically but in temperament too, of each breed. They also have to ensure that each dog bred finds a good suitable home with a caring owner for its full life. All potential puppy buyers should be interviewed by the breeder. (See also mating; puppies, care of; reproduction; whelping.)

This Act governs the commercial breeding and sale of dogs and regulates the welfare and veterinary inspection of dogs kept in commercial breeding establishments (two or more bitches kept for the purposes of breeding for sale), and the licensing of breeding establishments by local authorities in the UK.

Breeding and Sale of Dogs (Welfare) Act, 1999

See fractures.

broken bones

The two air passages leading from the trachea or windpipe, one to each lung, where they branch into many bronchioles or smaller passages diffusing air through the lungs.

bronchi

Inflammation of the mucous membrane lining the bronchi and bronchioles of the lungs. There are acute and chronic forms. Acute bronchitis is usually caused by an infection often of viral origin and is generally a worsening of colds and chills. It can also be caused by smoke or other airborne irritants and is one of the complications of distemper.

bronchitis

Symptoms of the acute form include an increase in the rate of and difficulty in breathing, rise in temperature and a loss of appetite. The dog may also cough and have a nasal discharge.

Chronic bronchitis, which can result from the untreated acute form, also sometimes affects aged dogs, particularly those which are overweight and/or which have a history of respiratory disorders.

Preventive measures include avoiding the conditions likely to produce chills, avoiding bonfire smoke, grain dust and other hazardous irritants the dog might breathe in, and avoiding obesity, which causes added discomfort and difficulty in recuperation.

Treatment consists of keeping the dog warm and free from contact with damp and draughts, feeding a diet of easily digestible food and providing peace and quiet. In chronic cases a waterproof flannel jacket, worn on walks in winter, can help. Veterinary consultation is

bronchitis	necessary in the early days as antibiotics will probably be needed to combat the infection.
bronchopneumonia	Inflammation of the lungs and bronchi caused by bacterial or viral infection. While bronchitis affects the larger air passages outside the lungs, pneumonia attacks the tiny alveoli inside. Alveoli walls are thin, to allow exchange of oxygen from air to blood, and carbon dioxide from blood to air. Consequently, fluid leaking from the inflamed blood vessels quickly clogs them.

The disease can be a direct infection, a worsening of bronchitis, or a secondary infection from such diseases as distemper. It is a serious condition and can cause death. A veterinarian should be consulted as soon as the condition is suspected and, if there is an earlier disorder from which it stems, veterinary treatment may form a preventive measure.

Symptoms include respiratory distress with breath blown heavily through the lips, particularly when acute (chronic forms may not be accompanied by heavy breathing if the patient is still), temperature rise, and sometimes a worsening exhausting cough and nasal discharge. The dog becomes lethargic as each breath brings it closer to exhaustion. Keep the dog warm and still, and stay with it to comfort and soothe.

During convalescence a nutritious, easily digested diet, fresh water nearby and gentle nursing are important. Avoid chills, draughts, excessive noise and any form of pollution in the air such as smoke.

brucellosis	This is a rare disease in dogs, being largely a bovine affliction. One strain of the bacteria, however, which is specific to dogs, has been isolated in the USA. A second strain can be passed on to the dog from the untreated milk of an infected cow. Any veterinary treatment of the disease is usually temporary and the disease can cause varying degrees of subsequent disability. Farm dogs are the most likely to become infected; prevention by keeping them away from a herd known to be infected is obviously the best approach. Vaginal discharge appears in infected bitches and, if pregnant, abortion may result. Dogs affected by the disease show symptoms of inflammation of reproductive organs. Infecting bacteria can be isolated in laboratory examination of urine, blood, milk, aborted pups or male semen.
bruise	A bruise, caused by a blow, produces rupturing of blood vessels and damage to tissue. While light bruising is not dangerous, heavier, deeper injury involving muscles rather than skin may result in haematomas from the bleeding of damaged blood vessels into the surrounding tissues. Apart from pain, extensive bruising results in both haemorrhage and shock.

Bone bruising can produce exostosis – the formation of a bony growth. Treat the area with cold compresses in the early stages and watch for any complications.

brush	See grooming.

Both burns and scalds are extremely dangerous to a dog and the utmost care should be taken to avoid them. Burns are caused generally by dry heat, and occasionally through contact with electricity, ice and some chemicals. Scalds are caused by hot liquid or steam. The effects of both injuries are similar.

Burns and scalds can be superficial, affecting only the skin, or deeper, damaging the area below the skin, including fat or muscular tissue or bone. Burns can usually be seen as the fur will probably be burnt or singed, but scalds are often not immediately visible as the hot liquid seeps through the fur. Blood vessels in the affected area dilate and escaping fluid from them gathers in the local tissue, making the skin surface moist and inflamed.

Shock, one of the most dangerous complications, is produced by the pain and by toxic substances from the burnt tissues being absorbed into the bloodstream. Death can result from a combination of toxaemia and pain – or either. Treatment of extensive or deep scalds and burns by a veterinarian is both essential and extremely urgent. In an emergency, lessen the dog's pain by placing it immediately under cold, slowly running water. Burns and scalds must not be contaminated, so subsequently cover the area with a sterile, dry, absorbent gauze dressing. Keep the dog warm and give cold water to drink if wanted.

Slight burns of the skin (slight does not necessarily mean *small*, since sometimes small can also be deep) can be treated by swabbing with a saline solution (see entry) or antiseptic and a special sterile gauze burn-dressing (tulle gras) or tannic acid jelly covered with sterile gauze, applied over a small area.

If the injury is caused by acids, bathe with an alkali (such as sodium bicarbonate). If the dog is burnt by an alkali (such as caustic soda) mix equal parts of vinegar and water and irrigate the wound before dressing with sterile gauze. For cresol (found in some plastics, dyestuffs and cleansers) and phenol (often present in disinfectants, household cleaning agents etc) burns, swab briefly with surgical spirit and cover with Vaseline.

Since burns and scalds are mostly caused in the home the following household rules will help as preventive measures: keep dogs out of the kitchen when hot food and drink is being prepared; keep all household chemicals in a cupboard where a dog cannot reach them and where they cannot fall and be spilt; keep dogs away from bonfires, fireworks (which are a considerable hazard to most animals), hotplates, hair-curling equipment and other heated electrical appliances, lighted cigarettes and matches, etc; use convector heaters rather than barred electric fires; protect gas and solid fuel fires with appropriate guards; do not place hot drinks where a dog can upset them; and if a hot-water bottle is put in the bed of a sick or aged dog make sure it is well covered and only warm – *never hot*. (See also accidents.)

Inflammation of a bursa – tissue which lies between tendon and bone to cushion friction and pressure. Elderly dogs sometimes develop chronic bursitis, particularly if they are thin animals

bursitis   which have spent much of their lives lying on a hard surface. It can occur in hock, knee, stifle and sternum and can be detected by a soft, fluid-filled swelling usually with little pain. Acute bursitis can occur as a result of a violent blow. Both forms of this disorder can be treated with anti-inflammatory agents.

The small, blind end of the gut or large intestine. The ileum joins the large intestine at the junction of the ascending colon and the caecum. The caecum is pouch-like and about 5cm (2in) long, often an irregular corkscrew shape. | **caecum**

The removal by surgery of the foetus through the walls of the abdomen and uterus. It is an operation performed by a veterinarian when natural birth, or whelping, is impossible due to breech presentation, inability of the cervix to dilate, uterine torsion, pelvic obstruction or a large-headed pup in a bitch with a small birth canal. It may also be carried out if the bitch becomes too weak to expel the pups normally. The incision is subsequently sutured and, providing the bitch is in good health with no added whelping complications, a caesarean section is usually successful. The patient will need peace and quiet and general post-operative nursing. (See also whelping.) | **caesarean section**

A soothing, mildly astringent lotion which is used to relieve irritation, for example in eczema and other skin disorders. | **calamine lotion**

A process which takes place when calcium carbonate is deposited in tissue through an inflammatory reaction in or around the cell walls, eg in artery walls. | **calcification**

See nutrition. | **calcium**

A stone resulting from the accumulation in body fluids of the salts of physiological minerals such as calcium, sodium, potassium or magnesium. Calculi are found most commonly in the urinary system (including kidneys, bladder and male urethra), in the gallbladder and bile-duct, and sometimes in the intestines where they are most often caused by mineral salts forming around a small foreign body which has been swallowed.

Calculi are generally diagnosed, following pain or tenderness and often obstruction, by radiography and if not passed may have to be removed surgically. | **calculus**

A unit of measurement for the calculation of energy requirements from food. A calorie is the amount of heat needed to raise the temperature of a gram of water by 1°C (33.8°F). (See also energy; nutrition.) | **calorie**

A cell-growth disease in which, for reasons at present unknown, a cell or group of cells divide, producing 'rogue' cells which eventually outnumber the surrounding healthy cells. Some may also detach themselves and travel in blood or lymph to another site where they lodge and begin their division again to form secondary growths. Such tumours can arise in most organs of the body and as leukaemia, sometimes known as cancer of the blood. | **cancer**

cancer   The most common form of canine cancer occurs in the mammary glands in the bitch (neoplasia). Regular examination of all dogs for any form of growth is important in order to detect the disease in its early stages. The dog should be seen by a veterinarian without delay if an abnormality is found. Primary growths can be removed by surgery, though some believe that such an approach may cause the rogue cells to spread and form secondaries elsewhere if any are left. Radium implants and treatment with X-rays are alternative courses of action. Hormone treatment, particularly in prostate gland cancer, and radiofrequency heat for skin cancer, are other approaches which are sometimes used. (See also leukaemia; tumour.

canicola fever   See leptospirosis.

canine teeth   The sharp, single-cusped teeth between the incisors and premolars, one on each side of the upper and lower jaws, adapted for tearing purposes. (See also teeth.)

canker   A general term for an ear disease symptomised by the dog shaking its head and hanging it on one side and by the presence of a brown, sticky, mud-like wax, reddening of the inside of the ear caused by inflammation, sometimes swelling and a smelly discharge. It is primarily caused by ear mites and can manifest itself in dry and wet forms. Clean the affected ears gently with wedges of soft cotton wool where access is easy; never poke anything down into the ear. Ear drops (there are several good proprietary brands available) slightly warmed, should be dropped into the ear regularly and the exudate cleaned away from the outer ear; but if the condition persists, see a veterinarian. Do not use powder in the ear; it clogs the delicate channels and will itself need to be cleaned out.

Preventive measures include keeping the outer ear dry and clear of matted hair, and regular inspection – especially of flap-eared dogs – while grooming to catch any signs of canker in the early stages, when rapid treatment can help to forestall more serious and long-standing complications. (See also ear; otitis.)

capillary   A tiny, thin-walled vessel. Capillaries form a fine and complicated network throughout the tissues of the body, joining the arterioles to the veins. Exchange of fluids between blood and tissues is effected across capillary walls governed by the opening and closing of a minute muscle in the arteriole wall.

carbohydrates   See nutrition.

carbon dioxide   A gas generated in body tissue as a waste product, transported by the blood to the lungs where it is exchanged for oxygen and expired during respiration. It is also used in anaesthesia to stimulate respiration.

carbon monoxide   A poisonous gas liberated in some solid fuel heating systems and in car exhaust fumes. A concentration as low as 1 per cent can cause death by saturating the haemoglobin of the blood. Adequate ventilation of kennels or other accommodation is important and an animal overcome by the fumes should be taken into fresh air and, if necessary, artificial respiration applied without delay.

carbon monoxide

A term used to describe certain forms of cancer.

carcinoma

Heart failure, which can occur when the demand for oxygen by the tissues is greater than the supply. During exercise, for example, muscles may need up to fifteen times more oxygen than when the dog is at rest. The heart usually has sufficient reserve to meet the increased need, but defects or disease can mean that it is unable to cope and an accumulation of blood arises in and around the heart, resulting in cardiac failure. (See also heart.)

cardiac failure

See electrocardiogram.

cardiogram

See electrocardiograph.

cardiograph

The dog, as in all land-living carnivores, has carnassial teeth, situated between the premolars and molars, which have developed from the first lower molars and last upper premolars. They are large, with diverging roots, and are designed for dealing with particularly tough food. They can be seen in use when a dog turns its head on one side during eating, for example a bone, in order to bring them into action. (See also teeth.)

carnassial teeth

A member of the family of Carnivora which includes dogs, cats, lions, tigers, wolves, seals, bears and other flesh-eating mammals.

carnivore

Name of two main arteries, situated one on each side of the neck. At the jaws they split into various branches to take the blood to the deep and superficial parts of the head, including the brain.

carotid

A group of bones forming the 'wrist' on the forepaw of the dog. (For drawing, see paw.)

carpus

Most dogs travel well but some suffer from motion sickness. A dog should be familiarised with travel at an early age; if it appears to be getting distressed, or pants and salivates, stop to let it out of the car for a short time before continuing the journey. It also helps to have a passenger who will talk to the dog soothingly and gently calm it down. With these methods and a lessening of any fear the dog may have of the car, it usually grows out of the problem as it gets older.

In extreme cases, or those where the condition persists to the dog's frequent distress, consult a veterinarian who will probably prescribe tranquillisers to be taken before a journey. (See also transport.)

car sickness

A hard but flexible connective tissue which, in its various forms, bears weight, reduces friction, cushions shock and exhibits high tensile strength. It occurs in such places as in the larynx and trachea (where its purpose is to prevent collapse from outside pressure), and

cartilage

cartilage around the ribs and joints such as the stifle. It comprises rows of cells embedded in gelatinous tissue without nerves or blood vessels running through. Conditions resulting from abnormalities in development of cartilage and its degeneration in old age sometimes affect dogs and their ease of movement, especially if it occurs in the joints. (See also hip dysplasia.)

castration The surgical removal (orchidectomy) of the testes, permanently preventing mating. It is also – and perhaps best – performed in cases of tumours and diseases of the testes and prostate gland. The operation curtails the flow of the hormone testosterone and if performed on the immature dog results in prevention of the full development of the sex glands. Castration in the adult dog often causes the build-up of fat due to a slower metabolism.

Castration should not be carried out as a cure for aggressiveness unless it is of a sexually-rooted form; nor will it necessarily stop so-called objectionable habits around the house, although if the libido of a highly sexually-oriented dog is reduced it may prove successful.

Neutering a dog by castration is sometimes done when the animal becomes a regular problem, either by escaping or becoming difficult to control, each time a nearby bitch comes into season. An alternative and less drastic form of male sterilisation is vasectomy.

catabiosis The ageing of cells by natural means.

cataract Opacity of the lens of the eye, which causes a dimness of vision and, as the condition worsens, loss of sight. Most cataracts occur in aged dogs, though some arise through injury and others, evident generally in young dogs, through a defective lens. It may also be due to diabetes. Some breeds, such as American cocker spaniels, beagles and golden retrievers, seem to be more likely to develop hereditary cataracts than others. Surgery is the only course of treatment, performed by a specialist veterinarian. (See also eye.)

catarrh An inflammatory condition of the mucous membranes accompanied by a purulent discharge from nasal passages. It can also occur in parts of the alimentary canal where it is mostly caused by irritation or infection.

Nasal catarrh generally occurs through cold, damp conditions and can deteriorate to produce more serious respiratory problems such as bronchitis. If the dog is feverish, a veterinarian should be consulted as to appropriate treatment. Sinusitis is a painful complication of catarrh.

catgut An absorbable suture material, produced from sheep's intestine.

catheter A tube, usually rigid for female use and flexible for male, which is inserted in the urethra to draw urine from the bladder when it cannot be passed by normal means. The skills of a veterinarian must be used in any form of catheterisation since inadvertent damage to the urethra and the occurrence of cystitis are just two possible dangers.

Of the tail end. The caudal part is nearer to the tail. | **caudal**

A tiny portion of protoplasm. Millions of cells, together with fluid and intercellular materials, make up the tissues of the body. Each cell comprises a nucleus with surrounding cytoplasm in a cell membrane. The cytoplasm contains a solution of protein and other nutrients. The nucleus, with its complicated system of proteins, is the control centre for cell activities. Most cells have organelles, which direct a specialised function, including mitochondria where combustion takes place to provide energy for the work of the cell, and genetic material such as chromosomes. | **cell**

Following fusion of two cells – a spermatozoon and an ovum – during fertilisation, cell division commences with that cell by a process of mitosis to 'build' an individual through a continuing increase in cell numbers which differentiate to become specialised for a variety of needs, eg nerve cells, skin cells, etc. This differentiation is largely controlled by genes in the cell nuclei. Cell division also occurs during healing, when uninjured cells divide to replace those destroyed, and when replacement cells are needed through wear and tear. (See also mitosis.) | **cell division**

See brain. | **cerebellum**

Normally a clear, colourless fluid, it surrounds the spinal cord and stem of the brain, acting as a shock absorber. It contains proteins, sugar, various chemicals and a few cells. It is produced in the brain ventricles at a rate of about 3ml per hour and eventually drains into the bloodstream.
   Laboratory examination of CSF assists in the diagnosis of brain diseases: bacterial presence denotes infection and blood cells indicate brain damage. Chemical changes from the normal constituents also provide valuable diagnostic information. | **cerebrospinal fluid (CSF)**

See brain. | **cerebrum**

The neck of the uterus which projects into the top of the vagina. It is usually closed by a muscle but expands substantially during whelping. | **cervix**

A class of endoparasites known as 'tapeworms'. (See parasites.) | **cestoda**

A useful antiseptic used for cleansing skin, dishes, glassware, etc. It is also contained in ointments. | **cetrimide**

See training. | **chain**

The use of chemical compounds to treat disease. Such compounds, including, for example, antibiotics, sulphonamides, etc, have bactericidal properties without causing serious harm to living tissue. | **chemotherapy**

49

chest	The area, also known as the thorax or brisket, which is bounded by the diaphragm and ribs, and contains principally the heart, lungs, bronchi, oesophagus, thymus gland and important nerves, arteries and veins. The thoracic cavity is lined with the pleura (which covers the lung surfaces) and the heart is surrounded by the pericardium. The heart, in the centre of the thoracic cavity, lies slightly to the left between the two lungs. The spinal cord is at the back of the chest.
chest, injuries of	Most chest injuries are caused by accidents involving vehicles, or by falls, kicks or fights. Any such injury should be dealt with by a veterinarian with extreme urgency; there may be internal complications which cannot be seen. Broken ribs, for example, can puncture a lung, impair respiration or damage the heart. The spine is also vulnerable. An injured dog should be soothed, kept warm and moved as little as possible before the veterinarian arrives. (See also accidents; wounds.)
chewing	See mastication.
cheyne-stokes respiration	An unnatural form of respiration which diminishes until almost imperceptible, gathers momentum until very rapid, and diminishes again. The process is repeated continuously in a sobbing manner. It appears with shock following violent injury, severe nervous trauma or sometimes collapse from heart or kidney failure. It should be considered a serious condition and can herald imminent respiratory failure.
children, living with	Children can have fine relationships with dogs providing they understand an animal's needs, reactions and capabilities. The first rule is to remember that a dog is not a child's toy. If a dog or puppy is poked, pulled around, teased or kicked – even in fun – it will become withdrawn, nervous, aggressive or irritable and often ill. Dogs, like children, need food, sleep and play at regular times; too much or too little of any will be reflected in ill-health, and a child who receives insufficient instruction on how to treat a dog will be neither loved nor trusted by that dog. Train the child to be consistently kind – and to understand the dog – from an early age, and the result will be a firm friendship for life, and consideration for other animals. If the child is very young, the association between dog and child should be supervised by an adult so that both are trained to appreciate the other's feelings and limitations. Owners should also be aware that a child's toys, such as marbles, counters, etc, are potential hazards, especially to a puppy. Care should be taken to ensure that the puppy is wormed and a veterinarian can advise on good hygienic practices so that the child does not pick up infection from the puppy.
chills	A shivering attack accompanied by a raised body temperature. It can lead to complications, being subsequently worsened by infection leading to bronchitis and other respiratory problems. Prevention is

relatively easy as chills are caused primarily by damp and cold. Make sure your dog is thoroughly dried with a large, clean dry towel after a wet walk, and warmed if cold. Dogs should not be left standing about for lengthy periods in cold, wet or damp conditions, especially if unused to doing so.

At the first signs of a chill a dog should be kept warm and dry and observed for any worsening of the condition – increased difficulty in breathing, faster respiration and a gradual or rapid temperature rise – when a veterinarian should be consulted.

chills

This antibiotic has a similar range of activity to the tetracyclines. It can be given orally and intravenously, but not intramuscularly as it is painful in dogs. Damage of blood cells and bone marrow is possible following prolonged use, together with hypersensitivity.

chloramphenicol

A highly effective bactericidal agent, commonly known under the trade name Hibitane. It is a useful medium in which to store instruments (as a 1 per cent solution in ethyl alcohol) and is effective against blood, pus, mucus, etc in cleansing. (See also antiseptics.)

chlorhexidine

See electrolytes; nutrition.

chloride

A useful drain cleanser for kennels made up as a solution 170g per 4.5 litres (6oz per gallon) of water.

chlorinated lime

A powerful anaesthetic, not in popular use today due to its toxic effects, and the risk of cardiac failure and often fatal liver damage. Even its use in euthanasia is now rare as stages of excitement and distress, followed by a depressed state, are experienced before the chloroform acts on the central nervous system to induce paralysis and death.

chloroform

Used as a premedication prior to anaesthetic, and as a tranquilliser. It is administered by intravenous injection (where it acts within a few minutes) or by deep intramuscular injection where about forty-five minutes are needed for appreciable results. Injected subcutaneously, it often produces a local reaction. As it has irritant properties a dilute (0.5 per cent) solution is mostly used.

chlorpromazine

This is an extremely dangerous condition which often proves fatal. Choking is frequently caused by a foreign body being partially swallowed and becoming lodged in the entrance to the trachea, thus blocking the supply of air to the lungs.

Prevention lies in not feeding the dog unsuitable bones and ensuring that all potentially hazardous small objects are kept out of its (and especially a puppy's) reach. Cure, if it is possible, must be the very speedy removal of the obstruction to allow the dog to breathe again. This is done by grasping the dog's tongue and pulling it forward and then attempting to pull out the foreign body with fingers, forceps or tweezers. The dog will be extremely

choking

choking	distressed as it fights for breath and the fingers may be bitten. However, drastic measures are necessary to give the dog any chance of recovery. 'Choking' is also used as a term to describe an obstruction of the oesophagus, producing symptoms which include vomiting, refusal of food and dejection. Here there will be time to call for the advice of a veterinarian. (See also accidents; bones; foreign bodies.)
cholesterol	A fatty substance made in the liver and found in the blood. It is a parent compound of some steroids and is chemically linked to various digestive acids and hormones. Bile salts and some sex hormones are produced from it. Its level is high in deficiencies of the thyroid and uncontrolled diabetes and low in wasting diseases such as tuberculosis and cancer. In some liver conditions the level is increased; in others decreased.
choline	The precursor of acetylcholine and a member of the B group of vitamins. It is present in meat, liver and egg yolk, and a deficiency in the dog, though rare, may be reflected in fatty liver and kidney disturbances. (See also acetylcholine; nutrition.)
chondritis	Inflammation of the cartilage.
choosing a dog	There are nearly 350 breeds of dog available and an additional large number of local breeds which predominate in one country or another. These are usually variations bred locally and generally confined to local areas. The choice among the cross-breeds or mongrels is almost infinite. Some people say that pedigree dogs are more intelligent or healthier than mongrels; others state the reverse. The fact is that dogs, like people, are individuals; each has its own character and personality. However, there are certainly some character types and variations between breeds, and temperaments common to a specific breed. Spaniels, for example, tend to be friendly, intelligent, affectionate, cheerfully eager and anxious to please. Terriers often show an aggressive friendliness, are good-humoured and generally playful. This does not mean that one who loves spaniels will find terriers totally unattractive or vice-versa; it does mean that people – and dog owners are no exception – have preferences. Some may prefer the affectionate, faithful intelligence of a Welsh Springer spaniel to the loyal but somewhat stubborn character of the Rottweiler or the wilful but beautiful Afghan hound. Some may prefer short-haired to long-haired dogs; small ones to large ones. What one owner finds exasperating in a dog others find amusing. Beauty, too, is often in the eye of the dog owner or breeder. A discussion on the various breeds and their respective merits is beyond the scope of this book, but there are many publications devoted to the subject (see Further Reading). However some guidelines on how to set about choosing a dog should be useful. Whether you decide to buy a pedigree dog or give a home to a mongrel, you should choose carefully. Forethought and planning will save another unwanted dog being abandoned or destroyed.

choosing a dog

The size of the dog is probably the first consideration. A large breed for instance, will be unhappy and possibly unhealthy in a small flat. The time and space available for exercise, the financial and moral responsibilities of dog owning and the provision of suitable accommodation are all vital factors. Much also depends on what the dog is wanted for. It can be just as a companion, as a show or working dog or principally for guard duties. It can also be a combination of all these but a show dog may be a very different animal from one chosen as an affectionate pet.

A pedigree dog should be purchased from a reputable breeder. Your local breed association will help, and the Kennel Club will provide lists of breed associations in your area.

If you decide to have a mongrel, the choice is equally wide. Battersea Dogs' Home, the NCDL (National Canine Defence League) and the RSPCA in Great Britain, and local rescue organisations and dogs' homes in most countries, welcome enquiries. Your local veterinarian will probably also know of a source for a sound, healthy mongrel. A mongrel pup can often be unpredictable in terms of size and temperament unless you know about its parents, but your veterinarian can give you a general idea of how big it is likely to grow. Local advertisements are another way of finding a dog. While the internet may be a good way of locating breeders and animal welfare organisations, it is never good practice to buy a dog via the internet. A personal visit to the breeder's premises is thoroughly recommended.

Sometimes the purchase of a fully-grown dog, especially if it is a mongrel, can be preferable to taking on a puppy with all the need for training, especially if the new owner is elderly or has limited time.

Do not buy from street traders or markets, where animals are often unhealthy, or from pet shops that are obviously unclean or badly equipped or unable to provide background information on the animal. Some pet shops, of course, are well run and do have some sound, healthy pups for sale, but a visit can soon show you what you need to know. (See also Battersea Dogs' Home; Kennel Club; mongrel; NCDL; pedigree; unwanted dogs.)

chorea

Also known as St Vitus's Dance, this is a serious condition and can follow an attack of distemper. It is marked by spasmodic movements of the limbs, face, head, etc, which, while sometimes remaining of a minor nature, often progress until the entire body becomes involved and the dog reaches complete exhaustion due to the continual effort and lack of rest.

Treatment consists of the administration of antispasmodics, a nutritious, easily digested diet, peace and quiet and gentle soothing, and a comfortable bed. In the last century dogs suffering from chorea were often dosed with very small amounts of the poison strychnos nux vomica – a drastic course of action which, while apparently curing many, also killed some!

Since the disease is frequently connected with distemper, prevention is best approached by immunisation against distemper when a puppy is about twelve weeks of age.

chorion	The outer of the three foetal membranes, being that closest to the uterine wall. (See also placenta.)
chromosomes	Thread-like particles present in the cell nucleus during cell division. Chromosomes contain DNA and genes which determine the hereditary nature of the body.
chronic	A chronic disease is one which is deep seated and of lengthy duration, in contrast to acute.
circulation of the blood	See vascular system.
cirrhosis	A disease affecting aged dogs rather than younger ones, although malnutrition can be a cause. It is usually associated with the liver but can also occur in other organs including kidneys and lungs. It is characterised by the replacement of normal healthy cells by fibrous scar tissue which hardens the organ. In advanced cases the hardening compresses surrounding blood vessels and impairs circulation.
	In some breeds, including Bedlington terriers, toxic excesses of copper in the liver lead to cirrhosis – apparently an inherited condition.
	A healthy, balanced diet throughout a dog's life will do much to prevent the disease.
clavicle	A bone, sometimes known as the 'collar bone', which is part of the foreleg and situated next to the scapula and top of the humerus. In the dog it is about 1cm (½in) long and a third as wide. It does not usually appear on radiographs.
claw	Horny, slightly curved skin substance with blood vessels and nerves running through it. The dog has five claws, covering the third phalanges of the digits (or toes). (See drawing under paw.)
	Much care must be taken when trimming claws during grooming to prevent haemorrhage by cutting too far back into the matrix or 'quick' where the blood vessels are situated. They grow rapidly and may curve under if left unfiled or untrimmed. This is particularly true of the dew claw, which is not subject to wear and can grow in a full circle back into the pad. Dew claws should therefore be inspected regularly and trimmed accordingly; their surgical removal by a vet, preferably while the dog is still a puppy, is usually advocated.
	Claws sometimes become torn and should be carefully cleared of jagged pieces by cutting with a pair of nail clippers. Fungal infections may attack claws but injuries are more common. (See also dew claw; onychomycosis.)
cleft palate	A gap in the hard palate or roof of the mouth. It is mostly a hereditary condition (violence can be another cause) which is rarely seen beyond the puppy stage of life since affected puppies are unable to suck and feed. They can, of course, be fed artificially and the defect corrected by surgery. Affected dogs should not be used for

breeding. Hereditary cleft palates may be associated with some breeds, including bulldog, daschund, German shepherd, shih tzu and Staffordshire bull terrier.

cleft palate

See grooming.

clipping

A small, knob-shaped organ of erectile tissue situated at the ventral angle of the vulva of the bitch. Its development corresponds to that of the penis in the dog.

clitoris

See coagulation.

clotting of blood

The blood-clotting process (and similarly coagulation disorders) is comparable in man and dog. Coagulation of blood occurs naturally in a wound and at the cut end of a vessel, so that a plug is formed to arrest blood loss. During haemorrhage, wound tissue and platelets release thromboplastin which reacts with prothrombin and calcium to produce thrombin, which in turn alters the protein substance fibrinogen to fibrin. A network of fibrin forms, trapping escaping blood cells. Platelets also stick together at the wound and a jelly-like clot is formed. This, however, is a simplified explanation of a complicated process involving at least eleven clotting factors.

Coagulation takes only a few minutes to accomplish and, after a few hours of non-disturbance, serum seeps out from the clot. (See also blood; haemophilia; thrombosis.)

coagulation

A coat made of warm, waterproof material can be useful for an aged dog or one convalescing during cold weather when chills or other adverse conditions are likely to be contracted during exercise. It should be fitted to wrap snugly around the body, protecting the chest and flanks, and tied loosely at convenient points away from the throat, groin, etc. A good example is the standard coat used for greyhounds and whippets. If a dog regularly wears a coat it should not suddenly be left off, particularly in cold or wet weather when a chill is likely.

coat

See grooming; hair.

coat care

See nutrition.

cobalt

An internal fungal disease affecting respiratory organs with secondary lesions there and elsewhere in the body. It is rare in the UK though identified in the USA, particularly California, Arizona and Texas, parts of South America and other arid regions. It seems to be associated with desert areas and may arise from eating, or making contact with, infected wild rodents. Boxers seem to be a susceptible breed. Symptoms include fever, lameness and skin nodules.

coccidiomycosis

A parasitic disease of the small intestine which is more common in other animals, including rabbits, sheep, goats and cattle, than in

coccidiosis

coccidiosis	dogs. It is symptomised by diarrhoea and diagnosed by microscopic examination of the faeces.
coccus	A round bacterial cell. Diplococci are such cells in pairs; streptococci are in a chain formation and staphylococci in bunches. (See also bacteria.)
cochlea	A spiral-shaped tube opening into the vestibule, or central part, of the inner ear. Its duct is concerned with the transmission of hearing impulses, via the sensory fibres of the vestibocranial nerve, to the brain. (See also ear.)
codeine	An alkaloid of the morphine group of drugs mainly used to ease pain and coughing.
cod-liver oil	A mineral oil obtained from the liver of the cod-fish. It contains vitamin D and increases the capacity of the dog to absorb calcium from the intestine. An occasional teaspoonful in the dog's food, therefore, helps the development of growing dogs and the prevention of rickets. It is also good for the coat of an out-of-condition dog and as a daily winter conditioner. A 100ml (4fl oz) bottle of pure cod-liver oil will last a dog such as a labrador or boxer, weighing about 30kg (60lb), around a month. Care should be taken not drastically to exceed the recommended levels continuously, since the action of Vitamin D contained in cod-liver oil eases the absorption of calcium from the intestines. Rancid cod-liver oil can produce a poisoning effect.
cold	See exposure; hypothermia.
colic	A term frequently used in the past to describe any one of a number of acute diseases of the abdomen with symptoms of pain and general ill-health. In modern times we are able to define intestinal and digestive disorders more critically.
colitis	Inflammation of the colon, or large intestine. It can be caused by infection through, for example, food poisoning, or the presence of a foreign body. It is characterised by pain and tenderness. The cause needs determining and treatment needs to be made by a veterinarian. Ulcerative colitis is a serious chronic form.
collagen	A protein found in bone, cartilage, tendon, skin and connective tissue. Collagenous fibres have high tensile strength.
collapse	A sudden breakdown under severe physical or mental strain. The lung is said to collapse when, for one or another reason, it ceases to fill with air. A dog can collapse from virtually any severe strain and will need immediate attention. Heart failure is one example resulting in collapse; heat stroke and shock are just two others.
collar	Every dog should have a collar and learn to wear it, with a lead during exercise, from puppyhood.

The first collar should be a cheap one as it will soon be outgrown. All collars should be large enough to fit loosely around the dog's neck but not so loose as to be easily pulled off over the head. Leather collars are best, with small dogs having light, rather narrow collars and the larger breeds heavier, stronger ones.

In most countries the law demands that dogs should wear collars when away from their owners' premises and that each collar should bear the owner's name and address on a tag or panel. It also helps if the dog's name is included. This sensible precaution is one which you will appreciate if your dog is ever lost. Another more recent form of identification is by tattooing. Collars may be removed in the home, since continual wear affects the hair on the necks of some dogs.

Proprietary flea collars are available which can be cut to size and worn with an ordinary collar, when necessary, to control such external parasites as fleas, ticks and lice. They are generally quite effective and can provide protection for up to about four months through all weathers. They should, however, be removed if the dog shows signs of skin irritation or allergy as some dogs are prone to reaction. (See also 'Elizabethan' collar; exercise; lead; legal and moral responsibilities; training.)

collar

Part of the large intestine running from the caecum to the rectum. The colon is divided into ascending, transverse and descending sections; it lies at the back of the abdomen and in shape resembles a shepherd's crook. The descending colon is the longest part the straight portion of the crook – and is about 12cm (5in) in length. (See also intestines.)

colon

The rich milk from the bitch which is secreted immediately after whelping and for three or four days subsequently. It is substantially higher in protein and has a somewhat higher fat content than the milk which follows and contains concentrations of vitamins A and D and the initial antibodies which provide the puppies with their first, temporary protection against infection.

colostrum

A deep form of unconsciousness with a lack of reflex actions. It is often the terminal stage of an illness such as that affecting the brain. It can also occur in some forms of poisoning, and in severe diabetes through either the terminal stages of the disease or the excessive or insufficient administration of insulin. (See also unconsciousness.)

coma

The better you know your dog – and the closer you are to it in terms of companionship – the better communication you will have with it. Communication means the transmission of information or the conveyance of a meaning between two individuals. Though there are various stereotyped forms of canine communication, eg tail wagging for pleasure, urination sometimes for marking territory, baring of teeth accompanied by growling and often barking representing anger and a warning to

communication

communication

others, each dog has its own way of communicating with its owner and friends. Facial expressions in dogs can often be interpreted correctly by those who know it well and actions can easily show when some form or another of attention is required.

Communication plays an important role in safeguarding a dog's health: an observant owner can easily recognise the signs of ill-health. Communication is also valuable when a dog is sick. Many grievously ill dogs have been nursed back to health (and provided perhaps with the will to live) by the soothing ministrations of a much-loved owner coupled to fine veterinary care.

Spending much time with a puppy helps to form a sound foundation for communication in later life. Continued companionship and careful observation and reaction add useful bricks to the foundation. (See also behaviour; social interaction; training.)

complementary medicine

The use of complementary (or alternative) medicine in veterinary work is steadily increasing around the world and good results can be obtained from treatment by trained hands. Additional research is needed in some areas but generally both the value and limitations of various treatments and techniques is becoming better understood. This approach to the diagnosis and treatment of illness and the preservation of health includes homeopathy, herbal medicine, acupuncture, physical therapy and massage therapy.

Homeopathy features the use of small doses of drugs that, in a healthy animal, produce similar symptoms to those in a sick animal undergoing treatment. Correct dosage is vital.

Herbal or botanical medicine makes use of plants and plant materials in treatment and, because some plant extracts can be toxic in inappropriate dosage, much care is needed in administration. Some proprietary herbal medication can be beneficial but checking with a veterinarian, especially if other veterinary treatment is in hand, is essential.

Acupuncture uses a range of fine needles accurately inserted for short periods of time at precise points on the body known to a trained acupuncturist. It is used in the treatment of a variety of diseases and conditions. The dog needs to be immobilised and a regular course of treatment is usually required.

Physical and massage therapies are non-invasive and are useful in treatment and rehabilitation, particularly for muscle and joint disorders.

Increasingly, veterinary practices are taking complementary medicine seriously and qualified veterinarians are undergoing the additional specialist training definitely needed to be able to make safe and effective use of these techniques.

conception

The fertilisation of the ovum by a spermatozoon which occurs during a successful mating.

concussion

A temporary loss of consciousness caused by a violent blow to or a fall on the head. It should last for only a few seconds and if unconsciousness is prolonged a veterinarian should be contacted as there may be some more serious damage to the brain.

concussion

In very mild cases, concussion does not cause complete loss of consciousness and the dog may stagger, sometimes vomit and show signs of shock. Slow, shallow breathing is evident and contracted pupils of the eye may not react to light, though equal in size. Complete rest and warmth is required, and no liquids must be given until the animal has recovered. Even on full recovery it is worth having the dog checked over by a veterinarian.

A term usually describing abnormalities transmitted from one generation to the next, but more accurately it means dating from or before birth.

congenital

A mucous membrane which lines the insides of the eyelids and transparently covers the cornea. It is filled with blood vessels and nerves. A fold of the conjunctiva forms the dog's third eyelid and is usually dark in contrast to the remainder. It is mostly hidden in the eye socket as the third eyelid and is very mobile.

conjunctiva

Inflammation of the conjunctiva. It is caused by infection, dust and grit in the air (sometimes due to the dog poking its head out of the window of a moving car), smoke and, in some individuals, pollen. It can also be produced by a vitamin A deficiency. The eyes water and often there is a discharge from them. Washing the eye out with a warm saline solution (see entry) is the first treatment: if the condition does not respond, seek the advice of a veterinarian.

conjunctivitis

This binds all other body tissues together. It also supports them and transports nutrients to and waste products from them in some cases. Strictly, blood is a form of connective tissue; so are collagen, ligaments, parts of the skin, tendons, cartilage, bone and haemopoietic tissue.

connective tissue

Infrequent passing of faeces. A common enough complaint, but it may be symptomatic of a more serious condition. If prolonged after laxative treatment a veterinarian should be consulted. The disorder is frequently due to incorrect diet, with insufficient exercise a secondary reason. Excessively dry food, obstructed anal glands and abdominal tumours are others, the latter being reflected in long-standing constipation. Observe the dog for other symptoms, since as a rule these will be apparent in more serious diseases.

constipation

Symptoms of constipation include small, infrequent or total lack of faeces, straining with no effect and sometimes vomiting.

A disease that spreads by direct contact. Mange is a particularly unpleasant example.

contagious

See bruise.

contusion

See nursing.

convalescence

convulsion	A violent involuntary muscle spasm and contortion. Convulsions are usually symptomatic of another, more serious, condition requiring veterinary treatment; epilepsy is perhaps the most common cause of canine convulsions – itself a symptom usually of canine distemper. Pressure from a brain tumour may produce convulsive activity, as can other brain diseases, hypoglycaemia, extreme stress, poisoning, and eclampsia in the whelping bitch.
copper	See nutrition.
coprophagia	The habit of eating faeces. Puppies sometimes adopt this rather unnerving behaviour but it is usually of a temporary nature. It is thought that it may have a bearing on stabilisation of gut flora, or be due to a lack of minerals in the diet, or just because some puppies have odd eating habits (chewing coal is another). If discouraged, the habit is soon discarded.
copulation	See mating.
cornea	The tough, protective, transparent structure over the front of the eye which allows light to pass through the pupil to the retina for vision. Transparency is due to the arrangement of collagen fibres and damage or oedema may affect sight through loss of transparency. (See also eye).
coronary thrombosis	See thrombosis.
corpuscle	A name given to red cells (erythrocytes) and white cells (leucocytes) in the blood. (See also blood.)
corpus luteum	A yellowish structure formed in the ovary following ovulation, when the ovum is released. About twenty-five days after conception it has filled the ovary and produces progesterone, stimulating the growth of the lining of the uterus for pregnancy. If conception does not occur it disappears, being formed again at the next oestrus in readiness for a possible pregnancy.
corticosteroid	A natural hormone (eg cortisone or hydrocortisone) secreted by the cortex of the adrenal glands, or a synthetic derivative such as prednisone or prednisolone. Corticosteroids are used as anti-inflammatory agents and sometimes against shock and serious allergic reactions. There are significant dangers in excessive doses and in prolonged treatment: healing may be impaired, for example, infections masked and similar reactions produced to those found in over-active adrenal glands.
corticotrophin	A hormone which controls the secretion of corticosteroids by the adrenal glands. It is produced in the anterior pituitary gland. Sometimes used as an injectable to stimulate inactive adrenals.
cortisone	A corticosteroid produced by the cortex of the adrenal glands.

Generally caused by irritation of the nerve endings of the larynx or by the presence of mucus, smoke, dust, etc. Coughing is also a symptom associated with many infections and the cause may be serious. When a dog coughs frequently, whether or not other symptoms are present, an investigation by a veterinarian is called for to discover whether it may be due to one or more of the following: obesity, tonsillitis, chronic bronchitis, emphysema, distemper, heart valve disease and pleurisy. (See also kennel cough.)

coughing

See paws.

cracked pad

An involuntary muscle contraction accompanied by pain in the affected muscles – usually in the hind legs. It appears to affect some breeds more than others. As perhaps would be expected, racing greyhounds are susceptible to cramp during substantial muscular exertion. A defective heart, tiredness from overactivity and dietary deficiencies are probable underlying causes. The occurrence of an attack is sometimes simultaneous with cyanosis which may indicate a heart problem.

cramp

Hunting dogs, particularly after strenuous swimming in cold waters, are also candidates for cramp and some strains of Scottish terrier frequently contract the complaint during puppyhood, indicating a hereditary cause in this breed. The puppy shows symptoms after exercise when there appears to be marked difficulty in walking. General symptoms of cramp include pain, slowing down of movement or collapse, and hardening and twisting of the stricken muscles. Rest and massage until normality returns is the best on-the-spot treatment.

See skull.

cranium

The turning point or sudden worsening in a severe illness.

crisis

See agglutination; blood group; transfusions and infusions.

cross-matching

When injected, this extract from trees of the Strychnos group is a deadly poison. It was first used in animals in the early part of the nineteenth century to reduce muscle spasm in tetanus and is still used by the veterinary profession as a muscle relaxant.

curare

An operation performed by a veterinarian to 'scrape' a wall of an organ surrounding a cavity. It is most commonly done to the walls of the uterus following abortion or whelping complications so that a new, healthy lining will form.

curettage

Caused by over-production of corticosteroids by the cortex of the adrenal glands. The dog becomes depressed and lethargic and anxiously increases its intake of food and water. Slowly the skin is affected by loss of hair and pustule formation. The abdomen swells and muscles begin to atrophy. It rarely appears in dogs younger than about five years of age.

Cushing's disease

Cushing's disease

Treatment is by surgical removal of the adrenals and intensive care. Post-operative attention includes regular administration of the hormones lost by the operation, usually by means of implants. (See also adrenalectomy.)

cut

See wound.

cyanosis

A blueness seen on tongue, lips, gums, etc, due to a lack of oxygen. It is a serious indication that the dog's heart is being overtaxed, either because it is defective or pushed beyond its normal capacity through overwork or disease. In some cases, such as pneumonia, it may be because lung congestion is preventing the absorption of sufficient oxygen. Immediate rest is as essential as an early examination by a veterinarian.

cyst

A growth or swelling filled with fluid. Cysts are soft and mostly benign. They are most commonly found in the ovary, in blocked sebaceous glands, or as hydatid cysts caused by tapeworm eggs in various organs including liver and brain, as interdigital cysts, as ranula in the mouth, and as dermoid cysts beneath the skin. If a cyst is not causing any problems, then it is usually best for it to be left alone, otherwise surgical removal is the only alternative. (See also tumour.)

cystitis

Bladder inflammation. Bitches are more commonly affected than dogs, the condition often being caused by an infection usually contracted via the urethra. Urinary calculi, kidney diseases or parasites can be other causes.

Frequent urination with some pain in the lower abdomen, straining, and sometimes blood-stained urine and constipation are symptoms. In chronic cases, urine retention is often part of the condition.

The dog should be seen by a veterinarian and a fresh sample of its urine taken along in a clean container for laboratory examination. Urinary antiseptics are prescribed if an infection is the cause and pain relievers may be necessary. The patient is encouraged to increase its intake of fresh clean water. (See also urination; urine.)

cytology

The study of cells, their structure and function. (See also histology.)

cytoplasm

The fluid medium, enclosed in a cell membrane, that surrounds the nucleus of a cell.

Dangerous Dogs Act, 1991

This Act (UK) prohibits persons from keeping dogs bred for fighting, or having characteristics of such a dog, and any dog that is deemed to present a serious danger to the public. It specifically names the pit bull terrier and Japanese tosa. The Act also prohibits breeding, selling, giving or exchanging any fighting dog or allowing it to stray, and requires muzzling and lead control of dangerous dogs in a public place. A full copy of the Act can be obtained in the UK from HM Stationery Office.

Dangerous Drugs Act, 1965

Aimed at the prevention of drug misuse. Addictive drugs, or narcotics, such as morphine, cocaine, pethidine, etc, are covered by the Act, which means that veterinarians can obtain them for animal treatment but strict records of their use must be maintained and the drugs must always be kept under lock and key. Only a veterinarian may prescribe, procure or possess drugs mentioned in the Act in the UK, and for this reason dog owners cannot obtain them elsewhere.

deafness

May be the result of disease, injury or heredity. It also occurs in aged dogs. Deafness is caused commonly by canker and by injury (externally from a blow or internally from damage by a foreign body to ear drum, Eustachian tubes, brain or auditory nerves). It also occurs congenitally in some white dogs, including bull terriers. Foxhounds, dalmatians and great danes are other breeds which may be prone to deafness.

Care of a dog's ears throughout its life does much to prevent deafness in later years. Any condition should be treated as soon as it occurs. A gradual loss of hearing is often mistaken for disobedience and, if in doubt, should be checked by observant testing. One of the greatest dangers to deaf dogs is traffic, and extra care should be taken to safeguard against accidents.

death

Sometimes a deep coma can be mistaken for death. In death the heart and respiration cease, the eyeball loses its firmness and the eyes glaze. Eyelids do not respond by flickering when a finger touches the front of the eye, muscles go limp and the jaw drops. Body temperature falls very gradually and in an hour or two rigor mortis stiffens the body which eventually relaxes again as decay commences.

debarking

Surgical removal of the vocal cords (devocalisation). The Royal College of Veterinary Surgeons considers this practice thoroughly unethical and an unnecessary mutilation. (See also bark; voice.)

defecation

The expulsion of waste products or faeces from the anus. Abnormal faeces or difficulty in defecating provide clues to the health of the dog. (See also constipation; diarrhoea.)

deformity

Can be inherited or acquired. Common inherited deformities include cleft palate, imperforate anus and bone malformations. If

deformity	serious deformities are present and evident at birth, euthanasia may be the best course of action. Dogs with inherited deformities should *never* be used for breeding.
dehydration	A serious condition caused by the loss of more fluid from the tissues than is absorbed. Dehydration can be produced by certain disorders such as diarrhoea, vomiting, heat exhaustion, gastro-enteritis, and extensive burns or scalds. Prolonged, hard exercise can also be a cause, producing stress and resulting diarrhoea.
	Dehydration arises when body water equivalent to 6 per cent of body weight is lost. Kidneys also react by reducing urine excretion, and eventually waste products which would normally be filtered off are returned to the bloodstream to add more danger to the dog's life. Symptoms include some distress, loss of skin elasticity, dry coat and often recession of the eyeball into its socket. Faeces, if passed, are small and dry and little urine is voided. The dog becomes increasingly dejected and coma may result if the fluid balance is not quickly returned to normal. The dog should be given a glucose/saline solution to drink (to half a pint of boiled and cooled water add a level teaspoonful of salt and a heaped tablespoonful of glucose) and examined by a veterinarian who may administer blood plasma and dextran intravenously and infuse a compound electrolyte solution. (See also transfusions and infusions.)
dental hygiene	A correct diet substantially contributes to sound teeth. Some dry food preparations, such as Canine Td can be additionally useful in cleaning teeth after a meal. Veterinarians will advise and many practices run special clinics for canine dental hygiene organised by qualified veterinary nurses. Regular inspection of teeth can be made part of the grooming routine. A build-up of tartar can be gently removed, either with the milled edge of a coin or, preferably, with the aid of a dental scaler which can be purchased from a reputable supplier of dog grooming equipment. Any painful or damaged teeth should be seen by a veterinarian and removed under anaesthetic if causing problems to the dog's health or comfort. (See also scaling teeth; tartar; teeth.)
dental plaque	See tartar.
dentition	The study of teeth arrangements, variations and eruption times. (See also teeth.)
depression	The effects of depression should never be underestimated. For example, a seriously physically ill dog that is also depressed will have a lesser chance of recovery than one that is mentally alert and happy. Whilst some diseases in themselves produce a depressive state (which can usually be counteracted by careful nursing and a caring companionship throughout the illness), prevention of boredom and subsequent depression is important in a healthy dog. This lies in a considerate, understanding companionship, a sound diet

with adequate nutritional requirements, a comfortable and interesting environment in which to live and regular exercise.

See eczema

dermatitis

The layer of connective tissue below the epidermis (the outer layer of the skin). The dermis carries blood vessels, nerve fibres and hair follicles.

dermis

This fairly common cyst occurs generally beneath the skin and in ovaries and testicles. It contains sebaceous glands and hair follicles from which hair grows. It is formed through the isolation of embryonic cells in surrounding tissue and may even contain a tooth or other body tissue foreign to the site, which usually touches the skin surface. Surgical removal by a veterinarian is the remedy. Some breeds are more prone to softer dermoid cysts than others; among these are boxers and German shepherds; and St Bernards, which tend to develop corneal dermoid cysts.

dermoid cyst

A soapy substance producing lather which is used for cleaning and washing. Feeding dishes, for example, should be washed in a detergent prior to being thoroughly rinsed, first in water, and subsequently in an antiseptic or disinfectant before a final water rinse.

detergent

The dog's fifth digit in rudimentary form; one appears on the inside of each leg. The origin of the name is obscure but it has been suggested that while all other claws touch the ground the dew claw merely brushes the dew from the grass. These claws, if left in place, tend to be a continual nuisance as they catch in undergrowth and in other objects when the dog is running or playing, causing painful tears in surrounding flesh. For this reason many veterinarians remove them shortly after birth, usually around the fourth day.

dew claw

Dew claws that are left on and tear back should be gently bathed with a warm saline solution (see entry) and bound to the leg until healed. If there is infection seek the advice of a veterinarian.

A synthetic plasma used in transfusions in serious cases of blood loss.

dextran

See glucose.

dextrose

There are two forms of diabetes: polyuria (the more common name for the less serious diabetes *insipidus*) and diabetes *mellitus* – the more dangerous condition. The *insipidus* form is characterised by the passing of large volumes of urine of low specific gravity and is the result of a deficiency of the anti-diuretic hormone vasopressin, which comes from the pituitary gland. Treatment generally consists of correcting the deficiency by injection.

diabetes

In diabetes *mellitus*, the hormone insulin, produced in the islets of Langerhans of the pancreas, is deficient. Since insulin is necessary for glucose to be converted to energy or stored, its deficiency

depression

diabetes

results in glucose being collected in the bloodstream and passed away in the urine. Pancreatic disease, which causes excessive insulin to be produced, dangerously decreases the glucose in the blood (hypoglycaemia). Diabetes *mellitus* is symptomised by hyperglycaemia (excessive glucose) resulting from an insulin deficiency.

Dogs suffering from diabetes show only vague symptoms, but they are generally thirsty, mostly overweight though they lose weight rapidly through the progress of the disease, and are subject to fits of trembling and restlessness. They often circle around and are generally dejected. Laboratory examination of blood samples (taken not less than five hours after a meal low in carbohydrate) will show high blood glucose levels and, in severe cases, glucose present in urine samples. Sometimes vision is affected, the abdomen swells and often the dog vomits. Appetite may remain unaffected.

The diabetic dog is treated by the regular administration of insulin by injection and can live happily under careful control for a full life. The insulin dose levels have to be carefully established by a veterinarian to reduce or eliminate glucose from the urine and provide stability to eating, drinking and weight. Dietary adjustments are also necessary to minimise or regulate carbohydrate intake. The food allowed must be fed in several small meals to ease the load on the endocrine system. Half the total energy requirements can be fed at midday and the remainder divided into two meals to be fed morning and evening. Exercise may need adjusting too, and the owner needs much patience and awareness and must be ready to deal promptly with changes in the progress of the disease.

Careful monitoring of the dog is necessary and care has to be taken to ensure the correct insulin dosage is given at predetermined intervals. In the event of an overdose of insulin being inadvertently given, or if food is refused following an insulin injection, hypoglycaemia will result, causing the dog to tremble and stagger around, probably salivating and urinating. Glucose or sugar (sugar lumps may be the handiest form) must be given rapidly to prevent collapse, coma and death. After counteraction by the glucose the dog rapidly recovers.

Disease of the pancreas, resulting in insulin imbalance can be caused by obesity linked to other causes. Viruses also probably play a part in the destruction of pancreatic cells and excessive cortisone may contribute.

Diabetes is more common in certain breeds, including dachshunds, King Charles spaniels and samoyeds.

diagnosis

The identification of a disease, illness or disorder by means of examination, observation, laboratory tests, etc.

diaphragm

A muscular division between thorax (chest) and abdomen. It is attached to the lumbar vertebrae of the spine and to the ribs and sternum. Its muscular dome is mobile to regulate the size of the thoracic, or chest, cavity, thus contributing substantially to respiration.

The frequent passing of abnormally soft, unformed faeces. It happens when water absorption in the large intestine is impaired and is a symptom of a great many diseases, often associated with infection. In itself it is a serious condition if prolonged, due mainly to subsequent dehydration which can be fatal if not quickly treated. Diarrhoea should never be allowed to continue for more than two days, even if no other symptoms are immediately apparent, without veterinary attention.

diarrhoea

Temporary diarrhoea can often be eliminated by dietary adjustments. Feeding liver, or commercial dog foods containing liver, more than once a week is probably the most common cause of diarrhoea in the dog. Owners should always carefully check the ingredients of dog foods (especially the canned variety) for the presence of liver. A sudden change in diet, or overfeeding, may give rise to temporary diarrhoea as, for example, can eating windfall apples (which dogs, especially puppies, are prone to play with and chew). In these cases give easily digested food for two or three days, excluding red meat and substituting cooked rice and a little boiled, boneless fish or chicken breast. Elimination of temporary diarrhoea in puppies (particularly those that are hand-reared which are more often susceptible) can usually be achieved by adding half a teaspoonful of cornflour to the feed. Chills and, rarely, a vitamin B deficiency may also cause temporary diarrhoea.

Blood-stained diarrhoea indicates a more serious problem and should be referred to a veterinarian.

Examples of the many diseases in which diarrhoea is a frequent sympton include: parvo virus, distemper, poisoning, intestinal tumours, pancreatic diseases, tuberculosis, leukaemia, gastroenteritis, haemorrhagic gastroenteritis, colitis, ulcerative colitis, hepatitis, stress, allergies and parasites.

A form of physiotherapy where high-frequency electricity is used to produce heat rays from a machine. The rays penetrate the body to give inner warmth and lessen pain in such conditions as rheumatism or, used more powerfully, to act against tumours.

diathermy

An organo-phosphorous compound sometimes incorporated into flea collars giving protection against fleas and ticks.

diazinon

An insecticide used primarily against fowl mites but sometimes incorporated in resin strips designed to be fixed to the inside of dog collars to prevent flea infestations.

dichlorvos

One of the most important facts to remember when formulating a diet for a dog is that, like all animals, dogs consume and digest food to provide themselves with energy; anything which the dog's digestive system cannot readily digest and convert to energy is useless, and sometimes harmful. A good, balanced and varied diet contributes substantially to a dog's health.

diet

Formulation of a dog's diet, for whatever breed, should be based primarily on four main principles: firstly it must be varied enough

diet

over, say, a weekly period of feeding to provide the optimum nutritional needs; secondly, it must be sufficient, and definitely not excessive, to provide the dog with the maintenance energy required for its normal weight, lifestyle and age (a large, young working dog will obviously need substantially more food intake than a small, elderly pet); thirdly, the balance of the diet – in terms of proteins, fats, carbohydrates, vitamins and minerals – should be consistently adequate; and, fourthly, the dog should *enjoy* it. Like any other animal, dogs have gastronomic preferences and, as there are many alternatives which can be equally suitable nutritionally, diet planning can be arranged with this in mind.

Protein is found in meat, eggs, cheese and fish; carbohydrate in dog biscuit meal, cereals and brown bread; and fats are contained in meat fat, milk (though a few dogs may be unable to tolerate the lactose content of milk, which can cause diarrhoea), and fish oils.

Meat can be varied to include beef, lamb, rabbit, chicken, liver, kidney, heart, tripe, ox-cheek, etc. A diet consisting of meat only should not be fed. One of the reasons is that it lacks calcium and phosphorus, a deficiency of which can lead to bone disorders. Bone meal, however, is a useful extra source of both of these minerals if prepared especially for canine consumption. Meat, especially if it is bought for canine consumption from a dealer or slaughterhouse, should always be cooked – primarily to kill any harmful micro-organisms which may be present. Meat and fish of all kinds should have the bones removed carefully before being fed to dogs.

There are some very good proprietary brands of canned dog food (and some nutritionally poor ones which usually cost less, having a low meat and high cereal content). The good ones, when mixed with a good proprietary biscuit meal soaked in gravy or warm water, offer a balanced, if not a very varied, diet. The better biscuit meals contain such minerals as calcium, phosphorus and magnesium with vitamins, oils, fats and cereals. The contents are usually listed on the packet and this factor may well be a good reason for buying branded – as opposed to loose, unlabelled – biscuit meal. Brown bread makes an acceptable alternative to biscuit meal.

Liver is a good supplementary source of vitamins A and D, also containing protein and fats. These vitamins are also found in cod-liver and halibut-liver oils. However, extreme care must be taken not to feed liver, or foods containing liver, more than once or twice a week as diarrhoea is caused. Many owners think that they must feed their dogs with liver almost every day and then fail to understand why the animal has loose faeces and/or diarrhoea.

The only bones to be fed to a dog should be large beef marrow bones or clean ribs. They have virtually no dietary use but are helpful in teeth cleaning and are interesting for the dog. Marrow can, of course, be extracted from the bone after the dog has chewed it, providing extra fat and protein.

Eggs are useful food, being rich in proteins, vitamins (including A, D and B_{12}), iron and other nutrients. They are best fed cooked, as raw egg whites are difficult to digest and contain a substance, altered by cooking, which prevents the dog absorbing a useful vitamin.

Some cooked vegetables are quite enjoyed by dogs, including peas and broad, French and runner beans which are fairly rich in protein compared with other vegetables and contain B vitamins. Cabbage, lettuce, cauliflower and Brussels sprouts are of little nutritional value to the dog; potatoes, while acceptable in small quantities, must be cooked for the dog to be able to digest them. Cooked carrots can be used and provide some vitamin A. While these vegetables, together with cooked rice, can be included in the diet in small quantities (probably as household scraps) they have bulk, rather than nutritional value to the dog and should not therefore form a major part of the diet. In some cases flatulence may occur when vegetables are fed and if this happens regularly, peas and beans, which will be the main culprits, should be excluded.

Specially formulated dry foods are also now readily available on the market; they are often cereal based, with additives to include the nutrients dogs require throughout their lives. They are 'complete' foods and should not be confused with dry biscuit 'mixer' foods. While the complete dry dog foods may well be more convenient to feed and store as far as the owner is concerned, there can be little doubt that most dogs will be happy on a diet varied to provide optimum nutritional and energy-giving requirements and sustain a continued interest in their food. In recent years the major diet manufacturers such as Hills, Petfoods etc have produced a wide range of diets to deal with specific problems such as obesity, kidney failure, diabetes etc. These diets are available from veterinary practices.

Water forms a vital part of all dogs' diets and should be available, fresh, clean and cool, at all times. A dog's metabolism (and health) is drastically affected if it is denied water. A working dog, for example, will be more than 50 per cent less efficient if it cannot reach water.

Just how much food a dog needs depends on weight and activity but in very basic terms, for the average, non-working but active dog, about 110 to 170g (4 to 6oz) of meat mixed with approximately 225g (8oz) of biscuit meal and 30g (1oz) of 'extras' such as suitable scraps, egg, cheese etc, is a useful guide for a daily intake per 9 to 11kg (20 to 25lb) of dog.

Special diets are discussed under aged dogs; nursing; obesity; puppies, care of; whelping. (See also digestion; feeding; nutrition.)

digestion

The purpose of digestion is to break down nutrients, taken into the alimentary tract as food through the mouth, into simple form for absorption through the walls of the digestive tract and transportation via the blood to the tissues for use in production of energy and for growth, maintenance and repair work. Digestion is carried out with the help of enzymes acting as catalysts, each with a special task to perform. Nerves and hormones are also involved in the digestive process, playing control or stimulatory roles.

Digestion commences in the mouth where saliva from the salivary glands starts the breaking down of food – minimally so, since most dogs tend to bolt their food, although some of it will be chewed. The enzyme ptyalin is found in saliva, which changes starch to maltose sugar – a task completed in the intestine. Perhaps

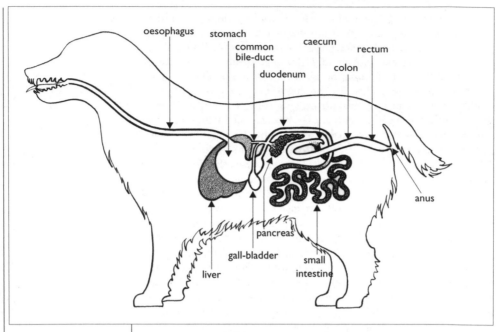

3 Schematic diagram of the digestive system

digestion

the most useful action of saliva in the dog is to lubricate the food, making it easier to swallow and speeding it on its way down the oesophagus, or gullet, to the stomach.

The stomach serves as a reservoir from which food is gradually released into the small intestine. The first part of the stomach (the corpus) is expandable to take food in bulk and the mucosal lining secretes mucus, dilute hydrochloric acid and enzymes which begin the protein breakdown. The second part of the stomach (the antrum) secretes an alkaline solution from its lining, and fat present in the food stimulates a hormone release which in turn causes cessation of acid production. Stomach contents, which at this stage are already transformed into a milky liquid, enter the small intestine through its upper section, known as the duodenum, where additional enzymes commence work.

Some enzymes come from the duodenal lining and others from the pancreas which also issues a secretion to neutralise the acidity in the partially-digested food, or chyme, as it is now called. Pancreatic enzymes assist with fat and carbohydrate digestion. Bile is also added to the chyme from the gall-bladder to help with digestion and absorption and to emulsify fats.

The small intestine, so-called because of its relatively narrow diameter, is an average of three and a half times the dog's body length – considerably longer than the large intestine which follows. It is in the small intestine that most of the digestive process takes place. It is more or less completed there so that proteins, fats and carbohydrates are converted to amino acids, glycerol, fatty acids, dipeptides and monosaccharides. These are then absorbed, mainly through the walls of the small intestine, though some have passed already through the stomach walls and small quantities pass later through those of the large intestine. As the newly-converted nutrients are absorbed through the digestive tract walls they enter the bloodstream for transportation around the body. Products of protein and carbohydrate digestion are mainly taken to the liver while those of fats (the fatty acids) enter the lymphatic system before arriving in the blood. The liver converts much of the absorbed glucose to glycogen and stores it until a reduction in the blood levels of glucose requires the conversion of glycogen back to glucose for energy for the tissues. Amino acids circulate in the blood for use by the tissues as they are needed.

digestion

Remaining material which arrives in the large intestine, divided into caecum, colon, rectum and finally the anus, is mostly expelled eventually as faeces. Bacteria are present in large numbers in the large intestine which have as their major purpose the dehydration of faecal contents, and act on residual fibre and remaining protein. Undigested materials are retained in the rectum to await expulsion from the anus, before which a considerable amount of water absorption back into the bloodstream occurs.

A compound made from the dried leaves of the foxglove plant. It stimulates a failing heart by adding strength to the heartbeat and prolonging the time lapse between beats. Its action also increases blood pressure through constriction of the walls of minor arteries and veins. Over-dosage can be dangerous.

digitalis

Having characteristics of both sexes. (See also hermaphrodite.)

dimorphism

A purulent exudate from a wound or orifice, usually indicating infection and certainly the need for professional diagnosis and treatment.

discharge

Substance that destroys micro-organisms. Strictly, steam can be used to disinfect, as can heat, but mostly chemical disinfectants are used to rid kennels of harmful micro-organisms and to ensure that infection does not take hold or spread. Chemical disinfectants include formalin, o-phosphoric acid and citric acid and a very wide range of proprietary products which are mostly supplied as liquid concentrates and need to be diluted before use. (See also antiseptics.)

disinfectant

Bone displacement within a joint. There is frequently pain and bruising in the affected area and some dislocations can be seen as well as felt on examination. Surrounding ligaments are sometimes torn and the dog will be lame. The skills of a veterinarian will be needed to reduce the dislocation under anaesthetic. While awaiting veterinary attention the dog should be kept as still as possible, lying on the opposite side to the injury. Cold compresses help to relieve swelling.

dislocation

Dislocation of the shoulder is rare, except in racing dogs, although some smaller breeds such as miniature poodles and pinschers, *dislocation* | pomeranians and griffons have a predisposition to it. Dislocation of the patella or 'kneecap', is relatively common, especially in smaller dogs where the problem may again be hereditary in origin. Perhaps the most common of all is dislocation of the hip, caused by a road accident or the result of a fall or an awkward jump. Jaw dislocations can be frightening for animal and owner alike, especially if the dog is unable to close its mouth. Such dislocations can be caused by chewing on large objects or by a sudden wrench on the lead during a walk. Stifle joint and elbow dislocations are also possible and are usually the result of a violent blow or wrench.

distemper | Canine distemper is a serious virus disease which attacks the nervous system of dogs, foxes and members of the Mustelidae family, including badgers, ferrets, stoats and mink. It is highly infectious, especially among young dogs, although it can be contracted by dogs of all ages. Those between three and twelve months are the most vulnerable.

Symptoms include a rise in temperature and a thickening discharge from nostrils and eyes. The dog becomes lethargic, depressed and loses interest in food. Respiratory complications may arise (including cough, bronchitis and severe bronchopneumonia) or those of intestinal origin (including diarrhoea, vomiting and abdominal infection), depending on secondary attack by bacteria. In some forms of the disease the pads of the feet become swollen, thick and hard, a condition known as 'hard pad'. Nervous conditions may also be present, especially in the later stages and sometimes convulsions occur with following paralysis.

Distemper is better prevented than treated since treatment is rarely effective and the disease often proves fatal. Even if the dog is lucky enough to recover through the use of medication followed by extreme care in convalescence to prevent rapid relapse, complications may arise in later life. Immunisation at ten to twelve weeks of age provides protection and regular boosters are advisable. No puppy should be allowed in public prior to its immunisation for fear of contracting distemper (or other serious diseases such as hepatitis and leptospirosis).

Widespread immunisation in the past has substantially contributed to the rarity of distemper in modern times. Never accept that a puppy or dog has been immunised unless supported by a certificate signed by a veterinarian. If in doubt, arrange for the immunisation to be carried out as soon as possible. (See also immunisation.)

distress | Generally caused directly by fear, distress can be the result of neglect, cruelty or thoughtlessness, or caused by accidents, wounds or severe disease. Frequent reasons for distress are respiratory blockage or foreign bodies. Evident distress in the dog (characterised by restlessness, an anxious expression and sometimes panting and high-pitched whining) should never be neglected. If unsure of the cause consult a veterinarian without delay.

diuretic | A substance used to increase the flow of urine from the kidneys. Diuretics are frequently used to relieve oedema and include thiazide, potassium citrate and potassium nitrate. They cannot be considered as cures for a particular condition but they assist in the treatment of the causative disease, usually originating in the kidneys, heart or liver.

diuretic

Removal of a dog's tail or part of it. Veterinarians and members of the public increasingly favour ending the practice of tail docking which is, after all, a mutilation for the purposes of fashion alone. It is extremely rare that docking is carried out for reasons of health.

docking

The Royal College of Veterinary Surgeons considers docking of dogs' tails to be an unjustified mutilation and unethical unless done for therapeutic or acceptable prophylactic reasons. Therapeutic docking to treat tail disease or injuries is acceptable in the interests of the dog. Docking is now an operation which may only be performed by a veterinarian. The Kennel Club allows so-called docked breeds to be shown with or without docked tails and Breed Standards now incorporate rules to show and judge both.

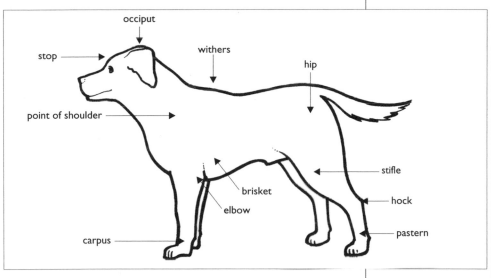

4 Main points of the dog

The dog belongs to the order Carnivora, family Canidae, genus *Canis* and species *familiaris*. Carnivora are a group of intelligent, flesh-eating mammals with developed canine teeth, molars which have adapted for cutting and grinding purposes and a comparatively short alimentary tract. They occur in most parts of the world and their ancestors were probably around some 70 million years ago.

dog (*Canis familiaris*)

There are about 350 breeds of dog and a wide and complex variety of hybrids or mongrels. The Chinese were among the first to breed pure-bred dogs and, later, standards were set up in the UK and USA, where respective Kennel Clubs (see useful addresses) maintain breed 'standards' and support dog shows to recognise and perpetuate the best in each breed.

dog
The term 'dog' is also used in contrast to 'bitch', to differentiate the sexes. (See also domestication; mongrel; pedigree.)

dolichocephalic
Long-muzzled with a narrow head. Such breeds include the collie, Afghan hound and saluki.

domestication
It is fairly certain that the dog was the first animal to be domesticated by man. The process began around 10,000BC in various parts of the world and the first dogs to be tamed were wolves, captured probably to assist in hunting, guarding and protecting and as companions. Social structures and patterns of behaviour in humans were very similar to those of dogs and were based on the need to hunt. The combination of canine and human skills resulted in much more successful ventures. From this alliance, bonds of companionship were developed.

Domestication was achieved gradually, by rearing wild pups away from their own society. The most placid and intelligent individuals were retained and, more importantly, survived through willingness to be part of the human group. Slowly, in this way, as these dogs flourished and bred, the wild temperaments and defensive reactions were bred out, resulting in more companionable characters.

The Egyptians and Greeks kept dogs as companions. Around 450BC the Greek historian, Herodotus, wrote of the watchfulness and fidelity of the dogs which were kept by the Egyptians. They thought so much of their dogs then that it was not uncommon for owners to shave their heads in mourning when a faithful canine friend died. Pythagoras (sixth century BC) mentioned that it was a belief that a man's spirit entered into an animal on his death. His own regard for dogs was high enough for him to hold a dog close to the mouth of a dying disciple to ensure that the departing spirit would enter the animal. Ancient Egyptian illustrations prior to 3000BC depicted dogs that resembled greyhounds, salukis and Afghan hounds, and some early Greek sculptures show dogs similar to the Newfoundland.

Today, more than 350 individual breeds have emerged as the result of selective adaptation, over many generations, for temperament and specific tasks; and there is also a wide variety of cross-breeds and mongrels.

dominance
A dominant gene is the one of a pair which is predominant and asserts its characteristics over those of the other (recessive) gene, although those which are dominated may appear in a subsequent generation of cross-bred animals. Exactly which factors dominate depends on the characteristics of each breed but can be seen best in mongrels: for example, a pup may inherit the rough coat of its collie sire over the smoother one of its labrador dam. Another may grow to the large size of one of its parents, in contrast to the smallness of the other parent.

Dominance is also a behavioural term referring to a form of high status obtained by some dogs over others. This is common in the wild and in groups of dogs living together as a pack, and is usually the result of aggression. Submissive, or subordinate, animals react to the one showing dominance by acts of appeasement.

dominance

A dog's sleeping quarters should always be in a place entirely free of draughts but well ventilated, to ensure coolness in summer and warmth in winter. A wet dog submitted to a draughty atmosphere may well contract respiratory or intestinal disorders, rheumatism, chills and many other forms of ill-health. (See also beds and bedding; kennel.)

draughts

Wound covering which affords protection against additional infection or injury and assists with healing. Some dressings are impregnated with substances to fight infection and promote healing; others are fixed in place dry. They should always be sterile; pre-packed and pre-sterilised dressings usually consisting mainly of gauze (which is probably the most widely used and effective dressing material), are readily available. A supply should always be kept handy for emergencies. (See also bandaging; wounds.)

dressing

See oedema.

dropsy

If a dog is totally immersed in water for four minutes or less it will drown. While most dogs are able swimmers, drowning accidents occur either because the dog is unconscious when it enters the water or has become exhausted through cold and/or struggling – for example, in mud or at the edge of surrounding ice, or while trapped by debris in the water. Frozen ponds, lakes and rivers are particularly dangerous places for dogs in winter as they may run onto ice which breaks under their weight. They become trapped in the resulting hole, unable to gain a foothold on the slippery edges of the ice, become exhausted, slip under the ice and quickly drown.

drowning

Rescued unconscious dogs should be swung back and forth by their hind legs, if they are small enough, before being laid on one side with the tail end higher than the head. Press and release the ribcage with the flat hand steadily and rhythmically at two-second intervals. Water should run from the mouth, and when this ceases it is time to turn the dog over to its other side and begin again. Also ensure that the dog's tongue is pulled well forward and not obstructing the flow of air into the lungs. On recovery, the patient should be towelled dry and well wrapped to keep warm. Pneumonia is a potential danger from the chilled body or the water-filled lungs. (See also artificial respiration.)

The upper part of the small intestine into which the stomach, bile-duct and pancreatic duct open. It is about 25cm (10in) long. Digested material entering the duodenum has a high nutrient content and it is for this reason that intestinal parasites can be found here rather than in other parts of the intestines. (See also digestion; intestines; parasites.)

duodenum

dusting powder	Dusting powder is most useful as a topical application to fight wound infection. It is usually easy to apply. Some sulphonamides and antiseptics are available in this form.
	Powders marketed for the treatment of external parasites, however, are less satisfactory to apply than sachet preparations which can be diluted in a warm bath. The dust particles may affect the eyes and nose (of dog *and* administrator) and are frequently shaken out – usually over the best lounge furniture! Such powder is best used for treating bedding, baskets and odd corners where fleas may be hiding; it can then be vacuumed away after it has done its work.
	Powder preparations should not be dusted into the ear to clear canker since they generally clog up sensitive channels.
dysentery	A collection of symptoms including discharge of blood with diarrhoea and mucus from the anus. Dysentery is accompanied by pain and results from severe irritation of the intestines. It is usually found specifically in such diseases as haemorrhagic gastroenteritis, ulcerative colitis, etc. Diagnosis of the underlying cause is essential so that appropriate treatment can be given.
dysphagia	Difficulty in swallowing. This may be a symptom of nasal disease, foreign body obstruction or tumours of the larynx. Severe inflammation of the pharynx, or tonsillitis, can produce dysphagia, and it is also seen in myasthenia gravis and tumours of the central nervous system. Food is often regurgitated through the nose and coughing may be caused by food particles in the trachea. There is also usually salivation and an unwillingness to eat. A veterinary examination is called for without delay to investigate the cause and treat urgently.
dyspnoea	Difficult breathing, often with pain. Respiratory obstruction is a common cause. The patient breathes with a grating sound and may be distressed, and the muscles of the abdomen move in an attempt to assist the diaphragm.
dystokia	Problematical whelping. Causes include uterine inertia, an incorrectly positioned pup, a head of a pup too large for the vaginal opening, uterine torsion, etc.
	The miniature breeds especially show a susceptibility to these whelping complications. (See also breech presentation; whelping.)
dysuria	Urine retention, which may be due to a number of causes; kidney or heart disease and obstruction of the urethra among them. Veterinary consultation is necessary for examination of the abdominal region and accurate diagnosis of the cause.

E

The ear comprises three sections: the external ear, the middle ear and the internal ear. The external section is the pinna or auricle (a flap which stands up in prick-eared dogs such as German shepherds, Welsh corgis and samoyeds, and hangs over in flap-eared dogs such as spaniels, dachshunds and basset hounds) and associated cartilage. The pinnae are mobile appendages which through muscular control can lift, by varying degrees, depending on the breed and type of ear, when the dog is surprised or attentive.

The middle ear consists of the tympanic cavity, the ear-drum or tympanic membrane and the auditory ossicles – a series of minute bones with associated muscles and ligaments. These bones are descriptively known as the hammer (malleus), anvil (incus) and stirrup (stapes). The cavity of the middle ear is connected to the nasal pharynx by the Eustachian tube.

The internal ear is in the form of a complex labyrinth containing the cochlea, a spiral, snail-shaped structure making three and a quarter turns and measuring about 7mm (¼in) in height, which houses the cochlear duct where mechanical stimuli are converted to nerve impulses and transmitted via the auditory nerve to the brain for interpretation based on previous experience. These mechanical stimuli are gathered as sound waves by the outer ear and channelled through the middle ear where they are transmitted as vibrations for the tympanic membrane through the fluid of the internal ear to the cochlea – the processing centre of the hearing system.

The internal ear is also concerned with balance and contains two basic parts which record balance information. The fluid-filled,

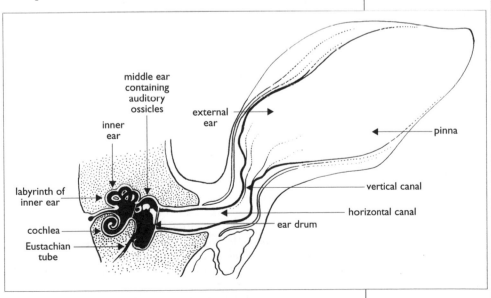

5 The structure of the dog's ear

ear   semi-circular canals have a sensitive arrangement of tiny hairs which records movement of the fluid inside as part of the process of muscle control of the eye, which maintains an object in view despite head movement. The second part also contains a system of hairs which records changes in posture and position and passes information along the auditory nerve to the cerebellum of the brain. (See also canker; deafness; grass seeds; haematoma; otitis.)

eclampsia   A condition caused by lack of calcium in whelping bitches. Though it can occur during pregnancy it is most common a few days after whelping and an urgent injection of calcium is essential to correct what can be a serious condition if left untreated. Symptoms include a stiff, unsteady walk and panting. The bitch ignores her puppies and becomes increasingly restless. Muscular twitching gradually worsens to reach convulsive proportions and, without treatment, coma follows. A veterinarian should be called at the first signs of eclampsia. Prevention lies in ensuring sufficient calcium is given in the diet before, during and after pregnancy, with an increase in calcium-rich foods such as milk (meat is low in calcium) after the fortieth day of pregnancy.

E coli   Bacteria (*Escherichia coli*) which are pathogenic in the urethra and bladder, causing infection. They are also causative organisms of enteritis. Unsterilised meat from knackers' yards can be a source of infection.

ectoparasite   A parasite which lives on the outside of the body, eg flea, mite, tick and louse. (See also parasite.)

ectopic   Outside the normal position, eg in ectopic pregnancy where the foetus develops outside the uterus.

ectropion   A possibly hereditary condition where the eyelids, through contraction of the skin of the lid, turn outwards. If marked, it can be corrected by relatively minor surgery. The converse condition is entropion.

eczema   Inflammation of the skin, usually due to an allergy. There are wet and dry forms of the disease, the former producing a moist, scaling, reddened skin surface with some watery discharge, and the latter a dry, greyish, flaking and wrinkling condition. There is usually considerable irritation and the dog scratches and bites the affected area, often breaking the skin and causing bleeding and secondary infection. The fur becomes matted and is often pulled out by the dog in its efforts to rid itself of the irritation.

Eczema occurs on the backs and sides, especially of long-haired dogs, between the toes and, in the male, frequently between the hind legs and around the tail. The dry form attacks especially the head, neck and legs.

Some breeds, such as West Highland terriers, seem more prone to the disease than others, indicating a hereditary origin in such cases.

The Chinese breed of 'wrinkled' dogs, the Shar Pei, are especially troubled by inflammatory skin conditions. Often, however, eczema is caused by sensitisation to flea bites – in which case fitting a flea collar can be a suitable remedy once the skin condition has been cleared up – or by a vitamin deficiency or an allergic reaction to any one of a variety of foods or contact substances. Eczema also tends to occur more frequently during warm weather when there is a higher incidence of mites.

Treatment, ideally, is to eliminate the cause of the trouble, although this may prove difficult. The condition should be relieved locally by the application of a topical preparation such as a mixture of coal tar, calamine and sulphur; sometimes calamine lotion on its own proves temporarily effective. First cleanse the area with a warm saline solution (see entry) and remove the surrounding hair carefully, then apply the lotion to the clean area. Antihistamine injections may be beneficial and, if the cause is a vitamin deficiency, vitamin supplements fed in a diet with an absence of fish will be of help.

There is a danger that ringworm or mange caused by parasites may be mistaken for eczema and for this reason, coupled to the need for a planned programme of treatment, a veterinarian should be consulted when the symptoms first appear. (See also allergy.)

eczema

The escape of fluid into body tissues or cavities caused by obstruction of vessels or infection, eg pleural effusion fluid abnormally surrounding the lungs.

effusion

See ovum.

egg

See diet; nutrition.

eggs (as food)

The act of expelling semen during copulation.

ejaculation

The joint at the top of the forearm.

elbow

An electric flex is an obvious and dangerous source of potential accident in the home. Puppies particularly are attracted to the snake-like coils; sharp teeth soon chew through and the result is electrocution – often proving fatal. Prevent such accidents by ensuring that unsupervised puppies have no access to electrical wiring or that electrical appliances are switched off at the wall or unplugged from the socket. Puppies can be trained to ignore electric flex and this should be an early accomplishment.

If an electrocuted dog is lucky enough to remain alive, urgent attention is vital. First, turn off the electric current *before touching the dog*. If this is not immediately possible, first insulate yourself quickly by standing on rubber, dry cloth, wood, glass or newspaper. Do not touch the victim with your hands but push it away from electrical contact with a wooden stick or broom, or even with the aid of rolled newspapers. The dog will probably have lost consciousness and be suffering from burns, especially to the

electric shock

electric shock   mouth. If breathing has stopped, administer artificial respiration after placing the dog on its side. Subsequently treat for shock and burns. (See also artificial respiration; burns and scalds; shock.)

electrocardiogram   The trace recording or output of the electrocardiograph or cardiograph.

electrocardiograph   An instrument which records, as electrocardiograms, the electrical changes which are produced during muscular activity of the heart. It is used to show irregularities of the heart's action as an aid to the diagnosis of disease or defect.

electrocardiophono-graph   An instrument which records heart sounds as an aid to the diagnosis of heart disorders.

electroencephalograph   This instrument is used in the diagnosis of conditions affecting the brain, and provides a graphic record of electrical impulses passing through the brain.

electrolytes   Minerals – sodium chloride (salt) and potassium – present in the body. They are supplied by correct nutrition.

electuary   A medicine which, when mixed with a convenient paste such as honey, can be smeared on the back of the tongue or pharynx. Its action is similar to that of a throat lozenge used in human medicine to alleviate coughs and sore throats.

'Elizabethan' collar   This useful aid to skin disease healing can easily be made out of a piece of plastic or other stiff material and fitted round the dog's neck to prevent it worrying wounds, sutures or sites of irritation

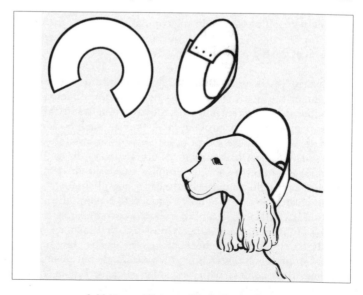

6 Making and fitting an 'Elizabethan' collar

with its teeth. To make such a collar, cut a circular piece of rigid plastic, about 45cm (18in) in diameter for the average-sized dog, and cut a circular hole large enough to fit over the dog's head with the collar resting comfortably on its neck. Cut out a V-shaped piece of the plastic, with the point of the V at the central hole, and punch out small holes (these can be made with the points of scissors) on either side of the V. Insert laces, fit the collar round the dog's neck and lace up hole to hole. It will resemble a shallow saucer when in place and will prevent the dog chewing or licking itself anywhere. If it is unsteady it can be clipped to the dog's own collar. Commercial forms are also generally available from suppliers of dog sundries.

'Elizabethan' collar

See castration.

emasculation

The blocking of a blood vessel, usually caused by a blood clot carried by the bloodstream from a larger blood vessel into a smaller one. It can also be caused by an air bubble or fragment of fat. It can bring death if it becomes lodged in a critical place, such as in a vessel supplying blood to the brain which often leads to a stroke. If blood supply to part of an organ is cut off by the blockage the tissues will degenerate and die, eg as the heart muscle in coronary thrombosis. (See thrombus.)

embolism

See foetus.

embryo

This is a list of conditions that demand immediate veterinary treatment. They are listed in random order. Other conditions may need urgent treatment too, but this list does indicate the kind of emergency that could occur with a dog.

emergency conditions

Cardiac failure	Bone fractures
Severe respiratory difficulties	Whelping complications
Massive haemorrhage	Prolonged diarrhoea
Severe wounds	Convulsions
Shock	Urine retention
Heatstroke	Evident pain
Penetrating wounds of chest or abdomen	Extensive burns or scalds
	Hernia strangulation
Coma or loss of consciousness	Swallowed foreign body
Spinal fractures	Grass seed in ear etc
Skull damage	Kennel cross-infections
Poisoning	Intussusception

A drug which induces vomiting. Some emetics are given orally while others are administered by injection. Perhaps the most common (and useful) oral emetic is common salt in water. Ipecacuanha and apomorphine can be injected by a veterinarian to make a dog vomit and morphine will have that effect if the dog has a full stomach. Emetics are useful aids in the treatment of poisoning.

emetic

emollient	An application used to soften skin, ease irritation and soothe topically. A plain soap has this effect to some degree and other examples are glycerine and various oils.
emotion	This complex and little understood state is the expression of certain moods by social signals eg happiness shown by tail-wagging etc. Emotion encompasses fear, anger (which stimulates aggression) and happiness. Charles Darwin was one of the first to study emotion and its expression. (See also behaviour; communication.)
emphysema	Over-inflation of air sacs – usually referring to the alveoli of the lungs and to 'air swelling' of a wound through air penetrating beneath the skin.
	In the lung, the condition is exacerbated by a gradual breakdown of the lining of the alveoli, demolition of the walls and a resulting enlargement of the air spaces. Exchange of gases in the lungs is impaired as small blood vessels are stretched and eventually destroyed. The heart is placed under increasing strain and congestive heart failure may result. It is usually a complication of chronic bronchitis and, in some cases, allergy. Obesity contributes to the condition in some dogs and prevention of this coupled to the rapid and effective treatment of any respiratory disorders (with rest being part of the treatment) helps with prophylaxis. An aged dog with emphysema may continue to thrive with care, rest and curtailment of strenuous exercise so that strain on the heart is reduced to a minimum.
empyema	An abscess with no wall. It occurs as a collection of pus in a natural cavity eg in the pleura – between lung and chest wall. Antibiotics are used to deal with the infection and, if necessary, a veterinarian may withdraw the pus-filled fluid from the cavity.
emulsion	A combination of immiscible liquids such as water and oil. One is distributed through the other and stabilised with an emulsifying agent, eg ammonium linoleate. Emulsions are taken orally and need to be shaken before use.
enamel	Hard white covering of the crown of the tooth. (See also teeth.)
encephalitis	Inflammation of the brain of which the most common cause is a virus. Bacterial infection of the brain, such as in meningitis, is mostly confined to the brain covering. Encephalitis may occur in rabies, distemper and other virus-related infections. The stricken animal is feverish, becomes distressed and has convulsions. Later, paralysis may occur and restless unconsciousness. Keep the dog quiet in the dark and call a veterinarian.
endocarditis	Inflammation of the heart lining and valve area. It can be caused by a parasitic worm or a bacterial infection, particularly if there is a congenital deformity of the valves. Diseased fragments may be detached in the bloodstream and become lodged elsewhere as

obstructions in an ulcerated form of the disease. Few symptoms may appear although the dog may be lethargic and even faint occasionally. Expert veterinary diagnosis is needed to confirm and treat the condition, otherwise permanent damage may be done to the heart.

endocarditis

The innermost of the three layers of the heart. It is continuous with the lining of vessels attached to the heart and connected by loose connective tissue to the muscular middle layer (myocardium) of the heart wall.

endocardium

A series of glands and organs which secrete hormones. It includes primarily the adrenal, parathyroid, pineal, pituitary and thyroid glands. The testes, ovaries, pancreas and placenta also have endocrine functions, and the kidneys, liver and thymus gland have endocrine functions which are secondary to their main tasks.

endocrine system

All components of the endocrine system are secretion centres, synthesising hormones, and are located separately around the body linked by the vascular and lymphatic systems. Endocrine glands assist and supplement the nervous system in releasing hormones to cells, tissues or organs to stimulate or alter activity.

Although well developed at birth it is only afterwards that the dog's endocrine system establishes co-ordinated activity, with the regulation of growth, internal activity, sexual maturity, metabolism control and involvement in the decline of body activity in old age being governed by the teamwork of the endocrine organs.

Ineffective endocrine action through malfunction of one type or another of any of the components can be dramatic in result. Such malfunction can, for example, cause diabetes, tumours, hyperthyroidism and behavioural disturbances.

Also known as the tunica mucosa, this is the thickest of the three mucosal lining membranes of the uterus. It is subject to inflammation (metritis) following whelping.

endometrium

A parasite which lives inside the body, eg lung or heart worm, or one of a variety of intestinal parasites including hookworms, roundworms, tapeworms and whipworms. (See also parasites.)

endoparasite

A tubular surgical instrument for examining the cavities of internal organs.

endoscope

A cell layer which lines some cavities and vessels, including blood and lymphatic vessels, peritoneum, pericardium and pleura.

endothelium

A fluid prepared for injection through the anus into the rectum and colon. There are four main reasons for use: as a means of evacuating accumulated faeces from the rectum, eg from severe constipation or impaction or prior to certain abdominal operations; as a means of administering some drugs or antiseptics; as a diagnostic aid, eg in

enema

enema	radiography of the intestines; and for nutritional purposes or to correct dehydration when other routes are impractical. The most common use of enemas is for evacuation of the rectum when the preparation is usually in the form of a tablespoonful of glycerine in a pint of warm water.
energy	Derived from nutrition. Food is broken down during digestion and the substances that result are absorbed through the intestinal wall and taken via the bloodstream to the cells where they combine with oxygen. This reaction produces energy and is mainly the oxidation of glucose which also forms carbon dioxide and water. It takes place through a lengthy series of steps so that the energy is not generated too rapidly for the cells to withstand the heat created. Released energy is either utilised immediately or stored for subsequent use. Energy is needed as heat to maintain body temperature, for the various activities of the internal organs, for voluntary and involuntary muscular action and for tissue growth and repair. Resting animals obviously require less energy than those active or working but energy production is constantly essential to maintain life. (See also calorie; digestion; nutrition.)
enteritis	Inflammation of the intestines, giving rise to diarrhoea and other symptoms and mostly due to infection. It is itself a symptom of various diseases. (See also gastroenteritis; haemorrhagic gastro-enteritis.)
enterostomy	The forming of an opening in the intestine by surgery. It is carried out when there is a need to drain the contents of the intestine.
entropion	The turning in of the eyelid perimeter. It is a harmful condition as the eyelashes brush against the cornea causing inflammation and discomfort. Surgery is needed before infection sets in and corneal ulceration arises. The converse condition is ectropion. Some breeds, such as the Shar Pei, are particularly sensitive to the disorder.
enuresis	See urinary incontinence.
enzymes	Organic catalysts which help or speed up a reaction in the body. They are complex chemicals made in the cells which assist in bio-chemical reactions and are particularly significant in digestion where each performs a specific task in the process. Some enzymes need the presence of vitamins and minerals to operate effectively and others require special environmental conditions, eg, the alimentary tract. Among those enzymes present in digestion are ptyalin in saliva and pancreatic diastase which convert starches to maltose sugars, and pepsin in the stomach, secreted in its inactive form, pepsinogen, and activated in the presence of hydrochloric acid which also provides optimum conditions for enzyme activity there. Pepsin, together with pancreatic trypsin, breaks down proteins to

amino acids, and lipase, secreted in the small intestine, transforms fats to fatty acids. (See also digestion.)

enzymes

A white blood cell with large granules (which show up red in the cytoplasm) and a lobular nucleus. There are relatively few seen in a normal differential white cell count of the blood, and any increase can indicate allergy, skin disorders, malfunction of the adrenals or the presence of parasitic worms. A decrease is to be found in distemper, over-activity of the adrenals and stress-related conditions.

eosinophil

An increase in eosinophils (eosinophilia) is probably triggered by histamine release and can sometimes be localised in an inflammatory tissue area. (See also blood.)

Outer layer of the heart wall.

epicardium

Outer layer of the skin, comprising several layers of epithelial cells. (The layer underneath is the dermis.) It varies in thickness across the body from about 25 to 40 microns. The surface layer of cells becomes dry, hard and protective and contains the protein keratin. A more concentrated amount of keratin is found in the claws – modified and hardened epidermis – to protect the toes. Epidermis of the digital pads of the foot (the smaller of the pads at the front of the foot) is about 1,800 microns thick in the adult dog. (See also dermis.)

epidermis

An elongated coiled tube, associated with the testis, which is a storage organ for spermatozoa prior to ejaculation. It also assists in the transportation of spermatozoa to the vas deferens – a slow process to allow them to mature properly.

epididymis

A cartilaginous organ in the throat shaped rather like a pointed spade with the point towards the soft palate. Its task is to protect the opening into the trachea and it drops back to prevent the inhalation of food and water during swallowing.

epiglottis

A nervous disease, sometimes of a hereditary nature (particularly in collies, German shepherds, poodles and keeshonds) and sometimes the result of scar tissue in the brain from injury or disease. Puppies may be subject to a form of the disease when cutting permanent teeth or when intestinal parasites are substantially present. Some forms of epilepsy (often described as fits) may be triggered by stress and hysteria. An attack starts typically with muscle spasms (convulsions) and loss of consciousness, sometimes briefly and on other occasions for a few minutes, during which time the dog salivates, jerks its head around and may become incontinent and 'gallop' with the limbs.

epilepsy

When the attack is over the dog appears bemused, wandering around and bumping into objects. It may also become aggressive and should not be handled or restrained but merely left to recover. Reduce lighting in the room and eliminate noise; if possible, protect objects with which the dog may collide with cushions or

epilepsy blankets. A veterinarian should be contacted, as the condition can be controlled by administering sedatives such as phenobarbital or anticonvulsants such as mysoline. Sometimes there is some 'trigger' which sets off an attack and careful observation could track it down. (See also convulsion.)

epiphysis The spongy end of a long bone. When a bone is growing, the epiphysis at each end is separated from the shaft by the epiphyseal cartilage which fuses with the shaft when the dog becomes adult and ceases to grow. Fractures sometimes occur along the line of fusion.

epistaxis Bleeding from the nose, which may be due to a violent accident or a blow to the nose. If there is a possibility of head injury, it may be a symptom of a fracture of the nasal bones or skull. It may arise from continued heavy sneezing, a foreign body, eg a grass seed, in the nasal passages, or a tumour of the nostrils. Apply cold-water compresses and keep the dog at rest. A veterinarian should be consulted to identify the cause.

epithelium A type of tissue. It covers external and internal surfaces and may be simple or stratified. The former consists of a single cell layer fixed to a membrane which lines internal organs and cavities. The stratified form is a stronger multi-layer composition and appears externally, taking harder wear than the simple form. It also lines the mouth, pharynx and oesophagus. Hair-like projections, or cilia, are present in ciliated epithelium – found in air passages, where they produce a 'sweeping' effect against dust and secretions, and in uterine tubes for movement of ova.

epsom salts Magnesium sulphate, used in small doses as a laxative and as an antidote to various poisons. (See also poisoning.)

equipment A dog owner's 'General Needs' list should include:

Dog shampoo	Salt
Anti-parasite treatment e.g. flea collars, spray or droplet preparations etc.	Brush
	Comb and tangle-comb
	Mat-splitter
Pure cod-liver oil	Clippers
Pure olive oil	Nail-file
Eye dropper	Clean towelling
Glucose	Thinning scissors
Honey	Round-pointed scissors
Suitable stainless-steel feeding bowl	Toe scissors
Drinking bowl	

erythrocyte Red blood cell. (See also blood.)

erythromycin An antibiotic sometimes used, eg to treat kennel cough, when a resistance to penicillin has formed. (See also antibiotics.)

ether

A volatile, highly inflammable liquid (diethyl ether) used as an anaesthetic. It can also be explosive and should not be used near an X-ray machine. It also increases secretion of mucus and saliva. (See also anaesthetic.)

ethology

See behaviour.

eucalyptus oil

Keep a bottle of this handy, for two purposes. It is a useful aid to the removal of contaminants from the coat and feet, especially the often unidentifiable smelly, oily materials a dog rolls in when out on a walk, and tar which can be picked up on feet from beaches and roads. Rub into the coat or contaminated part (keeping away from eyes and inside of mouth and ears) before washing in a dog shampoo and warm water.

Eucalyptus oil is equally successful in removing ticks from the skin. These should not be pulled out, as the head of the tick is usually left behind and can form an abscess. A drop of the oil should be applied to the tick and this usually makes it release its hold so that it can be removed and destroyed. (See also parasites.)

Eustachian tube

The tube which forms a connection between the nasal pharynx and the middle ear. Its purpose is to allow the air needed for hearing into the middle ear. These tubes may become inflamed, usually due to infection passing up from the nasal pharynx, causing temporary deafness. (See also ear.)

euthanasia

The act of producing painless and fear-free death. It should be used only when a dog is suffering from a painful condition which *cannot* be cured. In this way it is a last resort in releasing an animal from substantial suffering in a terminal disease. It is also used on aged dogs when it would be cruel to prolong their lives. Euthanasia is usually accomplished by a veterinarian injecting a lethal dose of barbiturates, such as sodium pentobarbitone, intravenously, so that the animal slips quietly away into a sleep from which it does not awaken.

evolution

Process of developing into a different form. The dog evolved from early carnivores, and was probably a forest dweller preying on small game. Limbs and feet were long, carnassial teeth were developed for cutting and the brain was becoming enlarged when compared with early Tertiary predators. There was subsequently little change in dentition but intelligence gradually improved as the brain grew larger.

By Miocene and Pliocene periods there was a variety of dogs – mostly large, heavy animals with long tails and even larger individuals with deep, heavy skulls and strong teeth. Later, in Pleistocene times, more canine branches were formed with wild dogs and wolves, foxes and the more specialised canids of Africa and South America. Dogs hunted in packs and lived together in family groups. From this point some became domesticated. (See also dog; domestication.)

examination

A dog must be restrained during examination to prevent additional damage following injury and to allay fear. The degree of restraint depends on whether or not the dog is in pain or shock and on the temperament or state of mind of the animal. It also depends on where and how the dog is to be examined. Some convenient methods of restraint for examination are described below. Wherever possible, stand the dog on a table or bench at a convenient height for comfortable handling.

To prevent a dog from turning its head or biting, stand in front of it, grip the collar or jowls on either side of the head just below the ears and press the heels of the hands firmly against the cheeks on each side. To examine the right side or ears pass the left arm under the neck and hold the palm of the left hand firmly against the dog's right shoulder, pressing the dog's body against your chest. The right hand is free to hold up the hindquarters or press them down, depending on the site of examination, or to steady the dog as it stands. Reverse the procedure for examination of the left side.

To place a dog on its side lift it correctly with a forearm under the front legs and the other hand firmly supporting the tail end. Holding the dog close against your chest, lean forward and place the dog on its side using your chest to push it down. From this position roll it over onto its back for examination of chest or abdomen.

A dog can be muzzled if necessary by using a bandage or stout strip of cloth (see illustration on p. 160).

Dogs should be examined carefully, not only in the event of accident or injury, but frequently, to ensure that all is well with their health. A routine examination from head to tail, using hands to feel along and around the body and observing any abnormalities in coat, eyes, ears, mouth, nose, chest, abdomen, genitals, anus, feet, limbs and spine, can be carried out as part of grooming.

excretion

Removal of waste products from the cells and from the body.

exercise

Vitally important to a dog's health; it keeps a dog interested in life and contributes to its mental, as well as physical, well-being.

Early mornings and evenings are the best times for exercise, especially during the summer. Weather, apart from heat, is not a problem although a wet dog should be thoroughly dried with a towel after exercise, particularly in winter.

How much exercise depends on the age, size and breed of dog (and, to a lesser extent, perhaps the owner's available time), with young animals needing the most, but an hour out, especially if spent running through fields and woods, will suit the average-sized young dog, although more is beneficial. If the dog can run free safely without a lead, so much the better, but if walking on a lead a brisk walk is better than a slow stroll. If the dog is running free it is often happier if its owner joins in occasionally, perhaps by throwing a ball. *Never* run a dog alongside a bicycle or car as the animal cannot pace itself – quite apart from dangers to the dog and to other road users, the method is injurious to health.

In pregnancy, gentle regular exercise is important to keep the muscles in trim, and in old age the dog should be encouraged to walk, but at its own pace and distance. Too much energetic exercise, where a dog is pushed beyond its limits of endurance, leads to exhaustion, or has a more serious effect, often on the heart, and in many cases shortens the lifespan.

Exercise should be regular – preferably at the same times each day so that the dog can know when to expect and enjoy it, and preferably either before meals or several hours afterwards. Neglect of exercise will lead to ill-health and produce a stodgy, uninterested and lethargic animal. (See also play.)

An overgrowth of bone, usually occurring near a joint or where a muscle joins a bone. Often it does not cause any problems, but surgical removal will correct the condition if necessary.

See importing/exporting.

Particularly dangerous to undernourished dogs. Extra food is necessary in cold weather for working dogs. Half to one teaspoonful of cod-liver oil per day mixed into the food in winter will also help. (See also hypothermia.)

A thin fluid containing cell debris which, as a result of inflammation, leaks from blood vessels into body tissues and cavities or through the skin, and dries hard on exposure to the air.

The eyeball is set in a mass of cushioning, protective fat inside a bony orbit which almost encircles the eye.

The conjunctiva, lining the eyelids, covers the front of the eye across the cornea from which light passes through the pupil and onto the retina, which is the reception centre of the eye.

exercise

exostosis

exporting

exposure

exudate

eye

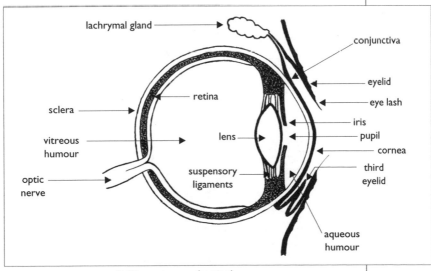

7 The canine eye (section)

eye

The pupil is the central orifice of the iris and is round when entirely dilated – an adjustment stimulated by strong light, and by focusing on near or far objects, which is effected by the muscle fibres of the iris. This action regulates the amount of light entering the eye. The colour of the iris varies with the breed but can be any one of a range of shades of brown or blue.

The tough outer coat of the eyeball is the sclera (modified in the front to form the cornea). The second coat – the choroid – of which the iris is part, is a vascular layer in which the choroid membrane holds a complex network of blood vessels. It is dark in colour but a portion is composed of light-reflecting iridescent cells known collectively as the tapetum. It is these cells that make a dog's eyes glow in the dark when a light is shone into them. The choroid membrane also forms the ciliary body which, by means of the ciliary muscles, allows movement of the lens associated with it to change its curvature for accurate focusing of light rays onto the retina.

The retina is the innermost layer of the eyeball. It is here that the fibres of the optic nerve and the nerve endings are interwoven. The fibres link up to the rods and cones of the retina – the specialist nerve endings which are highly sensitive to light. They 'sort' the visual stimuli, which then pass along the optic nerve to the brain for interpretation. The surface layer of the retina comprises absorbent pigment cells to prevent light received from 'bouncing off' into other regions of the eye – a secondary device to ensure that visual stimuli are efficiently absorbed by the retina. Seven ocular muscles surround the optic nerve, the fibres of which cross over on their way to the sight centres in the brain.

The anterior chamber of the eye, between the cornea and the iris, is filled with clear aqueous humour which helps to keep

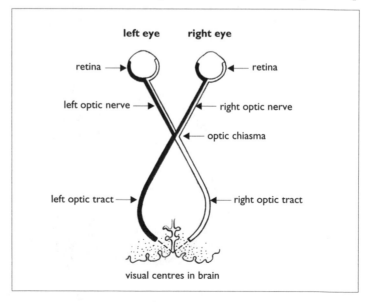

8 The visual path

the cornea in its correct shape. The lens is situated behind the iris and composed of sheaves of muscle fibres assembled in a similar fashion to an onion. The posterior chamber contains the jelly-like vitreous humour which keeps the eye itself in its normal round shape by maintaining ocular pressure.

Lachrymal fluid from the eye's lachrymal gland constantly washes the cornea to keep it clean and free of dust particles. The fluid drains into the nasolachrimal duct which passes through the face bones into the nasal passages. If drainage is inefficient, or if there is an excess of fluid generated, an overflow in the form of tears appears.

(See also blepharitis; blindness; cataract; conjunctivitis; ectropion; entropion; foreign bodies; glaucoma; ptosis; trichiasis.)

An eye-dropper is a handy object to have around. Dust or grit can often be gently washed from the eye by dropping in slightly warm sterile water (boiled and cooled water can be used). Antibiotic eye-drops are also a convenient means of fighting ophthalmic infection if prescribed by a veterinarian. (See drawing.)

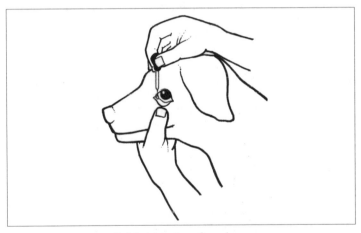

9 Administration of eye drops

The outer layer of the eyelid consists of hairy skin and subcutaneous tissue; the second is formed of muscles which open and close the eyelid; the third, fibrous layer contains forty to fifty sebaceous tarsal glands and the tarsus – a section of stronger fibrous tissue which stiffens the lid margin. The fourth layer forms the conjunctiva, a fold of which comprises the nictitating membrane or 'third eyelid'.

Long hairs grow from the upper lid margin but are absent from the lower lid. A tuft of long tactile hairs is present above, corresponding to the human eyebrow. In some dogs these tufts are of a different colour to that of the fur on the rest of the face. Shape of eyelids and the opening between upper and lower lids vary considerably with each breed. (See also ectropion; entropion.)

eye

eye drops

eyelid

face The face and its range of expressions give many clues to a dog's personality, emotional state and physical condition. Facial expressions (and accompanying body movements) vary between individuals and offer indications of the dog's needs.

In broad terms an affectionate expression with alert ears and wide-open eyes gazing into your face shows a gentle disposition, perhaps awaiting a response. Eyes that look sideways, laid back ears and twitching of the lips give warning that the dog may bite or is angry or frightened. Dull, vacant eyes with perhaps red or yellow tinges to the whites provide clues to illness in a similar way to a dry nose.

fading puppy syndrome There are various causes for this disease which results in the death of entire litters within a few days of their birth. Some may be passed through to the puppies in the colostrum of the dam. From about the third day the puppies become increasingly sleepy and weak, their suck reflex disappears and, since they do not feed, they may die of starvation and dehydration; attempts to feed them by hand are usually totally unsuccessful. Herpes virus, hypothermia and blood conditions have all been suggested as possible causes but sometimes a post-mortem examination does not reveal any definite disease.

faeces Excreta from the bowels, ie food waste from the intestine expelled through the anus. Owners should watch to make sure that their dogs pass normal well-formed faeces of a stodgy consistency at least once a day. Hard, dry faeces usually indicate a dietary problem, as may temporary diarrhoea, although the latter is dangerous due to dehydration if in evidence for more than a day or two.

Examination of faeces is important in the diagnosis of intestinal disease, parasites and other disorders. A veterinarian will be helped if information can be provided on the state of a sick dog's faeces or if a small sample can be taken to the surgery. Blood-stained faeces should always be a reason for a veterinary consultation. Grey, blood-stained faeces may indicate parvo virus and mucus-filled, blood-stained diarrhoea may herald cancer or ulcerative colitis. Rancid-smelling, foamy, putty-coloured faeces can be a symptom of a pancreatic problem. Pale faeces are usually lacking in bile or contain excessive fat. Drug treatment may affect consistency and colour – for example, iron produces black faeces. (See also constipation; diarrhoea; dysentery.)

fainting Fainting, or syncope, occurs due to a weak blood flow to the brain (usually from reduced action of the heart) and may arise following severe shock, emotional disturbance or because of a heart defect. It must be distinguished from other cases of loss of consciousness which may be due, for example, to head injuries, epilepsy, stroke or poisoning.

The dog is helped in recovery if its body can be propped up with the head lower. It needs soothing quiet as it regains consciousness and reassurance whilst resting.

The uterine tubes which join each of the two ovaries to the uterus. Eggs pass along the Fallopian tubes to the uterus, with fertilisation taking place in the funnel-shaped part of the tube (the infundibulum). Each tube averages about 4 to 7cm (1½ to 2¾in) in length and 1 to 3mm (⅟₂₅ to ⅛in) in diameter.

Fallopian tubes

Cysts sometimes occur in the Fallopian tubes and congenital stenosis (narrowing) of the tubes can be a reason for infertility. (See also reproduction.)

See pregnancy, false.

false pregnancy

See obesity.

fat

See diet; nutrition.

fats

See digestion; nutrition.

fatty acids

Dogs can become aggressive or withdrawn through fear. Training should never be based on fear, since the true personality of the dog will be suppressed and – more importantly – the dog will be both unhappy and unhealthy. (See also emotion.)

fear

The long, fine hair fringes at the back of the legs and under the tail of some breeds.

feathers

Capacity to breed.

fecundity

(Suitable foods are described under diet; the nutritional needs of the dog are dealt with under nutrition, and the digestive system under digestion.)

feeding

A dog should generally be fed two meals a day: the main meal in late afternoon or early evening if possible and a smaller one in the early morning. The dog's 'breakfast' can be something light (such as scrambled egg with milk and cereal, for example), while the main meal contains the bulk of the dog's food requirements for the day (see diet).

Feeding should take place as near as possible to the same times each day – and in the same place. A dog looks forward to meal times, which should be interesting and enjoyable events for it, and it should therefore know when to anticipate them.

If you have more than one dog in a family, planning is necessary to ensure that all are fed simultaneously. Unless one is especially aggressive towards the others they should be fed together in the same room but far enough apart to avoid interference with one anothers' meals. Often a dog which is over-fastidious about its food will more readily eat if in sight of another doing the same. Some dogs naturally eat slowly while others eat fast, so some supervision may be needed to make sure the slow eaters get their share. The majority of dogs 'gulp' their food and do not chew (masticate) it; this is entirely natural.

It is preferable to place the food bowl on a bench for long-legged dogs such as Afghan hounds, wolfhounds and salukis, so that they *feeding* do not need to bend their heads far down between spread forelegs – a contortion which may result in digestive and intestinal disorders.

Food containers should be adequate in size for the meal, preferably of stainless steel with a base larger than the top to prevent overturning. They should be thoroughly cleansed in boiling water after each feed and put away where they cannot become contaminated.

The meal should be fed warm and a little moist for maximum acceptability and ease of digestion. Never give a meal which is too hot, nor one which has just come out of the refrigerator. Stale food or any that has risked contamination by exposure to flies, pests, parasites or harmful bacteria should never be fed.

Clean, cool, fresh drinking water should be available at *all* times, not just at meal times when it will probably not be used. Dogs should never be fed in direct sunlight; a shady, cool place in summer is preferable.

Observation at feeding times reveals exactly what food is preferred in a varied diet and provides clues to the state of a dog's health. If it consistently refuses food over two or three days, it could be ill and other symptoms may or may not be present. If in doubt consult a veterinarian.

femur The thigh bone running from hip to stifle. It is the heaviest bone in the dog. In those breeds which are well-proportioned the tibia (shin-bone) and ulna (longest forearm bone) are generally a little longer than the femur, which is itself about 20 per cent longer than the humerus (upper armbone between shoulder and elbow).

The rounded head of the femur fits into the hip socket to form a synovial joint and at the lower end joins with the patella or stifle joint. The femur is a common site of fracture, at the head or across the shaft, usually the result of a road accident.

fertilisation The process which occurs when a male spermatozoon fuses with a female ovum in the Fallopian tube. After penetrating the ovum the tail of the sperm disappears and the head combines with the nucleus of the ovum in its cytoplasm. Each cell contributes an equal number of chromosomes and all body cells are produced subsequently by division from the one formed during fusion. (See also reproduction.)

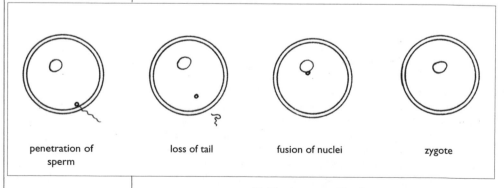

| penetration of sperm | loss of tail | fusion of nuclei | zygote |

10 The sequence of fertilisation

A raised body temperature due to infection and usually accompanied by a quickened pulse. A body temperature of over 41.7°C (107°F) is abnormally high and dangerous; 42.8°C (109°F) or over indicates that the dog's life is in danger if the fever is prolonged. Fever is itself a symptom of an infective condition, and associated symptoms vary but include loss of appetite, lethargy or distress, fast breathing rate and sometimes thirst. A feverish dog should be examined by a veterinarian as soon as possible. (See also temperature; thermometer.)

fever

The rapid, unco-ordinated twitching and contraction of individual groups of muscle fibres. It may be a symptom of heart disease and as such may be treated with drugs such as digitalis. Cardiac massage sometimes corrects the disorder if it is of a temporary nature. Fibrillation can also occur in other muscles, usually as a result of a nervous disorder.

fibrillation

A protein formed by the conversion of fibrinogen which occurs when thrombin is liberated during the process of coagulation of the blood. A further reaction during coagulation in the presence of calcium links fibrin molecules together to produce an insoluble fibrin clot. The process may occur similarly in appropriate pathological conditions to cause thrombosis. (See also coagulation; thrombosis.)

fibrin

A soluble plasma protein involved in the sequence leading to blood coagulation, being converted by thrombin liberation to fibrin. It is made in the liver and consumed during coagulation. Liver disease or thrombosis may cause fibrinogen deficiency and increases are sometimes evident in pregnancy, uterine infections and shock. (See also coagulation; thrombosis.)

fibrinogen

A tumour comprising fibrous tissue. Such growths are usually benign and slow-growing. Removal by surgery is the treatment. (See also tumour.)

fibroma

Granulation, ie a form of cellular change in chronic inflammation where fibrous tissue replaces normal cells. It arises when there is a continuous cause of inflammation or when the body cannot reduce inflammation rapidly enough. Fibrosis sometimes appears around chronic abscesses or when, for example, a neck chain constantly chafes the skin.

fibrosis

One of the two bones of the lower hind leg, running behind the tibia from stifle to hock. It twists slightly and is much finer than the tibia. Its main purpose is for the attachment of muscles.

fibula

If a dog has been in a fight it needs a very thorough examination for any form of wound; small puncture wounds can be as dangerous as severe gaping ones as they often form abscesses. Dogs seldom attack bitches and, although a bitch may drive off a pestering dog there is rarely harm in the encounter. Each may become involved in

fighting

fighting a fight with its own sex, however, and keen observation during exercise, watching for any signs of aggression in your own as well as other owners' dogs will do much to avoid what could be a nasty battle. Aggressive dogs should be kept under control at all times. (See also bite; wounds.)

filariasis A disease, occurring chiefly in the tropics, caused by filarial worms which infest the heart and occasionally the eye. Since the drug diethylcarbamazine eliminates the larvae of these worms, which are transmitted by mosquitoes, a daily dose in infected areas of tropical countries is an effective form of prevention. Symptoms of infestation include coughing and respiratory distress with lethargy and collapse.

fireworks Despite numerous warnings to owners, many pets, including dogs, are burned, injured and frightened each year by fireworks and bonfires. The method of prevention is simple: keep all dogs inside the house behind closed curtains when fireworks are being used. If, in an emergency, a dog must go outside, it must be accompanied and on a lead, and be brought inside again as soon as possible. The increasingly widespread mayhem caused by local firework parties puts ever more stress on some dogs who may need administration of a tranquilliser to calm them over the period of noise. Seek help from a veterinarian in advance if a dog is generally susceptible to this type of stress.

first aid Emergency measures to save life, ease pain and suffering and aid recovery while professional help is awaited. First aid is generally valuable in sudden illness and after accidents, and guidelines on various first-aid techniques are mentioned under individual entries in this book where applicable.

In order to save critical time it is advisable to keep a first-aid box stocked for the dog at all times in the home (and perhaps a basic one in the car). Suggested general contents are listed below. (See also artificial respiration.)

First-aid box contents

Dressings (gauze, sterile)	TCP
Round-tipped scissors	Eucalyptus oil
Round-ended forceps	Worming tablets
Clinical thermometer	Veterinary deodorant
Medicine dropper and rubber teats	Alugan sachets (flea shampoo treatment)
Plastic syringes (20ml)	Bandages
Stainless steel dish	Absorbent lint
Clean towelling	Cottonwool balls
Disprin	Double-sided surgical tape
Epsom salts	
Sodium bicarbonate	
Vaseline (tube)	
Acriflavine	

Lost and abandoned tackle can be as much of a danger to dogs as to water birds and other creatures. Fishing line can catch and tangle in dogs' feet, splitting pads and tearing claws, and is an especially dangerous hazard to swimming dogs. Barbed fish-hooks become embedded in tender noses, lips, ears, feet and other parts of the head and body and may require surgery to remove them. Swallowed lead weights cause obstruction and lead poisoning. Less seriously, anyone whose dog has found some of the smellier baits discarded and happily rolled in them will know just how difficult it is to remove the smell from the coat. (Eucalyptus oil is a useful decontaminant.)

fishing tackle

An ulcer or wound sometimes causes a fistula – an abnormal channel between internal organs, or between an organ or a natural cavity and the body surface. In dental fistulae a molar abscess in the root bursts upwards through the flesh of the face. Another example is an anal fistula which may follow sepsis of an anal gland rupturing on the perineal surface. Treatment consists of thoroughly clearing the infection plus the help perhaps of some antibiotic ointment. Healing can be problematical at times and surgery may be necessary.

fistula

See convulsion; epilepsy.

fits

Distension caused by gas in the alimentary canal. It is generally a symptom of indigestion and may be treated by giving a few charcoal biscuits and reducing fatty foods for a while. An adjustment in diet may be necessary since this may be the primary cause of the disorder. (See also diet; digestion.)

flatulence

See collar.

flea collar

See parasites.

fleas

Flies can transmit (or assist in the transmission) of many canine diseases including ear diseases (especially in parts of the USA), filariasis (in the tropics), skin infestations (particularly in South America, Africa and India), eye infections (and infestations in parts of the USA and tropical climates), and intestinal disorders.

flies

However, they mainly cause danger to dogs by contaminating food (resulting in infection) and possibly spreading kennel diseases, and they are a nuisance to dogs with skin diseases or wounds. Food should, of course, always be kept covered or refrigerated before use and no food should be left around if the dog has not cleared it from its dish. Any food suspected of fly contamination should be destroyed. Kennels should be kept clean and regularly washed with disinfectant to discourage flies, and patients with wounds and skin troubles should be kept away from fly-ridden areas.

Beware of some aerosol fly-sprays; they can be almost as dangerous to dogs as to flies.

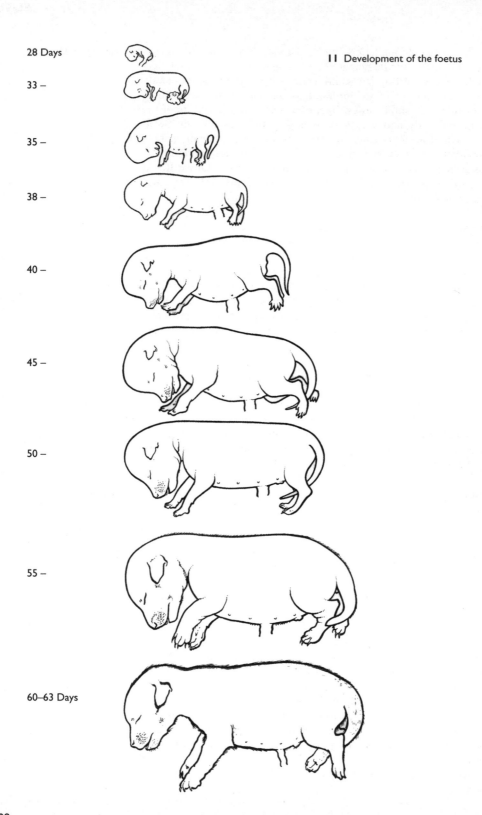

28 Days

33 –

35 –

38 –

40 –

45 –

50 –

55 –

60–63 Days

The developing canine embryo becomes a foetus after thirty-five days of gestation and growth in the uterus. It is then recognisable as a dog and major organ formation is accomplished. It will have grown to about 35 to 40mm (1¼ to 1½in) of the 160 to 185mm (6 to 7in) length it will be at birth if it is an average-sized breed.

At about thirty-five days after fertilisation, eyelids, ear-flaps and sex organs are evident; at forty days, paws and claws are formed and eyelids closed together; at forty-five days, the dog's colouring appears as hair begins to grow; and at fifty days the foetus is well-proportioned. Five days later the foetus is moving around in the uterus within the placental band with teeth well formed, and at sixty to sixty-three days it is no longer a foetus but a pup being born blind but well covered in hair. (See also whelping, and diagram opposite.)

foetus

See nutrition.

folic acid

A small pit-like structure such as that surrounding a hair-root. Graafian or vesicular follicles are found in the ovary and contain the ova; each follicle, under pressure from follicular fluid within, eventually ruptures to release an ovum (egg). (For drawing, see hair.)

follicle

The application of a hot liquid soaked into a sterile cotton or gauze pad, usually to accelerate the development of an abscess and the subsequent discharge of pus. Salt water is commonly used in such cases. Epsom salts in solution can assist in hardening a wounded area, eg cut pads of the feet. Test the temperature of the solution with a clean hand before application.

fomentation

See diet; feeding; nutrition.

food

Tweezer-like instrument with rounded or pointed tips designed for a variety of uses in surgery. Forceps are also used to place and remove sterile dressings aseptically; arterial forceps are used to clamp a bleeding artery and dental forceps are used in the extraction of teeth.

forceps

Part of the foreleg extending from elbow to pastern. The bones of the forearm are the radius and ulna.

forearm

A wide assortment of objects gain entry into a dog's mouth or other orifices. Common foreign bodies include grass seeds which become embedded in ears (particularly in the flap-eared dogs such as spaniels), between toes, in the nose and under eyelids and skin. They can cause inflammation leading to more serious conditions and should be removed without delay. If within reach of fingers or a pair of blunt-ended forceps gentle extraction can be carried out. If out of reach, however, such as deep in the ear, a visit to the veterinary surgery is an urgent necessity, and the offending object may have to be removed under local or even general anaesthetic.

foreign bodies

foreign bodies

This approach is the general rule for all foreign bodies: if easy, gentle removal is impossible, then a veterinarian must be consulted.

The mouth is another common site for foreign bodies, as is the entire alimentary tract. Sometimes a needle or a pin is collected on the tongue, or a fish-hook caught in the mouth. Pieces of carpet, rubber bands, coal, nails, corks, plastic bags and sheeting, large pieces of gristly meat, small balls (such as those used in golf or squash) and the vast range of small toys which children frequently leave around the house, are all potential dangers to a dog's health, and sometimes to its life. They can be wedged in the throat or swallowed to cause hazards elsewhere in the body. Stomach linings can become inflamed, or sharp objects can pierce the lining of the intestine, causing peritonitis and possibly death. Chronic gastritis can result from intestinal, rectal or anal obstruction.

Chop and chicken bones are dangerous, becoming swallowed or stuck in the dog's throat or wedged across the teeth or between the jaws. Small stones, picked up on the beach or in the garden are additional hazards to be avoided as these often remain in the stomach after being swallowed, where they cause obstruction, inflammation and other problems.

Symptoms of problems caused by foreign bodies vary but almost always include dejection or obvious distress, depending upon where the object is situated, sometimes vomiting (often with blood flecks resembling coffee grounds present in the vomit) and, over a lengthy period, loss of weight. In cases of sudden onset, such as a foreign body becoming wedged in the respiratory tract or the throat, the dog may fall over and its tongue turn a bluish-purple colour; its back will arch and signs of distress will be obvious. In extreme cases such as these, it is necessary to attempt to remove the object from the dog's throat or it will die quickly. If it cannot be pulled out, then pushing it down to a point where it can be swallowed is virtually the only course of action left.

Yelping during defecation may indicate the presence of a foreign body in the anus; constipation can be a sign of an intestinal obstruction. Surgery is often necessary and an X-ray will help in the diagnosis of the long-term problems.

Common sense can prevent most of the above mishaps. Keep all potentially dangerous objects out of reach (especially of a puppy), discourage dogs from rooting around in refuse bins and watch them closely on walks if they have a tendency to pick up anything. (See also accidents; bones, feeding of; grass seeds.)

fracture

The breaking of a bone. Virtually any bone in the dog's body can be broken by violence, a fall, accident or other injuries. Suspected fractures should be dealt with by a veterinarian as soon as possible and the patient meanwhile immobilised.

Symptoms of a fracture are usually, but not always, obvious. There is pain, possibly swelling and associated wounds at the site of the break, difficulty in moving and, if pain is prolonged, shock. Sometimes a grinding noise can be heard if the dog moves the fractured part, with extreme pain accompanying the movement.

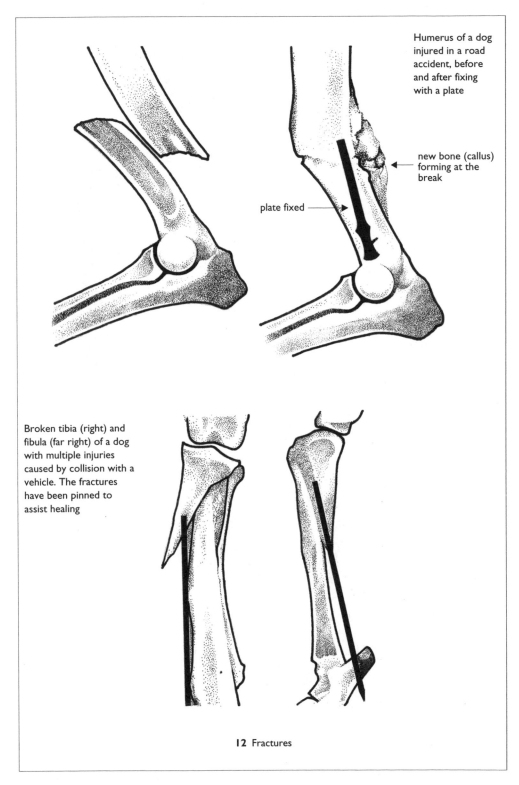

Humerus of a dog injured in a road accident, before and after fixing with a plate

new bone (callus) forming at the break

plate fixed

Broken tibia (right) and fibula (far right) of a dog with multiple injuries caused by collision with a vehicle. The fractures have been pinned to assist healing

12 Fractures

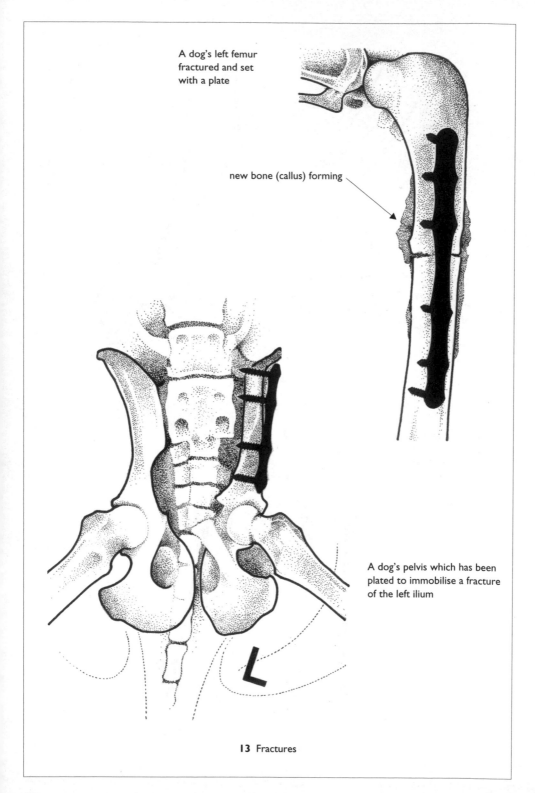

A dog's left femur fractured and set with a plate

new bone (callus) forming

A dog's pelvis which has been plated to immobilise a fracture of the left ilium

L

13 Fractures

There must be minimal and very careful, gentle handling. In the case of a broken limb, immobilisation with the aid of a temporary splint, with even padding between splint and skin, is a useful measure and the dog must be kept still, warm and comfortable until a veterinarian can set or effect a reduction of the fracture.

fracture

Fractures generally fall into one of the categories below:

A simple fracture is a broken bone without a wound from the break puncturing the skin. Simple fractures can be termed 'transverse' (a straight break across the bone), 'fissured' (cracked but not entirely broken) or 'spiral' (an oblique break).

A compound fracture is a broken bone with skin or mucous membrane torn to expose bone fragments to the air. Bleeding often occurs and there is a danger of infection from airborne organisms.

A multiple fracture occurs when there are several breaks in one bone at various distances apart.

A complicated fracture is any bone break complicated by damage to surrounding organs, joints, nerves or blood vessels. A simple or compound fracture can become 'complicated' through the dog moving around or being mishandled.

A comminuted fracture is a break where the bone is splintered or shattered.

A greenstick fracture is so called because the bone is bent and cracked, splitting like a green stick. It usually occurs only in young bones.

A depressed fracture is where a fragment of bone is depressed lower than its normal level. It often occurs in a skull fracture, for example, and can consequently be a serious complication.

A deferred fracture is a break which is incomplete, but which can be completed by an extra strain or jolt.

An impacted fracture is one where the bone pieces from the break become pushed into each other.

A hairline fracture is a very fine break.

A veterinarian will set the broken bones in place again, sometimes under a general anaesthetic, and keep the bone immobile until it has healed. This is accomplished by means of a splint or bandage, or, if internal fixation is required, by a metal pin or plate which may or may not be subsequently removed.

Bone heals like any other tissue. The healing process starts with inflammation with an increase of blood flow and white blood cells, fluid and protein arriving from blood vessels. The blood clot which occurs at the fracture site gradually disperses and is replaced by a spongy tissue similar to early scar tissue on skin. Chalky deposits harden this tissue, forming a firm mass. This new tissue, or 'callus', is finally replaced by newly-developed bone. Movement of the broken bone is to be avoided to prevent destruction of the callus.

The age and state of health of the dog, as well as the site and extensiveness of the injury, will affect the length of healing time. In general terms, however, about six weeks is needed for fractures to heal and lameness and swelling may persist for some months. Patience and common-sense nursing are important. (See also accidents; splint.)

frill	A mass of feathery hair on the chest of some breeds.
frustration	Frustrated dogs become unhappy, bored or aggressive, and usually unhealthy physically as well as mentally. Frustration can develop through tethering, lack of exercise, lack of companionship, confinement in a small space, teasing, etc. (See also behaviour.)
'frying-pan dangers'	These are now recognised as hazards in the home and have been known to kill dogs. Overheated fat gives off poisonous fumes and, in an unventilated room, a dog can be quickly overcome, with extreme difficulty in breathing, cyanosis and collapse. Polytetrafluoroethylene, which is used to coat non-stick frying pans, can also be dangerous when overheating, according to some reports. There is also a danger from fire spreading from overheated fat pans. Adequate ventilation is a preventive measure and, in any case, it is inadvisable to allow a dog to remain in an unattended kitchen when cooking is in progress as a variety of accidents are possible. (See also accidents; artificial respiration; burns and scalds.)
fumigation	After an outbreak of infectious disease in kennels, fumigation with formaldehyde gas and cleansing with disinfectant is necessary to eradicate any remaining organisms and prevent recurrence of the infection. If possible the kennels should be left empty for about a week after total fumigation.
fungal infection	See aspergillosis; ringworm.
fungi	Moulds and yeasts are fungi which, in various forms, can cause canine infections.

G

gall

See bile.

gall-bladder

A pear-shaped bladder which stores bile until needed in the digestive process. It holds about 15ml (½fl oz) of bile at any one time and measures about 5cm (2in) in length by about 1.5cm (½in) wide at the bulbous end. It lies between lobes of the liver and although rarely a source of trouble for the dog, can become inflamed and cause pain in the region of the liver. Gallstones may also cause pain.

gallstones

Hard, cholesterol-rich calculi which contain bile pigments and fill the gall-bladder or block the bile-duct. Such an affliction produces pain and probably jaundice. They may be passed or may require surgical removal.

gametes

Reproductive male (spermatozoa) and female (ova) cells which unite in pairs to produce new individuals or zygotes.

ganglion

A bunch of nerve-fibre endings and nerve cells found throughout the body. It is also a term applied to a cystic swelling associated with a tendon.

gangrene

The death of living tissue (necrosis). It may occur when a limb, for example, is deprived of its blood supply. It can be caused through wound infection by specific organisms, bacterial invasion, extensive damage or a combination of any of these. When bacteria are involved, complications can arise in the form of toxins from the bacteria and the formation of dead tissue.

The area becomes swollen and inflamed and soon turns a greenish-black colour, hair comes out and there is a characteristic smell of putrefaction with fluid oozing from the tissues. Irregular heartbeat, distressed breathing, pain and raised temperature accompany the condition. Surgical amputation is usually necessary, with substantial use of sulphonamides and antibiotics to deal with the circulating infection.

gas

For intestinal gas, see flatulence; for poisoning by gas, see poisoning.

gastric juices

See digestion; enzymes.

gastritis

Inflammation of the mucous membrane lining the stomach, usually caused by incorrect diet or overeating. Sometimes it is due to the presence of a foreign body but more frequently the cause is less dramatic. The dog rarely vomits with mild gastritis but will probably have some diarrhoea and a little abdominal tenderness.

The best course of action if the cause is thought to be dietary is to starve the dog for twenty-four hours and give only plenty of fresh water. Then give the dog some light food such as boiled chicken breasts and cooked rice. If the condition persists after two days, or if the dog is in pain, consult a veterinarian.

gastroenteritis	There are many causes of gastroenteritis, among them distemper, leptospirosis, tuberculosis, uraemia, anaemia, vitamin deficiency and dietary problems. Symptoms include extreme lethargy and gradual weakening, with excessive diarrhoea. There may also be vomiting. Partially digested and some undigested food passes along the intestines due to digestive failures and bacterial growth is consequently encouraged. Tissue invasion and septicaemia follow and toxins are absorbed. If the dog has diarrhoea and is also vomiting it needs veterinary attention without delay so that fluids can be injected to maintain fluid balance and counteract dehydration. Withhold solid food for twenty-four to forty-eight hours and feed glucose water (about 2 tablespoonfuls dissolved in ¼ pint of boiled and cooled water) with an egg beaten up in the mixture if it is not being vomited up. Antibiotics are required against the bacteria and possibly supplementary doses of vitamins A and B during recovery. A bland, easily-digested diet is needed in convalescence. (See also enteritis; haemorrhagic gastroenteritis.)
gauze	See dressing.
gelatin	A jelly made from animal bones and tissues, frequently used to contain drugs in capsule form. It melts in the alimentary tract liberating the drug for absorption. It has also been used in sponge form to arrest bleeding in a wound, being impregnated sometimes with antibiotic. It becomes absorbed as the wound heals.
genes	DNA (deoxyribonucleic acid) compounds, often called the basic units of heredity. They are contained in chromosomes and directly influence the characteristics of the offspring which are inherited from the parents. By a process known as mutation, a gene may exist in two or more alternative types known as alleles.
genetics	The study of inheritance or heredity and mutation.
genitalia	The male and female reproductive organs. (See also reproduction.)
genotype	The complete collection of genes held by one individual.
germicide	A substance or solution which kills germs, eg a disinfectant.
gestation	The period between fertilisation and whelping. In the dog it is sixty to sixty-three days.
gingivitis	Inflammation of the gums. It is usually accompanied by foul breath. An excess of vitamin A can be a cause but more commonly it is due to a build-up of tartar on the teeth. Superficial gingivitis is often seen in dogs fed soft, mushy foods for several years and may spread to deeper tissue and involve the dental alveoli, producing a purulent discharge and loosening of the teeth. If untreated the disease can eventually invade the jaw and

facial bones. Prevention lies mainly in a suitable diet and having the teeth scaled regularly to counteract an accumulation of tartar. (See also gums.)

gingivitis

Organs which produce and secrete substances to be used elsewhere in the body. (See also endocrine system.)

glands

A special hazard to dogs; broken glass encountered on a walk can cut feet and legs, even sometimes producing wounds extensive and deep enough to cripple a dog for life. Even the smallest cuts in the dog's pads on its feet are extremely difficult to heal and to keep free from infection.

glass

Accidents in the home resulting in broken glass can also be highly dangerous. Apart from the danger to feet there is the additional hazard that tiny pieces of glass, which may be mixed, for example, with milk spilt from a shattered bottle or with food such as butter from a smashed dish, may be licked up and swallowed. If glass is broken, immediately confine the dog away from the area while the pieces are thoroughly cleared with a vacuum cleaner, and ensure that even the tiniest particles are removed. Any dog which has swallowed glass should be seen by a veterinarian without delay. (See also foreign bodies; wounds.)

A condition characterised by swelling of the eyeball and impaired sight; it is due to an increase in intra-ocular pressure built up by the secretion of aqueous humour in the eye faster than it can drain away. It can also be the result of atrophy of the retina, dislocation of the lens, congenital defects or other eye diseases. Often the cause is difficult to determine. Pilocarpine, which constricts the pupil, is sometimes an effective drug for use against glaucoma, but surgery may be required.

glaucoma

Some strains of basset hound appear to be susceptible to glaucoma and some rough-haired terriers to dislocation of the lens, which may cause it. (See also blindness; eye.)

Inflammation of the tongue, symptomised by drooling and tenderness and generated by mouth ulceration, local infection, injuries, etc. An examination may reveal the presence of a foreign body such as a pin, needle or fish-hook – particularly in puppies which are over-enthusiastically prone to pick up objects on their tongues. Treatment of glossitis is generally carried out against the underlying cause. If it is due to a minor injury causing bleeding, a cold-water compress held to the affected area will stem the flow of blood. The tongue usually heals rapidly.

glossitis

A form of sugar. It is especially useful to sick dogs because of its ease of absorption through the intestine for direct conversion to energy without the need to use valuable energy in digestion. It is normally produced through the process of digestion from carbohydrate intake. Glucose is excreted in the urine in diabetes. (See also digestion; energy.)

glucose

glucose/saline solution	It is an ideal source of energy for sick dogs suffering from diarrhoea or intestinal diseases such as gastroenteritis and haemorrhagic gastroenteritis and also helps in maintaining fluid balance and overcoming the effects of dehydration. It can be given orally if there is no vomiting, or by injection or via the rectum. If the dog is reluctant to take the mixture orally it can be gently dripped down the throat by holding the head up, inserting the nozzle of a plastic syringe through the side of the mouth between two of the back teeth and slowly depressing the plunger, allowing the dog ample time to swallow. Glucose/saline for oral use can be prepared by adding a level teaspoonful of salt and a heaped tablespoonful of medicinal glucose – available from a chemist or drugstore – to half a pint of boiled and cooled water.
glycerin	An effective laxative in small doses and a purgative in large amounts when given orally. About 20ml (¾fl oz) injected rectally will help in the removal of impacted faeces in severe constipation. It is very soothing if painted on the inflamed inside of the mouth and throat and is frequently included in cough mixtures.
glycogen	A form of starch found in the liver and muscle. The liver converts excess glucose to glycogen for storage until it is needed for energy, when it is reconverted. (See also digestion.)
goitre	A disorder characterised by an enlarged thyroid gland and general lethargy. It is caused by iodine deficiency and is usually corrected by iodine injections, though some cases return to normal without treatment. Puppies are sometimes affected and some fox terriers and larger dogs from three to five years of age seem to be more susceptible than the smaller breeds. Care should be taken not to confuse goitre with laryngeal or thyroid tumours.
gonads	Male and female sex glands which produce gametes. (See also ovaries; testes.)
graft	The application of a piece of skin, bone or other tissue to similar tissue, usually on another part of the body. A graft can also be taken from an adjacent area by cutting and folding skin over the affected place.
granulation	See fibrosis.
granulocyte	White blood cell which exhibits granules in its cytoplasm. Granulocytes are neutrophils, eosinophils and basophils. (See also blood.)
granuloma	Granular tissue or 'proud flesh' which may result from continual licking of an irritating skin area. Dogs can become obsessed with licking when plagued with such conditions and an inflamed and ulcerated area develops leading to granular tissue formation. Treatment of the cause is the best method of prevention and an 'Elizabethan' collar (see entry) may assist healing. (See also tumour.)

Some dogs often eat grass. The action is considered to be both bene- **grass**
ficial and medicinal and it is probably no accident that the species
they tend to select is of the 'couch' family – *Elymus repens*. This
grass has been used for centuries for its medicinal purposes (the
Greeks and Romans both used it), to soothe inflammation of the
urinary tract and promote the flow of urine. It was also once considered to be of use in easing vomiting and diarrhoea and controlling
worms in children. Extracts from the plant are still used in
pharmacy today against cystitis, urinary tract infections and rheumatism, as it contains several useful pharmaceutical compounds.

Some breeds also occasionally take several long strands of rough
grass which they swallow to produce a single bout of vomiting,
apparently to rid the stomach of displeasing contents, excessive
mucus or bone particles which are difficult to digest.

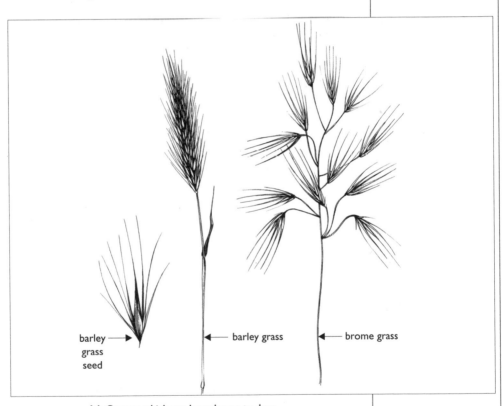

barley → grass seed   ◄— barley grass   ◄— brome grass

14 Grasses which can be a danger to dogs

The seeds of some grasses are, at certain times of the year, truly **grass seeds**
dangerous for the dog. During the summer and early autumn,
country, and indeed many urban, veterinarians are constantly
faced with canine patients which have grass seeds ferociously
implanted in different parts of their bodies, particularly ears, feet,
nostrils, anus and sometimes eyes. While the dog owner may be
able to extract those in the dog's coat and sometimes from feet and

grass seeds

skin, those in ears and nostrils especially will need urgent attention from a veterinarian as they are not only extremely painful but can cause severe complications if not removed quickly. Flap-eared dogs, such as spaniels, retrievers and dachshunds, are most affected in the ears by these dangers but all dogs are at risk, especially if they have long-haired coats.

The most injurious seeds (see drawing previous page) are from the wall or meadow barley grass, and some forms of the oat grass or brome. The seeds of the barley grasses, assembled in tiers on a stem and light brown when ripe, detach themselves loosely from their stalks to be blown away by the wind or distributed by other means in late summer and early autumn.

The sharp, spiked, pointed end of the arrow-shaped seed, with its rough flights sticking out behind it, catches into the dog's coat. The barbed flights prevent it falling off and assist its progress as it eases its way as if alive through the fur during the dog's movements. If caught in long, vulnerable ears, it can soon find its way into the ear opening and quickly descends into the interior where it becomes embedded deep in the horizontal ear canal next to the ear-drum, causing much pain, inflammation, bleeding and ultimately infection. An affected dog will shake its head with the injured ear held down, rub its cheek along the ground and cry out with pain. It needs immediate veterinary attention and possibly a general anaesthetic for the removal operation. After-care is important to prevent complications from the damage done by the seed, and the dog must receive antibiotics to combat or prevent infection and anti-inflammatory agents to reduce the inflammation and promote healing.

Similar veterinary attention is needed if a seed is sniffed in and becomes embedded in the nostrils. The dog snorts, shakes and paws its head and shows obvious distress from the pain, which is sometimes accompanied by copious bleeding from the nostril. In the feet the seeds make the dog limp and gnaw at its toes. If affected in the mouth the dog shows distress, rubbing its cheeks and probably coughing and retching; and if there is a barley seed in the anus the hindquarters are rubbed along the ground and the dog whines and tries to worry the area under its tail. Eyes are sometimes affected by small grass seeds (luckily, rarely by the half-inch barbs of the barley grass) and may be bathed out with warm water. If they are deeply embedded, then again the help of a veterinarian is needed.

The only sure way to avoid the hazard is by exercising your dog away from an area where these grasses are abundant and seeding, or where any long grass is in seed. Clipping the fur short during the relevant months will help too.

If your dog should encounter any grass seeds on a walk (and awareness of the potential danger, coupled to sharp observation will be your alarm system) call it immediately to heel and check it over for any signs of the seeds in the coat and remove them before they become embedded in the skin. (See also foreign bodies.)

greenstick fracture   See fracture.

Regular grooming is essential to good health. It should commence in puppyhood so that the dog becomes used to the brush and comb and enjoys the operation. Grooming should not only consist of coat brushing but should include attention to ears, eyes, teeth, mouth and feet. Bitches can be examined carefully around the mammary glands and abdomen for any signs of growths and the anus can be inspected for inflammation and anal gland problems.

Short-haired dogs need less brushing (and even less combing) than long-haired breeds, but all need some brushing to prevent dandruff, discourage parasites, cleanse the coat and clear tangles. It also makes healthy dogs feel better. A grooming session once a week is usually sufficient for all but the very long-haired breeds such as Afghan hounds, Pekinese, shih tzu, etc which need daily attention.

Grooming equipment for a short-haired dog should include brush, dental scaler, a chamois leather (or piece of velvet) and a dog's nail file (for claws). For long-haired dogs, these, plus one or more steel combs with varying distances between the teeth, a tangle-comb and mat-splitter, 'toe' scissors (for hair between the pads) and suitable round-tipped scissors, are all standard pieces of equipment. A stainless steel bowl with warm water, cotton wool balls and a pair of round-tipped forceps may also be useful for cleaning up the bench or for washing around some skin areas where dirt has lodged.

Bristle brushes are ideal (*not* wire) and the choice of comb will depend largely on the type of coat (and its thickness), which must be groomed without painful tugging. Dental scalers are needed to remove any accumulation of tartar on the teeth, particularly in older dogs, and a chamois leather or velvet cloth adds a fine shine to the coat after brushing. A tangle-comb (shaped rather like a miniature short-handled garden rake) is used with a mat-splitter to comb through after the scythe-shaped splitter has cut through the tangle (beware that the point of the splitter's blade does not poke into the dog's face or body while it is being used). Round-tipped scissors are helpful in clipping away extra long hair and levelling the trim (though Kennel Club rules may not allow owners of show dogs to use them).

A variety of electric hand clippers is available on the market should it be necessary to strip a dog during hot weather. There are instructions with most of these and lengthy books on how to use them. Most students of the craft learn by trial and error, and it is therefore advisable to purchase a pair with blades which are adjustable for depth of trim.

A dog should be groomed on a firm table or bench so that it is conveniently level with the chest of the groom. Talking a good deal to a dog while it is being groomed is soothing and it interests the dog in what is going on as well as giving it confidence. If grooming is made into an enjoyable operation, the dog becomes eager for the regular sessions, and the task is made easier. (See also bathing; shampoo.)

Achieved by cell division, which requires energy. The optimum energy production requires adequate diet and nutrition. Puppies

growth	double their weights very rapidly, with exact rates of growth varying with the breeds. During these times they will consume double the quantity of food of an adult dog of the same breed. Rates of growth will be reduced by lack of energy resulting from insufficient food although eventual size generally remains unaffected. Growth may also be stunted by disease which may or may not affect adult size depending on type of disease, severity and time of occurrence. (For 'growth' meaning pathological tissue, see tumour.)
gullet	See oesophagus.
gums	The dense fibrous tissues extending around the lower parts of the teeth down to the alveoli; they are covered with smooth mucosa filled with blood vessels. The gums are continuous with the hard palate on the upper jaw and the oral mucosa of the lower jaw. Pigmentation of the mucosa in some breeds is therefore also apparent in the gums. Pale gums can, with other symptoms, indicate anaemia and when inflamed signify a mouth infection. Yellowed gums are a sign of jaundice. (See also gingivitis.)
gunshot wounds	See wounds.
gut	See intestines.

H

The vomiting of blood. Clear blood usually indicates damage to the oesophagus while stale blood from the stomach resembles coffee grounds. Haematemesis should always be taken seriously and a veterinary examination made without delay. There are various causes of blood being vomited from the stomach; among them ulcers, foreign bodies and sometimes drugs or stress.

haematemesis

A test usually performed as part of a blood count carried out in the laboratory. It refers to the percentage by volume of the blood which is composed of red blood cells (the remainder is plasma and white cells). A blood sample is taken into a bottle containing anti-coagulant, transferred to a special haematocrit tube and spun down in a centrifuge so that the red cells are packed at the lower end. The reading is taken from the graduations on the tube. The test is also called 'packed cell volume' (PCV). The result varies with the age of the dog. When taken into account with other component results of the total blood count it presents useful evidence of disease, including anaemia.

haematocrit

The study of blood and its diseases.

haematology

A blood-filled swelling. Haematomas are most common in ear-flaps where, in response to irritation, continual head shaking and scratching cause a small blood vessel to rupture; the blood accumulates in one place producing the swelling, which is usually relieved permanently by surgical draining. Parasites in the ear are frequently the original cause of the irritation and treatment of this condition often prevents the arrival of the swelling.
   Haematomas can also be caused by violent blows to various other parts of the body and these, too, need draining.

haematoma

The presence of blood in the urine. The colour may be a smoky brown or red and its appearance at the end of micturition may indicate bladder damage as blood cells collect at the base of the bladder. Presence of blood when the dog begins to pass urine suggests damage in the genital region or to the urethra. Blood throughout the urine stream may mean kidney or ureter lesions.
   Haematuria is not only the result of damage to the urinary system but can also denote infection, inflammation, ulceration, tumours, urinary calculi, leptospirosis or even endoparasites. Observation of the dog's ability to pass urine and its colour and frequency, as well as the dog's demeanour, will help a veterinarian in diagnosis.

haematuria

The substance which gives the red colour to the blood. It absorbs oxygen from the lungs and carries it to the tissues. It is contained in the red blood cells and itself contains iron. When the cells break down the iron is collected by the liver, spleen and bone marrow and re-used as haemoglobin is regenerated.

haemoglobin

haemoglobin

A lack of haemoglobin in some anaemic conditions can be serious in that the tissues are starved of oxygen. In such cases blood transfusion may be required.

haemolysis

Breakdown of red blood cells. Sometimes this happens pathologically causing 'haemolytic anaemia'. It may be due to spleen or liver damage, leptospirosis, blood disease, snake bite or an infection which generates toxins, releasing them into the bloodstream and destroying the red cells. Another form is caused by an auto-immune reaction where the dog's body destroys its own red cells. A similar disease – 'haemolytic disease of the newborn' – affects newly-born pups and may be passed through the colostrum. Corticosteroids often reduce the reaction which is symptomised by haematuria, bleeding from gums, depression, anorexia and sometimes jaundice. Mismatched transfusions have also been the cause of haemolysis, particularly on the second transfusion, in which case kidney failure is usually the result. (See also agglutination; blood group; transfusions and infusions.)

haemophilia

A hereditary disease characterised by bleeding through impaired blood coagulation due to a complete or partial deficiency of one of the components of the blood coagulation reaction (Factor VIII). It is sex-linked, being carried by bitches and occurring in male dogs. It appears in bitches through mating haemophiliac males to carrier bitches. While it can arise in most breeds it is relatively rare.

Caring for a haemophiliac dog is difficult since it must be carefully prevented from fighting or bumping itself, even minor cuts or knocks being dangerous. Any form of damage can cause external or internal bleeding which can be very serious. Canine haemophiliacs fortunately often show no inclination to mate and, in any case, should certainly not be allowed to breed.

Frozen dog plasma containing the missing Factor VIII (or concentrates of it) is transfused to treat bleeding – provided it is available when needed. Owners of canine haemophiliacs should register with a local veterinarian so that preparation can be made for such an emergency. Diagnosis depends on thorough laboratory tests and symptoms may first be noticed through an excessive bleeding following a slight injury or by the repeated arrival of haematomas.

Breeds running a relatively higher risk than others of inherited haemophilia include beagle, husky, chihuahua, Irish setter, St Bernard, samoyed and weimaraner.

haemopoietic tissue

Tissue where blood cells are formed (haemopoiesis). This is mainly in bone marrow where red blood cells and most white cells are produced. Haemopoiesis also takes place in lymphoid tissue (also present in bone marrow) where lymphocytes are made. This is found in the thymus and spleen as well as in lymph nodes in various parts of the body.

haemorrhage

The escape of blood from a vessel. Bleeding from small blood vessels is soon curtailed under normal circumstances by the body's coagulation mechanisms. If large vessels such as veins or arteries are severed the situation is much more serious as the dog can rapidly lose a good deal of blood, suffer shock and, unless the bleeding is arrested, eventually die. In the event of any substantial haemorrhage a veterinarian should be called with a minimum of delay. Meanwhile first-aid measures are necessary.

If a vein is cut, dark red blood flows from the wound in quantity; if an artery is severed, bright red blood gushes out in a pumping action. A pad of clean cloth, gauze or clean handkerchiefs should be applied quickly to the area and, if insufficient, another added on top and bandaged over the wound. Apply pressure with the fingers, above the wound in the case of a bleeding artery and below if a vein. Maintain the pressure evenly to slow the haemorrhage and allow the normal coagulation process of the body to take effect. If a limb is affected a tourniquet may be necessary for stronger pressure. One can be made hastily from a double bandage or folded handkerchief looped around the limb, with a stick or pencil pushed through the loop so that a twist of the stick will tighten the tourniquet. This must be released gently after about ten minutes and should never be left on longer than fifteen or twenty minutes or permanent damage to the tissues may result.

Haemorrhage produced internally is usually manifested in vomit (haematemesis), urine (haematuria) or faeces and is dealt with under these headings. (See also wounds.)

haemorrhage

A serious intestinal bleeding disease which can be lethal. Early diagnosis and rapid start of treatment are needed, with much care and nursing to soothe the dog and give it the best chance of recovery. Symptoms are vomiting, diarrhoea (often bloodstained) and pain. Abdominal spasms and near-collapse follow, and severe dehydration, shock and hypothermia take their toll of the patient. Attacks can be very sudden and death can ensue before the disease has run its course of three or four days. Careful nursing is critical – day and night. The patient must be kept warm, quiet and comfortable, and gentle soothing will help. A veterinarian must be summoned as early as possible, and will administer intravenous fluids and electrolytes, such as lactated Ringer's solution and sodium bicarbonate. Sodium succinate and betamethasone are often effective with large doses of antibiotics. B vitamins and atropine are also often given.

Give the dog, every hour, night and day, for three days, a dessertspoonful of a mixture composed of one egg white, one tablespoonful each of boiled water and milk and a dessertspoonful of glucose or honey beaten up together. Give also boiled cool water with a teaspoonful of salt added to every pint.

On recovery, feed warm salty chicken soup for two to three days and then chicken breasts chopped in boiled rice for two days or until faeces are normal again. Boiled and cooled water should also be readily available. (See also enteritis; gastroenteritis.)

haemorrhagic gastroenteritis

The coat which covers most of the dog's body consists of cover or guard hairs (stiff, large hairs) and wool hairs (softer, smaller hairs)

hair

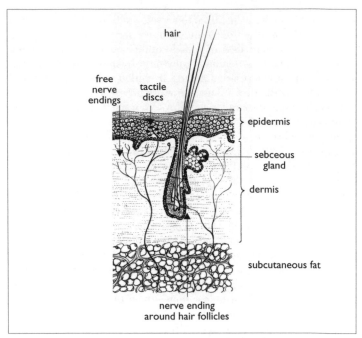

15 Section through the skin showing hair follicle

hair   or undercoat. Tactile hairs (whiskers) are present on the muzzle and above the eyes. Some dogs also have two small patches on each side of the face from which long hairs protrude. Eyelashes are the stiff hairs of the eyelids. Hair is thickest over the neck and back and grows faster in winter than summer.

The hairs are produced in hair follicles in the skin, with some growing in bundles, often from a single follicle. The density, types and lengths of dog hair differ between breeds. A short coat is genetically dominant over long, and hair colouring is genetically influenced, being produced by pigment cells in the follicle.

Genetic influence is also involved in moulting, together with environmental variations. When a hair ceases to grow it dies in the follicle and is shed in a moult. Short-haired breeds generally moult constantly, a little at a time, while longer-haired dogs usually moult twice a year. Grooming regularly each day limits a moulting season to about four or five weeks. Domestication has reduced the density of the undercoat in some breeds – particularly the poodle – and moulting of these animals is hardly noticeable.

An oily secretion from the hair-follicle glands keeps the skin in a supple condition and spreads along the hair to give it a gloss and some waterproofing. When a dog is sick the glands are not as efficient, and the coat consequently appears dull and dry. (See also grooming.)

halothane   A volatile and potent anaesthetic. (See also isoflurane)

handling   See examination.

See distemper.	**hard pad**

A deformity in the form of a break in the continuity of the upper lip. Puppies of the very small breeds sometimes display this defect and, if marked, sucking may be affected and hand rearing is needed. Hare lip often occurs with a cleft palate. Sometimes the deformity is corrected as the dog grows, but if not surgery may correct the condition. | **hare lip**

The red inside of the eyelid in such breeds as bloodhounds, cocker spaniels, etc. | **haw**

Dogs, like humans, can suffer from 'hay fever' (atopic disease) or a seasonal allergy to pollen or other protein particles which are inhaled. Itching occurs in some cases around feet, abdomen and face, eyes run, the skin around the eyes becomes bare and often the dog sneezes. Antihistamines are usually prescribed. (See also allergy.) | **hay fever**

These can include fractures, concussion, brain damage, superficial wounds, etc. Careful handling is of the utmost importance if head injuries are suspected and a veterinary examination with minimal delay is necessary for complete diagnosis. Even with superficial wounds, to exclude the possibilities of more serious, deeper and hidden injury, a check by a veterinarian is recommended. Convulsions, paralysis or haemorrhage from the ear may indicate brain damage. | **head, injuries to**

The healing process can take place efficiently and quite rapidly if conditions are ideal. A gaping wound may need suturing (stitching) or bandaging, but if infection is prevented and the dog is discouraged from putting strain on a vulnerable area, healing will run its course without impediment. | **healing**

The healing sequence begins with blood coagulation. The fibrin network produced spreads itself across the wound forming a bridge between the edges. This solidifies and toughens to create a scab under which the rest of the healing sequence can continue. Cell clusters, called granulation tissue, rise from deep in the wound, growing and thickening upwards towards the surface. Contaminants such as bacteria or minor dirt particles are dealt with by the arrival of phagocytes – white cells (mostly neutrophils) – to engulf such debris and clean up the wound area. As the new granulation tissue nears the surface, epidermal cells divide and multiply to repair the skin covering. Healing without complications can be complete in five to twelve days.

Healing of specialised tissue (such as nerve cells or brain tissue) is more complicated and very slow. Often fibrous tissue is formed rather than the specialised type, which may cause functional disorders. Glandular tissue, on the other hand, normally regenerates well, largely due to the fact that more is usually available than is actually needed. For example, the dog possesses between 20 per cent and *healing* 70 per cent more liver tissue than is required. (If this amount is removed for any reason, regeneration almost to original size can be expected in a few months.) Some 60 per cent of kidney loss can also be accepted under some circumstances without serious effect. (See also coagulation; wounds.)

heart The heart is the muscular pump of the vascular system. It is a cone-shaped organ and has four compartments: the left and right auricles in the upper half and the left and right ventricles below. Major blood vessels are connected to the heart by which blood is pumped to and from the lungs and around the body. Blood is received in the auricles (or atria) and pumped away by the ventricles. A series of strategically-positioned valves in the heart regulates blood flow to and from the heart.

Being contained in the strong, fibrous pericardium, the heart is situated in the chest cavity, lying roughly between the forelegs, and is normally largely covered by the lungs. The heartbeat may be heard on the left side of the chest just behind the dog's elbow. In young adult dogs the average weight of the heart is about 8g per kilogram (¼oz per 2lb) of body weight. (See also vascular system.)

heart failure See cardiac failure.

heart murmur Any cardiac insufficiency or valve defect will probably alter the heart's normal sounds, showing an irregularity or 'murmur'. Many dogs have heart murmurs and few are generally of a serious nature. Electrocardiography will assist a veterinarian in diagnosis and determining the degree of severity.

heartworm An endoparasite which affects dogs, mostly in the USA, Asia, Australia and USSR, as well as some parts of Europe. Heartworms are transmitted by mosquitoes and midges, although some are hosted by snails and slugs. (See also filariasis; parasites.)

heat See oestrus.

heat exhaustion See heat stroke.

heat stroke A dangerous condition frequently ending in a distressing death. It can almost always be prevented, since it is caused by human negligence. Most heat stroke deaths are caused by owners leaving their dogs in cars in direct sunlight. Even if windows are left open the interior of a car standing in the sun heats to well over 32°C (90°F) in the space of a few minutes. Dogs can also suffer from heat stroke through being left outside in the sun without access to shady places. Often owners forget that a dog left in shade will shortly be in direct sunlight due to the fact that the direction of the sun changes.

A trapped dog rapidly shows signs of heat stroke as it begins to lose control of its body temperature; it pants, becomes distressed, develops tachycardia and ataxia, vomits, passes diarrhoea and convulses. Internal organs may haemorrhage and the dog can die.

If an affected dog can be reached in time, emergency treatment consists of bringing it rapidly into the shade and dousing it with cold water (or immersing it if possible) to reduce body temperature. A veterinarian must be called to evaluate and treat the effects of dehydration with electrolytes and fluids if needed, to administer such drugs as dexamethasone, to prevent cerebral oedema, or mannitol to counteract it, to detect signs of internal bleeding from haematemesis, haematuria or faecal blood and to assess the condition of heart and liver, either or both of which may be damaged. Renal failure and other complications can arise several days later and careful observation and nursing during the immediate after-period are essential. The dog needs rest and comfort in quiet, well-ventilated, cool surroundings.

This is one of the easiest conditions to prevent and yet it claims many canine lives each summer. It is *never* worth risking a dog's life by leaving it shut in a car in direct sunlight, even for a few minutes, or by confining it in hot sun out in the open without access to permanent shade.

heat stroke

Paralysis of one side of the body. (See also stroke.)

hemiplegia

Inflammation of the liver. Infectious canine hepatitis, caused by a virus, can be lethal and frequently occurs with distemper. A combined vaccine is available for protection and this can be given when puppies receive their vaccination routinely at eight to twelve weeks of age.

hepatitis

Symptoms vary but include gastrointestinal haemorrhage, vomiting, diarrhoea, listlessness, high temperature, thready pulse and abdominal tenderness. Antiserum is used to treat the disease, together with glucose, water and vitamin K to help repair the clotting mechanism damaged by the virus and causing internal bleeding. Often dogs which have recovered from the disease remain as carriers and can infect non-vaccinated dogs through contact with urine.

High dietary copper appears to produce hepatitis (non-infective) and cirrhosis in some Bedlington terriers. (See also liver.)

Many herbs form the basis for a variety of modern pharmaceutical preparations used in treating various diseases and conditions. It is likely that some well-formulated herbal remedies produced by reputable herbalists will be effective in some way. Others, however, may be totally ineffective and their prolonged use may mean that another, better form of treatment is delayed, causing the dog unnecessary suffering. It is therefore advisable to keep a sense of proportion about the use of herbal remedies when a dog is sick. Discuss their use with a veterinarian who will be needed, in any case, to diagnose the illness in the first instance.

herbal remedies

Many successes are recorded regularly concerning the use of herbal remedies and few will do direct harm – apart perhaps from some of the individual vitamin supplements which may actually be contradicted in some conditions and situations. A dog which is fed a good diet should not require support from vitamin

herbal remedies	supplements as a general rule, and dosage may be an important factor if the dog is sick.
heredity	The relationship between successive generations which concerns the inheritance of various characteristics as they pass from one generation to the next. Half a puppy's genes are inherited from its dam and half from its sire. Grandparent characteristics become successively diluted by 50 per cent in each subsequent generation.

When breeding dogs, it is important to pass on only the characteristics which are the best in each breed; this means that dogs with any form of defect should *not* be used for breeding, although they may make good pets. However careful one may be in breeding, there is always the possibility of a disorder or abnormality coming through to another generation. Aggression, for example, unless very marked in a dog may not be noticed in a puppy until it grows and is influenced by its environment. There are many disorders which can be inherited, such as hip dysplasia and retinal atrophy, and passed from generation to generation subsequently though they are not caused *only* by inheritance. Some disorders, such as haemophilia, are entirely hereditary and, provided one is aware that a dog has the disorder, it is relatively easy to ensure that it does not pass it on.

hermaphrodite	An animal with sexual organs of both sexes. Some may have one ovary and one testis on one side of the body while others may possess an ovary on one side and a testis on the other.
hernia	The protrusion of an organ, or part of it, through its containing wall. Some hernias are hereditary and others caused through a weakness in the tissue wall, by accident or sudden exertion. Most frequently, hernias are associated with the abdomen. An umbilical hernia, for example, is where the omentum pokes through the umbilicus which may not have closed properly at birth. Inguinal hernia (in the groin area), which is more likely to happen to bitches, may have a portion of uterus protruding as well as omentum. Perineal hernias (genital/anal area) may result in bladder obstruction when part of the bladder pushes through the peritoneum. This sometimes occurs in aged dogs. Ventral (abdominal) hernia, which is mostly caused by violent accident (or, for example, where laparotomy sutures give way) is a tear in the muscular wall.

Those hernias that are reducible, ie, can be returned to normal by gently pushing the protruding portion in, or return to normal when the dog rests on its back, normally do not give cause for alarm. The chief danger with hernias is strangulation when they are not reducible. They may then cause sudden pain and become inflamed. Rapid breathing is noticed and the dog is obviously distressed. In these cases surgery is imperative since the blood supply will be cut off to the protruding portion and peritonitis and gangrene will result with probable death in twelve hours or so.

In diaphragmatic hernias the abdominal organs protrude through a tear in the diaphragm into the chest cavity. They are more common on the left side and are usually caused by trauma. As the condition worsens so does the accompanying respiratory distress. Fluid may need to be drawn off from the chest, with surgical repair following.

hernia

A disease associated with the genitalia of the bitch. Its presence can account for abortion, stillborn pups and the death of a litter immediately after whelping; it can also be a reason for infertility. Puppies can die quite suddenly from the disease which is transmitted through infected oral or vaginal secretions of the dam. Some puppies may be saved by a veterinarian performing a caesarian and rearing them in isolation in incubators, though this method is by no means certain of success. Symptoms in adult dogs include mild rhinitis and vaginitis and infected bitches produce antibodies which are passed in the colostrum to protect subsequent litters. At present no vaccine is available.

herpes virus

An active antiseptic against skin bacteria; soap containing it is useful for 'scrubbing up' prior to handling wounds, etc. This can cause poisoning in dogs, especially puppies if ingested.

hexachlorophane

See chlorhexidine.

hibitane

The hip joint is formed by the head of the femur, or thigh bone, fitting into the acetabulum – a socket in the side of the pelvis – as a 'ball and socket' joint. The combined strength of surrounding muscles and ligaments holds the joint in place.

hip

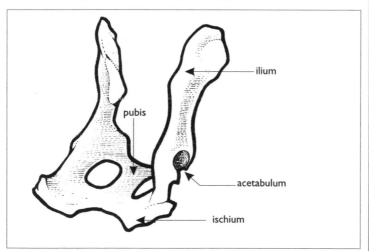

ilium

pubis

acetabulum

ischium

16 The hip bones

A developmental disease of the hip joint which is inherited. The head of the femur becomes dislocated from the acetabulum and gradually grows to deformity, worsening the condition. Larger, heavier breeds, such as German shepherds, Shetland sheepdogs and retrievers, seem to be more susceptible, though it can occur in some medium-sized dogs. Symptoms include pain when walking

hip dysplasia

hip dysplasia or exercising, and difficulty in rising from a sitting position, and often do not appear until the dog is five or six months old. Analgesics may be used to relieve the pain and, depending on the state of the disease, surgery may provide a temporary cure, lasting several years.

As the disease is inherited, no dog or bitch suffering from hip dysplasia should be used for breeding.

histamine A substance formed in the body by the decomposition of the amino acid histidine and used in muscle contraction and capillary dilation. Its action on capillaries produces a reduction in arterial blood pressure and consequently shock when large doses are liberated during massive infection, trauma or burns. It is normally circulated in the blood, lungs, liver and muscle. It also stimulates the secretion of hydrochloric acid used in digestion – an activity which is unaltered by antihistamines.

histology The study of the minute structure of tissue and organs. In laboratory studies, pieces of tissue for examination, eg from a tumour, are preserved and cut to extremely fine slices in a microtome (which is similar to an accurate bacon slicer). The slice, or section, is then mounted on a glass slide and treated with various stains which selectively dye specific tissues and cells in different colours for microscopical examination and diagnosis of tissue disease.

hock The tarsal joint or ankle at the lower end of the tibia.

honey A useful energy provider for sick dogs which find ordinary food indigestible. It is rich in glucose and soothing to the digestive system. It is best administered by diluting in boiled water that has been cooled to warm.

hookworm A blood-sucking parasite which lives in the small intestine in adulthood. Larvae can penetrate the skin, or infection can be transmitted orally or through uterine or mammary routes. (See also parasites.)

hormones Secretions of the endocrine glands. They stimulate action in other organs in various parts of the body. Some work in combination; some stimulate each other and others are antagonistic to each other. Their activities are complex and there is still much to discover about them. Hormone imbalance is known to produce a wide variety of symptoms and conditions; in the event of removal or disease of a gland, such as the thyroid or adrenals, it is often necessary to provide supplementary hormone therapy to make up for the deficiency if the dog is to be kept in good health. A veterinarian, however, will approach hormone therapy very carefully since inappropriate dosage is hazardous.

Hormones include insulin and glucagon from the pancreas, thyroxine from the thyroid, and adrenal and pituitary hormones. Sex hormones are used to treat infertility, pyometra, nymphomania, enlarged prostate and dystokia and to prevent abortion and conception.

Oestrogens are produced by the ovary, vasopressin and oxytocin by the pituitary, testosterone by the testis and progesterone by the ovary. All have stimulatory tasks in normal health and reproduction, and are dealt with under their own headings. (See also endocrine system.)

hormones

hospitalisation

There are advantages and disadvantages to hospitalisation. Advantages include regular professional attention with drugs given at appropriate times, careful response-monitoring in critical situations, and no loss of valuable time in an emergency following a sudden deterioration in the patient's condition. The dog can also be fed appropriate nutrients by the most acceptable route if oral feeding is impossible, or transfusions are necessary; wounds can be dressed regularly and expertly; and post-operative confinement may help prevent the dog damaging itself. Laboratory specimens can also be more easily obtained and handled, and the dog more simply observed by the veterinarian and veterinary nurse.

Disadvantages include disorientation of the dog, which may become anxious and tense if away from its owner and home surroundings. An owner who is calm and with whom the dog has a bond of trust and affection can often do much to speed a dog's recovery at home and this aspect should never be minimised. The sick dog also usually responds better to nursing by its owner than by a stranger. Cross-infection at a hospital is also a possibility for consideration, unless the hospital is well-equipped and staffed.

If hospitalisation is rejected by owner and veterinarian it must be remembered that careful home nursing with adequate facilities and strict adherence to veterinary instructions in peaceful, clean surroundings is essential. (See also nursing.)

house training

See training.

howl

A melodious, long sound produced by the dog expelling air through its partially-closed mouth, with lips pushed forward. Some breeds howl more than others and some dogs may never howl. A house-bound dog may howl as an expression of loneliness in order to seek company; another may howl in response to a particular sound such as church bells or a musical instrument.

Howling, which is a characteristic of canine pack animals, such as wolves, helps to keep members of a pack in contact with each other and is more often performed by those who are 'left behind'.

humerus

This is the dog's 'arm'. The head of the humerus forms part of the shoulder joint, and the lower end forms part of the elbow joint in the foreleg, joining with the radius and ulna. At the shoulder the joint is a 'ball and socket' and at the elbow a hinge.

hunger

A dog should always be ready for its food. If it is not hungry it may be unwell; if it shows no hunger signs for two days it is certainly unwell and should be observed for other symptoms. A dog should always receive adequate food each day and should not remain

hunger	hungry after its meal (nor should it be overfed). Cold surroundings and an empty stomach (with typical contractions) stimulate hunger which is controlled by the hypothalmus, and regular feeding routine, smell, taste and sight all enhance the feeling of hunger. (See also appetite; diet; feeding; nutrition.)
hybrid	Offspring of parents of different species. (See also mongrel.)
hydatid	Cyst produced by the larvae of a species of tapeworm (*Echinococcus granulosus*). It can be contracted by eating infected meat and passed on to man. Prevention is by means of regular worming. (See also parasites.)
hydrocele	A fluid-filled cyst occurring in the testis or spermatic cord of the male dog. It is a non-malignant condition and surgery, if necessary, is the usual treatment.
hydrocephalus	An accumulation of cerebrospinal fluid in the brain cavity. It may be present before birth, in which case the puppies are often stillborn and may cause whelping complications; or it may occur subsequently. Hydrocephalic puppies, if alive at birth, are likely to be weak in intelligence and uncoordinated, with a thin and vulnerable skull structure. Serious seizures can be expected from about three months of age and the prognosis is poor. Some strains of bulldog are particularly susceptible. The condition can also arise in adult dogs, due to an obstruction of the flow of cerebrospinal fluid, perhaps following meningitis or the growth of a tumour in the brain. The patient becomes lethargic, enters a deep sleep and frequently has convulsions. Euthanasia is usually recommended in such cases.
hydrochloric acid	Present in the stomach where it assists digestion by providing an acid medium for certain enzymes to work effectively.
hydronephrosis	A distension of the kidney which occurs when urine is trapped due to an obstruction or a kink in the ureter. The kidney becomes painful and also causes pain in the surrounding region due to pressure on other organs nearby. Surgery may correct the condition by eliminating the obstruction or straightening a twist in the ureter but, in cases where neither approach is possible, nephrectomy or removal of the affected kidney is necessary – provided the other is healthy.
hyoid	A structure of bones and cartilage supporting the tongue and larynx. It is trapeziform with larynx and tongue suspended from it.
hypercalcaemia	Excessive calcium in the blood. Causes can be dietary, with too much vitamin D being one example, or it can be due to parathyroid disorders such as a tumour. Affected dogs show symptoms of vomiting, lethargy, constipation and bradycardia. Radiography may show bone changes from calcium resorption. In severe cases the kidneys may be impaired by calcification resulting in dehydration and uraemia.

Over-activity of the parathyroid gland which may be caused by a **hyperparathyroidism**
tumour or a dietary insufficiency. There may be increased hormone
secretion from the gland to compensate for a mineral deficiency in
the diet, eg low calcium, high phosphorous with normal or low
calcium or lack of vitamin D. It can also appear during kidney
disorders.

Lameness in young dogs provides an indication of the disease
and other symptoms include lethargy and progressive weakness.

The enlargement or over-development of an organ or tissue area. **hyperplasia**
Vaginal hyperplasia may happen during the oestrus cycle of particu-
larly large bitches and often disappears at the end of the cycle.
Surgery may be necessary if it recurs. Hyperplasia of the adrenal
cortex sometimes appears due to the presence of a pituitary tumour.
(See also Cushing's disease.)

Abnormally high body temperature which can also be apparent in **hyperthermia**
some forms of insecticide poisoning. (See also heat stroke.)

Over-activity of the thyroid gland which produces an increase in **hyperthyroidism**
activity of the body. Symptoms include shivering, irritability,
anxiety and an increased heart-rate. It can sometimes be due to a
tumour or, in some breeds such as the Pekinese, it may be of
genetic origin. It is rare in dogs, but if it does occur veterinary
treatment must be sought.

An inflammatory disease affecting lungs and often with lesions in **hypertrophic**
the chest cavity. It may be associated occasionally with pulmonary **osteopathy**
disorders such as tuberculosis. The radius, ulna and tibia are also
affected and the legs swell as a result. Cutting the vagus nerve has
been a successful form of treatment. Causes are obscure.

The enlargement of an organ to take on extra work. It happens **hypertrophy**
sometimes to the heart when an obstruction stems the blood flow,
causing a back-pressure, or when a remaining kidney takes on the
work of two after one is removed through disease.

Breathing which is faster and deeper than normal, producing a **hyperventilation**
more rapid gas exchange in the lungs.

Drugs, including barbiturates, which have a soothing effect on a **hypnotics**
dog and help it to rest if it is uncomfortable or in pain. They are
often given post-operatively to ease the dog's discomfort and
prevent it damaging itself.

Low blood calcium. This can be the cause of eclampsia in **hypocalcaemia**
pregnant bitches and is evident in starvation and in absorption
disorders of the alimentary tract, dietary deficiencies of vitamin
D and calcium:phosphorous ratio abnormalities. Continued low
levels of calcium, particularly during growth of the young dog,
will lead to bone disorders.

hypochromasia	A deficiency in haemoglobin in the red blood cells, which consequently appear paler than normal.
hypodermic	Beneath the skin, ie subcutaneous. The term usually refers to a hypodermic syringe which is used to inject substances such as vaccines and antibiotics beneath the skin.
hypoglycaemia	Low blood sugar which can be the result of starvation. It is a condition which indicates problems with the absorption of nutrients through the intestines, or liver damage. It may also suggest glandular disorders since blood sugar is maintained at a normal level by the action of hormones secreted by the adrenal, pituitary, pancreas and thyroid glands. Symptoms vary depending on the underlying cause. (See also diabetes.)
hypoplasia	Under-development of an organ or tissue area. Hypoplasia of blood cells, for example, appears in some anaemias.
hypothalamus	A 'thermostat' in the brain which maintains body temperature and also influences appetite, urination and blood-circulation activities.
hypothermia	Subnormal body temperature, usually following exposure. In very cold conditions the body temperature is substantially reduced and, if as low as about 24°C (75°F), can cause death. A dog suffering from hypothermia should be handled gently and warmed gradually with covered hot-water bottles, blankets, etc, and kept in a warm environment. Recovery takes some time and, generally, medication should not be used until body temperature returns to normal. A weak dog suffering from prolonged exposure could die but if the animal is in good physical condition and has not been long exposed to the cold, the chances of recovery are good. (See also exposure.)
hypothyroidism	Under-activity of the thyroid gland. Signs of hypothyroidism include falling coat, rapid tiring and lethargy, intestinal upset (in the form of either constipation or diarrhoea), an intolerance of cold and often obesity. Treatment depends on the reason for the thyroid disorder.
hypoventilation	Shallow, slow breathing. It can occur after surgery, particularly on the chest or lungs. Administration of oxygen can be beneficial.
hysterectomy	Surgical removal of the uterus either because of disease or for sterilisation. (See also spaying.)
hysteria	A vague term for an over-emotional state which, while fairly common in dogs in the past is now much rarer. There are various theories on the reason for the decline of the condition which may be due to it being bred out genetically. Another theory is that a reduction in cases corresponds with the cessation of use of nitrogen trichloride as a bleaching agent in flour production. Certainly hysteria can be an inherited condition and resembles a form of 'fit',

the dog becoming over-excited with a blank stare and giving high-pitched yelps. If one dog in a group becomes hysterical others very often become affected similarly. An affected dog usually charges around apparently unaware of its surroundings, yelping and bumping into obstacles until it finally collapses exhausted. It can be induced by stress in some dogs and is also a symptom of lead poisoning. The best treatment is to place the dog in a dark, quiet room. Tranquillisers may be prescribed, often as a preventive measure in times of anticipated stress.

hysteria

I

ichthyosis   A development of a skin disorder which usually appears over the hock and elbow. The skin becomes dry and cracked and the cracks often become infected. Topical applications and antibodies are usually effective forms of treatment.

ileum   The short, terminal part of the small intestine, which is about 15cm (6in) in length and opens into the ascending colon.

ilium   One of the four bones of the hip which, during development, fuse to form the socket of the hip joint. It is also the largest portion of the pelvis.

imitation   See behaviour.

immobilisation   Usually refers to non-operative methods of treating fractures by means of plaster casts or splints, made from flat or gutter-shaped pieces of wood or plastic, padded and bound in place with bandages to keep the limb immobile.

A dog also needs to be immobilised for various forms of treatment or examination – which may be accomplished by physical restraint, by anaesthetics or by drug administration. (See also examination; splint.)

immunisation   A protection against a particular infection by inoculation with an appropriate vaccine. In cases of infection which can cause epidemics and death, this is of much importance and all dogs should be immunised by a veterinarian when they are in puppyhood.

A certain amount of immunity is carried to the puppy through the first milk (colostrum) from the dam and will protect it for several days after its birth. Some immunity is still retained after this period, which may last longer in small litters than in large ones and can interfere with immunisation if carried out too early. The best age to immunise depends on the disease involved and on veterinary advice. The diseases which are usually vaccinated against are distemper, hard pad, hepatitis, parvo virus and leptospirosis. Annual boosters are recommended.

In countries where rabies vaccination is applicable, the first dose should be given at three to four months, with a repeat dose after a year, and every three years subsequently.

implants   In hormone therapy, pellets of sterile synthetic hormone are sometimes inserted beneath the skin from where they are absorbed by the body over lengthy periods.

importing/exporting   Imported dogs are subject to various laws of the country into which they enter and full information, licences, etc, are usually needed long before the dog arrives. In some countries quarantine is required by law and immunisation may also be necessary. In the UK an import licence is required in advance from the Import

Licence Section of the Department for Environment, Food and Rural Affairs (DEFRA). Dogs smuggled in run the risk of being destroyed or re-exported and the owner would have to pay a heavy fine. A check needs to be made on restrictions in individual countries and this can be done through their commercial attachés. In Australia, for example, dogs are only admitted from the UK or New Zealand.

On arrival, imported dogs need immediate attention as they will be suffering from some degree of stress. They should be examined by a veterinarian and quickly housed, fed and watered.

When arranging export, clearance and veterinary certificates are needed, indicating that the dog to be exported is certified free of disease and fit to travel. There are shipping agents that specialise in the transport of livestock overseas. Entry regulations, as mentioned above, can be obtained from the appropriate commercial attaché well in advance. Advance bookings should be made with an appropriate airline to fly by the quickest route with the fewest possible intermediate stops and to arrive at the most convenient time for clearance and collection. Dogs travelling to hot countries, for example, should do so overnight so that their arrival is timed for early morning when it is coolest. Dogs must also be adequately housed for their journey in containers which are well ventilated and roomy enough for them to stand upright and to turn around and lie down comfortably.

Check and satisfy all local regulations for point of departure and destination well before the dog is shipped. Make sure that all paperwork is in order. In this way the canine passenger will have the smoothest possible passage. Finally, ensure that collection arrangements are reliable and efficient and details of shipping and arrival times are in the recipient's hands in good time. (See also quarantine; transport; Useful Addresses.)

impotence

Inability to perform the sexual act. It may be temporary, due to malnutrition or even starvation, and recovery can be aided by a sound diet and rest. In other cases it may be due to genital damage or disease. (See also mating.)

imprinting

This is the process by which a puppy recognises that an object has a certain function. Most dogs will form firm bonds with those with whom they come into agreeable contact during their early life. Such contacts are made for dogs between about three and twelve weeks of age. In the earlier part of the period, social contact among other members of canine society is important, eg the puppy's dam and litter companions, to provide canine social knowledge; in the latter period the contact is with its human owner especially. For this reason it is important to set aside a good deal of time to spend with the puppy; training it, talking to it, touching it and generally gaining its trust and affection. In this way a bond is formed which will last a lifetime. Conversely, neglect during the sensitive period, or leaving a puppy to its own devices and depriving it of the necessary contact, may result in a nervous or aggressive dog with little regard for human companionship. In older dogs the

imprinting	bonds of human trust and companionship can still be made, but extra patience is needed for a longer time.
incision	The surgical cut made when an operation is performed.
incisor	See teeth.
incontinence	See urinary incontinence.
incubation	The incubation period of a disease is the time between infection by micro-organisms and the appearance of the first symptoms. In some cases of food poisoning the interval may be only an hour or two while with other disorders incubation may take much longer, eg in distemper the period is anything between a few days and several weeks. Virus infections usually take longer to become established than bacteria. The incubation period for rabies can be up to one year.
indigestion	Failure to digest, usually caused by a dietary problem, correction of which frequently eliminates the symptoms. Discomfort is shown, flatulence may occur and the digestive system may respond with either constipation or diarrhoea. If symptoms persist the condition may be more serious and a veterinarian should be consulted after a few days, or earlier if pain is evident. Any vomiting must be checked as soon as possible as it can lead to dehydration. Indigestion can also be caused by diseases such as pancreatitis, or by deformities of the alimentary tract. (See also digestion, flatulence.)
infarct	Blockage or congestion of a major blood vessel leading to an organ, eg the heart, lungs, liver or kidneys. The obstruction is most commonly an embolism.
infection	Invasion of the body by pathogenic micro-organisms. Sometimes it is due to an organism being in the wrong place. Staphylococci, for example, are harmlessly found in dog skin but if pushed deeper into the body – perhaps by a wound – an infection can be stimulated as they multiply. Some infections remain localised in one patient and are not normally communicated to others. Other forms may be transmitted – particularly in close communities such as kennels – by some form of contact with the patient or its waste products, by airborne circulation of the organism or by passing via a contaminated carrier from one dog to another. Symptoms of infection include fever, elevated body temperature, general lethargy, poor coat, dull eyes and various others depending on the degree of severity and the type of infection. Infection is usually treated with antibiotics, some of which are specific to certain diseases and therefore antagonistic to the infecting micro-organisms.

Inability to conceive. The reasons for infertility are numerous: dietary causes are probably the most common, or the condition may by hereditary, or due to disorders or deformities of the reproductive organs of either sex. A lack of active spermatozoa in the dog, or the destruction of them by excessive acid in the vaginal secretions of the bitch, may be other reasons. Obesity can also be contributory, though unlikely in a breeding animal kept for that purpose. Both dogs and bitches are more active sexually and more likely to conceive during the months when the daylight hours are longer.

Infertility sometimes occurs in a breeding bitch after several litters for no apparent reason, although in most cases it is probably due to an undetected low-grade infection. A wide range of micro-organisms can be responsible. A hormone imbalance may arise which can be corrected in both dog and bitch after it has been diagnosed.

infertility

A defensive response by the body against tissue damage or irritation from, for example, trauma, excessive temperature (burns and scalds), corrosive attack or infection. Symptoms include redness and swelling, heat and pain. Inflammation is the first step in the healing process. Damaged cells raise the alarm by the production of a substance which causes blood and lymph vessels to enlarge and leak into surrounding tissue as they become more permeable to the passage of fluid through their walls. Tissue fluid floods the area of inflammation and white blood cells congregate to combat any infection. The fluid excess is the reason for swelling, additional blood accounts for the redness and heat and the pain is due to raised pressure in the inflamed regions and some interference with nerve endings. The fluid dilutes toxins and provides a slightly antiseptic medium in which the white cells can work to engulf and destroy invading bacteria, debris, etc. Pus may be formed from debris, including dead bacteria, and, since the generated fluid contains the same proteins as the blood from which it has seeped, fibrin is available to form a clot.

Inflammation can be acute or chronic. In the acute form, progress is more rapid and is usually unimpeded, provided the source of the inflammation is properly treated. In the chronic form (where treatment may be delayed or ineffective, or where a less definite response is provoked by slower-acting bacteria), an abscess may be formed by the accumulation of fibrous tissue and obstruction of the blood supply to the area of infection.

While inflammation is helpful towards healing, it can also be harmful if prolonged, by causing the replacement of functional cells with fibrous tissue and interfering with the activity of an affected organ and those relying upon it. Such a situation occurs in the chronic form. Treatment, therefore, is essential to eradicate the cause of the inflammation and allow healing to progress.

inflammation

Dogs can contract influenza, particularly Hong Kong influenza and para-influenza virus type SV 5, which has been isolated in the USA. Symptoms are similar to those in humans, with a noticeable

influenza

influenza	respiratory infection. The dog should be kept warm indoors and given antibiotics.
infusions	See transfusions and infusions.
inguinal hernia	See hernia.
inhalant	A substance which is breathed in to alleviate acute and chronic respiratory diseases. It is sometimes used with oxygen therapy. Inhalation moisturises air and mucous membranes in the respiratory tract, which relieves irritation and dilutes thickened bronchial secretions, making breathing easier. Moisture sprays can carry drugs such as antibiotics and mucolytics which find their way into the smaller airways for maximum topical effect.
injection	A drug, usually prepared as a sterile liquid, forced into the body through a syringe. Injections can be given intravenously (into a vein), intra-muscularly (into a muscle) or subcutaneously (beneath the skin) for absorption or dispersal around the body. They can also be given directly into an organ or cavity, eg intra-uterine (into the uterus), intraperitoneal (into the peritoneal cavity), or into a joint. Most work faster intravenously; others may cause a reaction if, for example, injected subcutaneously. In general terms, drugs injected intravenously take only a few minutes or less to act; those by the intramuscular route take about twenty-five minutes or so, and those given subcutaneously around thirty to forty minutes.

Small volumes only can be injected into the tightly-packed muscular tissues which cannot deal with bulk fluids, and injections are usually made into the muscles of the thigh or haunch. Subcutaneously, the skin folds of the neck or shoulder are used as the skin is slack over these areas. Intravenous administration is usually given into the radial vein of the foreleg. Sterility is important and the hair is clipped away at the injection site and the area swabbed with surgical spirit. Air is expelled from the injectable solution, after it is loaded into a sterile syringe, to avoid the extreme dangers of injecting bubbles into the bloodstream which could cause an embolism. After intramuscular or subcutaneous injection the area is gently massaged to disperse the liquid quickly and reduce any subsequent pain or discomfort.

All forms of injection should be given by a veterinarian or experienced veterinary nurse.

injuries	See accidents; wounds.
inoculation	Synonymous to vaccination, ie the introduction of micro-organisms into a dog to produce antibodies as a means of protection against disease; inoculation also refers to the introduction of micro-organisms into a culture medium where they grow, are identified and demonstrate their sensitivity to specific drugs. (See also sensitivity.)

Substance used to kill insects. Most insecticides should be kept well out of reach of dogs – especially puppies. There are, of course, specific insecticides for veterinary use and such preparations are clearly labelled for this purpose. These are in the form of dusting powders, etc, used to kill parasites in the dog's coat. (See also poisoning.)

insecticide

Blowing air, powder, gas or vapour into a body space or cavity. As in inhalation it has the advantage of topical application of drugs into small airways, spaces, etc.

insufflation

The dog's double coat helps to insulate it against cold but a thorough drying is essential if it becomes wet, especially in cold weather when chills can be contracted easily. Aged dogs suffering from joint disorders, etc, can be fitted with an additional fabric coat, if necessary, to increase protection against cold. Kennels should be well insulated against cold in the winter and the summer heat. A sound diet also adds significant insulation properties during winter months. (See also coat; hair.)

insulation

A protein hormone secreted by the pancreas. It stimulates feeding, and the utilisation of body glucose depends on insulin. It is an important hormone since, if insulin is not efficiently secreted, glucose remains unused for energy and is excreted by the body which then takes emergency action by using fat and protein substances, resulting in tissue degeneration.
Insulin secretion lessens during exercise but stays above the minimum level needed to ensure that sufficient glucose is available for the working muscles. (See also diabetes.)

insulin

In many countries, including the UK, owners whose dogs stray and become involved in accidents may have to bear the financial responsibilities eg if a car is damaged or recovery expenses and costs are claimed by injured persons. Most reputable insurance companies offer cover against such accidents and the premiums are usually quite low. Some companies also offer an insurance covering veterinary fees. (See also legal and moral responsibilities.)

insurance

Most dogs possess a lively intelligence though, like humans, the degree varies between individuals. Patient training, companionship and interest sharpen a dog's intelligence, which is well suited to its needs.

intelligence

These are quite common in dogs. They are roughly bean-sized and appear between the toes. They are usually caused by irritation and infection and contain pus, starting as hardened swellings and often rupturing as the dog continually licks them. The first signs of their presence are tenderness in the paw which may prevent the dog from putting it to the ground and much foot licking in the affected region. Sometimes the condition clears spontaneously, provided the foot is kept clean and secondary infection does not complicate

inter-digital cysts

inter-digital cysts

the condition. They do, however, sometimes recur repeatedly and may need surgical treatment to cleanse the seat of the infection. Often the condition is soothed by and responds to treatment by hot fomentations applied to the foot. If there is a recurrence or complications, however, a veterinarian should be consulted.

intestines

A major part of the alimentary tract, occupying most of the abdominal cavity. The small intestine ('small' in terms of diameter rather than length) leads from the stomach to the large intestine. It is the longest part of the alimentary tract, being about three and a half times the length of the dog's body. There are three main portions: the loop-shaped duodenum; the lengthy, mobile jejunum and the short terminal ileum.

The large intestine runs from the ileum to the anus and is more like that of man than other domestic mammals. It is slightly greater in diameter than the small intestine and whereas much of the digestive process is carried out in the small intestine, the large is primarily concerned with dehydration of the material which will become faeces. The large intestine consists of caecum, colon, rectum and anus.

The intestines comprise four main layers: the inner mucous membrane lining; a submucous followed by a muscular layer and the outer peritoneal coat. Together they measure about 3 to 6mm (⅛ to ¼in) in thickness.

Blood and lymph cells are contained in the mucous membrane lining (and in the submucous layer) and, in the small intestine particularly, are involved in the absorption process of digestive nutrients through the villi. Digestive and lubricating juices are also secreted in the mucous membrane lining.

The submucous layer, lying next to the mucous membrane and the muscular layer above it, cushions the muscular action and permits freedom of movement of both. Muscular movement of the intestines – or peristalsis – is important to healthy digestion.

The outer, peritoneal coating forms a tough covering which protects the layers beneath. (See also digestion.)

intramuscular

Into the muscle. (See also injection.)

intraperitoneal

Into the peritoneal cavity. (See also injection.)

intra-uterine

Into the uterus. (See also injection.)

intravenous

Into the vein. (See also injection.)

intussusception

Telescoping of part of the intestine into an adjacent part, causing obstruction. It can occur in small or large intestines, or as a combined condition in both. Sometimes the lower end of the intestine protrudes through the anus in a similar way to a rectal prolapse, which is less serious. Symptoms include the passing of dark red, mucoid faeces resembling strawberry jam, and abdominal pain. Radiography is frequently used to help diagnose the disorder which, if severe, can result in shock and subsequent death in the space of six hours if not treated urgently. A dog with suspected intussusception should be seen by a veterinarian without delay. The condition can be corrected by surgery with the affected part being removed and the intestine sutured together again. | *intussusception*

'In glass', a term used to denote tests carried out in the laboratory rather than in the body. | **in vitro**

'In the body', referring to tests carried out in the body rather than in laboratory apparatus. | **in vivo**

An element required by the thyroid gland for hormone production. It has antiseptic properties in solution and is sometimes used as a tincture (2½ per cent in solution) to paint skin disorders. It should not, however, be used on open wounds as this kills the cells which have been cut and delays healing. | **iodine**

See eye. | **iris**

See nutrition. | **iron**

Washing out. A warm saline solution (see entry) is often effective in cleansing areas such as wounds or skin and clearing away particles of debris. | **irrigation**

Posterior bone of the pelvis. It is one of three bones, the others being the ilium and the pubis. | **ischium**

An inhalation anaesthetic which is in increasing use, generally taking the place of halothane in veterinary surgery. | **isoflurane**

Once an infectious disease is suspected the patient should be isolated from other dogs until clearance is given by a veterinarian. No infected animal may be transported or taken out of the country until the infection is over in cases of notifiable diseases. | **Isolation**

In kennels, an isolation area should be kept permanently ready for use to prevent the spread of infection. The area must be apart from the living and exercising regions of the kennels and be well ventilated and easy to keep clean. The floors should be suitable for hosing down and swabbing with disinfectant and must not be dry-swept. Wet dusting should also replace dry dusting of furniture, equipment, benchtops, etc.

The isolation kennel should be fitted and supplied with its own equipment including feeding and drinking bowls, which is not taken outside the area. Rubber boots should be worn by kennel staff and visitors, and washed in a tray of disinfectant kept at the door on leaving the infected area. Rubber gowns should also be worn and kept in the area. Bins with closed lids for contaminated material, dressings, etc should be available and left in the isolation kennel until safe disposal can be made. Push-open doors should be fitted *isolation*

so that there is no risk of contamination of handles on the infected side of the door.

Facilities must be available for warmth to be increased when necessary and for the patient to be comfortable, quiet and adequately nursed, during the night if necessary as well as the day. There should also be room for the patient to be exercised during recovery without making contact with other dogs. (See also infection.)

isotonic

An isotonic solution is one which can be mixed with body fluids without ill effects. This is because it is of equal concentration and can diffuse equally with the fluid into which it is injected. Isotonic saline, for example, is a 0.9 per cent strong solution, used for injection into blood to correct fluid imbalance, as it is the same diffusion strength as blood plasma. Similarly, isotonic glucose is 5 per cent glucose in sterile water.

itching

See pruritis.

A condition caused by excess bile pigment in the blood. It is detected by a yellowish tinge to visible mucous membranes, particularly gums, mouth and eyes. It can be especially serious in the acute form and may be accompanied by an elevated body temperature, vomiting and lethargy. Clay-coloured faeces and a much slower onset of symptoms, with the dog becoming progressively weaker, characterise the chronic form; bile salts are deposited in the urine which consequently turns bright yellow or greenish-yellow. The dog also becomes constipated.

jaundice

Jaundice may indicate hepatitis or other disease of the liver or gall-bladder. It may also mean that red blood cells are being destroyed, or that the bile-duct is obstructed so that bile which cannot pass into the small intestine becomes reabsorbed into blood and lymph vessels and is deposited during circulation of the blood. Some forms of poisoning also show jaundice.

A veterinarian should be consulted immediately symptoms appear. (See also leptospirosis.)

The jaw-bones, or mandibles, are in two halves joined at the lower front and hinged at the back beneath the ears to join the skull. The temporomandibular joint is formed by the ramus – the toothless, vertical bony plate of the mandible – articulating with the temporal bone of the skull. The mandibles hold the lower teeth in the horizontal part or body which has alveoli in which the teeth are rooted.

jaw

Most forms of canine jealousy can be prevented by a thoughtful owner. A dog can become jealous if it feels its position in a home is downgraded or its relationship with its owner threatened because, for example, a baby or another dog is suddenly added to the household. The dog needs to be involved in the attention and affection given to the new arrival. If a puppy has joined the family, an older dog will offer it protection and enjoy its presence if not supplanted by it. It will also accept a new baby if it grows up with it; and a young child should likewise be taught kindness to the dog and learn that it is not a toy.

jealousy

A dog may also show jealousy of other dogs or people because of its strong bond of affection for its owner, guarding him or her against the possible 'dangers' of approaching strangers. Verbal correction and gentle patience usually solve the problem. (See also aggressiveness; behaviour.)

The middle portion of the small intestine, of which, together with the ileum, it makes up the greater part.

jejunum

Articulations formed in the skeleton when two or more bones are joined by tissue. A fibrous joint is short and situated where the need for movement is limited; cartilaginous ones also allow only restricted activity such as compaction and protraction. The most mobile joint is the synovial form and this can be a 'ball and socket',

joints

joints

plane, simple, compound, ellipsoidal, hinge, condylar, trochoid (pivot) or saddle.

In fibrous joints thickly-packed connective tissue serves as the connection; those such as are to be found in the skull are referred to as sutures. Cartilage is the connecting medium in cartilaginous joints. Both fibrous and cartilaginous connections may eventually be replaced by bone so that, in effect, the joints disappear. The synovial joints, such as those of hip, shoulder, stifle, etc, can be complex, with a variety of bones involved, or simple. Synovial fluid secreted by the joint's synovial membrane lubricates bone surfaces and also serves to transport nutrients and leucocytes to the area for replenishment and to clear away the products of wear and tear. About 0.2ml to 2ml of the fluid is present in, eg, the stifle of an adult average-sized healthy dog. In disease the fluid may dry, thicken or become more copious depending on the condition. (See also arthritis.)

jugular

The left and right jugular veins are the major vessels for the return of venous blood from the head. They are situated one on each side of the neck running down from the head and close to the trachea. Each is about 12cm (4¾in) long and 1cm (½in) in diameter in the average adult dog. They are sometimes used for blood collection by a veterinarian in very small dogs whose other veins may be too small to utilise.

K

kaolin

Powdered aluminium silicate which is effectively used in some intestinal disorders for the absorption of fluids and irritants in the intestine. It is often administered in tablet form combined with an antibiotic to combat a diarrhoeal infection, and is sometimes mixed into a paste and applied to areas of inflammation. A liquid compound of kaolin and minute quantities of morphine (to relieve pain) is also given to treat diarrhoea and can be of help in such diseases as ulcerative colitis.

kennel cough

So called because it usually affects groups of dogs in kennels. It is caused by a variety of airborne viruses and generates a respiratory irritation which usually disappears without treatment in about ten days, apparently leaving a temporary immunity lasting for approximately a year. Vaccines have been prepared but are not considered to be very effective. Dogs showing signs of kennel cough should be watched carefully as a worsening may be due to other respiratory disease or to a parasitic infestation. However, if the dog is otherwise healthy and well cared for, the condition usually clears up without complications.

kennel

If you plan to keep your dog outside, a well-insulated, adequately ventilated, draught-free, roomy kennel, sited in a shady place protected from the wind, rain, heat and cold, is the ideal accommodation. Some dogs sleep in barns, outhouses, stables, etc and, provided the chosen place has suitable bedding and meets the very basic requirements mentioned above (together with access to clean, cool drinking water at all times), a kennel may be unnecessary. Any dog kept permanently outside needs to be in good health with care and a good diet. It also needs to be one of the breeds which can cope with an outside life, eg working collie, hound, German shepherd, husky, etc.

Breeding kennels are, of course, a more complex matter and a lengthy discourse on the subject is beyond the scope of this book. If you consider building from nothing then it is good sense to discuss your requirements with the local licensing authority and a specialist architect, since mistakes made early cannot often be rectified later. (See also boarding kennel; breeding; beds and bedding.)

kennel clubs

These clubs, which are established in various parts of the world, set breed standards for pedigree dogs and promote shows and competitions to establish the standards and improve the finer points of each breed. They are often also involved in obedience training and working trial events. Kennel clubs provide details of local societies and clubs associated with each breed and give useful advice on where to buy pedigree animals.

All pedigree dogs and bitches for breeding should be registered with their national kennel club as should their offspring. (See also Useful Addresses.)

ketones   Also known as ketone bodies, these are poisonous substances, formed during gross metabolisation of fat, which accumulate in the liver and bloodstream to be excreted slowly in the urine. Ketones include acetone, acetoacetic acid and betahydroxybutyric acid.

ketosis   A condition, also known as acetonaemia, which arises when ketones are present in the body, often through starvation, a diet especially low in carbohydrates (producing a mild form) or diabetes. If the body cannot make full use of carbohydrates in metabolisation, more fats are utilised leading to fatty acid oxidation and ketosis. Symptoms include vomiting and diarrhoea with impaired liver function. Laboratory tests confirm ketone bodies present in the urine.

kidneys   The kidneys, of which there are two, are situated in the abdominal cavity, one on either side of the spine with the right more forward than the left. They are shaped like beans and in the average dog one kidney weighs around 28 to 35 g (1 to 1¼oz) and is between 6 and 9cm (2½ and 3½in) long, about 5cm (2in) wide and 4cm (1½in) thick.

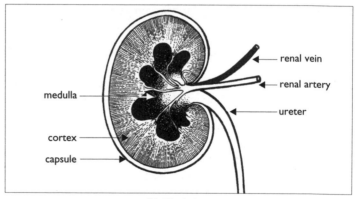

17 The kidney

A kidney acts as a blood filter, producing urine which contains waste products for excretion. It also has a prime role in the regulation of body fluid volume and composition. About 55 litres (12 gal) of blood are effectively filtered in a 10kg (22lb) dog each day and about 0.25 litre (½pt) of urine is passed as a result. Only waste products are filtered out when the dog is in good health although kidney damage and disease often cause a malfunction of the filtering system. Useful substances contained in the blood (amounting to about 99 per cent of the filtrate) are reabsorbed in the healthy dog.

A kidney consists of an outer cortex and internal medulla containing many nephrons – individual filtration units which contain the glomerulus, groups of capillaries through the walls of which filtration takes place. Blood pressure there is normally high to aid the filtration process (low blood pressure may consequently reduce the flow of urine).

kidney stones   See calculus.

An organism which occurs in several domestic animals and is associated with uterine infections. Although it is uncommon in the dog it can sometimes exhibit symptoms very similar to those of distemper with which it may therefore be confused. An overwhelming bacterial infection by klebsiella can also produce shock.

klebsiella

See stifle.

knee

Spinal curvature, occurring most frequently as an involuntary action in cases of abdominal pain though also a symptom of other diseases including tetanus.

kyphosis

L

laboratory tests and diagnostic aids	Laboratory tests are used in diagnosis to provide evidence of disease or disorder or to guide the course of treatment.

Tests in veterinary laboratories generally involve examination of body fluids (including blood, urine, cerebrospinal fluid (CSF) and various secretions), bone marrow, faeces or tissue. They fall broadly into four main disciplines: (i) haematology and serology, where blood cells and serum or plasma are examined to seek specific abnormalities found in various diseases and to group and cross-match blood for transfusion purposes; (ii) biochemistry, where blood, urine and CSF are studied to determine if standard levels of chemical components are normal, high or low and if organs are individually and collectively functioning correctly; (iii) bacteriology and microbiology, where micro-organisms present normally or pathologically are identified and evaluated, including often the 'culturing' of detected organisms *in vitro* from wounds or diseased areas against individual antibiotics, for example, to select the treatment which is most effective; and (iv) histology, where cells are studied, eg a small piece of tissue is taken either during a biopsy or post-mortem for a detailed microscopical examination to determine invasion limits, malignancy or, in the case of a dead animal, often the cause of death.

Diagnostic aids also include radiography and a variety of instrument-based studies related to specified organs such as electrocardiography, electroencephalography, etc. (See also under individual entries.)

labour	See whelping.
labyrinth	The inner ear containing the cochlea. (See also ear.)
laceration	A jagged, torn wound. (See also wounds.)
lachrymal fluid	See eye.
lactation	The production of milk. The first milk produced by the nursing bitch is the colostrum, which remains for several days. Afterwards, milk contents (proteins, fats, lactose and minerals) alter slightly and then remain normally consistent during the full lactation period until pups are weaned.

The lactating bitch has an enormous demand on her nutritional reserves and consequently requires increased nourishment during this time. High quality, high protein food is important and in general terms, the normal nutritional requirements are about doubled in the first week of lactation and trebled in the second or third to the seventh week. Typically, a lactating bitch with a litter of eight or more may eat her own weight in food at peak times around the fourth week. (See also nutrition; whelping.)

lactose	Sugar occurring in milk during lactation.

A surgical operation to open the abdomen. It is often of an exploratory nature, for example, in a case of gunshot wounds to the abdomen where internal organs are likely to be damaged. It allows inspection of the abdominal contents including urinary organs and also helps in the diagnosis and urgent treatment of calculi and tumours.

laparotomy

Inflammation of the larynx. Irritation causing the inflammation may be due to infection, enlarged tonsils or a foreign body such as a strand of cloth caught up around the back of the tongue. In infection it is often associated with bronchitis or influenza. Coughing and wheezing are symptoms and the mucous membranes swell, affecting breathing. A veterinarian should be consulted to diagnose the cause and commence treatment before the condition worsens.

laryngitis

An instrument used to view the larynx.

laryngoscope

The 'voice box', a complicated collection of muscle, cartilage, fibrous tissue and mucous membrane. It is situated in the throat at the entrance to the trachea, is about 6cm (2½in) long in the average dog and contains the epiglottis.

The larynx helps the production of vocal sounds and the passage of air. Muscular action in the larynx varies the tension of vocal ligaments, and subsequently vocal folds, and pressurised air from the trachea causes vibration of the folds. Volume and pressure of air passing through, coupled to resonance effects from the head, vary sound and pitch of the voice.

larynx

A medicine that loosens the bowels. Laxatives should not be needed if the dog is in good health and is fed a correct diet. If one is required, however, a half-and-half mixture of pure olive oil and castor oil, or alternatively a little syrup of figs, can be effective. Liquid paraffin is also useful as it acts as a lubricant. One dose should be enough – if constipation continues there may be a problem requiring the attention of a veterinarian.

laxative

Every dog should have a lead, even if it is trained to walk without one. In some areas (such as nature reserves) leads may be mandatory. It is essential that a dog is used to wearing one from puppyhood. It is also a useful training aid.

Use a lead of a weight suited to the size of the dog and long enough to reach at least from your knee to your shoulder. The first lead can be a cheap one, as it will need to be replaced when the dog reaches its full size. (See also collar; training.)

lead

See poisoning.

lead poisoning

Success or failure in the learning process has much to do with the teacher. Most dogs are capable of learning – responding to what they are taught – from a patient, kind and firm teacher who understands the dog's capabilities and limitations. Dogs learn most in

learning

learning

puppyhood, in patiently repeated sessions which are kept short but frequent, regular and interesting. The best age for training is from six to twelve months, when the dog is old enough to understand and not too old to learn. Owners lacking experience are advised to enrol in a dog-training class. (See also behaviour; training.)

legal and moral responsibilities

The responsibilities of keeping and caring for a dog are substantial. First and foremost are the responsibilities to the dog itself, including provision of a good diet, regular and adequate exercise, grooming, companionship, comfortable shelter, a stimulus for its intelligence and sound veterinary care.

In addition it is necessary to observe local and national laws on dog-keeping, which of course vary from country to country. Dogs imported into the UK, for example, are subject to quarantine regulations or the PETS travel scheme as a protection against rabies; and other countries have their own laws on this subject.

Control of dogs is a legal requirement in certain areas and local rules concerning dogs on leads should be observed. Special control of dogs is needed in places where livestock is kept, such as farmland. Sheep-worrying, for example, is an offence that may cost the dog its life. Training on this should be given in puppyhood. Aggressive dogs also need careful control, particularly in public places, where humans, or other dogs, can be attacked with surprising speed. Quite apart from the suffering this can cause, there is the possibility that financial damages might be claimed against the owner – as there may be also if a dog is involved in an accident on the road. Dogs should never be allowed to stray for such reasons. Dogs should always wear a collar, tagged with the owner's name, address and telephone number, when it is anywhere but in its own home.

A dog owner also has the responsibility of seeing that the dog receives adequate immunisation against dangerous diseases – both to protect itself and the rest of canine society.

The fouling of footpaths and parks by dogs is a problem that receives much attention in urban areas. There is no simple answer, as many owners lack garden space or a car to take the dog to rural areas. The best that can be done is to applaud the dog when it relieves itself in appropriate places, while ignoring it if it does so on the footpath. In some areas there are fines for owners allowing dogs to foul footpaths and some pet stores sell scoops which may be used to transfer faeces from footpath to road. Dogs trained to relieve themselves in the gutter run a real risk of being run over by vehicles in some areas, and more than a few dogs have had to go to a veterinary surgery as the result. (See also importing/exporting; immunisation; insurance; quarantine, unwanted dogs.)

legs

The foreleg consists of the shoulder or scapula joined to the humerus. Below are the radius, in the front of the foreleg, and the ulna leading down to the carpal and metacarpal bones of the foot. The humerus is the equivalent of the human upper arm; the radius and ulna form the forearm and the forepaw (hand), with the carpus (wrist) and metacarpus attached to main digits or phalanges.

The hindleg, commencing with the pelvic girdle and hip bones, consists of the femur (thigh), stifle (or knee joint), attached to the tibia, backed by the fibula, which lead down to the tarsus or ankle, with its digits – metatarsals, phalanges and sesamoid bones comprising the hind paw. (See also skeleton.) | legs

A feverish disease mainly occurring in tropical countries, including Africa, India and South America, where it is transmitted by midges and sand-flies. The dog rapidly becomes thin and is often partially paralysed. The condition is confirmed by laboratory tests, and is treated generally by antimony-based drugs. | **leishmaniasis**

See eye. | **lens**

A dangerous disease with a high mortality rate. Immunisation in puppyhood is the best preventive method. Leptospirosis is caused primarily by contact with infected rat urine, but transmission is also possible from one infected dog to another and the disease can be prevalent among kennelled puppies. One form of the disease is called 'infectious jaundice' and symptoms include the characteristic yellow tinge to mucous membranes common in jaundice as well as vomiting and clay-coloured or dark blood-stained faeces which are foul smelling. The dog may also develop diarrhoea, gastrointestinal bleeding and the kidneys may become damaged. Dogs which recover may carry residual infection in their kidneys for up to three years. | **leptospirosis**

Early treatment using antiserum and antibiotics is a prime need. Saline injections will also probably be necessary to combat dehydration, and careful, continuous nursing is of great importance in increasing the chances of recovery.

A medical term formerly taken to mean a wound but now frequently used to indicate any form of pathological change in tissue. | **lesion**

White blood cell. (See also blood.) | **leucocyte**

An increase in the numbers of white cells present in the blood. Such increases, particularly of immature leucocytes, can be expected in blood diseases, including leukaemia, although they also arise in infection and sometimes during pregnancy. | **leucocytosis**

A malignant disease of the haemopoietic tissue, often accompanied by tumours of the thymus gland or other organs, including the spleen. In some forms early blood cells, normally confined to the bone marrow, can be seen microscopically in the bloodstream although blood pictures vary in canine leukaemias and can be an unreliable form of diagnostic aid. | **leukaemia**

The affected dog rapidly loses weight, cannot eat and becomes progressively weaker. Sometimes the spleen is enlarged and there may be haemorrhage from the mucous membranes, and diarrhoea. Unfortunately, as in human leukaemias, a cure has yet to be discovered. (See also cancer.)

leucopaenia	A reduction in the numbers of white blood cells present in the blood. It can be a symptom of folic acid deficiency. It can also occur temporarily in viral infections, and can be found in certain bone marrow disorders, and in shock when leucocytes may be held in liver, spleen and lung capillaries.
libido	Energy associated with the sexual drive. In dogs a high libido may be noticed when a bitch in season is nearby and extra control will be needed to prevent the dog 'breaking out' in pursuit.
lice	See parasites.
licence	In some countries a licence is required to keep a dog and in most areas licences are needed for both import and export of dogs. (See also importing/exporting.)
licking	Some dogs lick their owners as a sign of affection. They also lick themselves as part of their self-grooming efforts and general toilet. Preventive measures should be taken where continual licking of a wound keeps the site open and impedes healing, and when a dog becomes obsessive about licking one particular area of its body where the tissue becomes granulated as a result. In this latter case there may be irritation which needs attention, and treatment (with steroids, for example) may be needed to rid the dog of the source of the problem. Fitting an 'Elizabethan' collar (see entry) will prevent continuation of licking while the area heals.
ligaments	Dense, fibrous connective tissues which bind and strengthen joints, usually running between and inserting into the bones of the joints. They can be in band, cord or sheet form and are elastic to varying degrees.
ligature	A strand of material, such as thread, silk, nylon, etc, used to tie off blood vessels during surgery. (See also suture.)
lightning stroke	A dog struck by lightning may survive but will almost certainly bear burn marks and needs a thorough veterinary examination, since it may suffer subsequent impairment of senses or movement.
liniment	A lotion used externally and massaged into muscles to ease strains and muscular pain. As such mixtures are for external use only, care must be taken to ensure that the dog does not lick them off the skin.
lipoma	A fatty tumour. (See also tumour.)
lips	Mobile, fleshy flaps forming the opening to the mouth. They are controlled by facial muscles which can draw the upper lips back from the teeth. They are pink on the undersides and the mucous membrane lining is also generally pigmented. The upper lips overhang those covering the lower jaw, which are somewhat serrated by about twelve peaked papillae. About two-thirds of the

area of the upper lips carries sparsely sprouting tactile hairs or whiskers. | *lips*

A surgical operation in which the bladder is opened. It is usually carried out for the removal of non-dispersive calculi. | **lithotomy**

A family of puppies. Litter size varies from breed to breed – generally the larger dogs tend to have more puppies, though there are other factors involved. Larger litters are evident in younger bitches, with fewer puppies born to bitches over three or four years of age, and older dogs also sire smaller litters. | **litter**

On average, smaller litters usually have more females than males. This may be influenced by less space being available for embryonic development in the uterus of smaller breeds as female embryos have more survival strength than males at this stage. Many embryos are reabsorbed by the bitch in very early pregnancy. More male puppies seem to appear in litters born in the last three months of the year. An average-sized bitch produces between three and seven puppies in an average litter. (See also whelping.)

The dog's largest gland, weighing on average over 400g (14oz) and representing nearly 4 per cent of body weight. It is deep red in colour, larger in the young dog than in the elderly, and is divided into four lobes and four sub-lobes. It is situated in the front of the abdominal cavity beneath the diaphragm and is almost entirely surrounded by peritoneum. | **liver**

The liver is an important organ and has many vital functions. Most of the blood circulating in the digestive system passes to the liver on its way back to the heart. About 80 per cent of the blood entering the liver arrives via the portal vein (the remainder coming through hepatic arteries). The portal vein is in contact with the liver cells and the blood carried through contains nutrients absorbed during the digestive process. In the cells of the liver, nutrients are stored, awaiting utilisation by the body tissues for energy, and some are prepared for metabolism. Glucose is converted to glycogen and stored until needed, together with iron and some vitamins; fats and some amino-acids begin an intermediary conversion process. The liver also breaks down old red blood corpuscles and extracts some toxic wastes. It manufactures protein materials used in blood-coagulation processes, including fibrinogen and prothrombin, and produces bile which is collected in small ducts and transported for storage in the gall-bladder via the common hepatic duct of the liver.

The liver has substantial regenerative powers and if damaged can often be replaced in large proportions by the body within about two months. (See also cirrhosis; hepatitis; jaundice.)

See tetanus. | **lockjaw**

A liquid preparation for external use. Lotions are usually alcohol or aqueous solutions or suspensions. Care should be taken to ensure | **lotion**

lotion	that those which are harmful are not ingested by the dog through licking after they have been applied to the skin. An 'Elizabethan' collar can be of assistance in prevention. (See also Elizabethan collar.)
lubricant	An oily substance used to prevent friction. The most common use of lubricants is to ease the passage of a veterinary instrument or tube inserted into an orifice, eg a thermometer inserted rectally to obtain a body temperature reading. Vaseline is suitable for this purpose. Liquid paraffin is also a useful lubricant in easing constipation.
lumen	The space surrounded by cell walls such as the interior of an artery, duct or intestine.
lungs	The two lungs almost fill the chest cavity, or thorax, and are situated close to the heart to which they are attached. Oxygen from the outside air and carbon dioxide from the body are exchanged in the lungs in the process known as respiration. (For drawing, see respiration.) The left lung has three lobes and the right four. Each lung is entered by a bronchus – an air tube leading from the trachea or windpipe with its beginning in the throat. The lungs, covered by pleurae, expand and contract as muscular movements of the chest and diaphragm create a partial vacuum or negative pressure in the cavity. Atmospheric (air) pressure then causes the lungs to fill with air. Consisting of elastic tissue filled with minute sacs at the end of bronchioles, lungs are normally a bright pink in colour, becoming pigmented in older dogs living in urban areas where air is more heavily polluted. (See also respiration.)
lupus erythematosis	A collagen disease characterised by skin lesions, thrombocytopaenia, anaemia and possible jaundice and haemorrhage from mucous membranes. Kidney failure can result, in severe cases. The disease is confirmed by laboratory examination of blood. Administration of corticosteroids and/or removal of the spleen are two courses of treatment.
lymph	Lymph is circulated around the body in the lymphatic system and is a colourless fluid similar in composition to blood plasma. It originates in blood, permeating through the walls of certain capillaries and into lymph vessels where it is used to bathe tissue, transport nutrients (particularly to areas where the vascular system does not reach, such as the cornea of the eye and cartilaginous tissue), carry antibodies and circulate those white blood cells known as lymphocytes – which are made in lymphatic tissue.
lymphatic system	Similar to the blood circulatory, or vascular, system except that lymph is circulated rather than blood. It comprises a fine network of channels connected to veins, together with capillaries, collecting ducts and filtering stations, or lymph nodes.

The lymphatic system can be considered as a subsidiary to the venous section of the vascular system and runs throughout the body, head, neck and limbs. Lymph tissue, apart from existing as lymph nodes, appears also in some organs, including the spleen and thymus, and in bone marrow.

lymphatic system

Capsules of connective tissue which act as filtering stations, preventing particles, bacteria, etc from entering the blood, and as manufacturing centres for lymphocytes. They are situated throughout the body in the lymphatic system. They can be found in places where they are protected by fat, for example in joints formed by the branching of larger blood vessels or in angles formed by bone joints.

lymph nodes

A variety of white blood cell present in the bloodstream. Lymphocytes are synthesised in lymph tissue and are an important part of the dog's defence mechanism which responds to micro-organisms (antigens).

Fewer than 1,000 lymphocytes per microlitre of blood (determined by laboratory investigation of a blood sample) indicates possible hormone disorders, especially where adrenal hormone production is accelerated, distemper and hepatitis. An increase (lymphocytosis) may denote a chronic infection, some virus invasion or lymphocytic leukaemia.

lymphocyte

See lymphatic system; lymph nodes.

lymphoid tissue

magnesium　　See nutrition.

malignant　　Virulent or life-threatening, eg as a disease or condition which has a tendency to worsen. The term is often used in reference to tumours which spread from a primary growth to produce secondaries in other parts of the body. (See also tumour.)

mammary glands　　The milk glands, marked on the bitch's abdomen by the presence of teats on which the puppies feed. There are usually between eight and twelve teats generally arranged in two rows from thorax to base of abdomen.

Each teat has several small orifices, through which the milk can be sucked, and a corresponding number of canals (often between seven and sixteen) leading down to the milk supply in the mammary glands which are swelled by milk after whelping.

Diseases of the mammary glands include mastitis and tumours. Acute infections can occur, usually affecting one gland, and can be felt as hot, painful swellings, often with a discharge. Chronic mastitis, which frequently affects several glands, is characterised by swollen, hard areas around the teat. Abscesses of the glands can also form. The teats should be regularly examined by the bitch's owner for any sign of growth or disease, which should be treated immediately by a veterinarian.

In pregnancy, mammary glands normally enlarge around the thirty-fifth day. Rudimentary mammary glands are present in the male. (See also mastitis.)

mandible　　See jaw.

manganese　　See nutrition.

mange　　A skin infection caused by parasites. There are two main forms, both of which are contagious and can be serious. Sarcoptic mange produces intense irritation and consequent continuous scratching. Hair falls out in patches and the infestation usually commences in the armpits, insides of the thighs and edges of ears and spreads throughout the entire body area.

Follicular mange parasites, as the name suggests, invade the hair follicles, and with this form there is little irritation to annoy the dog. Hair falls out, however, the skin thickens and flakes and a secondary infection by bacteria can easily follow as a serious complication.

Any dog infected with mange should be treated quickly by a veterinarian so that the disease can be arrested as early as possible. The affected dog should be kept away from other dogs (do not, for example, sit with other dogs in the waiting room of the veterinary surgery but arrange for an appointment or, preferably, a visit). Bedding should be burnt and replaced by clean newspaper which should be changed regularly with the used paper burnt. The patient needs a special shampoo (probably gammexane) and possibly antibiotics.

A drug obtained from the hemp plant. Poisoning with this drug causes vomiting, increasing dejection and unsteadiness on the feet. It can last for about two days during which time the dog can suffer seriously from dehydration.

marijuana

Dogs purchased in markets can frequently be sick, weak or with suspect ancestry. Buying and selling dogs in this way is to be discouraged, it is hoped eventually by law; potential owners should deal only with reliable and reputable breeders. (See also choosing a dog.)

market trading

See bone marrow; bones, feeding of.

marrow

Chewing. Dogs tend to bolt (swallow) their meals, although suitable bones are chewed. Food should be cut up small enough to allow safe passage without mastication as large chunks can become lodged in the oesophagus.

mastication

Inflammation of the mammary glands. In the acute form an abscess is usually formed in the gland and the patient is feverish and irritable. Antibiotics are needed and cold compresses assist in pain reduction. If the condition occurs when a litter is being fed the puppies run the risk of weakening due to lack of milk, or unsatisfactory milk, and may need to be hand-reared. If only one gland is affected and treatment is rapidly effective the teat can be taped to prevent feeding from it. Mastitis is both painful and dangerous if not treated; early detection is therefore of special importance. (See also whelping.)

mastitis

Mating can take place usually from the age of about fifteen months or the bitch's third season. Timing is critical in most bitches – around the tenth to fifteenth day of oestrus. The exact time – which varies with individuals – is mostly determined by the bitch herself and readiness indicated by a sideways movement of the tail when she is approached by the male or when gently stroked down the loin.

mating

Some bitches are receptive at unusual times during oestrus, and if conception regularly fails after what appears to be a successful mating a veterinarian can determine the most appropriate time by microscopic examination of vaginal smears taken at intervals. Some males are more successful at certain times of the year and successes should be noted with a stud dog for future reference.

Mating may require supervision, especially with inexperienced dogs, and it is advisable to remain at hand during the procedure. Sufficient space for the pair to move around and 'court' will be needed in an area which is not too large for easy control. Introduce the dog to the bitch slowly (preferably on a lead) at first, so that they can become used to each other, and then let them loose.

The mating 'tie' is achieved by the introduction of the dog's penis into the vagina of the bitch (sometimes the bitch will lower her hindlegs and initially you may need to support them gently). The

mating

pair will subsequently turn back-to-back – a position they may maintain for twenty minutes or more. During this time they are best supervised closely to forestall one pulling away from the other and causing pain or damage. Eventually muscular relaxation allows them to part naturally and mating is complete. (See also breeding.)

mat-splitter

A scythe-shaped hand tool with a blade to split matted hair, used in conjunction with a tangle-comb in grooming long-haired dogs. Some, however, have sharp points and care must be taken not to injure the dog during the process. (See also grooming.)

maxilla

The upper jaw. (See also jaw.)

meat

No dog should be fed on an all-meat diet. Meat must be obtained from a reliable source and care should be taken to ensure that it is not contaminated or infected. (See also diet; nutrition.)

medicine, administration of

Medicines to be taken internally fall broadly into one of three categories: liquid, powder or tablet. Most dogs can be persuaded to take them mixed up in food – provided, of course, that they have a healthy appetite. Generally, however, sick dogs are reluctant to eat. In these cases a tablet will almost certainly be refused; even the usually recommended practice of placing it on the back of the tongue with the dog's head held up, closing the mouth firmly and massaging the throat to encourage swallowing may be unsuccessful, with the patient cunningly concealing the tablet until the coast is clear and then depositing it behind a chair!

If a medicine cannot be hidden in food it can be administered with the aid of a 10ml *plastic* disposable syringe. Tablets can be crushed to a powder and turned into solution with boiled and cooled water; this solution (or any liquid medicine) can be drawn

18 Holding a dog ready to give medicine or tablets

19 Giving medicine with a syringe inserted between the teeth and directed towards the throat

into the syringe. Holding the dog conveniently on a table or bench, take the muzzle firmly in one hand, keeping it closed and tilted upwards slightly. With the other hand holding the syringe, part the dog's lips and insert the syringe nozzle in a gap between the back teeth. Pointing the nozzle towards the throat, expel the fluid gently by slowly depressing the plunger, allowing the dog time to swallow as the liquid enters its throat across the back of the tongue. When the syringe is empty continue to hold the mouth closed with the nose tilted and gently massage the throat. Never use a glass syringe, which can easily be broken and is therefore dangerous, nor a metal one, which causes the dog discomfort when inserted between its teeth.

All medicines, whether for dogs or humans, should always be kept in one place, locked away. It is useful to keep a first-aid box of medicine, dressings, etc suitable for use when required. Old and out-of-date medicines should be discarded and replaced with fresh supplies. (See also eye drops.)

medicine, administration of

Approximate volume equivalents

15 drops from average dropper = 1ml
1 teaspoon = 4ml (5ml plastic dosing spoons are available from chemists and drugstores)
1 tablespoon = 15ml
1oz = 30ml
Average glass tumbler holds about 240ml (8oz)
Average teacup holds about 180ml (6oz)
1 pint = 473.2ml
1 quart = 946.4ml
1 litre = 1.06 quarts (1000ml)

Weight equivalents

1lb (16oz) = 453.6g (0.4536kg)
1kg (1000g) = 2.204lbs
1oz = 28.35g
1g = 1000mg
1mg = 1000mcg

A process of cell division which takes place in the reproductive organs – ovaries and testes – when gametes (ova and spermatozoa) are formed. When a spermatozoon fuses with an ovum, the egg or zygote which results then starts dividing by mitosis.

meiosis

A dark pigment existing as granules in the cytoplasm of body cells called melanocytes, which give a dark colouring to the body area where they appear. It is produced by an enzyme system which makes use of copper for melanin formation and is largely found in hair and skin.

melanin

A dark-pigmented tumour which is often a form of malignant cancer known as sarcoma.

melanoma

membrane	A tissue film. There are various types of membrane, including foetal, cell and synovial, and in some places they act as filters while in others they play a protective role or assist in absorption from one area to another. (See also mucous membrane.)
memory	See behaviour; learning; training.
meningitis	Inflammation of the membranes covering the brain and spinal cord. It is a serious disease which can follow injury or be caused by an infection elsewhere in the body, such as the ear. A dog stricken with distemper, for example, may contract meningitis as an additional complication. Restlessness, loss of balance and circling are usually the first symptoms, and convulsions may follow, together with a raised temperature, rapid pulse and feverishness. The dog may subsequently be dull and depressed and paralysis often occurs on one side of the body or in the hindquarters. A veterinarian should be called as soon as possible and sedatives, together with antibiotics or sulphonamides, may be prescribed. If the condition follows a head injury the dog should also be examined for skull fractures. While awaiting the veterinarian the dog should be kept as quiet as possible in a darkened, peaceful room.
mephenesin	An antispasmodic drug which may be useful in lessening spasms in tetanus.
mepyramine maleate	An antihistamine drug used in the treatment of urticaria.
mercury poisoning	See poisoning.
mesaticephalic	Having an average-shaped head of medium proportions. This classification embraces most dogs. Breeds include spaniels, setters, German shepherds, and retrievers.
mesentery	A doubled peritoneal fold which attaches the intestine to the abdominal wall and serves to transmit nerves and vessels to the organ as well as a form of support.
metabolism	The chemical and physical processes by which the life of the body is maintained and energy produced for living.
metacarpus	The area of the forepaw between the carpus and the digits (toes). There are five cylindrically-shaped metacarpal bones, larger at each end of the shaft to form the base and head of the bone respectively. A synovial joint is formed at each end of all five, and the first bone is shorter than the other four.
metastasis	The means by which a tumour spreads through the body – especially in malignancy. Cells break away from the primary tumour and are carried via lymphatic channels or blood vessels to other organs or parts of the body where they become lodged and grow as secondary tumours.

The area of the hind paw between the tarsus and the digits (toes). **metatarsus**
The metatarsal bones are similar in arrangement to those of the
metacarpus of the forepaw.

Inflammation of the uterus. This can be a serious disease which is **metritis**
often fatal if veterinary treatment is delayed. It is likely to occur
after whelping if a placenta or dead puppy is retained, following
abortion or a particularly difficult birth, or delivery in unclean
surroundings. It can be transmitted from a vaginal infection or, less
commonly, an adjacent infection such as salpingitis.

In the acute form a reddish-brown, foul-smelling discharge
appears from the vagina and the bitch becomes depressed, disinter-
ested and feverish. The temperature is raised and she may vomit.
Abscesses may form in the uterine mucous membranes where
bacteria can take hold and multiply readily. If a litter has been born
it will need to be hand reared while the bitch receives treatment
from a veterinarian.

Chronic metritis can follow the acute form or can arise from an
infection with virtually no discharge. Uterine glands will become
cystic and often a hysterectomy is necessary. Bitches should be
closely observed a few days after whelping for any signs of the
acute form. Useful aids to prevention include taking all possible
precautions in terms of cleanliness during whelping and having the
bitch checked over by a veterinarian soon afterwards to make sure
the uterus is clear. (See also whelping.)

A useful lifetime identification technique for pets and one which is **microchipping**
recommended for *all* dogs. The technology has been available in
the UK since 1989. An electronic 'chip' the size of a rice grain,
coded with a unique number which can be read with a hand-held
scanner, is painlessly implanted under the dog's skin, usually
between the shoulder blades. The microchip is contained in a
bio-compatible material similar to that used in human heart
pacemakers. No anaesthetic is required and the veterinarian
accomplishes the microchipping procedure in a matter of seconds.
Puppies can be microchipped at the time of vaccination.

It is estimated that around 10,000 scanners are in use throughout
the UK at veterinary practices, local authorities and animal welfare
groups. The scanner reads the dog's personal identification number
and this is checked with a central register. If a dog strays or is lost it
can be identified by its own implanted microchip when found and
returned to its owner. A collar and tag can be lost and tattoos fade
with age – a microchip is permanent. (See also Battersea Dogs'
Home; NCDL; unwanted dogs.)

A vital instrument for laboratory diagnosis. It consists of a system **microscope**
of lenses which obtain magnified images of minute objects,
including blood and tissue cells, bacteria, etc.

The act of passing urine from the urinary bladder to the exterior of **micturition**
the body.

milk	See diet; nutrition.
milk fever	A fever, mainly caused by hypocalcaemia due to low dietary calcium, which may occur in bitches following whelping. Consciousness is lost and often there is paralysis, especially of the hindquarters, with lowered temperature, rapid but weak pulse and dilated pupils. In the last century, when the mortality rate was substantially higher than it is now, the condition was known as 'parturient apoplexy' and deteriorated to coma. Today it can be treated successfully by injection, or prevented by a sound diet in pregnancy.
milk production	The production of milk is influenced by hormone activity associated with pregnancy and impending birth. Milk is generated from the mammary glands as the puppy sucks and extra fluids given to the bitch for the first two or three days after whelping (including cow's or goat's milk fortified with glucose or honey, and meals of beef broth) help the milk flow and the bitch's strength. A bitch with a small litter (or stillborn puppies) may have excess milk which needs relieving by standing her on her hind legs and gently pressing the milk through the teats with thumb and forefinger. Milk production can be curtailed by a veterinarian giving a hormone injection if there are no puppies left to feed. (See also lactation; mammary glands; whelping.)
mineral deficiency	A sound diet, fed regularly, should provide a dog with all essential minerals. (See also diet; nutrition.)
minerals	See nutrition.
misalliance	An unplanned mating. Conception can be avoided if a veterinarian is consulted as soon as possible. Such a course of action is more advisable than allowing the birth of unwanted puppies or risking the life of the bitch if she is in ill-health. Dogs and bitches with hereditary diseases and defects should not be allowed to breed and such a misalliance would also be a reason for preventing or terminating pregnancy. A misalliance between a pure-bred bitch and a mongrel leaves no ill effects on the bitch and does not prevent her from subsequently producing pure-bred pups from a pure-bred dog. (See also abortion.)
mites	See parasites.
mitochondria	Often referred to as the cell's 'power plants' or 'furnaces', these are rod-, filament- or granule-shaped bodies in the cell cytoplasm which consist largely of protein with some fat. Hundreds or thousands of them are present depending on the activity of the cell and their main purpose is to release energy for cellular activity with the help of the enzymes they contain.
mitosis	The usual method of cell division, which occurs so that the chromosomes are distributed equally to the daughter cells. The nucleus

of the cell divides, resulting in daughter nuclei which are alike in every way, with the same genetic composition as the nucleus from which they came. In this way characteristics of one generation are passed on to another. (See also heredity.) *mitosis*

Drug solutions or suspensions in liquid to be administered orally. (See also medicines, administration of.) **mixtures**

See teeth. **molar**

A hybrid or dog of mixed breed. Mongrels can be as companionable, intelligent and healthy as pure-bred dogs if cared for correctly and if their parents have not passed on any defects. More mongrel puppies become unwanted in adulthood merely because they grow larger than their owners expected, consuming more food and requiring more exercise and room to move. It is wise, therefore, before acquiring a mongrel pup to have some knowledge of its parenthood. If this is impossible, an experienced veterinarian will probably be able to provide advice on future size and temperament. There are many stray dogs' homes and rescue centres where an abundance of fully-grown mongrels seek good homes, and to acquire an adult animal in this way eliminates this problem. (See also choosing a dog.) **mongrel**

One of the varieties of white blood cell present in the bloodstream. Monocytes are phagocytes and are present in increased num bers in chronic inflammatory disease and acute stress. (See also blood.) **monocyte**

A dog with only one testis. The condition is sometimes due to the fact that only one testis has descended into the scrotum. In pure bred dogs it may be an obstacle to them entering shows or field trials (certainly according to UK Kennel Club rules). It is considered to be usually an inherited condition and therefore the dog should not be used for breeding. **monorchid**

An alkaloid contained in opium. It is useful in appropriate dosage as a narcotic analgesic and as a premedication in critical care. It is unsuitable for euthanasia since high dosage produces vomiting and uneasiness. Morphine is a dangerous addictive drug which, by law, must always be kept under lock and key and accounted for by the veterinarian. **morphine**

See car sickness. **motion sickness**

The mouth, which contains the cheeks, lips, gums, palates, teeth and tongue, is supported by the upper and lower jaws. The bones of the upper jaw serve as both the roof of the mouth cavity and the floor of the nasal passages, forming the hard palate. The far end of the hard palate becomes the musculo-membranous soft palate, and reaches as far as the larynx in short-faced dogs such as Pekinese and bulldogs, rather restricting the passage of air to the larynx and consequently making respiration more difficult in these breeds. **mouth**

mucolytic	An agent which disperses mucus. It can be a useful drug where mucus congests air passages. An example is acetylcysteine which is administered by nebuliser.
mucosa	See mucous membrane.
mucous membrane	The lining of many organs and passages, including the alimentary tract, respiratory tract, and urinary and genital passages. It is formed of epithelium and lubricated by mucus.
mucus	A secretion of the mucous membranes which normally lubricates their surfaces in small quantities. In response to inflammatory conditions of the membranes, however, copious amounts of mucus are secreted. An example is catarrh arising in the air passages. Mucus contains water, contaminant particles from the membranes, white blood cells and acidic glycoproteins called mucins.
multiparous	Bearing several young at birth.
mumps	An inflammatory virus disease which can be transmitted to dogs from humans. Mumps causes inflammation of the parotid glands, situated at the hinge of the jaw below the ears, which become enlarged and somewhat painful to the touch. The dog may be feverish and apathetic. Symptoms also include enlarged lymph nodes and salivary glands. However, these symptoms apply to many other forms of infection and a veterinary examination should be made.
murmur	See heart murmur.
muscle relaxant	See anticonvulsant.

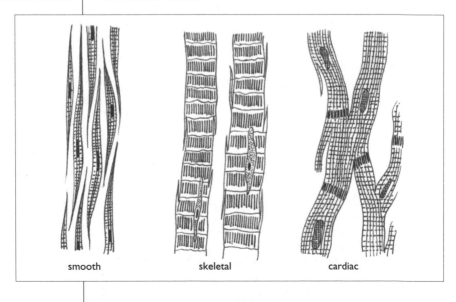

smooth   skeletal   cardiac

20 Muscle tissues

Muscles provide power for many functions including movement, respiration, digestion, circulation, etc, as well as for an indication of emotional changes (eg barking, tail wagging, lip curling, etc). They are controlled by nerve impulses originating by volition or reflex in the brain or spinal cord. Energy for action is created in muscle with the aid of glucose and oxygen to fuel activity.

Muscles generally comprise more than a third of the body weight and make up the 'flesh' of the dog. They are composed of cells arranged in fibres which can be classified as skeletal (mostly voluntary), smooth (mostly involuntary) and cardiac (heart).

Skeletal muscle, which attaches to the skeleton, is formed of long, cylindrical bundles of cell fibres enclosed in a sheath of connective tissue. These cells have many nuclei.

Smooth muscle cells each possess a single nucleus and are spindle-shaped. This form is associated with the walls of hollow organs, the eyeball, hair follicles in the skin, blood vessels and glands.

Cardiac muscle, arranged largely in network form, is able to contract rhythmically and makes up most of the heart.

There are over 300 major muscles in the dog, each with its own Latin name and some, especially skeletal forms, can be grouped under descriptive headings relating to their activity eg flexors (influencing joint bending), extensors (straightening joints), etc.

A rarely occurring change in the identity of a gene which produces a different characteristic in the following generation. Some exotic breeds may have appeared originally through a mutation which breeders subsequently exploited; other mutations are incompatible with the normal development of the affected dog and may die out.

Some forms of mutant cells grow abnormally, eg into tumours, or may cease to grow, producing a stunted deformity. Exposure to radiation in large doses has also produced mutations of this kind.

Excision of the vocal cords carried out to prevent a dog barking. It is performed surgically under general anaesthetic and is not recommended unless, for example, a dog continually barks to 'cause a general nuisance' and as a result is the subject of a court order for control. The reason for continual barking, however, may be boredom or distress and removal of the cause of the stress is a more acceptable approach in such cases. In general, debarking a dog is considered to be unethical as it is an unnecessary mutilation. (See also barking.)

The front of the upper and lower jaws and the facial section of the respiratory system. (See drawing under nose.) Short-faced dogs have short muzzles which contributes to respiratory difficulties associated with these breeds.

The term 'muzzle' also means a device, usually made of leather straps, which fits over the dog's own muzzle to prevent it from biting. An improvised muzzle for use during a veterinary examination can be made from a length of tape crossed over the dog's

muscles

mutation

muting

muzzle

muzzle   muzzle, taken under the ears and tied behind the head in a bow for quick release. For short-faced dogs this is more difficult and a small hand-towel rolled lengthways and drawn under the ears to a place where it is held close behind the head usually suffices as a temporary form of restraint.

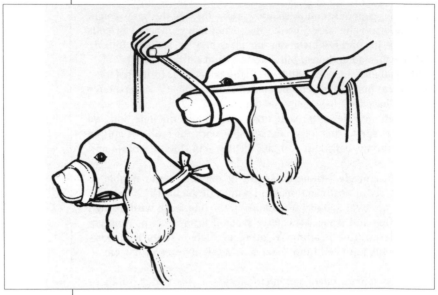

21 Two simple steps in muzzling a dog if necessary before examination or treatment of a painful wound

myasthenia gravis   A neuromuscular disease which produces weakness in all four limbs to the degree of collapse. Weakness is first noticed on exertion or exercise and is accompanied by a dilated oesophagus with difficulty in swallowing (dysphagia). Sometimes food is regurgitated and breathing may also be affected. It is relieved by rest and drugs.

mycosis   A disease caused by fungus. Among such diseases are aspergillosis, actinomycosis and ringworm.

mydriatic   A drug which produces mydriasis – exaggerated dilation of the pupil of the eye. Belladonna is an example.

myelocyte   A cell of the bone marrow which, as it becomes older and divides, eventually becomes one of three forms of white blood cell – neutrophil, basophil or eosinophil. In some diseases (such as leukaemia) these 'early' cells can be found freely in the bloodstream and identified microscopically in the laboratory.

myocarditis   Inflammation of the myocardium (muscle) of the heart. It frequently results from some other disease or severe infection and may occur as a secondary condition to heart failure. In some cases it results in

sudden death, but generally symptoms include ventricular prema- | *myocarditis*
ture heartbeat, tachycardia, weakness and fatigue worsening to a
state of collapse if untreated. A variety of drugs can be used
for treatment, depending on the origins of the disease, and rest is
essential. Some dogs seem predisposed to the disease, including
boxers and St Bernards.

The muscular middle layer of the heart wall consisting of cardiac | **myocardium**
muscle cells.

The outer layer of the uterus. It is itself in two layers: a thin outer | **myometrium**
coat and a thicker inner layer of involuntary muscle which
contains blood vessels and nerves.

Inflammation of a muscle. It can follow injury or be caused | **myositis**
by other bacterial infection. Affected muscles become swollen
and very painful and movement becomes difficult. One form of
the disease is caused by eosinophils (a type of white blood cell)
invading the muscle. German shepherds particularly seem
vulnerable to this form of myositis and the muscles of the jaw are
most likely to succumb.

An anticonvulsant drug which is used in the treatment of epilepsy. | **mysoline**

Adult hypothyroidism characterised by slow metabolism, falling | **myxoedema**
coat and dry skin.

One of a number of virus groups which cause influenza. | **myxovirus**

N

nail See claw.

narcolepsy A disorder of the central nervous system where a dog may suddenly fall asleep. The condition is rare and sometimes accompanies exercise, eating or other occasions for excitement. It is considered to be hereditary in some animals (particularly dobermann pinschers). Diagnosis is usually confirmed with the aid of electroencephalography, and the intravenous administration of imipramine provokes response.

narcosis A state of stupor. Narcosis can arise in some diseases but is usually induced by drugs to various levels and may supplement light, local or regional anaesthesia.

narcotics Drugs used to induce a state of narcosis. They include promazine, chlorpromazine and opium. High dosage may produce depression and some toxicity and for this reason they are rarely used alone for anaesthesia.

naso-lacrymal duct This carries the lacrymal secretion (which bathes the eye) from the conjunctiva to the nasal chamber. The 'healthy nose' of a dog owes its wetness in part to the secretion brought by this duct (and otherwise to the secretion of the nasal glands). (See also eye.)

NCDL (National Canine Defence League) This organisation is the largest dog welfare charity in the UK, founded in 1891. Its mission statement reads 'The NCDL is working towards the day when all dogs can enjoy a happy life, free from the threat of unnecessary destruction'. The NCDL maintains 16 rehoming centres around the UK, rehoming 8,000 dogs each year. All dogs leaving an NCDL centre are neutered, vaccinated, microchipped and passed fit by a veterinarian. They also leave with a collar and lead and free veterinary insurance for six weeks. A free advisory and back-up service is in place for the life of each dog. New owners sign an agreement to return the dog to the NCDL if for any reason they need to part with it.

On the preventive side, the NCDL operates a variety of initiatives to reduce the number of unwanted dogs. Reduced cost neutering and microchipping schemes are available around the UK for those on means-tested benefits. The value of education is also recognised as a longer term solution and free materials are provided for all school age groups linked to the curriculum. NCDL is a registered charity relying on donations and legacies for its work. (See also microchipping; unwanted dogs; Useful Addresses.)

navel See umbilicus.

necrosis The death of tissue while still part of a living body. On some sites the dead cells may 'slough' or part from the healthier tissue associated with them and thus allow healing to progress. In other situations, usually as a result of injury or disease, necrosis can appear in parts of organs which are deprived of their blood supply, become isolated and begin the process of dying.

necrosis

A sewing needle can be a potential danger to the dog as a foreign body.

needle

Hollow needles of various sizes are used with syringes by veterinarians to give injections or to take samples of blood from a dog's vein for laboratory examination prior to diagnosis. Special needles of varying shapes and sizes are used as part of sutures for 'stitching up' after a surgical operation or repairs after a road accident or dog fight.

An antibiotic with action similar to streptomycin. It is useful against some skin infections as a topical application but is generally avoided as an injection due to resulting toxicity and kidney damage.

neomycin

Another name for a tumour.

neoplasm

Inflammation of the kidneys. It can arise in aged dogs – sometimes prompted by chill winds and prolonged exposure to cold – in bitches where a vaginal infection has passed in through the urinary system to the kidneys, or through various other infections. It also occurs in leptospirosis.

nephritis

Symptoms include loss of appetite, increased thirst, raised temperature, stiffness in walking, vomiting, and loss of weight. In extreme cases an odour of ammonia on the breath or severe mouth ulcers characterise a very sick dog with advanced kidney problems.

A veterinarian may prescribe antibiotics to combat infection and the patient should be kept warm and away from draughts. A special diet may be needed, fed in small meals several times a day rather than in large amounts, and chicken breast and fish should replace red meat in a reduced protein diet. Milk and honey or glucose will be beneficial. Intake of water at any one time should be reduced (though clean, cool drinking water should not be denied) to avoid the dog vomiting it back. (See also kidneys.)

Damage to the filtering tubules of the kidneys. It may be part of other diseases of the kidneys, including nephritis, or the result of attack by toxins in the bloodstream. (See also hydronephrosis.)

nephrosis

A surgical operation where an incision is made in the kidney to remove calculi or as the start of a more complex operation.

nephrotomy

See nervous system.

nerves

An emotional condition that can be defined broadly as exaggerated timidity. Much of this can often be traced to causes in puppyhood when the young animal is bewildered by its environment. For this reason some precautions when introducing a puppy to its first home or a new family are worth observing. Soft words, smooth

nervousness

nervousness

movements, gentle handling and an absence of loud, sudden noises help a puppy to become accustomed to its environment at its own pace and help to prevent timidity in later life. A puppy which learns to trust its handler will be self-assured in his or her presence as it grows. Avoid sudden movements, loud, sudden noises, picking up a puppy suddenly, rough handling by children, teasing in all its forms and leaving it alone for hours – especially in a noisy or unfriendly environment.

A nervous dog needs careful handling; it also needs to be kept on a lead at times and in places where its nervousness is likely to be hazardous. Extreme nervousness can be hereditary and nervous dogs should not be used to breed.

nervous system

The nervous system in basic terms consists of the brain and spinal cord acting as a 'control centre', and a complex network of nerves which spread throughout the body. The nervous system is the body's communication system and has been compared to a telephone system with the brain as the central switchboard, the spinal cord as the main cable and the nerves as the wires of transmission with receivers and transmitters in the tissues throughout the body.

The task of the nervous system as a whole is to receive information in the form of stimuli from within the body and from its environment, to process and analyse these stimuli and transmit appropriate response information to the tissues to provide responsive action. Special tissue is used by the system and this is made up of nerve tissue cells, known as neurons, which respond to stimuli by creating an electrical wave or nervous impulse. A neuron comprises a cell body and a combination of processors. Only one of these processors carries impulses *away* from the cell and is called an axon. The remainder are known as dendrites and carry impulses *to* the cell. Impulses pass from one neuron to another across a junction or synapse – always one way from the axon to the cell body or dendrite of the next.

The nervous system can be divided into individual responsibilities in various terms within the main operation, and perhaps the simplest division is as the 'central' and the 'autonomic'. The central, with brain, spinal cord and nerve network, controls the voluntary muscles of head, body and limbs and their movements, sensation in muscles, skin and bones and the sensory organs (eyes, ears, etc). Nerves are supplied to limbs and cavity walls of body and head, outer muscles and skin surface. The central nervous system is concerned with sensation, control of voluntary muscle movement and reflex action. The brain controls sight, hearing, touch, taste and smell, the vital actions of respiration and blood circulation and mental activity including memory, emotion, etc.

The autonomic nervous system is concerned with automatic activity where an organ is self-controlled – the involuntary muscles in the alimentary tract, for example, the heart and the urinary system as well as the blood vessels. A double nerve supply is used in this system (the sympathetic and parasympathetic) with one stimulating action and the other slowing it down. These nerves receive their stimuli from emotional sources, for example, the sight of food and the accompanying excitement stimulates the flow of digestive juices.

nervous system

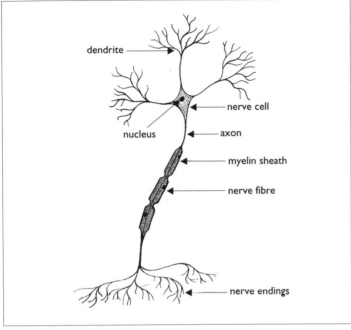

dendrite

nerve cell

nucleus

axon

myelin sheath

nerve fibre

nerve endings

22 A neuron

Inflammation of the nerves. Some virus infections produce neuritis, as can some forms of poisoning. Allergies also exhibit neuritis as a symptom: for example, an allergy to protein (eg horsemeat) may be characterised by neuritis of the nerves of the foreleg as well as vomiting and body skin irritation.

neuritis

Sterilisation of male and female dogs; a useful practice in the control of canine populations. (See also castration; spaying; vasectomy; unwanted dogs.)

neutering

A white blood cell. A normal white cell count has more neutrophils than any other white cell. Their main purpose is bactericidal and they originate in the bone marrow before maturing and entering the bloodstream. Lack of neutrophils in the blood may indicate an infection such as metritis, pneumonia, etc, due to the migration of the circulating neutrophils to cope with the infection. The cause may also be due to impaired production in the bone marrow. They are recognisable in a stained blood film under the microscope by their horseshoe-shaped or lobed nucleus.

neutrophil

See nutrition.

nicotinic acid

nictitating membrane | The so-called third eyelid that covers the front surface of the eye when the two outer eyelids close.

night blindness | Progressive retinal atrophy. (See also retina, atrophy of.)

nikethamide | Also known as N-diethylnicotinamide, this is used as a cardiac and respiratory stimulant in shock or cardiac failure and administered in solution by injection.

nipples | See mammary glands.

nocardiosis | A relatively rare condition in dogs caused by a fungal infection. The symptoms are similar to those of actinomycosis, and the affected animal may also have diarrhoea and increase its uptake of water. Brain or liver may be affected with adverse prognosis.

noise | Dogs generally dislike noise, some breeds being more sensitive to it than others. They react badly, especially to loud, prolonged or sudden noises. For this reason, among others, a sound training of a specialised type is necessary for gundogs (which, in any case, are best bred from gundog parents). Noise can produce stress in dogs and has very bad effects on sick animals and whelping bitches which have a particularly low noise tolerance level. The least disturbance they have the better; peace and quiet aid recovery.

noradrenaline | One of the hormones secreted by the medulla of the adrenal glands. It is similar to adrenaline in composition and physiological action.

nose | The nose can be divided into the external nose with associated cartilage, forming a bony case enclosing a mobile cartilaginous structure, and the internal nose or nasal cavity.

Nostrils, or nares, are part of the external nose, separated by a channel or philtrum. The nostril area is slightly crinkled and this forms a pattern which is individual in each dog – making 'nose-prints' a potential form of canine identification in a similar way to finger-prints in humans. The external nose also contains an olfactory organ or organ of smell, known as the vomeronasal organ or Jacobson's organ. It is shaped like a tubular pocket of skin surrounded by cartilage, and is paired. It is thought to play a role in sexual sensing and recognition of other dogs.

The internal nose is divided longitudinally into two halves into which right and left nostrils lead. Each comprises bony, cartilaginous and membranous sections and each has a respiratory and an olfactory portion. Mucous membranes coat the nasal cavity and it also contains receptor and sensory nerves for the dog's sense of smell. When sniffing to sample the air the nostrils are dilated and larger quantities of air are taken in and directed to where the receptors are located deep in the cavity. Mucous membranes of the nasal cavity generally carry hair-like projections known as cilia which wave around and help to filter dust and small particles, enclosed in secretions from the membranes, into the throat where they may be

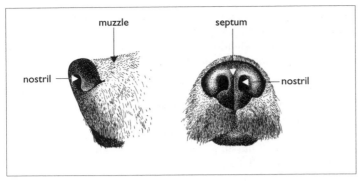

23 The canine nose

swallowed. Secretions from the membranes also moisten and warm the incoming air during the first stages of respiration.

The nasal cavity leads into the pharynx and subsequently into the trachea where air passes on its way to the lungs.

A cold, wet nose is said to be a sign of good health, and often this is a fairly reliable pointer since a dry, warm nose *may* be accompanied by fever although this is not always so.

Any discharge or bleeding from the nose indicates the need for examination by a veterinarian since the cause may be of a serious nature.

nose

See nose.

nostrils

The control centre of the cell. It is contained in a nuclear membrane which is the 'communicating door' between the nucleus and the surrounding cytoplasm which makes up the remainder of the cell. The nucleus contains chromosomes and DNA (deoxyribonucleic acid) and, on division of the cell, passes hereditary material to the next generation.

nucleus

While a dog is sick it needs peace and quiet, gentle handling and soothing reassurance. It requires the administration of prescribed medicine and a special diet (probably including glucose or honey as well as nourishing broths) fed punctually at predetermined times. (If in doubt write the times down.) It usually needs to be kept warm without being uncomfortably hot, and provided with clean bedding, to be changed as necessary.

nursing

Hygiene is of special importance during nursing. Scrupulously clean hands (preferably with short fingernails), feeding and drinking vessels, nursing and veterinary equipment are vital. Isolation may be recommended, especially if a communicable disease is involved when barrier nursing, with careful adherence to a strict and special routine to prevent cross-infection, is necessary – particularly in kennels or dog families.

If changing dressings is part of the nursing programme much care must be taken to do so gently and with utmost cleanliness, scrubbing and washing hands in a disinfectant and making sure that new dressings are sterile before application. Assistance may be necessary in dressing wounds or administering medicines and such arrangements should be made beforehand to allay the dog's natural fears and minimise discomfort. A good light for these occasions is also helpful and disturbance should be minimal.

If medicines or food are spilled on the dog's coat these should be gently wiped away. Food remaining after one feeding session should be disposed of and fresh prepared at each subsequent feed.

During convalescence, gentle grooming should be carried out if possible with soft brushing and special attention to eyes (wiping with cotton wool balls dipped in warm boiled saline), external ears (cotton wool soaked in warm, pure olive oil) and anal and urinary areas (cotton wool or gauze pads dipped in warm boiled water). Exercise, as prescribed, should be gradual with patience and understanding of the dog's recovery rate. The dog should not be encouraged to do too much too quickly nor should the care for its general recovery, including keeping it warm and quiet, for example, be slackened.

Light nourishing meals in small regular amounts allow the dog's digestion to return to normal at its own pace. Check with a veterinarian when formulating a diet for a sick dog. Some cases need special diets, others require the elimination of certain foods or may benefit from supplements. There are, however, some general points to remember in considering the dietary needs of a sick or convalescent dog:

1 While food intake is reduced generally in sickness, the body's nutritional requirements are higher.
2 Feed small meals four to six times a day, rather than two larger ones.
3 Make food wet, warm it to about 37°C (98°F), and feature highly digestible food with protein sources including, for example, cooked eggs and cottage cheese. Glucose, fat, milk and liver are often beneficial in sickness and convalescence. Encourage the patient to drink lots of cool, clear water.
4 Salivation is usually diminished, and a little fat added to the meal should compensate and improve palatability.
5 Avoid excitement at feeding times and allow long intervals between exercise (if any) and eating.
6 In fevers a 1 degree temperature rise means a roughly 10 per cent metabolism rate increase. A 10 degree rise virtually doubles the dog's metabolic rate with more enzyme activity and a need for more high quality, easily-digested protein.
7 If food is entirely refused a raw egg beaten up in milk with glucose, a little water and a pinch of salt added is often acceptable and, if not, can be administered by being gently squirted onto the back of the tongue from the nozzle of a plastic syringe inserted between the back teeth.

Nursing is usually best done by the dog's owner in its own home, though this depends not only on the nature of the dog's illness but on facilities and available time. A dog that is nursed away from home is unable to understand the reasons for a sudden change to a totally unfamiliar and probably frightening environment. Continuous close care by a calm and efficient owner pays dividends in speeding recovery. (See also hospitalisation.)

nursing

See digestion; nutrition.

nutrients

A series of processes of nourishment by which the animal body transforms food materials for growth, activity and repair.

nutrition

Nourishment – or nutrition – is brought about by the dog taking in food and converting it to suitable forms for use in these ways. The nutritional needs of the dog consist broadly of proteins, fats, carbohydrates, water, vitamins and minerals – all of which are found in a balanced, varied diet suited to the digestion of the animal. Such a diet rarely lacks adequate nutritional requirements, and the prevention of ill-health lies in sound dietary planning as far as possible. However, the dog may contract illness for other reasons and then it may be necessary to adjust the normal nutritional intake to compensate. Diarrhoea is such an example where a canine sufferer requires a low protein diet, and probably additional vitamin B which is destroyed by the micro-organisms causing the diarrhoea; a lack of vitamin B can in itself cause diarrhoea, thus creating a continuous cycle of illness unless treated. Additional nutrients may also be needed, not only to effect recovery from a disease, but to prevent a relapse or recurrence. Dietary adjustments may be needed to compensate for these changed needs. Elderly dogs may require supplementary nutrition to cope with disorders associated with old age or merely because the growth and repair processes are sluggish or the digestion slow.

If the normal nutritional needs of the healthy dog are understood then it is easier to adjust diets or to add supplementary nutrients if and when required.

Proteins help with the growth and repair of body tissue through their amino acids which are also energy producers. The vast number of permutations in which amino acids can occur results in a very large number of natural proteins.

Fats are highly efficient producers of energy and also repair fat wastage. They provide about twice the energy per unit weight of proteins and carbohydrates and add palatability to dog food.

Carbohydrates also provide energy and can be converted to body fat. They are, however, of less value to the dog's metabolism than fats or proteins.

Water, while not actually a nutrient, is essential to nutrition and to life.

Minerals such as calcium and phosphorus, which are used in bone and tooth growth and repair, are present in larger amounts than the trace elements – minerals which exist in tiny quantities, such as iron, zinc, selenium and iodine. Calcium and phosphorus function in the dog on a closely-related basis and are also linked to vitamin D requirements. Calcium is at the higher level in the calcium:phosphorus ratio and the normal balance (from 1.2 to 1.4:1) appears to be essential to good health. Calcium is also necessary for several stages of the blood-clotting process and for nerve activity and muscle contractions, and a deficiency can lead to spasms and paralysis as well as bone disorders. The calcium:phosphorus balance is doubly important to the whelping bitch. If calcium falls below the level of phosphorus in the dog, bone formation and repair will be affected. High calcium may also be harmful. Phosphorus itself is involved in the work of many enzymes and in energy conversion processes.

Sodium chloride and potassium are major minerals known as electrolytes. Sodium chloride occurs as common salt and, usually as such, is absorbed in small amounts in the dog's diet, as is potassium which appears widely in foodstuffs. Sodium is needed in the fluid outside the body's cells, while potassium is needed inside, for fluid balance, nerve impulse transmission and effective muscle operation.

Magnesium is a mineral which is found in both bone and soft tissues and, similar to the association between calcium and phosphorus, there is a bond between calcium and magnesium and between the electrolytes and magnesium. The correct balance between calcium and magnesium is important for efficiency in the operation of muscles around the skeleton and heart. Magnesium is also useful in enzyme activity and is unlikely to be deficient in a normal diet.

One of the best known trace elements is iron, a deficiency of which leads to anaemia. Too much iron, however, is toxic and symptomised by anorexia. Iron is present in the haemoglobin of the blood, where about 60 per cent of it occurs, and plays a part in respiration. Copper, another trace element, is closely linked to iron activity and may act as a catalyst for iron in haemoglobin formation. It is also involved in the activity of some enzymes associated with collagen so that a deficiency may contribute to bone disorders as well as anaemia. Excessive copper in some breeds, however, may lead to liver damage.

Zinc is needed by the dog to prevent skin problems, loss of weight and anorexia, and helps with growth of tissues. It is present in the general diet, as is selenium. This latter serves to protect cell membranes and its activity is linked both to vitamin E and two amino acids (cystine and methionine). Like magnesium, its deficiency can impair the action of muscles around skeleton and heart, but over-dosage is dangerous.

Other trace elements present in the dog's diet under normal circumstances include iodine, which helps to make thyroid hormones for the thyroid gland (its deficiency as well as excess resulting in thyroid disorders) cobalt, which is present in vitamin B_{12} and manganese, which influences growth and acts to stimulate some enzyme activity.

There are fourteen main vitamins essential for the health and growth of the dog. Vitamin A helps vision, and growth of bones, teeth and skin, and has some anti-infective properties. Deficiency can cause skin and respiratory tissue disorders, conjunctivitis and other eye problems. Excess of the vitamin may result in gingivitis or serious bone disease.

Vitamin B_1 (thiamin, aneurin) safeguards against serious nervous diseases and anorexia. It is progressively destroyed by cooking. It is a tool in carbohydrate metabolism and the need for it is therefore relative to carbohydrate consumption. Vitamin B_2 (riboflavin) is needed for cell growth, and skin and eye disorders may result from a lack of it. Vitamin B_6 is used in amino acid production and various enzyme activities. Diets deficient in it will contribute to anaemia. Vitamin B_{12} is a very essential vitamin involved in the production of nerve tissue and fat and carbohydrate conversions. It is absorbed in the intestine with the aid of a special substance (intrinsic factor), and a dog's inability to absorb B_{12} will lead to pernicious anaemia and nerve disease. It is the only vitamin which contains a trace element (cobalt).

Vitamin C (ascorbic acid) is not needed normally in the diet as the dog is able to make it with glucose which is 'burnt' for energy, though a deficiency in the body may contribute to some skeletal diseases such as hip dysplasia.

Vitamin D operates as a stimulant to stabilise calcium and phosphorous at levels needed for bone manufacture and repair. It is essential for puppies, when bone is growing steadily, and in fracture repair. Substantial reductions from the normal level cause rickets and other bone-related diseases. Adult dogs apparently synthesise this vitamin in the skin when exposed normally to sunlight.

Vitamin E helps to develop muscle and process fat. It is destroyed by rancid fats in a diet. Its deficiency is associated with muscular dystrophy, reproductive disorders and nerve failure. Its action is linked to the presence of selenium.

Vitamin K is used in the liver to synthesise blood plasma components essential to blood clotting processes. While this vitamin is highly unlikely to be deficient in the dog except in malnutrition, malabsorption or intestinal disorders, lack of it may be expressed by dangerous internal haemorrhages.

Pantothenic acid is necessary in the processing of fats, carbohydrates and amino acids and in dogs a deficiency may cause alopecia and gastro-intestinal and liver problems.

Nicotinic acid (niacin) is converted physiologically to nicotinamide which is an important component in the processing and use of nutrients. The amino acid tryptophan can be converted in the body to this vitamin. Mouth inflammation and ulceration (see black tongue) are symptoms of its insufficiency.

Biotin, another B vitamin, assists in the combination of amino acids with proteins. A dry, flaky skin disorder may reflect inadequacy occasionally caused by very large quantities of raw egg whites in the diet or by continued antibiotic administration.

Folic acid is useful in the production of red blood cells in the bone marrow. Lack of it will consequently contribute to anaemic conditions.

nutrition Choline is important in nerve impulse transmission and a deficiency of it may lead to liver and kidney problems.

Those items mentioned above are the main nutritional 'ingredients' needed by a dog to maintain good health. By providing your dog with a balanced, varied diet, deficiencies will normally be prevented. If they should occur, or be caused by disease, a veterinarian must be consulted for treatment and to ensure that a controlled supplementary administration is made if needed during the dog's recovery, as some, though not all, vitamins and minerals may produce toxic conditions in excess as well as in insufficiency. A careful monitoring of levels will then be necessary to make certain that the correct balance is attained and not exceeded. (See also diet; digestion; feeding.)

nymphomania An excessive desire on the part of the bitch to mate. Often, however, the bitch will refuse the dog when a mating is arranged. The desire is due generally to a hormone imbalance or to ovarian cysts. Hormone therapy may correct the condition or, if the bitch is not to be mated, removal of the ovaries may be necessary, especially if they are cystic.

nystagmus Involuntary movements of the eye which occur independently of normal motion. If co-ordination between the balancing mechanism of the middle ear and the eye is upset, or if other associated nerves are affected by a brain disorder, nystagmus may result.

nystatin A fungicidal antibiotic often used in the treatment of moniliasis and other fungal infections, including those of the skin.

It is essential that a dog is obedient in a few matters and its life may at sometime depend on it. It should certainly come when it is called, sit when told to do so, walk to heel, stay on command and 'leave' anything it has found or is worrying. It is useful to teach a dog to lie down, drop objects from its mouth, be quiet when told and 'fetch'. Obedience in terms of performing tricks is unnecessary. Working dogs (and show dogs) are, of course, required to be obedient in more wide ranging subjects. (See also training.)

obedience

Excessive fatness – perhaps the single greatest danger to a dog's health in civilised society, with the possible exception of neglect and cruelty. In a way obesity is also caused generally by either neglect or a form of cruelty by kindness. Neglect in providing a correct diet – in terms of nutritious quality and daily amount of the right kind of food – is as common a cause of overweight as believing it is kind to feed a dog as much as it wants to eat. Some dogs are literally fed to death by their owners.

obesity

Obesity affects around 35 per cent of the canine population and is more common in bitches than in dogs. It is usually caused by overfeeding and/or an unsuitable diet coupled often to insufficient exercise. It can, less commonly, be caused by a hormone imbalance or other disease. Aged dogs, too, run a higher risk of obesity as their dietary needs change and they take less exercise. Mostly, for example, they will need less carbohydrate and more protein than when they were young.

An overweight dog is certainly less healthy and its heart, kidneys and respiratory and digestive organs are strained beyond normal limits. Obesity is the direct cause of many illnesses, reduces potential lifespan, adds to orthopaedic complications and reduces the dog's resistance to infection.

Obesity occurs, in physiological terms, because the energy input is greater than the output, so treatment must lie in either reducing the intake or increasing the output, or, preferably, both. The obese dog needs a properly-formulated reducing diet, a subsequent carefully-formulated maintenance diet for when its weight returns to normal, and an exercise plan to be implemented gradually. On a reducing diet about 15 per cent body weight loss in around ten weeks is not too ambitious. These diets vary and advice from a veterinarian, who can set a target weight and provide instructions for the owner to follow strictly, will be helpful. Titbits and 'treats' must be abandoned or the diet will prove useless. The dog should be weighed each week and its weight recorded on a graph. Once a reduction occurs weight loss usually continues steadily and the dog becomes happier and more active, responding by its own initiative to an increase in exercise which, after all, will be a more comfortable, enjoyable event for it.

A reducing diet can for example be based on the following combined ingredients: lean minced beef, carrots, green beans, peas and cottage cheese. To this a suitable vitamin-and-mineral supplement

obesity

should be added. Quantities given depend on the breed and the circumstances of the obesity. As a general rule, feed some 60 per cent of the normal calorie requirements for the dog's target weight and give plenty of cool, clean water. Remember that even one dog biscuit can represent an additional 100 calories. If no reduction is seen after keeping to a strict routine for a week, cut the calorie intake again by 20 per cent. If no reduction is seen after six weeks of this dieting, consult a veterinarian.

An alternative approach to calorie reduction is starvation, giving a vitamin-mineral supplement and water only. This can be dangerous without veterinary supervision.

When the weight-reduction target is achieved, keep the dog on a normal diet without returning to overfeeding. Follow up weight tests at three-monthly intervals.

Prevention of obesity is of course the best approach to the problem. Normally there are only two rules to follow: firstly, feed a nourishing diet regularly, and ensure that the amount given is not excessive for the dog's weight; and secondly, see that the dog gets as much *regular* exercise as it needs.

obstetrics

The study of the management of pregnancy and labour. (See also breeding; whelping.)

occiput

The back of the head or skull. The occipital bones are in the shape of a circle around the entrance of the spinal cord. The top of the occiput is particularly prominent in cocker spaniels and setters.

odour

If the breath is malodorous, decaying teeth could be the cause. It may alternatively be due to mouth ulcers or tonsillitis. Severe kidney disorders, including nephritis, produce a smell of ammonia on the breath – indicating a very sick dog. In ketosis, acetone can sometimes be detected on the breath and in serious lung infections a decaying smell may be present.

Body odours may be noticed in some aged dogs but regular grooming and bathing at appropriate times can accomplish much in diminishing or eliminating these.

oedema

An accumulation of fluid in tissue spaces or body cavities. It is usually an inflammatory reaction (although it can be due to severe mechanical restriction if, for example, a collar or chain is too tight or a child has wound an elastic band around a dog's leg – an all too frequent occurrence).

Inflammatory oedema is due mainly to massive infection, allergy, injury, scalding or burning when the protein balance between blood and tissue fluid is upset. This balance may also be disturbed, for example, due to malnutrition when the body is starved of protein, when liver disease impairs the synthesis of protein or when protein is lost in urinary excretion due to kidney disease.

Lungs can become 'waterlogged' with oedema when, for example, a dog is overcome by fumes or suffering from pleurisy or some forms of poisoning. Oedema of the abdomen is known as ascites.

Diuretics assist the condition but the underlying cause of the oedema needs appropriate treatment.

oedema

The oesophagus or gullet commences at the back of the pharynx, running to the left of the trachea down to the stomach. In average-sized dogs it is about 30cm (12in) long. Diameter varies along its length and thickness of the wall is also variable, between about 2.5mm and 6mm ($\frac{1}{10}$ and $\frac{1}{4}$in), due to its ability to dilate. There are four layers of the oesophagus; two inner are mucosal, one is muscular and the outer fibrous. Food passes down the oesophagus by peristalsis to the stomach to begin the digestive process.

oesophagus

Disorders of the oesophagus may be symptomised by regurgitation which may be accompanied by pharyngitis and, in some instances, by pneumonia. Such disorders may include the presence of foreign bodies or other forms of obstruction, pneumothorax, diseases of the mucous membrane lining or a hiatal or diaphragmatic hernia. Report symptoms to a veterinarian and, if a foreign body is present, confirmation will probably be obtained by radiography and surgical removal accomplished under general anaesthetic.

Ovarian hormone of the female. (See also oestrogens.)

oestradiol

Ovarian hormone of the female. (See also oestrogens.)

oestriol

A group of hormones, including oestradiol, oestriol and oestrone, which are secreted by the female ovaries and are concerned with sexual activity. They stimulate oestrus, prepare the genitalia for reproduction and activate the mammary glands. Oestrogens are also produced by other endocrine glands and can be prepared synthetically when they are utilised primarily for inducing or prolonging oestrus and stimulating the desire to reproduce.

oestrogens

Ovarian hormone of the female. (See also oestrogens.)

oestrone

The period when a bitch is 'in season' or 'on heat', ie the time when oestrogens are active in the body and the female is ready for mating. Oestrus lasts for between eight and eighteen days generally and at the appropriate time the bitch will accept the dog for mating. It usually occurs twice a year, around late spring and late autumn, although this may vary between individuals. Basenjis, for example, have only one season a year.

oestrus

The first oestrus occurs when the bitch is around eight months old and its approach is signified by a slight swelling of the vulva followed shortly by a discharge of bright coloured blood when the bitch is said to be 'showing colour'. This is due to the shedding of the endometrium as the oestrus cycle begins. (See also gestation.)

Semi-solid medicament for external application to the skin. Ointments with a large fluid content are called creams and some well-tried ointments and creams are made up in the veterinary dispensary, often with bases of lanolin or lard.

ointment

old age	See aged dogs.
olfactory system	This is concerned with the sense of smell, which is highly developed in most breeds. It is a relatively simple system based on the testing of air for the small particles of a scent or 'smell' and sending of messages to the brain for evaluation and interpretation. In the mucous membranes of the nasal cavity at the back of the nose lie buried nerve fibres associated with receptive hairs or cilia which make contact with the scent particles as the indrawn air passes over them. These particles are dissolved in the secretions of the mucous membrane and provide a chemical stimulus to the hairs passing to the nerves which transmit impulse messages to the brain via the first cranial nerve. The dog uses its keen sense of smell in the recognition of many different objects including friends, enemies, 'unknowns', offspring and mates. It can interpret odiferous messages left by others in a form of communication, locate food and familiar objects and people, track by following a scent trail left by another species, and it can obtain diverse information brought by scents on breezes or wind movement diluted enough to remain undetected by human senses. Its sense of smell also helps it to tell when a mate is ready for reproduction. Since a dog's sense of smell is both sensitive and delicate, pungent odours readily start a dog sneezing. (See also nose.)
oliguria	The passing of insufficient urine for the rate of metabolism. It is often the start or the end of anuria and is closely associated with uraemia. It can be caused by dehydration, hypotension or heart problems. It can also arise through urinary obstruction, perhaps by calculi, or kidney damage.
olive oil	An occasional half to one teaspoonful of pure olive oil on food helps the coat retain the glossiness of good condition. It is also a useful mild laxative when given to constipated puppies and dogs (about two teaspoonfuls for the average sized adult dog).
omentum	Part of the peritoneum which fills spaces between coils of intestine and helps to support them. There are folds of the lacy omentum from the stomach down to the bladder (known as the greater omentum) containing fat, and veils of the lesser omentum loosely spread over other abdominal organs from duodenum to the liver.
onychomycosis	A fungal infection of the claw which can set up an inflammatory condition in the root if not treated. A suitable fungicide is usually prescribed which can be applied topically.
oophorectomy	The surgical removal (or ovariectomy) of the ovaries. This may be called for because of tumours or cysts and one or both ovaries can be removed. Often the uterus is also removed, when the operation is known as 'spaying'.

An instrument similar to a small torch with a built-in mirror with which the eye and its interior can be viewed by means of reflected light. **ophthalmoscope**

See medicine, administration of. **oral administration (of medicine)**

The surgical removal (or orchiectomy) of one or both testes. This operation is performed, under a general anaesthetic, to render a dog infertile or because a testis is diseased. (See also castration.) **orchidectomy**

The inflammation of a testis. In severe cases this can be a very painful condition in which the affected testis swells and is extremely tender. Treatment with corticosteroids reduces swelling and antibiotics are generally given to eliminate the infection causing the inflammation. **orchitis**

Bone formation or osteogenesis – the transformation of cartilage into bone. A chemical change occurs in the cells and magnesium and calcium salts are deposited. During the process special bone-building cells known as osteoblasts enter the cartilage from the bloodstream and convert the soluble salts of magnesium and calcium in the blood into insoluble salts – chiefly calcium phosphate – which hardens the cartilage. Another type of cell, an osteoclast, is responsible for the reabsorption of any unwanted bone, changing the solid salts back into soluble form for the bloodstream to carry away. Both forms of cell are active during bone development in normal growth and such repair as is required following a fracture. **ossification**

Skull bones, although still formed in the ossification process, are different in that they develop from fibrous tissue instead of from cartilage.

See arthritis. **osteoarthritis**

A bone-building cell which converts soluble mineral salts into insoluble form for bone formation. **osteoblast**

A cell which operates in the bone formation process to convert any unwanted bone to soluble salts for reabsorption into the blood. **osteoclast**

Defective bone formation, largely caused by a calcium deficiency coupled to normal or excessive phosphorus intake affecting the calcium:phosphorous ratio. A common reason is the dog being fed an all-meat diet. The high phosphorus and low calcium content affects the secretion of hormones from the parathyroid gland and bone formation is impeded. Kidney problems where phosphorus salts are retained produce a high phosphorus content in the blood with a similar effect. **osteodystrophy**

The patient usually suffers from swelling of the bone with inflammation and pain. This is noticeable at first from difficulty in

osteodystrophy	walking and lameness in the forelegs. Young dogs are mostly vulnerable during the time of bone development.
osteogenesis	See ossification.
osteomalacia	See rickets.
osteomyelitis	Inflammation of the bone marrow. It can be caused by an abscess in the bone, injury, wounds, contaminated fractures or other forms of infection. If an abscess is present the pus it contains has no opportunity to escape and spreads along the interior of the bone infecting the marrow. If untreated the blood supply may eventually be restricted and dead bone may result which retains bacteria and remains unaffected by the drugs which cannot reach it through the bloodstream. Surgery may then be necessary to remove the dead bone and repair the damage. This chronic stage should, however, be prevented if the patient receives antibiotics early enough to combat the original source of infection before it spreads and worsens. Early symptoms include pain and tenderness at the site of infection, an elevated temperature and often dejection and loss of appetite.
otitis	Inflammation of the ear which occurs through a variety of causes, in some cases from the presence of a foreign body such as a grass seed or from a disease commonly known as canker, usually caused by an ear mite parasite. The dog scratches its ear and shakes its head. Examination by a veterinarian is needed so that a suitable remedy can be prescribed. Drops are usually inserted into the ear to reduce inflammation and attack the root cause. If penetration of drops into the affected inner ear is impossible due to swelling caused by chronic inflammation, aural resection may be necessary. This condition should be attended to as soon as the first signs appear to prevent the need for a surgical remedy later and also to avoid worsening and the danger of loss of hearing or even death if the disease spreads past the inner ear. Otitis is most common in flap-eared dogs such as spaniels where there is reduced ventilation of the ear canal. (See also canker; ear; grass seed.)
ovariectomy	See oophorectomy.
ovaries	The female sex glands, or gonads, where ova are produced. There are two ovaries, which are generally a little larger than the size of a pea, relatively smooth but becoming roughened on the outside in bitches which have produced several litters. They are situated in the abdominal cavity behind the kidneys and are connected by the Fallopian tubes to the uterus. Each ovary weighs less than ½g in a 10kg (22lb) bitch. The medulla of the ovary contains nerves and blood vessels while the cortex contains the follicles which mature to commence ovulation.
	Ovaries sometimes become cystic and can be so when there are tumours of the mammary glands. Surgical removal is frequently necessary in such cases.

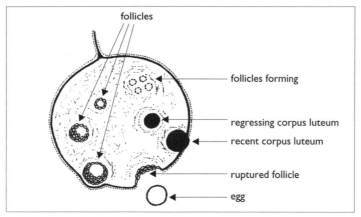

24 Section of the ovary showing follicles

The process by which a mature egg (ovum) is released from the ovary. Ovulation occurs during oestrus and commences with the ripening of one, or sometimes two, follicles within the ovary. As they mature a cavity is formed filling with follicular fluid. Inside, a slight protuberance appears containing an ovum or egg cell. As the fluid fills the cavity it exerts increasing pressure from within until the weakest point of the follicle ruptures, releasing the ovum into the Fallopian tube.

Ovulation begins a few days after oestrus has started and the ovum lives for about four days. After fertilisation by the sperm it takes about four days to reach the uterus, and implantation in the wall of the uterus is achieved about nineteen days after ovulation has ended. Development of the embryo then commences.

After ovulation a minor haemorrhage occurs in the follicular cavity and the corpus luteum is produced from associated cells. If the ovum is fertilised the corpus luteum is retained during pregnancy and disappears after whelping. If fertilisation is not achieved, shrinking of the corpus luteum sets the cycle in motion again for the next oestrus and ovulation.

ovulation

The female egg produced in the ovary and released into the Fallopian tube for fertilisation by a male sperm during ovulation.

ovum

The most vital element for sustaining life. It is drawn in from the air during the process of respiration and exchanged for waste carbon dioxide in the lungs. It is absorbed by haemoglobin in the red blood cells as it passes through capillary walls into the bloodstream, and is transported by the blood to combine in tissue with products of the digestive system to make energy. Much more oxygen is utilised during exercise – up to thirty times more when a dog is running at 20mph than when at rest – and any weakness in respiratory organs or heart will be more noticeable during increased activity.

In respiratory disease or insufficiency the administration of supplementary oxygen may be indicated; sometimes it is required during anaesthesia. While a face mask or other appliance can be

oxygen

oxygen

used while the dog is anaesthetised, it cannot be used effectively when the dog is conscious. A dog will strongly resent the application of a face mask, for example, and frightening an already sick animal in this way causes energetic struggling which further increases the degree of respiratory insufficiency. Oxygen tents, though relatively rare in veterinary practices, are probably the best form of equipment (especially for small and medium-sized dogs) to provide oxygen.

oxytetracycline

An antibiotic member of the family of tetracyclines.

oxytocin

A hormone secreted by the posterior lobe of the pituitary gland. It activates the release of milk from the mammary glands of the whelping bitch and stimulates the muscles of the uterus to contract.

Oxytocin can be administered to bitches suffering from uterine inertia during whelping and is useful following whelping when it is given, often with a long-acting antibiotic such as ampicillin, to ensure that the uterus is clear. In this way it does much to prevent metritis.

See paws.

pads

A symptom of many diseases and disorders. Since the dog is unable to say where it hurts, it is up to the owner to detect its presence as soon as possible. Depending on the severity of the pain the dog may be merely restless or extremely distressed. It may whimper or whine and may try to get at the source of the pain by licking or even chewing at the approximate location. Respiration rate will probably increase with the dog panting and often the eyes take on a somewhat glazed, staring appearance. The dog will probably yelp when the affected part is touched gently. Symptoms should be noted, first-aid measures taken to relieve the pain if this is possible and a veterinarian contacted immediately. An attack of pain should never be left to see if it subsides; even if it does lessen it is likely to recur with added violence since pain is the body's indicator that something is wrong.

pain

See analgesic.

pain reliever

The palate is formed by the floor of the nasal cavity or the roof of the mouth. The front portion is the hard palate which has bony ridges to help the tongue move food down to the back of the mouth. At the rear of the mouth and continuous with the hard palate is the soft palate which is composed of muscles. Both hard and soft palates are covered with mucous membrane. The palate effectively forms a partition between the respiratory passages above and the digestive passages below.

The soft palate, which normally begins just beyond the level of the last upper molar teeth, is particularly long in the dog compared to other mammals and, in short-faced breeds (such as bulldog and Pekinese) may be so long that it restricts the passage of air into the larynx causing breathing difficulties. In the average dog it is about 6cm (2½in) long.

Tumours sometimes arise in the soft palate and inflammation of the mucous membranes there (stomatitis) is not uncommon. Hereditary incompletion of the soft palate is a cause of chronic nasal discharge. (See also mouth.)

palate

Examination by touch. The hands and fingers may be used to examine the surface of the body and, with special knowledge, the internal organs. Veterinarians are, of course, skilled in examining dogs in this way but certainly the owner should, for example, regularly palpate the area around the mammary glands of the bitch. If this is carried out, perhaps during grooming, early warning of any mammary tumours or mastitis can be obtained. Palpation also gives indication of skin tumours, or irregularities in the spine or other bones, and evidence of pain in various parts of the body. The examination should be done gently with clean, warm hands softly feeling for anything abnormal. A regular session will help you to

palpation

palpation

get to know your dog so that anything abnormal can be detected quickly and reported to a veterinarian for further study. (See also examination.)

pancreas

The pancreas gland is roughly V-shaped, consisting basically of two lobes with a body area at the junction. It is composed largely of tubular cells and connective tissue and is situated in the abdominal cavity near the liver and kidneys. It weighs about 30g (1oz) in an average-sized dog and is about 25cm (10in) in length. The right lobe is around 15cm (6in) long and the left about 10cm (4in).

The pancreas has a double role to play: it secretes a digestive juice, emptied via at least two ducts into the duodenum, which contains enzymes, including those for the conversion of proteins (trypsin), fats (lipase) and carbohydrates (amylase). Insulin, a hormone which regulates blood sugar levels, is also produced by the pancreas in a part of the gland known as the Islets of Langerhans.

Bicarbonate salts as an alkaline solution are also secreted by the pancreas to neutralise acid from the stomach during digestion. Pancreatic secretion is controlled by two hormones, secretin and pancreozymin. The former is secreted when intestinal acidity becomes high, in turn triggering the release of more bicarbonate salts for neutralisation activity. Pancreozymin is secreted when partially-digested food is abundant in the intestine and in turn stimulates enzyme release from the pancreas to help the digestive process.

Damage to the pancreas can be caused by a sudden blow or other 'blunt' injury such as those sustained in road accidents. Symptoms

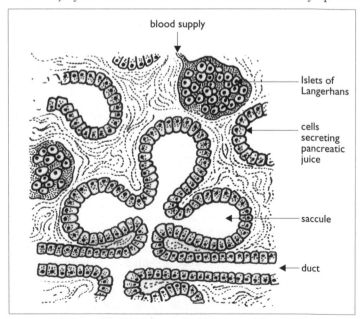

25 Cross-section of pancreas tissue

include vomiting, increasing abdominal pain, loss of appetite and shock. Diagnosis is aided by laboratory tests for pancreatic function, including the evaluation of the blood levels of amylase and lipase, and by radiography which shows a dappled area between gas-filled bulges of the small intestine.

Disease of the cells of the Islets of Langerhans can cause diabetes and the pancreas can become inflamed in pancreatitis. (See also digestion.)

pancreas

Inflammation of the pancreas. Acute inflammation often results in necrosis and can be linked to obesity. Symptoms include pain and tenderness of the abdomen, depression, a rise in blood sugar levels and shock. Smelly, pale, fatty faeces appear later as the condition becomes chronic and a ravenous appetite is evident – leading to further increase in obesity.

pancreatitis

Pancreatitis is most likely to affect middle-aged, obese bitches and can include complications such as toxaemia and cardiac problems. Dehydration can occur through persistent vomiting. Treatment generally consists of the administration of suitable antibiotics, and other drugs to control pancreatic secretion. A special diet is usually necessary, which can include boiled rice and cooked eggs. Dehydration needs to be treated with urgency to replace lost fluid. Laboratory tests are needed to evaluate pancreatic function and eliminate other diseases with similar symptoms.

Pancreatitis can be haemorrhagic, producing the general symptoms mentioned above, plus a stiff walk, diarrhoea and fever. The critical period is usually the first twenty-four to forty-eight hours, when the dog's life is most at risk.

See nutrition.

pantothenic acid

Tiny, conical-shaped projections of soft tissue from, for example, the wall of parts of the alimentary tract, the surface of the tongue and the skin. Their purpose is to increase the available surface area for nerve endings and blood vessels, eg in places where touch is most sensitive.

papillae

A wart-like tumour which is frequently benign. It arises from abnormal growth of papillae in mucous membranes or skin. (See also tumour.)

papilloma

Liquid paraffin is sometimes used as a laxative, or as a lubricant when, for example, a thermometer is inserted rectally (Vaseline is perhaps more suitable). It is also sometimes used as a basis for ointments. Commercial paraffin, or kerosene, however, should never be applied to a dog either internally or externally. It will cause poisoning. Spilt kerosene (and petrol) has a harmful effect on a dog's feet and produces a stinging sensation. If a dog is affected after stepping in a pool of it on the road, for example, the feet should be washed in soap and warm water, rinsed and dried carefully to ensure that nothing remains.

paraffin

paralysis Loss of muscular power due to interference with nerve supply. It is generally caused by damage to, or interference with, the brain, spinal cord or nerves. It can be partial or total, temporary or permanent.

There are many reasons for paralysis and while prognosis is bad in some cases, in others recovery can be expected. A veterinarian should be consulted immediately a dog shows any sign of paralysis, even in the mildest form.

Paralysis can follow head or back injury; it may be a result of distemper, encephalitis or brain tumour. In one particular form, known as brachial paralysis, a foreleg is affected and becomes totally useless due to damage to a nerve centre called the brachial plexus. In this instance amputation of the limb is often the only course of action, from which most patients make a good recovery and are active on three legs after practice. A deficiency in calcium, phosphorous and magnesium in the diet can also cause paralysis. In some cases, although there is a loss of use and movement, pain may still be present and careful handling is important. The dog may also be distressed and tranquillisers will be needed to calm it while analgesics may be prescribed to reduce the pain.

Nursing is important if there is to be a chance of recovery and, if the dog is unable to raise itself with its forelegs it needs to be gently turned at least two or three times a day to prevent lung congestion and body sores. (See also paraplegia.)

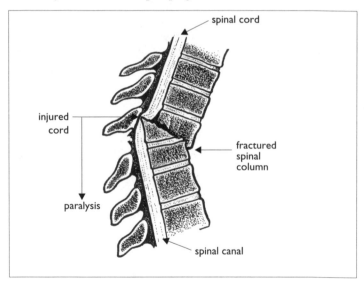

26 Fracture of the spinal column showing a 'pinched' spinal cord below which paralysis results

paraplegia Paralysis of the hindquarters involving the limb and usually the muscles, including those controlling the passing of urine and faeces. It can be caused by direct injury, for example, from road accidents, spinal fractures or violence.

Dachshunds (and other long, low dogs such as Pekinese and sealyhams) are particularly vulnerable to paraplegia from a 'slipped' disc in the spine. This condition is frequently due to obesity. The spine supporting the long body of the dachshund cannot take the extra weight and one of the shock-absorbing discs between the vertebrae protrudes and pinches the spinal cord producing partial paralysis and pain. A slipped disc can also be the result of an injury.

paraplegia

The patient may recover from paraplegia, and complete rest and gentle, patient nursing are of the utmost importance. A soft, cushioned bed is helpful, as are light meals and plenty of cool, clean water to drink. If the dog has lost control of its bladder, urination can be encouraged about twice a day by supporting the patient in a standing or squatting position and very gently pressing the abdomen with both hands. Faeces need only be passed every second or third day and this can be stimulated by a warm soapy enema if necessary. In severe cases, surgical intervention to reduce the pressure on the spinal cord is likely to be advocated by your veterinarian.

Recovery can often be helped by gentle massage and by supporting the hindquarters with a towel held at each end and stretched underneath the rear body as the dog moves along with its forelegs. Some dogs which have remained partially paralysed but without pain have lived happy lives with assistance from a specially-built trolley to carry their hindquarters and give them mobility.

A wide variety of parasites can attack the dog though, in most cases, prevention is relatively simple and eradication more difficult but possible. There are two basic forms of parasite: ectoparasites which live externally on the dog causing irritation, infection and sometimes disease, and endoparasites which inhabit an internal organ and damage the host by individual means.

parasites

Ectoparasites

Perhaps the most well-known, and most common, ectoparasite is the dog flea (*Ctenocephalides canis*). It is a small, flat-sided, wingless insect with mouth parts suited to blood sucking. A similar infestation to that of the dog flea can occur with the human flea (*Pulex irritans*) and sometimes with hedgehog fleas. The flea completes its life cycle away from the dog, usually in bedding, etc, and its presence can be detected by the dog scratching and nibbling at its fur. Some dogs pay little attention to the activities of fleas while others can become quite frantic and also become sensitised to them, which produces eczema. Fleas breed rapidly in warm weather and can be destroyed by specially-prepared veterinary shampoos, while bedding is regularly disinfected or destroyed. The dog flea is also a carrier of the endoparasite *Dipylidium caninum* or tapeworm. Flea larvae become infested with tapeworm eggs which develop in the adult flea and are swallowed by the dog when it cleans itself.

Flea collars generally give effective protection for three to four months. Such collars also provide protection against 'jiggers', 'keds' or ticks. Special spray or drop formulae are also available and effective against fleas, ticks and lice. A veterinarian will advise

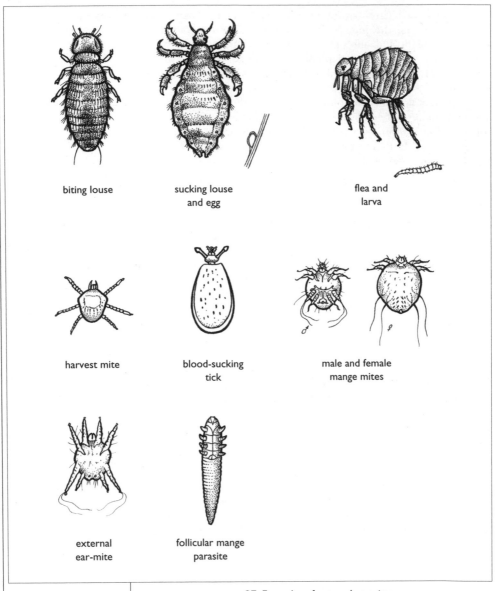

biting louse

sucking louse
and egg

flea and
larva

harvest mite

blood-sucking
tick

male and female
mange mites

external
ear-mite

follicular mange
parasite

27 Examples of external parasites

parasites on the most suitable programme for all purposes. Ticks are ferocious creatures with eight legs and vicious mouth parts armed with cutting and boring mechanisms and a set of hooks to bite into their host and cling on. Some burrow deeply under the skin, setting up inflammation around them. Such insects should not be pulled off as they will leave their mouth parts behind to exacerbate the infection: a drop of eucalyptus oil will usually relax their hold when dropped onto the visible part and they can subsequently be destroyed when they fall off.

parasites

A common tick in the UK, USA and Western Europe generally is *Ixodes canisuga* although *Ixodes hexagonus* (also found on hedge-hogs) attacks dogs in these countries as well as parts of Africa. There are many other ticks, including the so-called 'harvest mites' (*Trombicula*) which attach themselves to the skin and are rapidly evident as a spot in the centre of an inflamed patch of skin. These are orange-red in colour and sometimes infest the spaces between the dog's toes where they cause much irritation.

The smaller mites are responsible for several debilitating and problematical diseases including the two forms of mange and some otitis in the ear. They invade the external skin (though ear mites find their way deep into the ear itself) and eggs, larvae and adults are very resistant to treatment. There are also 'nose mites' which can enter the nasal passages and cause a nasal discharge.

Lice are another troublesome form of ectoparasite. They have flat brown or whitish bodies with strong claws to prevent themselves being dislodged when the dog scratches. They spend their entire life cycle on their host, clinging to hair and laying eggs on indi-vidual hairs. There are two types, biting and sucking, and both take the blood of their host, which can lead to infection and anaemia.

Most forms of biting lice live on birds, but there are over 500 species in the UK alone, and some infest dogs, including for example *Trichodectes canis*, which is also an intermediate carrier of tapeworms.

Sucking lice, of which there are a mere twenty-five species in the UK, invade only mammals, including dogs. *Linognathus setosis* is a common example. This species sucks blood with a toothed proboscis and a set of stylets which pierce the skin and draw blood out.

Lice can best be destroyed by the use of an appropriate veterinary shampoo which kills both adults and eggs.

Apart from the dog's obvious irritation, ectoparasites can be detected by their droppings, which often appear like grains of coal dust when the dog's hair is parted.

Endoparasites

There are many species of endoparasite which live inside the dog in various stages of their life cycles. The most common of these are several species of worm. The name 'worm' is vernacular and applies to most elongated, legless creatures; the name 'helminths' is that which describes most parasitic worms. Among these the most common in the dog is the roundworm which, as the name suggests, has a round cross-section. Some of these are also known as thread-worms or pinworms.

Roundworms can infest adult dogs as well as puppies but the earliest danger is to the puppy which inherits the disease through the placenta of the dam. One of the roundworm varieties (*Toxocara canis*) is responsible for the disease toxocariasis which mostly affects puppies some two weeks after their birth. The larvae develop in various internal organs and grow to adults to inhabit the intestines. The life cycle recommences internally when thousands

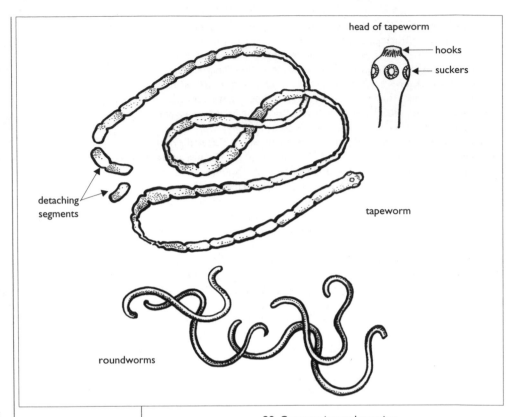

head of tapeworm

hooks

suckers

detaching segments

tapeworm

roundworms

28 Common internal parasites

parasites

of eggs are laid a month or two later. They can cause vomiting, abdominal pain, loss of weight, obstruction and even convulsions if the infestation is severe. Treatment for roundworm is usually by means of piperazine, or proprietary compounds containing this anthelmintic, given when pups are about two to three weeks old and subsequently at intervals of two to three weeks until three months of age. The worms are expelled in the faeces and are generally small and pointed at both ends. Other species of roundworm, apart from causing the symptoms mentioned above can also produce muscular cysts; some do not appear in the intestines until the puppies are four to eight weeks old.

In the oesophagus, the reddish *Spirocerca* roundworm, which uses cockroaches as intermediate hosts, can produce tumours, coughing fits and vomiting. Heartworms, in the form of *Dirofilaria* roundworms, can gain entry to the dog by infected mosquitos; others are hosted by snails. Most occurrences are in tropical countries, though they are not unknown in parts of Europe. Infested dogs exhibit limb stiffness, dejection and loss of weight. Treatment with levamisole and dithiazine iodide have been effective.

Bladder worms, causing cystitis, may be the result of infection with the roundworm *Capillaria*, and the kidneys may be badly damaged by a large worm known as *Eustrongylus*. Coughing and vomiting, followed by loss of weight and breathing difficulties, may indicate the presence of a roundworm (*Oslerus*) in the trachea and can become a serious problem in young dogs especially. Thiabendazole has proved an effective treatment against this worm.

As well as the fluke attacking the lungs there are two other forms of roundworm (including another member of the *Capillaria* family) which can live and reproduce in the respiratory passages. Eggs are coughed up and swallowed, passing into the faeces, and hatched larvae find their way into molluscs which are in turn eaten by various creatures, including rodents and birds. Scavenging dogs then ingest the larvae, which penetrate the mucous membrane lining the stomach and intestines, travelling subsequently via the lymphatic system to the lungs. The liver, too, can be damaged by migrating parasites, including several forms of roundworm.

The other major group of internal worms are flatworms – they are flat in cross-section. The commonest tapeworm found in the dog is *Dipylidium caninum*, which is frequently introduced by the dog flea, which carries the eggs. Lice may also carry them. Other forms of tapeworm have as intermediate hosts rats, sheep and rabbits. This form often causes intestinal inflammation by damaging the mucous membrane lining with the hooks on its head. Tapeworm heads bear suckers or hooks, depending on the species, and otherwise resemble dirty white tape when whole. Individual segments (which can each be mobile) sometimes appear in the hair round the anus, like small maggots or grains of rice, though a complete tapeworm may be as long as 45cm (18in) or more. Each segment operates individually and carries eggs. Intestinal obstruction can be caused by tapeworms but symptoms are often difficult to diagnose. There may be a vague indigestion and sometimes increased appetite. The tapeworm *Taenia* makes its appearance in a variety of forms, and its larvae penetrate the intestinal wall producing cysts. Some of these tapeworms develop into bladderworms, and the most common type of *Taenia* to infect the dog has the rabbit as its intermediate host. Scavenging dogs and some farm dogs are particularly vulnerable to tapeworms and a sound diet is important in prevention. Treatment is by means of a special anthelmintic such as mebendazole, praziquantel or bunamidine.

Hookworms are blood feeders and attack the external skin of dogs (eg between toes) where they cause irritation, and also internally where they damage the intestinal wall, keeping an open wound to take a constant flow of blood as nourishment. Dogs infested with hookworm are anaemic, lose weight and become dejected. Young puppies may become infected through the milk of a dam which has not been wormed prior to whelping. Treatment is by means of a suitable anthelmintic including mebendazole, pyrantel pamoate and, for older dogs, dichlorvos.

Whipworms inhabit the colon and caecum and produce symptoms which include diarrhoea and a dull coat. Eggs ingested can live for up to five years and adults for almost a year and a half. Eggs are often passed in the faeces though they may be difficult to

parasites

detect. Repeated treatment with such drugs as mebendazole is necessary and careful hygiene to prevent reinfection is important.

While flukes in various forms can infect the livers and lungs of dogs in tropical climates and in parts of Europe and North America, they are relatively uncommon in the UK. In the USA particularly, a form of fluke ingested when eating salmon can cause gastrointestinal poisoning and patients require treatment with oxytetracycline and fluid therapy. Liver flukes which normally attack sheep and cattle in the UK can sometimes cause trouble in dogs, though cases are rare. In America and Asia the fluke *Paragonimus* can infect the lungs, producing lesions that may be mistaken for tuberculosis, as well as bronchitis.

Much prevention of worm infestation can be achieved by giving the dog a sound diet and wherever possible stopping it scavenging or devouring rubbish or carrion. Feeding cooked meat (or prepared dog foods) reduces the risk of infestation. Regular worming is an important preventive measure against the common endoparasites. Regular grooming, coat care and early effective use of suitable dog shampoos are the best forms of protection against ectoparasites. (See also anthelmintics; bathing; worming procedures.)

parasitic diseases

Many organs can be affected by the ravages of parasites. While ectoparasites attack the skin (and some are vectors for the eggs of endoparasites and so contribute to a double infestation), endoparasites cause damage to such organs as lungs, liver, heart, kidneys, trachea, oesophagus, bladder, stomach and, most commonly, to the intestines. Among the general parasitic diseases of the dog are coccidiosis, jaundice, leishmaniasis, toxoplasmosis, and trypanosomiasis, although localised inflammation and infection in an organ may cause additional complications and disorders. (See also parasites.)

parasitology

The study of parasites and associated disease.

parathyroid

There are two pairs of parathyroid glands, one on each of the right and left lobes of the thyroid gland. Each measures about 2 to 5mm ($\frac{1}{12}$ to $\frac{1}{5}$in) in the average dog. The secretion of parathyroid hormone from these glands controls the level of calcium and its relationship with phosphorus in the blood. Reduced secretion will cause muscular twitching, tremors and possibly convulsions. Overstimulation causes a loss of calcium by the bones into the blood from where it is filtered by the kidneys and excreted in the urine. Urinary calculi develop and bones soften.

parenteral

By injection.

parotid

The parotid gland is a salivary gland situated at the junction of the head and neck. There are also accessory parotid glands on both sides and all have ducts opening into the mouth. (See also salivary glands.)

Inflammation of the parotid gland. Most commonly caused by the mumps virus, although bacteria can also produce inflammation which may lead to the formation of an abscess in the parotid. Symptoms include pain and tenderness at the junction of the head and neck. **parotitis**

See whelping. **parturition**

A highly dangerous virus-based disease which claims many canine lives. It is easily passed from one dog to another and can be a scourge of kennels and dogs' homes. In breeding kennels, adult dogs may be infected first and puppies which contract the disease are especially vulnerable, with a mortality rate often as high as 90 per cent, some dying within the space of twelve hours. Those that survive build an immunity which, it is hoped, will last the dog's lifetime. **parvo virus**

Some dogs appear to have only mild attacks which produce an immunity, and bitches affected in this way pass on immunity to their pups. Large litters, though, with each pup receiving less colostrum from the dam can expect a lower resistance than small litters.

In kennel outbreaks it has been found that blood samples taken from dogs affected mildly and evaluated in the laboratory can form the basis for providing immunity to others. The serum is separated from the cells and used to inject five-week-old pups with a high rate of success. Proprietary vaccines are also available and each dog should be immunised routinely in puppyhood with repeat booster injections later in life. This cannot, however, always provide total protection against parvo virus.

Dehydration is one of the most hazardous complications of parvo virus disease which produces severe diarrhoea, gastroenteritis and gastrointestinal bleeding. The patient rapidly becomes weaker, is in considerable pain and, while some breeds (and individuals) fight for life better than others, many succumb within the first forty-eight hours. Myocarditis is an additional complication which occurs in some patients as the virus attacks the heart.

The rapid administration of fluids to counteract dehydration is essential, and careful, continuous nursing offers the patient a better chance of survival. In kennels, dogs and puppies should be nursed in isolation wards.

The lowest part of the leg below the knee or hock and above the foot. **pastern**

The knee-cap. This is an oval-shaped bone which forms the joint of the knee with the lower end of the femur on the hind legs. The patella is the dog's largest sesamoid bone (one which is formed in tendon to ease its passage over another bone surface). (See also stifle.) **patella**

A micro-organism or substance which causes disease. Some micro-organisms which exist harmlessly in one area of the body may become pathogenic in others. **pathogen**

pathology The science which studies the causes and nature of disease and the changes brought about in the body as a result.

paw The dog's paw is the equivalent of the human hand (forepaw) and foot (hind paw). The skin of the digital pads is the toughest part of the dog's skin and is thick and pigmented. The roughness of the surface is due to conical papillae which may become rounded if the dog is exercised regularly on concrete or otherwise roughened ground.

    Dense connective tissue forms the epidermal layer beneath this tough surface and also provides a base for the papillae. The digital cushion below consists of fibrous adipose tissue in which the sweat glands (with ducts through this and the layer above to the surface) are situated. This tissue acts as a cushion for the metacarpal (and metatarsal) bones and for the joints between phalanges. (See also cyst.)

    The pads of the feet can sometimes become cracked through much activity on rough ground, or they can be cut by sharp objects such as glass, or stone-bruised. Such injuries may cause lameness and wounds, of course, require careful attention. Healing is often difficult due to the fact that the feet are constantly in use but, after gentle cleansing with a warm saline solution (see entry) and, if necessary, dressing with a suitable ointment, the foot may be cushioned with a large pad of cotton wool and lightly bandaged. A tight bandage can impair circulation and cause serious damage to the foot. If a cut is severe, sutures may be necessary. (See also claws.)

pedigree A pedigree dog is one of pure blood. A document which provides details of the parentage and ancestry of a pup should be passed to the new owner by the breeder and will have the pup's 'kennel name' added when registered and approved by the Kennel Club. If a dog is subsequently used for breeding, its own name, together with that of its mate and those of their respective immediate ancestors, appear on the pedigree forms of its offspring. The document also carries the registration number allocated by the Kennel Club which may be needed for shows, etc.

pellagra See black tongue.

pelvis The hind limb girdle which consists of the lower part of the spine (sacrum) and the two hip joints. It is a ring of bone with the sacrum at the centre, and its main purpose is to attach the hind limbs to the skeleton. The pelvis is broader and deeper in the bitch than in the dog to facilitate whelping. It encircles (in most dogs) the rectum and the prostate gland and neck of the bladder in the male, and the female reproductive organs.

    The pelvis may be fractured in, for example, road accidents and this may also result in rupture of the bladder.

pencils Puppies find pencils and crayons irresistible to chew. Many contain aniline dyes, however, (as does shoe polish) which destroys

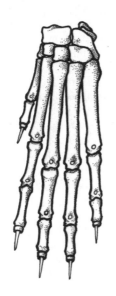

29 Skeleton of left forepaw

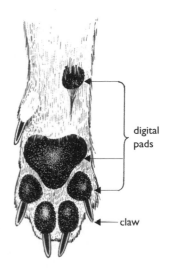

digital
pads

claw

30 The right forepaw showing pads and claws

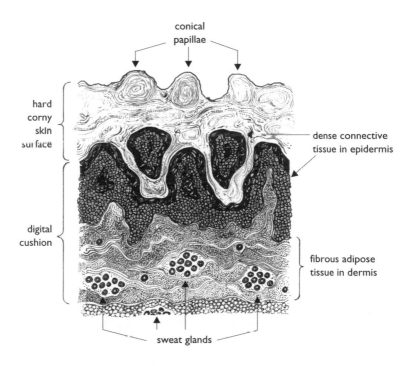

conical
papillae

hard
corny
skin
surface

dense connective
tissue in epidermis

digital
cushion

fibrous adipose
tissue in dermis

sweat glands

31 Cross-section of the digital pad

pencils | the haemoglobin of the blood. Symptoms of poisoning include vomiting, apathy and sometimes convulsions. A dog which has ingested aniline in this way may need its stomach washed out by a veterinarian, and oxygen and/or a blood transfusion may be necessary, together with drugs.

Chewed pencils can also be a potential hazard as foreign bodies. Pieces can become lodged in the throat, oesophagus or intestine causing damage and obstruction.

penicillin | The first antibiotic to be discovered and used. Other closely related antibiotics have subsequently been produced from it and it is effective against a wide range of infections. Its action is based on attacking the development of the cell walls of susceptible micro-organisms and rendering them useless.

penis | The penis is a tubular organ at the end of the urinary system which passes urine from the bladder, by means of the urethra which it accommodates, to the exterior. It is also the male reproductive organ with the task of depositing the male sperm into the vagina of the female during mating. It contains erectile tissue which fills with blood to stiffen it, facilitating entry into the vagina. The outside of the penis is covered with a skin sheath known as the pre-puce into which it retreats when not erect, and the free end, or glans, contains a bone – the os penis or baculum. This bone has a groove along which the end of the urethra passes.

pentobarbitone sodium | An anaesthetic (sodium ethylmethylbutyl barbiturate, also known as Nembutal), usually administered intravenously and used quite extensively to produce a variety of depths of unconsciousness. It can also be injected intraperitoneally, when its action is slower and recovery takes longer.

pepsin | An enzyme which is secreted by the walls of the stomach. Its task is to break down proteins in food to peptones during digestion for eventual absorption in the small intestine. It works best in an acidic environment and in the stomach this is assisted by the secretion of acid during the process. (See also digestion.)

peptides | 'Building bricks' for proteins. They are formed when two amino acids are joined together (more than two produces polypeptides), an action which binds all proteins.

pericarditis | Inflammation of the pericardium of the heart. It is a disease which usually develops over a period of time. It can be caused by an infection which produces a thick, copious fluid in the area which may interfere with the heart's action and have to be drawn off by a veterinarian. It can also be caused by a sharp foreign body puncturing the diaphragm.

pericardium | The surrounding outer sac of the three coats of the heart. It consists of a fibrous outer layer and an inner serous membrane which, in good health, keeps the heart surface smooth and moist by means of the serum secreted from it.

pericardium

The tissue area between the anus and the scrotum in the male dog and between the anus and the vulva in the bitch. Rupture may occur in whelping, requiring suturing, and sometimes in elderly male dogs.

perineum

The connective tissue which surrounds and protects bone. It is rich in blood vessels carrying nourishment to the bone. If torn away, the bone beneath will die but if disease or injury should destroy the bone leaving the periosteum intact, new bone will be generated by the provision of cells from the periosteum to repair the injury. Periosteum is not present on joints but is replaced by cushioning cartilage.

periosteum

The muscular action which propels food from the top of the oesophagus down to the stomach and subsequently from the stomach through the remainder of the digestive system. The action is the result of a series of muscular contractions and dilations by the muscle coat of the oesophagus and intestines.

Peristalsis also occurs elsewhere in the body: for example, in the ureter which possesses a muscular coat and uses peristaltic contractions to push urine towards the bladder from the kidneys. If a blockage should occur in the ureter this muscular action is impeded, resulting in spasm and the pain associated with renal colic.

peristalsis

A serous membrane lining the abdomen and surrounding the organs in the abdominal cavity (the pleura is its equivalent in the chest cavity).

The peritoneum serves to carry blood vessels and nerves to the abdominal organs, to attach some organs to the abdominal walls for support and to prevent friction between organs and the wall of the abdominal cavity, secreting serum for lubricating and moistening contacting surface areas. The fluid produced is constantly drained away into the lymphatic system.

peritoneum

Inflammation of the peritoneum. It is due to infection or irritation within the abdominal cavity and is one of the most dangerous complications of a number of abdominal disorders, including ulcerative colitis, strangulated hernia, intestinal puncture from accident or disease, extension of inflammation from other regions, damage to the urinary system (with urine contaminating the area) and foreign bodies. The liberation of bile or pancreatic enzymes into the abdominal cavity can also result in peritonitis.

In the acute form, large volumes of fluid build up in the abdomen. As the infecting bacteria are absorbed, toxaemia follows with an increase in body temperature, rapid pulse and respiration, sometimes vomiting, shock and collapse. Pain and tenderness, often severe, are present in the abdomen and abdominal muscles are

peritonitis

peritonitis	frequently hard and rigid. Paralysis of the small intestine can contribute to the death of the patient unless treatment is received as soon as the first symptoms appear.
	Treatment of peritonitis is similar to other abdominal infections though urgency is of the utmost importance if the dog's life is to be saved. The infection must be fought with antibiotics and the effects of dehydration need to be counteracted with fluids. Blood calcium levels should be monitored and shock treated. Surgery may be necessary to drain any abscesses, etc. Useful antibiotics include penicillin, ampicillin and gentamicin.
perspiration	See sweating.
Perthe's disease	A deformity of the head of the femur, characterised by lameness. It shows up during radiography. It may be caused by interference with the blood supply to the area due to an injury (even a minor one). It often clears up on its own though assistance can be provided by a temporary splint to provide support while the bone grows normally.
pessary	A drug compound for insertion in various cavities and orifices of the body. Pessaries are useful for treating infections in the uterus, where they dissolve to allow their contents to act locally. Pessaries can also be used to prevent conception immediately after a misalliance.
pesticides	Many pesticides, including those used to control household and garden pests, and contained in agricultural sprays, can be hazardous and frequently lethal to dogs. Check with manufacturers (and preferably a veterinarian) before using any pesticide in areas where dogs will be. Keep dogs clear of farmland when crop spraying is in progress and away from all areas suspected of being dressed with pesticides. (See also poisoning.)
Pet Animals Act, 1951	An Act which covers (among other issues) the licensing and inspection of pet trading establishments in the UK. The Pet Trades Association runs symposia and examinations in pet shop management and any owners of premises which appear to be below standard can be prosecuted under the Act. If pet shops are selling dogs which are sick or being held in less than adequate conditions, a report of the situation should be made to the local authority and the Royal Society for the Prevention of Cruelty to Animals.
pethidine	A useful analgesic, administered by injection to relieve pain. It has a similar action to morphine, to which it is related.
phagocyte	A devouring cell. The white cells of the blood engulf and ingest bacteria as a means of overcoming infection. The process is known as phagocytosis. Those white cells known as polymorphonuclear leucocytes are phagocytes of which the principal type is the neutrophil. Others are basophils, eosinophils and monocytes. (See also blood.)

A book published in various countries to provide details of the standards on individual pharmaceuticals, eg British Pharmacopaeia, European Pharmacopaeia, US Pharmacopaeia. Doses and origins of each drug are listed and information is given on associated laboratory tests. (See also veterinary codex.) **pharmacopaeia**

Inflammation of the pharynx. The most common cause is catarrh and it is a symptom of other disorders such as tonsillitis and various throat infections. Severe pharyngitis may be due to an irritant in the air breathed in or to the presence of a foreign body such as a chip of wood lodged in the pharynx. **pharyngitis**

The chamber at the back of the throat which commonly serves the respiratory and digestive systems. There are nasal, oral and laryngeal regions of the pharynx and it is divided by the palate into the upper nasopharynx leading from the nasal passages, and the lower portion where food is passed from the mouth into the oesophagus. The laryngopharynx is mainly concerned with the act of swallowing, receiving food from the back of the tongue and, by muscular constriction, passing it to the oesophageal entrance. **pharynx**

While air passes into the nasopharynx from the nasal region, it is also drawn in orally when the dog pants and this air combines with that from the nose in the pharynx to pass into the trachea.

The epiglottis is situated at the back of the pharynx and the Eustachian tubes lead from the ear into the nasopharynx, where the tonsils are.

An antipyretic (anti-fever) drug which reduces pain and lowers the temperature but does not combat infection. **phenacetin**

A sedative drug, obtainable through a veterinarian, which is useful in nervous disorders, particularly hysteria, and as an anticonvulsant. It can be administered by injection intramuscularly and intravenously, or orally in tablet form. Sedation can last for several hours. **phenobarbital**

A group of chemicals found in household cleaning agents, domestic disinfectants, etc; they are toxic when ingested and often when in contact with the skin. (See also poisoning.) **phenols**

Characteristic produced by the interaction of genes and environmental influences, eg a dog may be black spotted or liver spotted, of a large or small strain. Various combinations of parent genes and environmental situations produce a wide variety of appearances to be passed on to subsequent generations. **phenotype**

A useful analgesic in joint and muscle disorders to reduce pain and inflammation. It has been used with success in arthritic conditions. It can be given orally or by injection. **phenylbutazone**

A drug, diphenylhydantoin, used as an anticonvulsant. It can be given orally, often with phenobarbital. It is prescribed rather for **phenytoin**

phenytoin	long-term prevention than for emergency use: it is poorly absorbed by the gastrointestinal tract and several days of treatment may be needed before results are evident.
pheromone	A substance which acts as a chemical communication signal. Pheromones are contained in various body scents and their effect on individuals of the same species results in a change in behaviour. In some ways they resemble hormones, being produced in glandular tissue. A bitch in oestrus produces an odour containing pheromones which attracts and excites the male sexually.
phlebitis	Inflammation of a vein or, strictly, of its lining. Phlebitis is caused when a vein is damaged by, for example, a blood- or lymph-borne infection, a nearby abscess or, more rarely, by the use of a catheter in the vein after or during surgery. Blood cannot normally coagulate in a vein but if the vein's smooth lining is damaged blood-flow slows and platelets congregate, providing optimum conditions for thrombosis to occur. In a reverse situation, phlebitis may arise as a result of thrombosis in a vein – which may damage the lining of the vein by its obstruction. Treatment consists essentially of rest and the administration of anticoagulants in a carefully-monitored procedure by a veterinarian. If an infection is involved antibiotics may be prescribed.
phlebotomy	The surgical cutting of a vein; nowadays it refers to venepuncture, usually for the removal of a blood sample for laboratory examination. The radial vein of the upper foreleg is most commonly used for this purpose in the dog. In early veterinary medicine it was regular practice to 'bleed' a patient as a treatment for a variety of disorders, but this has long been recognised as useless.
phosphorus (in diet)	See nutrition.
phosphorus poisoning	See poisoning.
phymosis (or phimosis)	A condition where protrusion of the penis is impeded by a narrowing of the prepuce. The disorder is remedied – essential if a breeding dog is affected – by surgery in which the prepuce is cut to make the aperture wider.
physiology	The study of the ways by which living creatures operate their life processes. This study is usefully linked with anatomy to provide a total view of how the animal is 'assembled' and how its body works.
physiotherapy	The physical treatment of disease and disorders. Generally, the methods used most frequently involve the application of heat, cold, programmed exercise, massage and electricity, depending on the condition to be treated. Two basic forms of heat can be used, ie superficial and deep. Superficial heat can be produced by infrared lamps penetrating

only the surface of the body with their heat which is dispersed by circulation of the blood. This method can be useful for some skin problems but should not be used for inflammation. A more efficient method of applying superficial heat is often by means of hot, wet towels which produce a gentle heat but may be more uncomfortable for the patient in sensitive areas. These hot packs are helpful in arthritis and myositis. Deep heat, which can be produced by shortwave diathermy (currents from special electronic oscillators), ultrasound or microwave techniques have specific uses, and many contraindications. Such methods should be used only by specially-trained and experienced operators.

physiotherapy

Cold is relatively simple to apply and useful in such cases as acute inflammation and trauma – although prolonged treatment can cause frostbite. Cold packs used in a damp towel are convenient and cold immersion baths (with care taken not to overchill) can be used in heat stroke. Cold constricts the blood vessels, reduces pain and blood flow.

Careful exercise in therapeutic terms can strengthen muscles and bones, improve mobility and assist respiration and cardiac capability. It should be limited to the capacity of the patient's heart output and respiratory system. Such exercise during illness or while a patient is recovering should be carried out only on a programme determined with the help of a veterinarian. Passive exercise can also be useful, particularly in paralysis, paraplegia and when a slow recovery from injuries prevents active walking.

Massage, using hands gently to manipulate muscles and tissue, can be employed with warmth, heat or even cold treatments under appropriate circumstances. It soothes the patient, helps blood circulation and reduces oedema. Its main advantages lie in relaxing tightness in muscles, tendons and ligaments and in reducing chronic oedema. Firm, fast strokes will stimulate while soft, slow movements soothe and relax the dog.

Electricity, useful in such conditions as arthritis, neuralgia, and atrophy and weakness of muscles can also be used with an expert understanding of the subject.

Physiotherapy is a specialised form of treatment and, with the possible exception of some specific applications in first aid (such as the application of cold packs in heat stroke) and the use of massage for soothing purposes in appropriate conditions, it should only be practised by experts or under expert guidance. Before attempting any form of physiotherapy as a regular treatment of a sick or convalescent dog, discuss the matter with a veterinarian who will set up a programme if it is appropriate in improving the dog's health, speeding its recovery or relieving pain or other symptoms.

The function of this gland is somewhat obscure. It certainly has some form of inhibitory effect on the sexual drive though it is thought that it may have other roles to play. It is situated in the front of the midbrain, measures about 3mm by 1.5mm by 1mm in the average dog and is wedge-shaped and cream in colour.

pineal gland

pinna	The flap or entrance to the ear.
piperazine	A useful anthelmintic (diethylenediamine) for the treatment of roundworms. It is frequently found in proprietary compounds for worming dogs. (See also parasites; worming procedures.)
piroplasmosis	Also known as canine babesiosis, this is an uncommon disease in the UK and USA but well-known in the Far East. It also appears in parts of Europe. Sometimes called tick fever or malignant jaundice, it is caused by a parasite of the blood which is passed on by infection from a specific tick (*Babesia canis*). Red blood cells are destroyed by the parasite, producing anaemia, fever, raised temperature and rapid pulse and respiration. The spleen becomes enlarged, the dog weaker and often membranes of the mouth and eyes are tinged with yellow. Careful nursing is an important part of the treatment which includes the administration of such drugs as diaminodiphenyl ether.
pituitary	The pituitary gland, or hypophysis, takes its name from the early Greek word *pituita* meaning phlegm. It was once thought that this gland was responsible for the production of catarrhal secretions.
	In fact the pituitary gland is of major importance in the body for its control of the entire endocrine system and its part in influencing interrelated activities of the endocrine and nervous systems. Consequently, it has often been referred to as the 'master gland' of the body.
	The pituitary is situated on the underside of the midbrain and varies substantially in size between breeds as well as between male and female. (It is usually larger in the female if all other criteria are equal.) There are two lobes of the pituitary: the anterior and posterior. The anterior pituitary secretes a growth hormone which regulates the development and enlargement of all body tissues, and others which influence activities of the thyroid and adrenal glands. It also produces a group of sex hormones stimulating growth and activities of the testes of the male and the ovaries of the female. The posterior pituitary releases vasopressin and oxytocin; the former to act on the kidneys to prevent excessive water loss and the latter to cause contractions of the uterus and the flow of milk from the mammary glands during whelping.
	Laboratory tests are used to evaluate the competence of the pituitary if a deficiency is suspected. (See also endocrine system.)
placenta	The afterbirth which follows each pup at its birth or whelping. It develops from the outer layers of cells from the wall of the uterus at the point where the ovum became embedded in the endometrium. It includes the three foetal membranes, the chorion, amnion and allantois, and is part of the growing foetus, receiving the bitch's blood from the uterine wall and the developing pup's blood from its umbilical cord. It is in the placenta that the pup's blood absorbs nutrients, oxygen and water from its mother as they pass through a network of capillaries where they are exchanged for the waste

products from the pup's blood to be returned via the bitch's circulation for eventual excretion.

placenta

The placenta also produces hormones which pass into the bitch's circulation to maintain a state of pregnancy. (See also foetus; whelping.)

The fluid in which the cells of the blood are suspended. It is straw-coloured, containing water, chemical salts, nutrients, protein, waste products, antibodies and hormones which are transported in the blood circulation system to and from the tissues. It also contains coagulation components, which serum (the fluid of clotted blood) does not.

plasma

There are normal levels of most constituents of the blood and raised or reduced levels indicate specific diseases. Evaluation is carried out by means of laboratory tests. (See also blood.)

A white plaster, made from gypsum, which is used for casts to keep fractures immobile. Bandages impregnated with plaster of Paris are the most useful form, with padding provided between the surface of the limb and the cast itself. The application of plaster casts requires the expertise of a veterinarian since there is always the danger of localised pressure and resulting necrosis. A cast which is too heavy can cause a greater degree of muscle weakness and limb atrophy than would normally be anticipated from an immobilised limb. There is an additional hazard in that the dog may wish to chew the cast unless prevented, perhaps by an 'Elizabethan' collar (see entry).

plaster of Paris

A double danger to dogs and especially to puppies. Chewed and ingested plastic can cause obstruction in the alimentary tract, or in the trachea or throat, preventing breathing. Suffocation can also occur if a pup becomes enveloped in plastic sheeting or bags while playing.

plastic bags

Thrombocytes, originating in the bone marrow as early cell fragments and released into the bloodstream to assist in curtailing bleeding. They congregate to form a barrier at the entrance to a wound to reduce blood loss. When bleeding occurs they release an enzyme called thromboplastin which is a component of the blood coagulation mechanism. There are normally between 100,000 and 400,000 blood platelets per microlitre of blood. (See also blood; coagulation; thrombocytopaenia.)

platelets

Constructive play helps puppies grow and assists in the development of their personalities and intelligence. It is important for all healthy dogs, though older ones may be less interested.

play

Play can be a stimulatory form of behaviour, a utilisation of surplus energy, a repetition of rewarding activities and a process of learning to adjust to other creatures and environment, perfecting skills and assimilating information. Dogs most certainly enjoy a game, eg retrieving a thrown ball, particularly when their owners

play

participate. In play with canine contemporaries, mock aggression or simulated mating may be part of the exercise and, when playing alone, puppies in particular enjoy chewing and manipulating objects around them.

Planned play helps in training, stimulates mental alertness, improves muscle control and assists in forming a bond between dog and owner. Never play too long so that the pup or dog tires or becomes bored. Regular sessions, for example, on a walk, keep a healthy dog's interest alive and ensure that its exercise is of maximum benefit. (See also exercise; training.)

pleurae

The serous membranes which line the walls of the thoracic cavity and cover the lungs and diaphragm. They are in the form of two 'envelopes', one on each side of the chest cavity, and are known as pleural cavities although they are not cavities in the true sense of the word unless a lung is prevented from expanding. The serum secreted by the pleural membrane lubricates and moistens the organs and chest walls, reducing friction. In disease, fluid may collect in the pleural cavities, hampering the movement of the lungs. The pleurae are equivalent to the peritoneum in the abdominal cavity.

pleurisy

Inflammation of the pleurae, sometimes called pleuritis. It is usually caused by a bacterial or viral infection in the chest area or even spreading from the abdomen in some cases. Perforation of the chest wall can be a source of the infection or, as is often the situation, it can be a complication of pneumonia, tuberculosis or a secondary condition of lung disease. Fluid secreted by the pleurae increases as a result of the inflammation and a fibrous deposit on the lungs may attach them to the chest wall. If fluid volumes are large a lung may collapse.

Symptoms include much difficulty in breathing, dejection, fever, pain on the affected side and sometimes a dry, rasping cough. Early veterinary attention is essential and fluid may need to be drawn off. Treatment includes the use of antibiotics and analgesics with rest and restriction of movement on the affected side to reduce pain. Patient, compassionate nursing is required in a warm, draught-free, peaceful environment to increase the patient's chances of recovery.

pneumonia

See bronchopneumonia.

pneumothorax

Air in the pleural cavity which collects between the chest wall and the lungs reducing the lung's capacity to expand and restricting respiration. It can be caused by air leaking out from a diseased lung or by a penetrating wound of the chest. Symptoms of distressed breathing and some pain following an accident or fall may indicate pneumothorax and treatment may include aspiration of the air from the cavity. Sometimes a puncture of the chest can occur in a dog fight and any chest wound, however minor, should be immediately covered with a dressing to prevent the entry of air; if possible use a thick lint pad held in place with surgical tape or sticking plaster. A veterinarian should be consulted as soon as possible.

A dog can be accidentally poisoned by many substances and liquids. Puppies are the most vulnerable since they are more inquisitive and uninhibited by training. The great majority of canine poisoning cases, however, could be prevented by awareness of the dangers and elementary precautions on the part of owners. Generally, household chemicals, garden pesticides and herbicides and human medicines cause the most damage to dogs. Among specific substances the following is just a representative selection: household cleaning agents, fuel oil, fire extinguishers, pencils and crayons, shoe and furniture polishes, matches, paint and paint remover, paraffin, turpentine, laundry and perfumed soaps, quicklime, hair lacquer, cosmetic accessories, antifreeze, rubber solvents, adhesives, weed and pest killers, many household aerosol sprays, alcohol, washing powders, bleach, putty, mothballs, tobacco, golf balls, some linoleum and most human medicines in the quantities that the dog is likely to absorb them. Most acids and alkalis are extremely poisonous and those substances which are likely to poison humans are equally likely to be poisonous to the dog – although in much less quantity.

In cases of poisoning it is important to contact a veterinarian with minimal delay, if possible giving information on the poison itself. Immediate first-aid measures include making the dog vomit by means of an emetic (unless strong acids or alkalis have been ingested, in which case give sodium bicarbonate to neutralise the acid, or vinegar and lemon juice to neutralise an alkali). A strong salt solution or a teaspoonful of salt on the back of the tongue are the best emetics. If given quickly they may lessen the damage by preventing absorption of the poison into the digestive system. After the dog has vomited, egg whites beaten with milk may be given and the vomit retained for veterinary examination. If the skin is contaminated wash liberally with water.

Few poisons have specific antidotes though, for example, Epsom salts are useful against lead, phosphorus and arsenic, and butter or other fats against strychnine. These usually only have a palliative effect and it is essential that the effects of the poison on the dog are treated by the veterinarian when as much of the poison as possible is washed or purged from the system.

Symptoms of poisoning vary considerably though perhaps the common aspect of all forms of poisoning is that the dog is obviously unwell, and may even be in a coma. Respiration may be fast or slow, the dog may be dejected or excited or even in a state of collapse. There may be some evidence around that the dog has ingested a poison, so be observant and search for clues if necessary. There is often vomiting and diarrhoea (but not always) and sometimes salivation.

Some pollens can cause sensitivity. Those individuals that are sensitised may be affected by symptoms of hay fever, urticaria or respiratory problems. (See also allergy.)

A polymorphonuclear leucocyte or white blood cell with a lobed nucleus. It is a phagocyte and is present in the blood in increased

polymorph	numbers during acute inflammatory disease. Neutrophils, basophils and eosinophils are all termed 'polymorphs'. (See also blood.)
polyp	A term describing various tumours, all identifiable by a stalk-like attachment to the tissue from which they emerge. While most polyps are benign, some may prove malignant. Polyps, which are treated by surgical removal, are found generally in the female reproductive organs, the nose and in the bladder. (See also tumour.)
polypeptides	See peptides.
polysaccharides	Complex carbohydrates, including starch, glycogen, etc, which are made up of many simple forms of sugar. They are present in food-stuffs and in the nutrients formed from some carbohydrates by the process of digestion.
polyuria	Passing of excessive amounts of urine. Normal amounts are around 25ml per kilogram (approximately ⅔fl oz per lb) of body weight per twenty-four hours; over 50ml in a twenty-four-hour period for every kilogram of body weight (1¾fl oz per lb) can be considered excessive. Polyuria can be a symptom of kidney inflammation, liver disease or diabetes. It can also be the result of nervousness or even cold on a temporary basis, but continued polyuria indicates that there is a need for additional veterinary investigation, especially if other symptoms are apparent. (See also urination.)
portal vein	The major vein to the liver which collects from various branches the absorbed products of digestion for diffusion into the liver by a fine network of capillaries. It carries blood from the alimentary tract to the liver.
posterior	Situated behind. The opposite of anterior.
post-mortem	See autopsy.
post-operative	Following a surgical operation. (See also nursing for post-operative care.)
post-partum	Following whelping.
potassium	See electrolytes; nutrition.
poultice	A substance used for applying heat to a particular body area to dilate the blood vessels, accelerate healing by encouraging an influx of white cells, and to reduce oedema, the fluid being carried away from the area in the dilated blood vessels. The usual material used for poultices is kaolin (bread is a substitute). It is made into a paste and heated before being spread on a pad of gauze. An additional piece of gauze is used to cover it, making a 'sandwich' to prevent the kaolin sticking to the fur or skin. It should be applied to the skin only if the heat can readily be

borne on the back of the hand. A thick pad of cotton wool on top of the poultice when it is in place helps to keep the heat in.

Medicines are sometimes administered in powder form, often mixed into solution before being given orally to the patient. Fine powder particles can also be used for topical application, eg an antibiotic powder puffed onto a wound. Powders are not recommended for use inside the dog's ear (eg for otitis treatment) since they cannot drain away naturally and, for this purpose, liquid preparations are considered preferable. (See also dusting powder.)

powders

A synthetic corticosteroid used as an anti-inflammatory drug. It has also been utilised in the treatment of viral pneumonia.

prednisone

The period between conception and birth, or whelping. A bitch should receive special care during pregnancy.

pregnancy

Diagnosis of pregnancy is made usually around the twenty-third day after mating when the several foetuses can be felt by expert hands, arranged rather like a series of beads. Around the thirtieth day, fluid surrounds the developing foetuses and they are therefore more difficult to detect by palpation. By the fifth or sixth week they are again evident as they have grown substantially. During pregnancy some (or even all) of the foetuses may be reabsorbed by the bitch, often around two or three weeks after mating.

The bitch should not be subjected to highly active exercise during pregnancy; a gentle, steady walk is, however, beneficial and she should not be allowed to become fat.

Mammary glands develop noticeably around the sixth week and the nipples become enlarged. By this time the increase in size of the abdomen will show visible evidence of pregnancy. (See also breeding; foetus; gestation; whelping.)

False or pseudopregnancy is fairly common and is a condition where all the signs of pregnancy are apparent but there is no foetus. The bitch's abdomen enlarges, the uterus swells and mammary development frequently occurs with limited secretion of milk. The bitch is often somewhat bewildered herself and may be especially attentive to her bed or make a 'nest'. Some carry pieces of bedding or other soft objects around and may become possessive over them.

pregnancy, false

This condition can affect a virgin bitch or one which has previously been mated, and usually wears off with the organs and tissues returning to normal. Hormone treatment is sometimes necessary. In some untreated cases pyometra or mastitis may occur. Spaying may be considered in such situations.

See whelping.

premature birth

The administration of such drugs as tranquillisers prior to surgery. Apart from having a calming effect such drugs eliminate two difficult stages of anaesthesia which may occur before the state of general surgical anaesthesia is achieved. These are the stages of,

premedication

premedication	firstly, voluntary excitement where the dog may hold its breath, struggle and become distressed, and secondly, involuntary excitement which may include irregular respiration, exaggerated reflexes and violent movements of the limbs when consciousness is first lost.
prepuce	The sheath of skin covering the penis of the male dog. Inflammation sometimes occurs inside the prepuce giving rise to a yellowish discharge. It is the result of an infection from a specific organism (mycoplasma) and requires treatment with appropriate drugs by a veterinarian. Foreign bodies such as grass seeds can also become trapped under the prepuce causing extreme irritation and subsequent infection.
presentation	The way the pup is produced from the vagina during whelping. Anterior presentation is head first and posterior presentation is when the tail comes first. (See also breech presentation; whelping.)
preventive medicine	Preventing a disease or disorder is far better than curing it. Many cases of ill-health in dogs can be prevented with awareness of certain potential hazards and by taking appropriate precautions. Of course, some diseases cannot be prevented because the circumstances are such that the dog has no chance to avoid them.

Basic preventive 'medicine' begins with a sound diet and correct nutrition, regular exercise and adequate housing. In such cases as heat stroke, for example, the large majority of cases which arise could be prevented with no more than a measure of common sense. Accidents on the road and in the house can be avoided if sensible precautions are taken (such as keeping a dog on the lead when traffic is around, or shutting it out of a kitchen when boiling water, hot fat, etc, is being handled). Most cases of poisoning can be prevented if household and garden chemicals are stored and used out of a dog's reach.

Immunisation is an important aspect of preventive medicine – avoiding with comparative ease not only individual illnesses (and frequently death), but also the spread of disease. (See also accidents; immunisation; poisoning.)

primigravada	A bitch undergoing her first pregnancy.
procaine hydrochloride	A substance used as a local anaesthetic. It is considered less toxic and equally efficient as cocaine and is sometimes combined with adrenaline to reduce haemorrhage in minor surgery.
progesterone	A female sex hormone originally from the corpus luteum of the ovary. It is secreted by the ovary in the early stages of pregnancy and subsequently by the placenta. It maintains the state of pregnancy and stimulates the uterus to support the fertilised ova, reducing associated muscular activity so that they are not dislodged. The activation of the mammary glands, commenced by oestrogens, is also maintained by progesterone.

A forecast of the course and likely outcome of a disease or illness, with some emphasis on recovery. Various factors are considered in making a prognosis: knowledge of the disease, condition of the patient and severity and effect of symptoms.

prognosis

See retina, atrophy of.

progressive retinal atrophy

A hormone secreted by the anterior lobe of the pituitary gland which stimulates lactation following whelping.

prolactin

The misplacement of an organ. Most frequently it affects the uterus or the rectum. Uterine prolapse, which may occur after whelping, is a serious condition requiring urgent veterinary attention. Anaesthesia is needed while the uterus is replaced, which may or may not be relatively simple to accomplish. Surgery may be needed, together with the administration of antibiotics and possible treatment for shock. Sometimes a complete hysterectomy is the only course of action.

prolapse

Rectal prolapse is most common in puppies but can also happen to older dogs. It can be the result of colitis, the presence of foreign bodies or tumours. Severe, prolonged attacks of diarrhoea can cause it and, under such conditions, the weakened dog seems more vulnerable to prolapse. Veterinary assistance is essential and surgery may be needed under anaesthetic.

The condition can be recognised as the misplaced organ usually protrudes quite clearly from the associated orifice (the vagina in the case of uterine prolapse and the anus where rectal prolapse is concerned).

Prolapse of discs of the spinal vertebrae is also not uncommon in dogs. Pressure on the spinal cord or injury to the spinal nerves results, producing pain and paralysis.

A member of the phenothiazine group of tranquillising drugs, used both as a tranquilliser and as a premedication prior to general anaesthetic for surgery. It can be given by intramuscular or intravenous injection.

promazine hydrochloride

Preventive medicine, such as immunisation, which helps to prevent a specific disease. A prophylactic is an agent which helps to prevent or protect against a disease, especially an infectious form.

prophylaxis

A group of substances present in most tissues and derived from fatty acids. They may have similar effects to hormones, are known to stimulate the uterus, inducing labour, and are artificially used to control oestrus.

prostaglandins

The prostate gland is a male accessory sex gland, adding its secretions to semen. It surrounds the urethra at the neck of the bladder and has several openings into the urethra.

prostate

prostate	Enlargement of the prostate occurs in some aged dogs or as a result of an infection. The condition is usually treated either with injections of stilboestrol or, as a last resort, castration which curtails the activities of the gland, allowing it to atrophy. Symptoms of an enlarged prostate include stiffness of the hind legs when walking, pain and discomfort in the region of the pelvis. The passage of urine is usually obstructed and, if the gland is much enlarged, there will be difficulty in defecation due to pressure on the rectum.
	The action of hormones, including androgens, can apparently influence disease of the prostate since excessive androgen release experimentally produces prostatic enlargement. Malignant disease of the prostate is uncommon in dogs but does arise occasionally.
prosthesis	Replacement of part of the body by an artificial appliance. It is rarely performed in dogs since, for example, if a limb is amputated, the patient can usually manage better on three legs than with a new encumbrance. (See also amputation.)
Protection of Animals Act (1911)	An Act designed to protect animals in the UK from cruelty and malpractices.
proteins	See nutrition.
proteinuria	Protein being passed in the urine. They may appear when a dog has been excessively exercised, in cases of stress or following convulsions, or merely because the dog has eaten substantial amounts of protein. Excessive protein secretion in the urine may be associated with kidney disease, inflammation of the lower part of the urinary tract, enlarged prostate in male dogs, or a genital tract infection. Protein levels in urine can be detected by laboratory tests.
prothrombin	One of the components of the blood-clotting mechanism, sometimes known as Factor II. It is produced by the liver in a process for which vitamin K is essential. Prothrombin is normally present in the plasma of the blood and thrombin develops from it as a stage in the coagulation process.
protoplasm	A general term which has been adopted to mean all parts of the cell, ie the nucleus, cytoplasm and membrane.
protozoa	Single-celled primitive organisms which can cause infection inside the dog. An example is trichomonas which causes an inflammatory infection of the vagina and alimentary tract. They can be detected by laboratory examination of faeces. The causative organisms of leishmaniasis and trypanosomiasis are both protozoan.
pruritis	Inflammation of the skin giving rise to itching. This symptom is associated with various skin diseases, allergies, ectoparasites and sometimes reactions to certain drugs. It can also be produced by a lack of grooming where a dog's hair becomes matted and dirty.

Sometimes it is the result of boredom or depression when a dog scratches as a form of stereotyped behaviour. Skin weals occur and often there is encrusting of the skin with bleeding. Treatment consists of eliminating the cause and healing the affected areas of the skin.

pruritis

The study of diseases of the mind. The dog can be seriously affected by stress caused by ill-treatment, an adverse environment, excessive prolonged noise, etc, which in turn is manifested in physical illness. Dog psychiatry, which is being developed in the USA, is an infant science – largely because communication between a human psychiatrist and a canine patient is difficult. An owner who knows his dog well can be most effective in eliminating a stimulus to psychiatric problems if and when they arise.

psychiatry

The study of behaviour and the working of the mind. Much is still obscure about the mind of the dog but studies have been made of the dog's ability to learn and respond and about the effect man and environment have on canine behaviour. While man's ability to use language helps him to teach and learn in a variety of complex ways and to absorb information rapidly, a dog has no such advantage and communication must be basic and simple if it is to be effective. If the human teacher is efficient most dogs are intelligent enough to learn all they need for a contented and rewarding life. (See also behaviour; communication; training.)

psychology

A drooping eyelid due to nerve paralysis associated with the muscle which activates the raising of the eyelid. It is often part of a more extensive paralysis and can follow head injuries. Unless damage is permanent or extensive through traumatic injury the condition usually disappears gradually.

ptosis

An enzyme of the salivary glands. It is released into the mouth where it mixes with food to reduce starch in carbohydrates to maltose sugar in preparation for absorption in the alimentary tract during digestion.

ptyalin

The earliest age at which a dog is capable of reproduction. Puberty in the dog is reached between six and thirteen months for both the bitch and male dog, though it is unwise to breed from a bitch before she is fifteen months old.

puberty

A curved piece of bone which makes up the front wall of the pelvis. Three bones are included in the pelvic girdle: the pubis, ilium and ischium.

pubis

Associated with the lungs, as in pulmonary arteries, pulmonary veins, etc. De-oxygenated blood returns from the body to the right side of the heart which pumps it into the pulmonary artery. This divides into two branches – the left and right pulmonary arteries – which carry the blood to the lungs for re-oxygenation. The

pulmonary

pulmonary   purified blood leaves the lungs via the four pulmonary veins which empty into the left side of the heart for eventual pumping round the body.

Excessive fluid in the lungs is known as pulmonary oedema and this may be associated with cardiac failure or with such conditions as heat stroke, shock, poisoning, electrocution, etc. In this disorder the fluid becomes frothy and rattles in the throat, obstructing the air passages. A veterinarian may spray the airways with anti-foaming substance, such as a 12 per cent solution of alcohol in water, by means of a nebuliser. (See also lungs.)

pulse   The expansion and distension of the aorta in response to the heart-beat produces a wave of distension and recoil which travels along the elastic arteries producing the sound of the pulse as an echo of the heartbeat. Consequently the rate of the pulse and heartbeat should be similar (around 70 to 140 beats per minute, varying according to size with fewer in larger animals, and in puppies substantially faster, up to about 210 per minute). The dog has a slightly irregular pulse normally and a veterinarian will often take the pulse with one hand while checking the heart-rate with the other.

The pulse is measured by applying the fingers to the inside of the thigh where the femoral artery can be felt close to the surface of the skin. It requires practice to find the exact spot. Alternatively, the inside of the foreleg can be palpated.

Pulse-rates can help to determine the health of a dog, usually together with other symptoms. The rate is faster in fevers, for example, and weak, thready pulses are found in shock and various heart conditions. A dog's pulse-rate is normally much faster following strenuous exercise but, in a healthy dog, quickly returns to normal. In sleep the pulse is slower.

Changes in pulse-rate are more significant than the exact rate at any given moment. After injury, for example, a pulse-rate may be in the normal range but increase subsequently indicating the possibility of internal bleeding.

pupil   A circular aperture in the centre of the iris of the eye through which light passes to reach the retina. (See also eye.)

puppies, care of   The care of puppies immediately after birth is dealt with under whelping. When puppies are purchased from a reputable breeder the new owner is usually provided with the pup's pedigree, a suggested diet sheet for the first few weeks in its new home and details of immunisation. The breeder will also give information on the basic needs of the pup as it grows.

A new home should be prepared before the pup arrives. A dog's immediate needs include a warm, draught-free place to sleep with adequate ventilation and room to move around, even at night. A suitable bed is required, together with bedding, a feeding bowl and dish for drinking water. Utensils should be easy to clean. An appropriate sized collar and lead are needed and a few safe toys (such as a ball no smaller than a tennis ball, perhaps an old leather belt with the buckle and decorations removed, a sterilised large bone, etc) will be acceptable to a playful puppy. A brush and other grooming equipment should also be included. The garden fence may need attention to prevent the loss of an inquisitive puppy which will seek out places to hide and escape. Poisonous chemicals, household cleaning agents, medicines, etc, together with dangerous objects should be removed to a place of safety where a pup cannot reach them.

In the early days it is best to provide the food suggested by the breeder so that the pup's diet is not suddenly and drastically changed at the same time as its environment. Some puppies take longer than others to settle to dietary changes. After weaning a puppy needs four meals a day until it is about three months old. A typical diet is made up as follows:

8.30am	Breakfast of milk and cereal (such as rusks or Shredded Wheat).
12.30pm	Beef mince and puppy biscuit meal in equal amounts.
4.30pm	Scrambled egg with brown bread soaked in milk. Rice pudding is an example of an alternative.
8.30pm	Repeat of the 12.30 meal.

Pork, liver or adult canned dog food should not be fed at this stage. Possible meat alternatives to minced beef include chicken, lamb, white fish or tripe. After three months of age a reduction to three meals a day can be made, for example, by gradually reducing the gap between the midday and afternoon meal until the latter can be eliminated. After four months of age two meals a day can be fed, again by reducing the interval between afternoon and evening feeding.

During the first few weeks at home the puppy's drinking water should be boiled and cooled before it is offered, and should be available at all times.

Puppies are usually wormed by the breeder and require additional worming by the new owner at around three months of age. Immunisation is carried out later.

While a puppy is young its life consists mostly of sleeping, eating, playing, urinating and defecating, and it should be allowed to do so at its own pace. Sleep is a vital part of the pup's life pattern and essential to its health. It must not be considered a toy to be woken when the family is ready to play: wait until the pup wakes of its own accord and wishes to play. While play is also necessary in developing the pup's personality and learning patterns, an excessive amount is harmful, causing over-excitement. It should never include any form of teasing.

A pup normally wants to urinate and defecate after a meal and house training can begin by regularly taking the pup into the garden and praising it when it is successful. It will often wish to urinate when it awakes from a sleep, too, so be prepared.

puppies, care of

Gentle grooming can be started when the pup is young; it is useful to allow it to familiarise itself with the equipment and procedures, making it a pleasurable process.

Consistency in commands, training, feeding and grooming is important if the pup is to learn what is expected of it. Be affectionate to a pup – it likes contact and much enjoys sleeping on an owner's lap, for example, which gives it a feeling of security.

Puppies are lively, if they are healthy; they also chew, lack control over bladder and bowels, and need almost as much care as an infant human. It is essential, therefore, that any prospective owner is prepared for the disruption to the household. Other members of the family, particularly children, should also be prepared and should be briefed about the pup's requirements. (See also beds and bedding; docking; choosing a dog; immunisation; microchipping; toys; training etc.)

purgative

A medicine which stimulates bowel action, nowadays rarely recommended for use. Laxatives, which have a much more gentle action than purgatives, are generally used instead. Some purgatives cause irritation of the lining of the intestines; some act only on the first portion of the alimentary tract and have no effect on the large intestine. Purgatives should only be considered on the advice of a veterinarian.

purpura

A bleeding disorder characterised by small haemorrhagic spots on the skin or mucous membranes. The cause is usually due to a platelet dysfunction or to a weakness of the capillary walls. There are various forms of purpura and in some, swellings are noticed around the mouth and parts of the body. Antihistamine injections are sometimes beneficial, indicating an allergic origin in some cases.

pus

A yellowish fluid which suppurates from abscesses, cavities and other sites of infection. It is a product of inflammation and consists of dead bacteria as a result of white blood cells attacking them, plus serum and debris of tissue damaged by the infection.

pyemia (pyaemia)

Pus in the bloodstream. The blood becomes infected with bacteria from an area of sepsis within the body, pus circulates in the bloodstream and other abscesses arise in other parts of the body.

pyloric stenosis

A narrowing or constriction of the pylorus of the stomach. It is generally due to a congenital defect which is fortunately rare in dogs, although obstruction of the pylorus can produce similar symptoms. There is vomiting when solid food is taken and only liquids can be retained, Surgery is the usual remedy.

pylorus

The strong sphincter muscle which is situated at the exit from the stomach. It prevents food returning to the stomach after it has passed through during the course of digestion. It also regulates the amount of food being released into the small intestine, opening and closing in response to nervous stimulation, so that gradual digestion can take place.

pylorus

A disease which results in the accumulation of pus in the uterus. Metritis may follow. Cystic changes occur in the mucous membrane lining the uterus due to a glandular dysfunction and excessive progesterone generation with the production of bacterial toxins. Two forms can affect the bitch and, while one is associated with a vaginal discharge, the other has no such symptoms, though pain and tenderness and often fever can be detected together with an appearance of restlessness and discomfort. It is most common in middle-aged virgin bitches although it is sometimes associated with a false pregnancy.

pyometra

Treatment is usually by means of surgical removal of uterus and ovaries. There may be complications involving the kidneys and the few days after the operation require very careful nursing to maximise the chances of recovery.

The word literally means 'flowing of pus' and has now become associated specifically with the discharge of pus from the gums due to inflammation and infection. If untreated the condition can undermine the teeth, damaging roots and loosening them. It is most frequently caused by a build-up of tartar on the teeth producing tiny pockets where bacteria can be harboured, setting up a site of infection which spreads along the gums. Treatment is generally by means of antibiotics, and prevention of at least some cases is possible by regular cleaning and descaling of teeth, especially when a dog is fed entirely on soft food.

pyorrhoea

Fever.

pyrexia

Vitamin B_6. There are, in fact, three related compounds: pyridoxine, pyridoxal and pyridoxamine, and a deficiency in diet causes weight loss and anaemia. Skin and coat disorders can also be the result of such a deficiency. (See also nutrition.)

pyridoxine

Pus in the urine with an abnormal presence of white blood cells which are seen microscopically in clumps. It occurs as a symptom of inflammation somewhere in the urinary tract and further investigation is usually required to determine the site of infection. Other associated symptoms may include fever, pain in the kidney region and retention of urine.

pyuria

quarantine

Virtually all mammals, including dogs but excluding farm live-stock and horses, are subject to quarantine regulations. However, dogs that qualify for the Pet Travel Scheme (PETS), introduced in February 2000, can enter and re-enter the UK without quarantine if they meet certain criteria. In the following sequence pet dogs must have an identification microchip implanted, be vaccinated when at least three months old against rabies, subsequently blood tested as evidence that the vaccine provides sufficient protection against rabies, and issued with an official PETS certificate. This document is completed and issued by a government-authorised veterinarian in the animal's home country. Under the PETS scheme, dogs also need to be treated against tapeworms and ticks and issued with certification of this treatment by a similarly authorised veterinarian. Approved routes of travel apply and the dog must not have been outside certain countries in the six months prior to travelling. The dog's owner will also be required to sign a declaration of residence for the dog. No dog is allowed to enter the UK under PETS until six months after the date of a successful blood test result.

Quarantine regulations vary around the world and it is always best to check these out with the embassy of the country of entry well before making travelling plans. (See also microchipping; rabies; Useful Addresses.)

quinsy

An abscess on the tonsil. This can be a complication of tonsillitis.

rabies

A highly infectious virus disease, fortunately non-existent in the UK due to its island position and the strength of the quarantine laws. In other countries the situation is less agreeable, although dogs can be protected by immunisation. There are, however, exceptions to this rule and it has been known for vaccinated dogs to contract the disease later.

Rabies is caused by a virus which attacks the nervous system and can affect a wide variety of warm-blooded creatures including man. This fact emphasises the need for quarantine enforcement since, if this law was relaxed, a single case in contact with stray dogs or wildlife would be sufficient to spread the disease out of control. It is almost always fatal.

Rabies produces a form of madness in dogs with other symptoms including anxiety following a slightly feverish condition and restlessness. The dog often cowers and hides and its temperament is frequently reversed. Vomiting and muscle spasms occur and the dog may sound a high-pitched bark, salivating and snapping at anyone who comes near. Lower jaw paralysis follows, extending to other parts of the body until the victim collapses with convulsions and eventually dies. The course of the disease is run up to about ten days.

This disease is often very difficult to diagnose in its early stages as symptoms are not specific to rabies and any suspect should be confined and isolated from human and animal contact. The incubation period varies with individuals from a week up to twelve months, hence the need for adequate quarantine and veterinary supervised precautions.

radiation

A process by which heat is transferred from a source to a point of reception without heating the intervening tissue. It is not generally used in veterinary medicine until other approaches have been exhausted as it is a somewhat drastic form of treatment which is not without its dangers to the patient. It can, however, be useful in cases of malignant growths or tumours where treatment may need to be repeated every seventy-two hours for a specific period.

radiography

Registering images on photographic material by means of X-rays. It is useful in medicine since the images depend on the various degrees of absorption of the substances through which the X-rays pass. This means that the thicker, solid substances amid the softer tissue can be seen with some clarity. In diagnosis, therefore, of such conditions as fractured bone, foreign bodies causing obstruction and dense tissue masses produced by tumours, radiography is a valuable aid. It is also widely used for the confirmation of the presence of gallstones, calculi and lung disease.

radius

A long bone of the forelimb between the humerus at the top and the carpus at the foot. It is one of two forelimb long bones, the other being the ulna. The radius is the main weight-supporting bone of

radius	the front limb, is shorter than the ulna which runs parallel with it, and has major forelimb muscles attached to it.
ranula	A swelling appearing beneath the tongue, either on the underside of the tongue itself or on the lower mouth. It is caused by blocked salivary ducts and, if necessary, can be removed by surgery.
rash	A term used to describe skin inflammation which is spread over one or more areas. It can be due to an allergy, local irritation or spots appearing as a manifestation of disease such as distemper or eczema.
rat-killer poisoning	See poisoning; strychnine.
rats	A source of disease for dogs. Apart from the fact that a cornered rat can be extremely vicious and inflict damage by biting, rat urine can carry the organisms of leptospirosis. A large percentage of rats are infected with this disease and dogs that are in constant contact with rat-infested areas run a substantial risk. Rat bites also cause infection, and wound cleansing is essential if a dog is bitten; the victim may also need treatment with antibiotics or sulphonamides.

Rats can also be responsible for food contamination in kennels where all food storage containers, as well as housing, should be rat-proof. They breed fast and, if conditions are attractive to them with an ample supply of food for the taking and adequate shelter, they will multiply and colonise the area. Local authorities usually employ a pest control officer and this service should be called upon to dispose of the pests in a way which does not harm other livestock on the premises.

The brown rat (*Rattus norvegicus*) is widespread in town and countryside and can be detected, not only by teeth marks and gnawed wood and piping, but by characteristic 'smears' where its greasy coat has rubbed along a wall in a regular pathway. Droppings are large and cylindrical, about 17cm (6in) long by 6mm (¼in) wide and extensive tunnel systems are constructed under floors, or hay ricks with nests usually at ground level.

rectal temperature	See temperature.
rectum	The portion of the large intestine between the descending colon and the anal canal. It is straight, about 5cm (2in) in length and 3cm (1¼in) in diameter. It is approximately level with the vagina in the bitch and the urethra and prostate in the male dog. The rectum is a reception area for faeces passed from the colon and held until evacuation from the anus is prompted. The lining is pitted with tiny lymph nodules which make faecal retention easier.

Foreign bodies sometimes lodge in the rectum although they have passed successfully through the remainder of the alimentary tract. Impaction of faeces also occurs and inflammation results. Rectal prolapse is not uncommon in dogs, and abscesses and tumours may also arise.

Symptoms of rectal disorders include difficulty passing faeces, haemorrhage in varying degrees, pain and discomfort with the dog turning round to its tail, or persistent diarrhoea. (See also intestines.)

rectum

The treatment of fractures where the ends of the broken bones are brought back into their correct position and maintained there by pinning or other means while the healing process takes place.

reduction

The ejection of undigested food, as opposed to vomiting. It can be due to an obstruction high up in the alimentary tract, most frequently in the oesophagus. Bitches feeding a litter of pups also sometimes regurgitate food for their pups to take. Such behaviour is not abnormal.

regurgitation

Failure of the kidneys. Kidney disorders are among the most common canine ailments. There can be many reasons for renal failure, including kidney disease, cardiac failure, obstruction of blood vessels to the kidneys, poisoning by antifreeze or, for example, by lead, arsenic or mercury. Accidents are a frequent cause, especially where there is damage to the urinary tract. In acute renal failure, death can occur within forty-eight hours, due largely to toxaemia as non-filtered waste products are retained in the bloodstream. Most acute cases of failure can be treated successfully, provided the patient can be kept alive long enough for the tissues to heal, usually a period of between ten and fourteen days. Since one of the kidney's main functions is to regulate the fluid balance of the body, dehydration needs to be corrected and stress may be a further complication. A special diet in convalescence is important. Such ingredients as boiled rice, scrambled eggs, milk, honey and toast are acceptable.

renal failure

Most bitches have two oestrus periods a year during which, at a specific time, they are ready for mating. Fertilisation of the female ovum by the male spermatazoon is effected in the Fallopian tube after injection of the sperm by the male penis into the vagina of the female. Division of the resulting zygote occurs within several hours; conception has taken place and pregnancy begins.

Around the eighteenth day of gestation the implantation of the blastocyst (the earliest stage of the embryo) takes place in the wall of the uterus. The embryo develops gradually within the uterus. It is crescent-shaped amid a yolk sac and connected to the physiological system of the dam by embryonic membranes which form the placenta. It is about 5mm ($\frac{1}{5}$in) in length by the twenty-third day. (See also breeding; foetus; mating; pregnancy; whelping.)

reproduction

Surgical operation in which part of an organ or bone is removed. Common examples include the removal of dead bone, diseased intestine or part of the ear damaged by chronic otitis.

resection

A process which may take place during early pregnancy in which some embryos are absorbed by the body. The process is usually

resorption

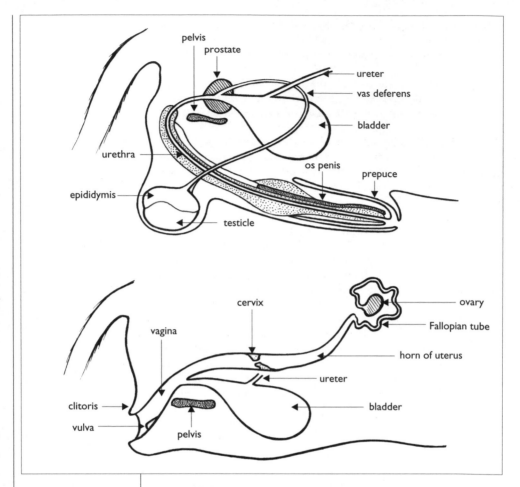

32 The male (above) and female (below) reproductive systems

resorption   partial and the mummified bodies of the embryos affected are delivered, along with the living, fully-developed members of the litter. Occasionally an entire litter is affected in this way and a cause may be a deficiency of vitamin A during early pregnancy or over-dosage with fertility hormones. An alternative reason for resorption is an infection and in such a case the expelled embryo may appear to be partially decomposed with a yellowish fluid surrounding it.

respiration   The process by which oxygen is taken into the body and exchanged for carbon dioxide. It takes place in the lungs which contain minute air chambers or alveoli with thin walls associated with the tiny blood vessels known as capillaries. Oxygen passes from the air into the blood, being absorbed by the haemoglobin of the red blood cells, and carbon dioxide passes from the blood to the air. Due to the difference in composition between blood and air a physio-logical attempt is made to equalise the composition which brings about the exchange – an attempt which remains unfulfilled because of the constant changes in both blood and air during the process of exchange and the two consequently never mingle.

The act of respiration is achieved by the body's respiratory system, consisting of a series of air passages and the lungs to which they eventually lead. Air is drawn in by means of muscular effort which involves the muscles and cartilage of the thorax and the dome-shaped diaphragm which contracts during the act of breathing in or inspiration. The effort enlarges the chest cavity and forces the expansion of the lungs to fill the resulting vacuum, sucking air down the passages. These passages comprise the left and right nasal cavities of the nose (where the air is warmed, cleansed and moistened), the nasopharynx, pharynx, trachea, and left and right bronchi which lead finally to the lungs.

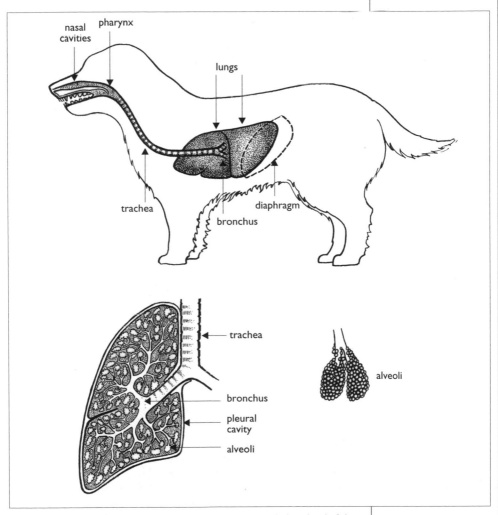

33 Schematic diagram of the respiratory system, including detail of the lung and alveoli with trachea and bronchus

respiration

Breathing out, or expiration, is achieved by a recoil effect involving the diaphragm, which pushes forward as the abdominal organs, displaced by its contraction for air intake, push back, and the action of the ribcage muscles and cartilage which complete the process.

Respiration is controlled by the nervous system and is under the direction of the medulla oblongata of the brain. The normal respiration rate of a dog at rest is ten to thirty times a minute. (See also lungs.)

responsibilities

See legal and moral responsibilities.

rest

Puppies need rest to revitalise themselves after play or energetic exercise and adult dogs should also be allowed to take rest as and when they feel like doing so. For a dog which is recuperating or convalescing, rest is important in promoting a full recovery.

Before the development of appropriate drugs, some diseases, eg tuberculosis, relied upon prolonged rest as the most effective form of treatment. In cases of severe inflammation rest promotes healing and, if infection is the cause, prevents a spread of bacteria. However, too much rest in some cases, particularly where injuries are concerned or where surgery has been carried out, may result in loss of function later. When in doubt it is often best to allow the dog to make the decision by resting when it wants and, when mobile, to supervise its movements if any part, such as a limb, is especially vulnerable to damage through increased activity.

restraint

See examination.

resuscitation

The act of restoring to life. Artificial respiration is the commonest method. External cardiac massage is another, used particularly for puppies which appear to have difficulty commencing breathing after delivery. The pup should be held in a head-down position and, if possible, the umbilical cord severed only after respiration has started. Some drugs are used after the first attempts at resuscitation, especially in cardiac patients. Victims of cold and exposure may benefit from prolonged attempts at resuscitation since cold reduces the body's need for oxygen. The patient should not be re-warmed rapidly since, for each rise in temperature of 10 degrees, between 2.5 and 3 times more oxygen is required. When cardiac and nervous system death have been indicated for about thirty minutes of continued resuscitation, and only after that time, survival chances are minimal. (See also artificial respiration.)

retained placenta

A complication of whelping which, unless the bitch is treated, can cause infection and metritis. There should be one placenta for each pup delivered and if one is missing it has almost certainly been retained (it may have been eaten by the bitch unobserved, of course). It is always sound practice after whelping to have the bitch checked over by a veterinarian who will give an injection of oxytocin to clear the uterus of any remaining debris and an antibiotic to prevent the establishment of any infection. At least 25 to 30 per cent of bitches retain some uterine debris following whelping.

retained placenta

See vomiting.

retching

Immature red cells of the blood. Their presence is significant, because increases or decreases indicate specific disorders. An increase in reticulocytes in the blood (seen microscopically in a specially stained blood-smear or 'film') can be indicative of internal bleeding. There is also a high reticulocyte count after splenectomy and in some forms of anaemia. A decrease may be due to damage or infection of the bone marrow.

reticulocytes

The reception centre of the eye which is light sensitive and contains two types of cell (rods and cones). (See also eye.)

retina

This disease is often known as 'progressive retinal atrophy' or night blindness since it is most evident when the light fails. A gradual atrophy of the nerve cells of the retina occurs and is demonstrated by the dog's staring expression as the pupils dilate widely, even in strong light, to correct the fault. As light diminishes at the end of the day the dog becomes more vulnerable and often bumps into objects it has avoided successfully during the day. It is a disease for which there is apparently no cure and the condition worsens until the victim becomes blind. No animal having the disease should be used for breeding as it is at least partially hereditary in origin. Some strains of red setter used to show progressive retinal atrophy as a hereditary defect and a special programme was established by breeders to eliminate the disease. (See also blindness.)

retina, atrophy of

A term used to denote virtually any painful disorder of joints or muscles which is not directly due to infection or injury. It affects aged dogs more than younger ones, although puppies are sometimes susceptible to an acute form. While there is no guaranteed cure for this disorder, pain relieving drugs help to alleviate symptoms; phenylbutazone, for example, is useful. (See also arthritis.)

rheumatism

See arthritis.

rheumatoid arthritis

Inflammation of the mucous membrane lining of the nasal cavities. It may be caused by infection, obstruction or tumour and is characterised by discharge of a frequently purulent fluid from the nostrils. It often accompanies catarrh and other respiratory disorders and is also a symptom of distemper.

rhinitis

Vitamin B_2. It is found especially in eggs, meat and milk. Its deficiency can cause eye problems, skin disorders and under-development of the testes of the male. (See also nutrition.)

riboflavin

The ribs form most of the skeleton of the thorax or chest. They are flat bones, sloping and curving downwards towards their back and

ribs

ribs front attachments and making the thoracic cavity they enclose roughly cone-shaped. The dog has thirteen pairs of ribs, attached at the back to the spine and the first nine pairs at the front to the sternum by strips of cartilage known as costal cartilage. The remaining four pairs consist of three joined to the cartilage of the rib above and forming the costal arch, and the thirteenth pair ending freely in muscle. This last pair is small and known as 'floating ribs'.

The ribcage protects the contents of the chest (heart, lungs, etc) and is also instrumental in the mechanism of respiration.

Rib fractures can be dangerous, especially if they puncture a lung, and suspected damage should be confirmed by radiography as soon as possible. Symptoms include localised pain and evidently painful breathing. Patients should be sedated initially and have supervised rest while healing takes place. Chest bandages may also be necessary.

rickets A disease which is fortunately less common in modern times since greater attention has been paid to an adequate diet. It is caused by a lack of vitamin D which is needed in the body for the synthesis of calcium salts used in bone development. Lack of sunlight can be a contributory factor and puppies fed inadequately while being kept in dark areas are most vulnerable. The disease mostly affects puppies and young dogs at a stage when bone formation and development is at its greatest. Bony swellings occur at the ends of the long bones of the limbs and on the ribcage. Bone shafts also bend and warp out of shape.

Pure halibut-liver oil or cod-liver oil is the best form of corrective treatment to provide concentrations of vitamin D. Excessive dosage with vitamin D in healthy animals can be hazardous. (See also nutrition.)

34 Dog with rickets

rigor mortis Temporary stiffening of the muscles which sets in several hours after death. This later disappears as the process of decay commences.

ringworm A contagious type of skin disease caused by a specific fungus (of which there are several forms). The skin lesions which provide evidence of the disease vary with the type of fungus involved, but irritation is a clear symptom and a yellow crust on the affected areas can be seen in some forms. The patches of skin denuded of hair by ringworm are frequently roughly circular and appear mostly on the head though they can affect the limbs and other parts of the body.

Treatment is by means of drugs, such as griseofulvin, with specific action against fungal infections. Hair around the lesions should be carefully clipped away and burnt to destroy traces of the fungus and the immediate areas around disinfected with gentian violet.

See parasites.

roundworm

Dogs enjoy a certain amount of routine, particularly if it involves food, exercise and play. Feeding should be carried out at the same time each day and exercise at regular daily times gives the dog something to look forward to. It also helps the dog's bowels to act in a routine way. If a dog can anticipate a play session at certain times it is another stimulation of its interest.

routine

See hepatitis.

Rubarth's disease

Can be a danger to dogs. It has been known for children to wind them around a dog's leg, for example, where they remain undetected in the dog's hair, causing loss of circulation and, if not removed, eventual gangrene. Dogs can also swallow these bands which may become entangled internally or obstruct the back of the throat. Keep them away from dogs, and especially puppies who find them fun to chew, often with disastrous results. (See also foreign bodies.)

rubber bands

A relatively unusual condition which may occur in some cases of chronic nephritis. Bone softens and may be replaced by fibrous tissue. There is no satisfactory treatment.

rubber jaw

A mild blistering agent which, when rubbed into the skin, causes inflammation to speed the elimination of sprains and strains. The heat generated is comforting to the animal and soap liniments are sometimes used in this connection.

rubefacient

Bursting or tearing of an internal organ or structure. Kidney, liver, spleen and bladder are examples of those most often affected by rupture caused by damage, severe strain or accident. Tumours also sometimes cause rupture of an organ.

There is always pain associated with a ruptured organ, often haemorrhage, shock and sometimes coma. Peritonitis may occur, especially in bladder and liver rupture. In rupture of the bladder pain may be less and the dog may vomit, progressively developing toxaemia and uraemia with increased pulse, temperature and respiration.

Treatment of a ruptured organ often includes surgery, and drainage of fluid-filled cavities may also be needed. One of the main dangers is shock for which the patient will require urgent attention from the veterinarian. (See also hernia.)

rupture

S

sacrum The last three vertebrae of the spinal column before the tail. They are fused together as a single unit in the adult, and are roughly wedge-shaped. Spinal nerves pass through the centre. The pelvis and hind limbs are attached to the sacrum which is equidistant from the crest of each of the two hip bones.

saline solution A solution of sodium chloride (salt) in water distilled or boiled and cooled is a useful antiseptic (about a teaspoonful of salt for every half-pint of water).

saliva Secretion of the salivary glands, the flow of which increases before and during feeding and in certain conditions and diseases (such as rabies and choking). It is also a symptom of oral problems such as a bone wedged across the teeth, inflammation of the tongue or gums, etc.

While saliva contains an enzyme (ptyalin) used in the early stages of digestion its main function is to lubricate and ease the passage of food down the oesophagus.

salivary glands A collection of glands which pour saliva into the oral cavity. They are the parotid, mandibular, sublingual and zygomatic glands.

The mandibular gland is a little larger than the parotid, weighing about 8g (¼oz) in the average dog, while the sublingual is the smallest of the four weighing about 1g (⅓₀₀oz). The zygomatic gland (found only in the dog and cat among domestic animals) is situated close to the zygomatic arch of the skull and weighs about 3g (⅒₀oz). All are connected to the interior of the mouth by a system of ducts.

salmonella A group of micro-organisms which can cause food poisoning in man and produce gastrointestinal troubles in dogs ranging from a mild fever to severe gastroenteritis during which the dog's life may be threatened. Vomiting and diarrhoea are symptoms of the infection and in severe cases convulsions and pneumonia may develop. Dogs infected with salmonella also usually suffer liver lesions causing some cell necrosis. Some dogs may carry the organism without noticeable ill-effects though it is uncommon outside hot countries where there are many strays. Cooking destroys salmonella organisms if they should find their way into food.

salpingitis Inflammation of the Fallopian tubes or oviducts. It usually appears in conjunction with infections of the uterus such as metritis and has been known to cause sterility.

salt Sodium chloride – see antiseptics; nutrition; saline solution.

sarcoid A small tumour which much resembles the malignant sarcoma but frequently disappears of its own accord in a few months in a similar fashion to a wart. It is reddish-brown in colour and appears on the dog's skin. It should not be cut and if it remains to cause discomfort a veterinarian should be consulted. (See also tumour.)

sarcoid

A malignant tumour which can arise in bone, muscle or connective tissue. Sarcomas are perhaps the most malignant of all growths and often bleed at the slightest provocation, spreading cells to other parts of the body to form secondaries. Sometimes a sarcoma can be in the form of a painful swelling on the leg of a dog; in other cases it can appear just beneath the skin, in lymph nodes, or around organs such as the kidney or liver. Treatment by radiation is sometimes effective. (See also tumour.)

sarcoma

A group of parasitic mites which are responsible for mange. They burrow into the skin, producing complex tunnel arrangements and giving the skin a scaly, fissured appearance. The skin becomes infected with bacteria due to the damage perpetrated by the mites, and to some extent by the dog suffering from intense irritation and attacking it with teeth and claws. (See also mange.)

sarcoptes

See mange.

sarcoptic mange

A proprietary ointment containing cetrimide – an antiseptic for external use.

Savlon

An encrustation which forms over a sore or open wound, usually as part of the healing process. It protects the vulnerable tissue beneath as it grows together and strengthens.

scab

See burns and scalds.

scalds

A useful part of grooming to prevent a build-up of tartar on the teeth as the dog grows older. Scaling can be carried out with an instrument known as a dental scaler and, if done carefully, is quite painless. (See also dental hygiene; tartar.)

scaling teeth

The shoulder blade; a large flat bone, triangular in shape, with a cup-shaped socket at the lower end into which fits the head of the humerus. It lies close to the thorax and is divided into two sections by a well-marked 'spine' on the outer surface. Many muscles are joined to it to help support the trunk.

The scapula is rarely fractured but after an accident or violent blow when other bones are broken it can be overlooked since there is generally little haemorrhage or swelling. Lameness may be a symptom, however, accompanied by a dropped shoulder. Retaining the scapula in place by bandaging across the chest side speeds recovery.

scapula

A permanent mark left on the skin after the healing of a wound, burn or other injury or operation. It may be due to the edges of the cut tissue growing together unevenly in which case it may be

scar

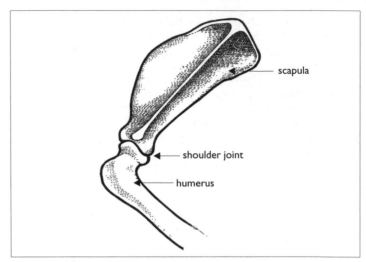

35 The scapula or shoulder blade

scar	ridged or it may be only a smooth mark which gradually disappears as time passes.
scent	Dogs are generally keenly sensitive to scents and some breeds have been developed to make use of this ability for tracking, sniffing out hidden explosives, drugs, etc and for retrieving. Scent contains minute particles of the substance from which it originates, and pheromones. (See also nose.)
sclera	The tough, fibrous outer coat of the eye. It forms a dense network of collagen and elastic fibres and varies in thickness. At the point where the optic nerve passes through it to leave the eyeball it is arranged rather like chicken wire with the nerves passing through the apertures. It is impermeable to light rays and affords much protection to the eye. (See also eye.)
scleritis	Inflammation of the sclera of the eye. The sclera is normally white or bluish-white and becomes bloodshot when inflamed. Scleritis may be associated with conjunctivitis and treatment for the latter condition usually clears it.
sclerosis	Thickening or hardening of tissue, such as arteriosclerosis (hardening of the arteries).
scrotum	The skin pouch which contains the male testes. It is lined with a membrane and divided into two with a testis, epididymis and part of the spermatic cord in each compartment. Contraction of the scrotal lining and associated muscles pull the testes closer to the body for protection and to regulate temperature for the testes and epididymis.
	Minor scrotal injuries cause the dog to lick the area and infection sometimes results. Sedation and restraint (or the fitting of an

'Elizabethan' collar) may be needed to allow healing to take place without interference.

scrotum

See oestrus.

season

While seawater is lightly antiseptic and may actually assist some skin conditions, the disadvantages of a bathe in the sea may outweigh the advantages in a normal healthy dog. The salt makes the coat sticky and uncomfortable and grains of sand can become lodged in skin crevices, orifices, etc, causing irritation and inflammation. There are also additional hazards in the sea, including sharp rocks, shells and debris like broken glass which may cut or crack the pads of the feet. There may also be jellyfish and sea anemones which inflict stings resulting in pain, swelling, cramps and nausea, and sea urchins which produce a burning sensation, inflammation and paralysis. Furthermore, dogs at the seaside should always be provided with shade and fresh water to drink. While humans may well wish to sunbathe, exposure to the full rays of the sun for lengthy periods is likely to produce heat stroke for the dog. (See also stings.)

seawater

Glandular masses sited at the base of each hair follicle which produce an oily secretion called sebum. This gives the coat its glossy appearance in good health and keeps the skin flexible, protecting it against drying and from moisture. Failure to function properly is associated with general ill-health and with malnutrition when the coat becomes dull and dry. There are also sebaceous glands in the eyelids, and in the external ear where their secretion is mixed with ear wax. (See also hair.)

sebaceous glands

Small doses of hypnotics or tranquillisers. They have a soothing, calming effect on the dog, making it drowsy while reducing anxiety and fear. Larger doses send the patient to sleep.

sedatives

See nutrition.

selenium

The reproductive, or seminal, fluid of the male. It contains the spermatozoa from the testes mixed with a secretion from the prostate gland which is thought to provide an optimum medium for survival of the sperm, though little is understood about the source of energy for them. A laboratory analysis of canine semen, in which the spermatozoa are examined, gives information about fertility. The amount of semen ejaculated by the mating dog varies between about 12ml (⅖fl oz) in a small dog to 60ml (3fl oz) in a large breed and may be passed gradually over a period of ten to twenty minutes. (See also spermatozoa.)

semen

See imprinting.

sensitive period

Carried out in the laboratory to test *in vitro* the sensitivity of specific organisms to antibiotics. The organisms are cultured in a

sensitivity testing

sensitivity testing	nutrient medium and discs of antibiotics are placed around them. After incubation a clear zone around the disc indicates that the antibiotic in the disc has diffused into the surrounding medium and inhibits the growth of the organism. There are other methods which can also demonstrate the resistance or sensitivity of an organism to a particular antibiotic and such tests as these are valuable with organisms which are known to have resistance. By this means, the appropriate antibiotic, ie that which will do the most damage to the infecting organism, is chosen with minimal delay.
sensitisation	The administration of an antigen to provoke an immune response from the body so that, when challenged later, a more vigorous secondary response will be encountered. Immunisation is an example. (See also allergy.)
sepsis	An invasion of the body by bacteria. Wounds are particularly vulnerable to sepsis, and burns and scalds exceptionally so. Sterile procedures in dressing and handling are essential to prevent this.
septicaemia	See toxaemia.
septum	A partition separating two cavities, eg the nasal septum which divides left and right nasal cavities.
serum	Plasma without the components of the clotting mechanism. It is said to be defibrinated plasma. When blood coagulates a heavy straw-coloured fluid separates away from the blood clot itself; this is the serum. Some chemical constituents vary between plasma and serum and, for this reason, certain laboratory tests are carried out using one rather than the other. The majority of clinical chemistry tests are, however, performed on plasma. (See also blood.)
sesamoid bones	Rounded nodules of bone embedded in certain tendons. Their main function is to protect tendons which are subject to substantial friction. They usually have one surface associated with a joint and move on a flat or convex surface of such bones as the femur. The patella is an example of a sesamoid bone.
shampoo	There are many shampoos available on the market for canine use. Sometimes an insecticidal shampoo is useful in keeping parasites at bay, and special shampoo treatments to eliminate certain forms of parasite are also obtainable. Dogs are often allergic to scented shampoos and on no account should human shampoos be used. (See also bathing.)
sheep worrying	An offence which may cost a guilty dog its life. Train all puppies that farmstock is to be avoided and certainly not to be chased. In the UK at least, a farmer has the legal right to shoot any dog caught worrying his sheep. If your dog is older and beyond training in this respect, it should be kept on a lead when farm animals are around.

A method of producing heat by means of rapid muscular contractions. Energy is constantly lost to the outside and is replaced by the intake and process of food and oxygen. After a dog is fed, for example, there is an increase in heat production which in cold weather may warm the body when it is most needed. Dogs exposed to cold generate fast muscular contractions in the form of shivering to produce the heat needed to replace that used up by the cold. When returning from a cold wet walk, a dog needs drying thoroughly without delay to prevent exceptional heat loss and the consequent possibilities of a chill.

Dogs suffering from debilitating diseases often shiver, since heat is being used up by fever or other illness. Those which are starved or affected by malnutrition shiver since there is insufficient 'fuel' for the body heat requirements for normal activities such as breathing and movement. Fear may induce fits of shivering, perhaps in part to cope with the need for more energy for a faster heart-rate and the generated anxiety and to build up additional energy reserves for flight. Some dogs, such as fox terriers and airedales appear to shiver at times for no apparent reason. (See also spasm; tremor.)

shivering

A complex cycle of events, which varies depending on the cause, affecting many organs and functions of the body. While the sequence of events in the cycle may vary the end result is much the same. For instance, drastically reduced blood-flow through the brain when blood pressure is low, and cardiac failure, can both be caused by shock and can both prove fatal.

Substantial haemorrhage is a common cause of shock. Here the loss of blood is too great for the blood vessels to contract sufficiently and quickly enough to maintain the even pressure needed throughout the circulatory system. If the blood circulation is impaired for any reason, the heart, blood vessels, brain and other tissues will receive less oxygen and capillaries may also be damaged. Some organs can cope with a temporary lack of oxygen but the brain is unable to do so as its cells die. The heart's pumping action also becomes weaker, blood vessels dilate, blood pressure falls and the flow lessens.

In extensive burns large quantities of fluid are lost from the blood to collect in the burnt tissue, with similar effects to those produced by severe haemorrhage.

During the cycle of shock various other actions are triggered: pain and fear (usually associated with the original condition) put extra strain on the circulatory system, and other organs react in different, but harmful, ways. The pancreas, for example, may produce a hormone which has a depressing effect on the heart and other hormones become involved in abnormal activity, causing kidney damage and inhibiting the use of glucose by the tissues to produce energy, at a time when additional energy is needed. The blood undergoes other biochemical changes, including those of electrolyte balance, and dehydration is an added complication. Lung damage can also occur as part of

shock

shock | the circulatory problem, still further reducing the availability of oxygen.

It can be seen, therefore, that shock is not only complex but far-reaching in the damage that it can cause, exerting a substantial strain on various body organs and systems when weakness from the original injury or disease is already causing havoc. The life of the canine patient is therefore doubly at risk and the veterinarian (who must be called as speedily as possible while the patient is kept calm and comfortable) has to deal with the original cause of shock while treating shock itself.

The clinical signs of shock include tachycardia; increased, shallow respiration; weak, irregular pulse-rate; pale or bluish-grey mucous membranes of the mouth, gums, eyes, etc; sub-normal temperature; weakness; and some disorientation. The body may be cold and the dog may shiver. Vomiting may also occur and the pupils of the eyes are often dilated. Loss of blood and pain should be minimised and the patient calmed as much as possible. A blood transfusion may be part of the treatment, together with the administration of other fluids including those to counteract dehydration. The main approach is to compensate for loss of fluid volume by replacement and to administer oxygen as it is needed. Septicaemia may be an added complication due to the generation of toxins as part of the body's reaction and this effect may therefore also need special treatment.

While shock can be lethal, it can also be reversed by skilled evaluation of both cause and effect and urgent treatment to correct the many imbalances which are produced in the reaction.

shoulder | See scapula.

showing | A good deal of time and some financial investment is needed if showing is to be a serious pastime. Apart from the cost of the initial equipment, which is relatively small, consisting largely of grooming instruments and materials probably purchased for the dog anyway, travelling costs can be high and entrance fees to shows have also to be paid.

Showing can be extremely interesting, however, especially if you possess an outstanding example of a particular breed. It is also of some importance to breeders not only because offspring of champions command higher prices at sale and male champions can expect larger stud fees, but also because it helps to keep breeds pure and to perpetuate the best strains.

A dog can enter from the age of six months in the UK and USA, and there are 'Puppy', 'Junior', 'Yearling', 'Open' and many other categories to suit the age of the dog. Winners obtain certificates and, as they progress, championships. Entrants conform to appropriate standards of the Kennel Club which sponsors the events in each country. There are also working and obedience classes in shows, usually open to most dogs.

An entrant to a show needs to be in fine health with a glossy coat, bright eyes and an alert manner. It must be trained to behave when being examined by the judge, to walk correctly and to stand well. Before a show it will need special attention, including bathing and detailed grooming.

showing

A term which refers to the onset of oestrus when the bitch 'shows colour' in the form of a discharge of bright-coloured blood from the vagina. She is not ready for mating at this time but between ten and fifteen days from showing colour she will be most receptive, although the exact time varies with each individual. (See also mating; oestrus.)

showing colour

A ligament or tendon joining muscle to bone.

sinew

A hollow cavity, usually in a bone such as those behind the nasal cavities of the head, where they are known as the maxillary, frontal and paranasal sinuses. The term is also used in pathology to refer to cavities produced internally by disease. There are natural venous sinuses, eg the veins of the cranial cavity of the head and of the spinal canal.

sinus

Inflammation of the mucous membrane lining the sinuses of the head. It usually spreads from the nasal cavities during an infection, or sometimes from a diseased tooth socket in the upper jaw. Tumours of the sinuses can also be a cause of prolonged sinusitis which, as with infection, is accompanied by pain and a purulent discharge from the nose.

sinusitis

The bones of the body. Those of the head and trunk form the axial skeleton to which most other bones are directly or indirectly attached. The remainder of the skeleton is made up of the bones of the limbs and their girdles, by which they are attached to the axial skeleton. There are two girdles: the shoulder and pelvic girdle. Those bones which are not part of the axial skeleton are often known collectively as the appendicular skeleton.

skeleton

The axial skeleton simply consists of the skull, the bones of the vertebral column (vertebrae) and those of the thorax or chest (the ribs and sternum).

The appendicular skeleton includes the thoracic or pectoral girdle (shoulder) with scapula and clavicle. To this is attached the humerus (upper arm). The radius and ulna (forearm) are joined at the top to the lower end of the humerus and at their lower ends to the forepaw which consists of the carpus (wrist), metacarpus and finally the phalanges or digits.

At the rear of the dog the appendicular skeleton comprises the pelvic girdle and the bones of the hind limbs. The hip of the pelvic girdle is made up of three bones: the ilium, ischium and pubis. The upper leg or thigh comprises the femur which is joined at its lower end by means of the patella (kneecap) to the tibia and fibula of the leg. These two bones lead to the hind paw – the tarsus, metatarsus and phalanges or digits.

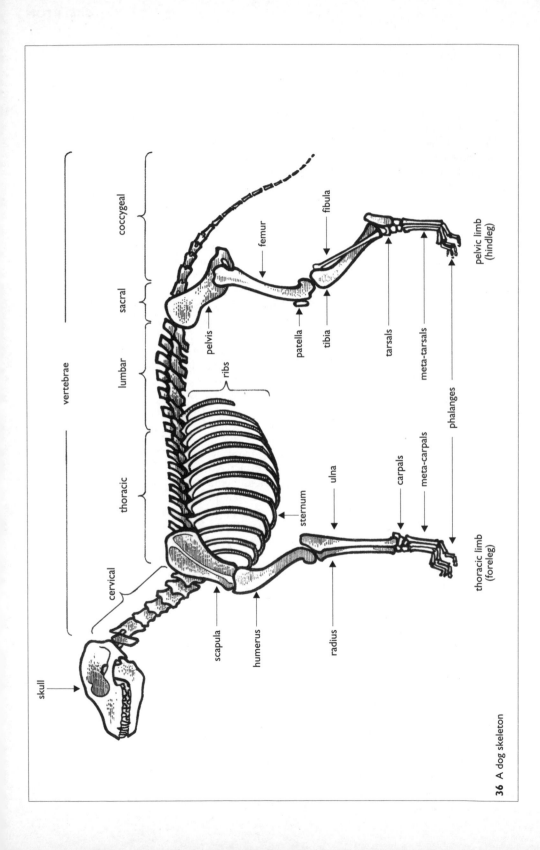

36 A dog skeleton

The purpose of the skeleton is to provide support and protection for the body and its organs and to act as a framework to which muscles can attach to provide a system of mobility. (See also under individual bones.)

skeleton

Connective tissue containing blood vessels, nerve endings, lymphatics and cutaneous muscles. It covers the body and is continuous with mucous membranes at the body's orifices. The outer part of the skin, or epidermis, consists of several layers of elastic epithelium. This is where hair begins to grow, but the epidermis has no blood supply. The underlying dermis of the skin not only carries blood vessels but also nerve fibres and glands.

Skin has many functions. It acts as a sensory organ, reacting to touch, temperature changes, pressure and pain. It serves as a protective covering, providing a barrier against the invasion of organisms and contaminants and against minor damage. It prevents the body from drying out and from becoming too moist with the aid of its glands which waterproof and lubricate it. With the help of sunlight it is a factory for the manufacture of vitamin D and, in a limited way, it assists in the regulation of the body's temperature by acting as a blanket together with subcutaneous fat layers immediately below to conserve heat. By changes in condition (and in some cases colour) the skin can also indicate ill-health in the dog. The skin can suffer from allergic attacks (such as eczema), inflammation, fungal infections and parasites.

skin

The bones of the head. It varies somewhat in shape depending on breeds but is divided into the cranium and the facial or frontal area. The cranium encloses the brain with its covering and vessels and the nerve fibres leading to and from it. The facial part of the skull consists of the nasal cavities and bones surrounding them, the hard palate and upper jaw. It is substantially reduced in short-faced dogs and longer in such breeds as the greyhound.

The skull protects the delicate mechanisms of hearing, sight and smell. It also supports the apparatus for mastication.

skull

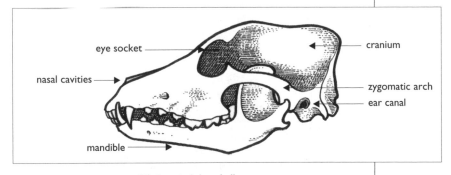

eye socket

cranium

nasal cavities

zygomatic arch

ear canal

mandible

37 A typical dog skull

As essential for dogs as it is for all creatures. For puppies it is especially important and they need much more sleep than the adult dog.

sleep

sleep The need for sleep is still little understood but dogs do sleep a good deal during which tissues rest and are repaired. They are light sleepers and can be disturbed by noise or activities in unfamiliar surroundings.

In sleep, respiration and heart-rate are slower and body temperature falls, apparently due to the cessation of nerve control over body heat production. There are periods of rapid eye movements (known as REM) during which time the dog may also twitch its limbs and sometimes make little whimpering noises. As REM in man generally corresponds with dreaming it may be safe to assume that the body movements are also connected with the dog's dreams. REM is considered to be the most important (or refreshing) period of the sleep pattern.

Deprivation of sleep can cause ill-health and also alter a dog's personality. Puppies need to be allowed to sleep peacefully whenever they wish to do so, in a warm, comfortable resting place which provides security.

The dog prepares for sleep by seeking out a special place, circling round and round its bed before settling down in a particular sleeping posture, often curled with its head down to its tail. The circling and curling up behaviour may perhaps be a legacy from the wild days of the dog when sleeping outside entailed finding a sheltered spot and turning round and round to make a circular hollow in which to curl up to retain body heat.

A sick dog is helped in many cases by peaceful sleep, allowing healing to take place and tissues to be repaired undisturbed by other body activities. Anxiety, which uses up much energy, is also reduced while the patient is asleep.

smell See odour; olfactory system.

snake-bite Death from snake-bite is rare in the UK since the only venomous snake likely to be encountered by a dog on a walk in the countryside is the adder or viper. While the adder varies in description between individuals there is little difficulty in distinguishing it from the other two British snakes. The adder has a dark zig-zag stripe down the middle of its back and there is usually an inverted V or X-shaped mark on the head. The iris of the eye is copper-coloured. It is found in many types of countryside throughout the British Isles, though it shows a preference for open places where sun is plentiful; on sandy heaths, moorland, hillsides, open sunny spaces in woodland and rough common land, for example. In the spring, groups of them, recently emerged from hibernation, may be seen together.

In the USA a variety of snakes may be found, though the most common are the various pit vipers. In tropical countries the selection is greater still and snake-bite may present a more substantial problem to the canine population. While all venomous snakes are dangerous, the degree of deadliness depends on several factors, including the toxicity and quantity of venom, size of snake and the type of venom injected.

Symptoms of snake-bite vary but usually include nausea and vomiting, pain in the area of the bite, dizziness and nose-bleeds. Convulsions and coma may follow. The dog should be treated well within four hours of the bite to provide a sound chance of recovery. It should be kept still and quiet while awaiting the veterinarian. An incision is made at the site of the bite, where fang marks appear amid some swelling, and mechanical suction applied to the wound to remove as much of the venom as possible (the dog's owner can perform this first aid as soon as the bite has been made). The venom is neutralised by the appropriate antidote and analgesics administered if needed. It may also be necessary to treat for shock, give tetanus antitoxin and include antibiotics to prevent a secondary infection. | **snake-bite**

A growling sound, usually delivered with the upper lip curled back as a sign of aggression. A snarling dog should be taken seriously; if provoked further it may well bite. If the object of its aggression is another dog it should be taken as a warning that the aggressor intends to start a fight. Sometimes dogs on leads set up a fearful snarling against other dogs but when walking free often ignore them under similar circumstances. In this case it may be more of a defence than an act of outright aggression. (See also aggressiveness; behaviour.) | **snarling**

A sudden expulsion of air through the nasal passages to expel irritants and protect the mucous membranes against attack. A dog may sneeze when dust or pollen are drawn in through the nose or when inhaled smoke produces a stinging sensation in the nasal cavities. A dog will also sneeze violently if a grass seed has been sniffed in or when mucus gathers due to inflammation. The dog's keen sense of smell is also often assaulted by such scents as after-shave or petrol fumes and these, too, irritate and cause sneezing. | **sneezing**

A dog which sneezes continuously for prolonged periods should be taken to a veterinarian urgently since it is most likely that a foreign body or an insect is lodged in the nasal cavity. While the latter may present little problem when it is dead (though it may have stung the delicate lining of the nose), foreign bodies can cause much pain as well as discomfort.

When bathing a dog, human soaps are to be avoided. Use only those especially formulated for dogs. Ingested soap, particularly if perfumed, can be poisonous, so keep it out of reach. (See also bathing; shampoo; poisoning.) | **soap**

Where two or more dogs live in a household, it can be seen that in play and other activities one dog purposely stimulates another to obtain a reaction. Each learns the others' responses in certain regularly occurring situations and may act deviously to obtain such a response. Dogs also behave similarly with their owners, for example, at dinner or exercise times, when attention is sought in various ways to obtain the required response. (See also behaviour; communication.) | **social interaction**

sodium	See electrolytes; nutrition.
sodium bicarbonate	A useful acid neutraliser. It can be used in solution to treat acid burns in an emergency or if any acidic compound has been swallowed. It may also be administered by a veterinarian to alleviate acidity in cardiac arrest and as a blood volume replacement solution in the treatment of shock. (See also poisoning.)
sodium chloride	Salt.
soporific	A drug (also known as a narcotic) which induces a deep sleep.
sore	See ulcer.
spasm	Uncontrolled contraction of muscles which may precede convulsions, paralysis or unconsciousness and can be a symptom of many disorders. Spasms can be muscular or neurological in origin and can be painful if severe. Cramp is one common form of muscle spasm. Hollow organs are also subject to spasm producing, for example, colic in the intestines. (See also convulsion; shivering; tremor.)
spaying	Removal of the female ovaries (and often the uterus) by surgery under general anaesthetic. A bitch may be spayed due to disease of ovaries and/or uterus, or to prevent conception.
	Many stray bitches which are housed by animal rescue organisations are spayed prior to being found new homes, as a measure to prevent the birth of additional unwanted dogs.
	Spaying is a major operation and is therefore less traumatic in the younger than in the older bitch. It is usually successful and recovery uneventful, though some individuals suffer side effects which may need post-operative hormone treatment, but these are rare.
	Diabetic bitches may be spayed to prevent oestrus which can affect their tolerance of the disease. It is also a cure for nymphomania and should be carried out in bitches suffering from hereditary and other defects and disorders which make them unsuitable for breeding. Obviously the removal of ovaries and uterus eliminates the possibilities of infection in these organs and, more significantly, reduces the risks of malignant mammary tumours, though this factor alone is a rather inadequate basis for a decision to have a bitch spayed. (See also neutering; unwanted dogs.)
speculum	An instrument for the visual exploration of internal cavities and passages. It is hand-held and sometimes equipped with a battery-powered light. It is frequently used for examination of vagina or anus, for example.
spermatic cord	The spermatic cord runs between the abdominal cavity and the scrotum of the male in the left and right inguinal canals and from it the testis is suspended. It consists of the duct (the vas deferens)

which conveys the spermatozoa from the testis to the urethra, together with associated nerves, blood vessels and lymph vessels. This bundle is covered with a serous membrane.

spermatic cord

spermatozoa

The male sex cells which are formed in the epididymis of the testes. During fertilisation they fuse with the female ova at the beginning of the reproduction cycle.

Each spermatozoon is equipped with a flagellum or tail to assist its onward movement during its journey from the testis of the male to the Fallopian tube of the female.

sphincter

A muscle which contracts to close or reduce an orifice. There is one, for example, at the duodenal end of the bile-duct and others at each end of the anal canal, in the bladder and at the lower portion of the stomach which opens into the duodenum.

A sphincter's purpose is to act as a control mechanism to regulate the escape of the contents of an organ or duct. It is controlled by the nervous system, and paralysis (as well as other conditions) results in loss of control and, for example, incontinence.

spinal cord

Part of the central nervous system extending from the medulla oblongata of the brain at the back of the skull through the spinal column, and terminating at the middle of the sacrum in a bundle of nerves, called the cauda equina as it resembles a horse's tail.

The H-shaped cord consists mainly of white matter on the surface and grey matter inside, as does the medulla. It contains nerve fibres and its dual function is that of a connecting link between the brain and the nerves supplying the outer parts of limbs and trunk, and a centre of nerve reflex action. In this latter role it uses a system of motor and sensory nerves, without cerebral involvement, to provide rapid reflexes. For example, should the nose of an inquisitive dog touch the sharp spines of a hedgehog the dog's head is quickly drawn away by reflex action. Similarly, if a paw touches the hot ash of a bonfire the heat sensation stimulates the reflex action of pulling the paw away, triggered in the spinal cord.

Damage to the spinal cord, through injury or disease, generally causes paralysis or paraplegia. (For drawing, see paraplegia.) Limitation of movement may occur in arthritis of the spine but cord inflammatory conditions produce symptoms which may include pain, weakness, dragging hind feet or loss of limb co-ordination.

If spinal injuries are suspected the dog should not be moved until the arrival of a veterinarian who will administer tranquillisers and pain relievers before any movement is attempted; the animal is usually examined on a wide board to eliminate flexion, extension or twisting of the spinal column. Prognosis will depend on the extent of the damage and the possibilities of reversal.

spine

The backbone, also known as the vertebral or spinal column. It is a bony column consisting of a series of vertebrae which enclose and protect the spinal cord. It reaches from the base of the skull to the end of the tail. The vertebrae vary in size and shape in each of spine | the spine's five regions: cervical (neck), thoracic (chest), lumbar (back), sacral (pelvic) and coccygeal (tail). The spine comprises approximately fifty bones, supports much of the body and serves as a flexible frame in locomotion. (See also vertebrae.)

spleen | This gland, which has no duct and no direct connection with any other organ, is situated in the abdomen and loosely attached to the stomach. It is irregular, roughly tongue-shaped and plum coloured. It is an aid to the circulatory system and possesses many blood vessels.

The spleen and its workings are still insufficiently understood but it acts as a filter, production centre and storehouse. It plays a similar role to the liver in cleansing the blood of degenerated red blood cells and utilises them in the manufacture of some bilirubin which is passed to the liver. Iron is extracted from the remaining haemoglobin in the spleen to be used by the bone marrow to produce more red cells. The spleen is also a production area for some lymphocytes and monocytes and is involved in antibody production for the body's defence mechanisms. It serves as a store for blood, changing size to accommodate varying supplies, and releasing it when needed.

Injury to the spleen or the presence of a tumour is often treated by a splenectomy.

splenectomy | Surgical removal of the spleen. This operation may be performed following injury, such as rupture, or disease, such as a tumour. The body is apparently able to exist without the spleen since splenectomy patients usually recover fully if there are no additional complications. Compensatory enlargement of lymph nodes may occur.

splint | Appliance bound to an injured limb to prevent movement. Splints are mostly used as a temporary measure in suspected fractures to rest the broken limb and prevent pain and additional damage.

There are preformed splints available commercially made of wood, tin, aluminium or wire, and also roller bandages impregnated with plaster of Paris (frequently used on a more permanent basis while healing is in progress).

Improvised splints can be made from flat or gutter-shaped pieces of wood, light metal or plastic, padded carefully between the injured limb and the splint and bound firmly (but not too tightly) in place with bandages. Stiff corrugated cardboard or pieces from a child's Meccano set are two alternatives. Internal splints are mainly metal pins or plates.

spores | Reproductive cells of fungi and other plants. They are often wind-borne and resistant to general environmental changes. Tetanus bacteria also produce spores at a dormant phase of their life and remain viable for many years. Instruments suspected of contamination should be sterilised by steam compression in an autoclave since spores may even survive boiling water immersion. Formaldehyde is mostly effective against spore contamination and can therefore be useful in kennels.

spores

This is the result of a sudden awkward movement of a joint which stretches adjacent tissues such as ligaments. The injury causes inflammation and pain. Rest and cold compresses help to reduce inflammation and analgesics may be needed to relieve pain. A bandage carefully bound to support the joint often helps to speed recovery.

sprain

Secretions of the nose, throat, bronchi and lungs which accumulate in these passages and contain bacteria during infection. Collection of sputum by means of a throat swab often assists in obtaining identification of the invading bacteria and allows rapid treatment with the most aggressive antibiotic.

sputum

Turning of the eyes in different directions. It is a possible symptom in tetanus, but more usually a defect of nature or heredity.

squint

A dull coat which has lost its usual healthy gloss. The condition is frequently a basic indicator of ill-health and the dog should be observed for other symptoms. A lack of fat in the diet can be one cause. (See also hair.)

staring coat

Lack of food and nourishment. The complications of the body's response to starvation still require investigation but in basic terms starvation means the body is unable to produce energy required, not only for activity, but for such essentials as breathing, heart action, etc and the patient will eventually die unless the situation is reversed.

starvation

An animal which is starved responds by utilising fat stored in adipose tissue as an energy source. This process gradually produces its own problems in the form of a condition known as 'fatty liver' and ketones which accumulate in the liver and bloodstream and cause ketosis. Glycogen stores in the liver may also be depleted within twenty-four hours of starvation and, when fat and glycogen reserves are depleted, amino acids, which contain nitrogen, are broken down.

In normal digestion the amount of nitrogen passing from the digestive system is equal to that being excreted in urea in the urine. In starvation, however, there is no nitrogen entering via the food, though it is being excreted from amino acid breakdown. The result can be lethal unless a combination of amino acids and carbohydrates is administered.

Any dogs found starving in a very weakened state should be treated urgently by a veterinarian since the side effects of starvation, as well as the condition itself, may need attention. (See also diet; feeding; nutrition.)

The constriction or narrowing of any internal passage, usually through disease. It is often due to the production of scar tissue in a

stenosis

stenosis tubular structure following damage to the lining or walls. It may occur, for example, in the pylorus, aorta or pulmonary vessels, eventually causing obstruction. Treatment depends on the cause and surgery is sometimes necessary.

sterilisation See spaying; castration.

sterilisation of equipment There are various means of sterilising equipment. Boiling for thirty minutes in water can be effective or instruments may be placed in a hot-air oven for twenty minutes at 180°C (358°F) or autoclaved to eliminate most pathogenic organisms. Cloths and gloves may also be autoclaved. Chemical sterilisation can be an alternative method, especially for equipment that cannot withstand high temperatures. Ethyl and isopropyl alcohol can be used as an 80 per cent solution for fat solvency; and chemicals of the cresol group, though highly toxic to living tissues, can be effective in 1 per cent solution against vegetative organisms and are useful in cleansing floors and contaminated grooming equipment, etc, provided a good rinsing follows. Formaldehyde is also highly effective against spores and viruses as well as bacteria but should not be used in the presence of animals. It can, however, be a valuable fumigating agent in kennels, etc. Other examples of chemical sterilising agents include centrimide, chlorhexidine and benzalkonium chloride. (See also autoclave; fumigation.)

sternum The breastbone; a series of eight segments of bone which form the floor of the thorax. It is vertically compressed and the ribs join it by connection with the intersternebral cartilages between each sternal segment. The first sternebra is longer than the others and is known as the manubrium; the last is rectangular with a thin cartilaginous plate at its end.

Damage to the sternum, usually caused by substantial force, can often heal without attention but, since the heart lies behind, suspected fractures should be X-rayed to ascertain the extent of the injury.

steroid See corticosteroids.

stethoscope An instrument for listening to internal sounds of the body. It consists of two earpieces attached to tubes joining a central diaphragm which is placed, for example, against the chest to listen to the amplified heartbeats, or against the abdomen to detect intestinal sounds.

stifle The knee joint of the hind limb. It is a synovial joint with the femur above and the tibia and fibula below. Examination of the stifle joint often requires general anaesthesia, especially as ligaments may be ruptured causing much pain. In acute dislocations lameness is always evident but in chronic conditions only a stiffness of the leg with the toes pointed forward may be apparent. (See also patella.)

An oestrogen which may be used in its synthetic form to treat pyometra or uterine inertia during whelping. It may also curtail lactation when a litter has been lost. It has also been used (as stilboestrol dipropionate) in the bitch to prevent conception after a misalliance and to treat dogs with enlarged prostate.

stilboestrol

Birth of a dead puppy. Causes of stillbirth include various infections, including that of herpes virus. Placental problems and hormone deficiencies may also produce stillbirths, although abortion or foetal resorption are more likely.

stillbirth

Drug or agent which increases the lapsed activity of an organ. Caffeine or digitalis, for example, are administered in cardiac disease as an expedient measure, or carbon dioxide is given to stimulate the respiratory system in failure. Adrenaline can be described as a stimulant since its action increases organ activity under normal circumstances.

Many so-called stimulants actually have a depressing effect on tissues, particularly in normal health. Alcohol (eg brandy) depresses the tissues, though its intoxicating action may have a temporary relaxing effect which gives the impression of stimulation. It also dilates the blood vessels and neither this nor any other stimulant is advisable during or after haemorrhage.

stimulant

Perhaps the most common form of sting is that made by bees and wasps since dogs (especially puppies) are prone to investigating the buzzing. They may pick up insects and be stung in the mouth or, more dangerously, in the throat, where swelling can cause suffocation. Feet are also frequently stung.

While wasps do not leave their stings in their victims, the bees do, and the stings should be removed if visible with a pair of forceps or tweezers. The area can be swabbed with a solution of bicarbonate of soda (a dessertspoonful in a pint of water). If the swelling is substantial inside the mouth or throat a veterinarian should be called. Some dogs are more affected than others by such stings and symptoms may vary from mild pain and irritation (and often salivation if the mouth has been stung) to weakness and pain spreading through the body, vomiting and fever. The condition and symptoms can worsen over a period of six to forty-eight hours after the sting. Antihistamine drugs are used routinely in treatment.

Dogs frequenting the seashore may also be stung by jellyfish, urchins or sea anemones where symptoms may include nausea, pain, swelling and cramps.

Cold packs help to relieve the pain of stings and analgesics may be necessary. In very severe cases additional drugs such as epinephrine and calcium gluconate may be administered by a veterinarian.

stings

The stomach is a musculoglandular organ situated in the abdomen between the end of the oesophagus and the beginning of the small intestine. It receives food during the digestive process and its

stomach

stomach function is to store and mix food (by muscular contraction and peristalsis) which various digestive agents, including enzymes and hydrochloric acid, act upon to break down.

The dog's stomach varies considerably in size between breeds and depending upon how much food is accommodated. It actually displaces part of the liver, behind which it lies, and other organs when full. Its capacity is usually about 0.5 litres up to almost 8 litres (1 to 14pt) in the largest breeds – such as an Irish wolfhound weighing around 54kg (120lb). (Puppies generally have greater capacities in relation to their size than older dogs.) A rough estimation of adult stomach capacity can be made by allowing about 100 to 250ml per kilogram (1¾ to 4½fl oz per lb) of body weight.

Food remains in the stomach for between ten and sixteen hours while several types of gland in the mucous membrane lining secrete hydrochloric acid, mucus and pepsin. Meanwhile the stomach moves rhythmically to mix and chop the food it contains.

The stomach has an outer serous coat which covers a muscular wall. There is a submucous layer between this and the mucous membrane lining. The stomach inlet is known as the cardia and the outlet the pylorus.

stomach torsion Twisting of the stomach. Generally, the condition is rare but may affect the giant breeds. Symptoms include pain in the abdominal region, and sometimes the dog vomits. Swelling of the abdomen usually follows and distress increases. Urgent veterinary attention is essential as the condition can be fatal.

stomatitis Inflammation of the mucous membranes of the mouth. It can be the result of infection in various forms; it can follow damage to the inside of the mouth from electrical burns or, for example, chewing wood, or it can be a symptom of various diseases, including uraemia, diabetes or dietary deficiencies.

There are three basic forms. Catarrhal stomatitis is symptomised by swollen, inflamed mucosa which can readily be seen on the pharynx or soft palate. It may be the result of infection, chemical or physical injury or respiratory disorders.

Vesicular stomatitis is characterised by mouth blisters on the tongue, hard palate and lips. This condition may appear during distemper, leptospirosis or various virus-based diseases.

Ulcerative stomatitis is diagnosed when ulcers are present, invading the submucosal layer of the mouth. The breath is particularly foul and healing is likely to be protracted.

General symptoms of stomatitis include distress on eating, excessive salivation, foul breath, pawing at the mouth and retching. The source of the condition needs treatment as well as localised attention.

stones Never encourage a dog to play with pebbles or stones. Always take away immediately any stones a dog may pick up in its mouth, and train puppies to ignore them. Apart from damaging the teeth they could be swallowed to cause internal obstruction and are consequently very dangerous. (See also foreign bodies.)

See calculus.	**stones, kidney**

A depression at the junction of the nose and cranium. It is prominent only in so-called short-headed (brachycephalic) breeds and is sometimes known as the glabella.	**stop**

See sprain.	**strain**

Unnatural effort during urination or defecation may indicate obstruction, inflammation or infection, or all three conditions. If straining is noticed during urination the cause may be cystitis or blockage of the urethra by calculi. The inability to pass urine properly should be considered as serious and an examination made without delay by a veterinarian. Straining during defecation can point to intestinal obstruction or to infected anal glands. The advice of a veterinarian is needed if the straining continues or is associated with pain, and if blood is passed in the faeces then it is a matter for some urgency. (See also urinary retention.)	**straining**

See hernia.	**strangulated hernia**

An antibiotic which, while effective against various bacterial diseases, can be very toxic and has been known to cause deafness as it affects the auditory nerve. (See also antibiotics.)	**streptomycin**

A physiological condition which arises through environmental and psychological pressures. A dog subjected to an excessive degree of stress is a candidate for a wide variety of diseases and conditions of a physical as well as mental nature. The body reacts to constant or excessive stress as a chain does, by breaking at its weakest point. Stress depresses the production of red blood cells, releases adrenaline and impairs other hormone activity, inhibits effective digestion and energy. Heart-rate increases, loss of appetite occurs and there may be reproductive incapability and cardiac failure. The stress patient is much more prone to infection, stress anaemia, gastric ulcers and even bone fractures; dormant disease such as tuberculosis may suddenly manifest itself. Dietary deficiencies may occur due to an increased demand for protein and vitamins, such as A, C and E, and minerals including calcium, magnesium, potassium, copper, iron and zinc. Symptoms vary from obvious nervous distress to excessive drinking, vomiting, hysteria and eczema. Diarrhoea may occur and result in dehydration to further complicate the effects of stress. Causes of stress are also varied. If a dog is particularly nervous, a noisy children's party or a loud argument between two humans may be all that is needed. Even a dog which is not over-nervous can be stressed by a large number of situations: being left alone for lengthy periods, boredom, attacks by other dogs, irritable or indecisive owners, frustration, anxiety, uncertainty, regular incomprehension of commands and teasing are common causes. A dog	**stress**

stress	which is overworked or subjected to regular exhausting exercise with little rest will be stressed; dogs that are lost, move to new homes or spend lengthy times in boarding kennels are also vulnerable. Prevention is largely by means of human consideration for the dog and awareness and understanding of its needs and tolerances. Treatment lies in removal of the cause of the stress and in suitable remedies for its physical manifestations.
stricture	The narrowing of a body tube or passage. It is a term usually associated with the urinary system where stricture may occur due to scar tissue forming after damage to, for example, the urethra. This may be the result of urinary calculi or other temporary obstruction. (See also stenosis.)
stripping	A heavy-coated dog may need to be 'stripped' for comfort during hot weather. This consists of reducing the amount of coat and is usually performed with clippers and scissors. (See also grooming.)
stroke	This is another term for apoplexy – a sudden loss of consciousness and paralysis caused by cerebral haemorrhage or cerebral thrombosis. It most frequently occurs in old animals and symptoms may include vomiting before the attack and/or loss of balance as paralysis begins. The patient is distressed and there is often a continuous to-and-fro movement of the eyeballs. The dog should be kept very quiet in a peaceful, darkened room. While a little water may be taken if needed, stimulants should be avoided. A veterinarian should be called to determine the cause and if possible prescribe treatment. Physiotherapy may help to aid recovery at a later stage.
strychnine (nux vomica)	A poison used in rat bait – toxic in the dog, causing respiratory paralysis and death if not counteracted with speed. Urgent gastric lavage is needed followed by the administration of activated charcoal and probably pentobarbitone to relax the patient, and other drugs to treat the effects. (See also poisoning.)
Stuttgart disease	'Canine typhus', which often occurs as a result of leptospirosis or during the course of a virus infection. It produces several symptoms that include vomiting 'coffee grounds', thirst, foul breath, mouth ulceration and gastroenteritis. Death can occur in less than seventy-two hours, usually from kidney failure, unless veterinary treatment is given quickly.
subcutaneous	Beneath the skin. (See also injection.)
suffocation	See asphyxia; heat stroke.
sulphonamides	A group of drugs which includes sulphanilamide, sulphathiazole, sulphadiazine and many others. Sulphonamides are widely used in veterinary medicine and, although they have been displaced somewhat by the success of antibiotics in combating infection,

they are still considered highly effective, particularly against
bacteria which are resistant to certain antibiotics. They are easy to
administer and relatively inexpensive, and are sometimes also
used in conjunction with antibiotic therapy.

Sulphonamides (or 'sulpha drugs' as they are often known) are
especially effective against such infections as metritis, pneumonia
and various forms of enteritis and associated diseases. In powder
form they are used topically in wound treatment and opened
abscesses.

This group of drugs operates with an antibacterial action depending on similarity to para-aminobenzoic acid which bacteria absorb
and apparently require to live; bacteria absorb sulphonamides and
are poisoned from within.

sulphonamides

See heat stroke.

sunstroke

Small cylindrical mass of glycerine containing drugs. Suppositories
are for insertion into the rectum and liquefy at body temperature
releasing the drug which may, for example, be an analgesic, or an
agent to reverse constipation.

suppository

The formation of pus. It is a phase of inflammation which occurs
if the body's defence mechanisms cannot deal with the cause
quickly enough or if treatment with antibacterial agents (such as
antibiotics, sulphonamides, etc) has not been used to aid these
defences.

suppuration

Above the kidney. (See also adrenal glands.)

suprarenal

An operation to treat, repair or alter a condition, or to remove something which interferes with or threatens the normal functioning of
the body and its life mechanisms.

Surgery should be carried out only by a qualified veterinarian
and requires local, regional or general anaesthesia. Post-operative
nursing is an important aspect of recovery.

surgery

A surgical stitch used to close a wound or an incision following
operation. Sutures are usually supplied to the veterinarian sterile
and attached to curved, straight, cutting or round-bodied needles.
Various types of material are used for different tasks in internal and
external suturing and can be non-absorbable (such as silk, nylon,
linen, stainless steel, etc), or catgut, made from sheep intestine,
which is absorbed by the body in a predetermined length of time,
thus obviating the need for removal after healing has taken place.
After suturing, the needle is snipped off, leaving the stitches in
place. Absorbable materials are usually applied internally unless
they are to remain permanently in position.

After an operation with external, non-absorbable suturing it is
advisable to prevent the dog licking or chewing at the sutures.
Sedation or the use of an 'Elizabethan' collar are two possible
approaches to the problem.

suture

suture	The term 'suture' is also used to mean a line of junction between bony structures, such as may be found in the cranium of the skull. (See also 'Elizabethan' collar.)
swab	A piece of sterile material such as gauze and cotton wool which is used to mop up blood, discharges, etc. A swab can also be a stick wound with absorbent cotton wool for taking a sample of secretion or discharge from an orifice or wound for bacteriological examination.
swallowing	See foreign bodies.
sweating	A dog does not sweat in the same way as a human because it does not have sweat glands as such in the skin. While a limited amount of sweating is done through the hair follicles of the skin, sweat is mostly issued from glands situated in the pads of the feet. Although sweating excretes some waste products its main purpose in man is normally for the regulation of body heat. In the dog, however, body heat cannot be lost rapidly through sweating since the process is confined to only a small area. Panting, after exercise or in hot weather, brings some relief but the limitations of the process make the dog very vulnerable to such conditions as heat stroke. Under normal environmental conditions the dog's heat loss through its body surface is balanced by heat production but excessive heat is distressing and dangerous to it.
symptoms	The evidence of a disease or disorder. Symptoms of ill-health are obvious to the observant owner who should take note of them in order to be able to diagnose the problems and give treatment, or to pass them on in detail to the veterinarian. While some individual symptoms are common to many different conditions, when connected with others a picture can be formed of the disease, and the correct treatment commenced without delay. Examples of symptoms which require further investigation are vomiting, diarrhoea, convulsions, prolonged loss of appetite, coughing, discharge or swelling, respiratory distress, loss of energy and alertness, pain, etc.
synapse	The region where one nerve cell makes contact with another through which nerve impulses pass by means of diffusion of transmitter substances such as acetylcholine.
syncope	See fainting.
synovial fluid	The lubricating fluid, or synovia, found in mobile joints and tendon sheaths. It is secreted by the synovial membrane which lines the area. Examination of synovial fluid can provide an aid to the diagnosis of various joint problems, including arthritis. (See also joints.)
syringe	Instrument for injecting fluid into the body. Apart from being used in giving injections, a disposable plastic syringe can also be useful

for administering medicine orally and for feeding premature puppies. (See medicine, administration of; whelping.) *syringe*

The rhythmical contraction of the heart. A high-pitched sound known as a systolic click is sometimes heard with a stethoscope and may be a warning of a diseased mitral valve of the heart. **systole**

tablets

Drugs or other compounds which are compressed from powder or paste into small cakes for convenience of strength and dosage. If dogs refuse to swallow tablets or have difficulty taking them, crushing them again into powder and suspending them in solution is often the answer. (See also medicine, administration of.)

tachycardia

Unusually rapid heartbeat. It can be a symptom of heart disease such as myocarditis. It can also be due to stress, pain, toxaemia and sometimes anaemia and may be evident in heat stroke. If severe the patient may be in a collapsed state and emergency veterinary treatment will be needed.

Tachycardia is considered to exist at heart-rates of more than 160 beats per minute in average-sized adult dogs (about 180 beats per minute in toy breeds).

tail

The bones of the tail, or caudal vertebrae, form an extension of the spinal column though there is no spinal cord enclosed. In the average (undocked) tail there are about twenty vertebrae. In a docked tail only about five may be present. The tail is otherwise composed of muscles with nerves and blood vessels running through.

The tail is used as a component of expression, often together with body and ear attitudes. Tail wagging (with a loose movement of the body in the larger breeds) is an expression of friendship, excitement or happiness (often a combination of all three). Puppies also wag tails when soliciting food. In intimidation behaviour the dog's tail moves slowly and stiffly from side to side or may stand straight up. If the tail is tucked between the legs with the body in a cowering position it is a sign of fear. Jerky tail (and head) movements occur in play signals. The sideways cocking of the tail by the bitch during oestrus when approached by a male dog usually signifies the correct time for mating.

Since the dog's tail is such an expressive appendage it is perhaps a pity that many are docked for the sake of fashion and the veterinary profession in the UK is seeking legislation to make it illegal. (See also docking.)

tangle-splitter

See mat-splitter.

tapeworm

See parasites.

tarsus

Seven tarsal bones form the tarsus, or hock, of the hind paw, situated at the lower ends of the tibia and fibula and above the metatarsus.

tartar

A solid deposit, usually brown or yellowish-brown in colour, which can build up on the teeth. It is mostly calcium phosphate and may contain food particles. In any case food particles and bacteria collect in its crevices and often decay of the teeth results unless regular scaling is carried out during grooming. Prolonged presence of tartar can cause bad breath, digestive problems (due largely to the discomfort from associated gum infections) and eventual loss of teeth unless removed. (See also dental hygiene; scaling teeth.)

tartar

The sense of taste is centred around the tongue and its superficial sensory cells, known as taste buds, which act as receptors. These are arranged in groups so that sour sensations are tasted in the centre of the tongue, sweet in the front and salt at the back. Nerve fibre endings reach into the taste buds and convey messages to the brain. Taste is enhanced in solution and is closely aligned to the sense of smell. (See also tongue.)

taste

A permanent mark on the skin, made with pricked-in pigment. Tattooing is a relatively new idea as a precaution against theft or loss. The dog is tattooed on the ear, usually with a number or mark of identification, so that if it is stolen or strays it can be identified easily by the owner, or the owner traced by the finder. Central registers can be kept by animal organisations or local authorities corresponding to appropriate identification marks with the individual marking added.

tattoo

An end product of sulphur amino acid metabolism produced from the amino acids methionine and cystine, which contain sulphur. It is contained in meat and a deficiency sometimes results in visual disorders due to degeneration of the retina.

taurine

The secretions of the conjunctival and lachrymal glands of the eye. The purpose of this clear fluid is to bathe the eye, keeping it free of dust and other harmful material. If tears are excessive the fault could lie in an obstruction of the lachrymal ducts taking excess fluid down into the nasopharynx, chronic irritation of the eye or inflammation of the iris. Diagnosis by a veterinarian is made easier with the help of a dye.

tears

See mammary glands.

teats

Whilst there are variations in the numbers and arrangement of teeth in a dog's mouth depending on its breed (short-faced dogs such as pekinese, pugs, bulldogs, boxers, etc, have fewer teeth), the average adult dog has 42 teeth. These are arranged as follows: upper jaw, 6 incisors, 2 canines, 8 premolars, and 4 molars; lower jaw, 6 incisors, 2 canines, 8 premolars and 6 molars. The fourth premolar in the upper jaw and the first molar in the lower are the dog's carnassial teeth.

teeth

Incisors, found at the opening of the mouth, are cutters and tearers; the canines, situated on each side of the upper and lower jaws behind the incisors, are relatively useless in domesticated dogs having been developed as fighting teeth; next in line are the premolars which, with the molars, are known as cheek teeth and used for grinding and chewing.

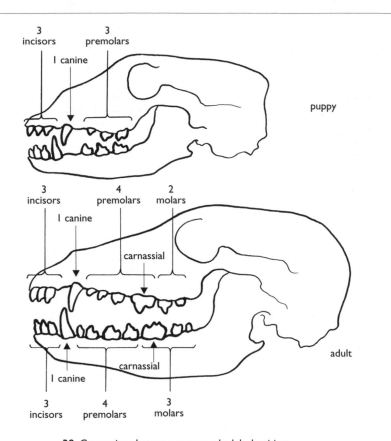

38 Comparison between puppy and adult dentition

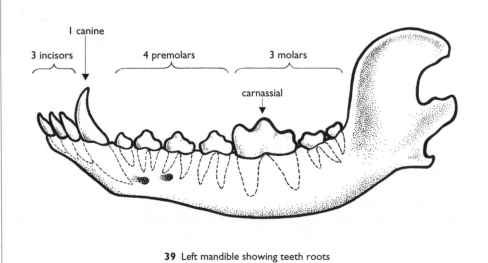

39 Left mandible showing teeth roots

The centre of each tooth is made up of pulp containing nerves and blood vessels, and it is from the pulp that dentine is formed to make up most of the tooth. The crown, the portion which emerges above the jaw, is capped with hard enamel and the remainder by 'cement' which is a tissue similar to bone and softer than dentine.

teeth

In the dog there are two consecutive sets of teeth: the deciduous or milk teeth and those that remain permanently, although molars have no deciduous predecessors. Puppies are born with no teeth and temporary canines are the first to show through in about three to four weeks from birth. Incisors follow during the next week or two with the first three cheek teeth. When the dog is about four months old, permanent premolars appear with permanent canines erupting at about five to six months of age (in toy breeds about a month earlier) together with the first three permanent cheek teeth. In the next two months the remainder of the permanent cheek teeth erupt so that, in most breeds, all permanent teeth are in use at the end of eight months of age.

It is impossible to discover the age of a dog with any accuracy by its teeth. (See also dental hygiene; diet; tartar.)

The natural disposition of an animal. A dog's temperament is partly due to heredity, but environmental influences and training also play important parts in its formation.

temperament

If bred from parents of good temperament dogs normally grow up to show affection to those they know and trust – it is canine nature to do so. Those they do not trust they may be permitted to show some wariness of until they come to know them better, though aggression should be discouraged or it may get out of hand as a dog grows up.

Sudden changes in temperament – from a gentle, affectionate disposition to an aggressive one – can be due to ill-health. It is, for example, one of the symptoms of rabies and distemper and can also be due to a brain tumour or a virus infection. (See also aggressiveness; behaviour.)

The dog's body temperature is usually taken rectally and should normally be between 38.3° and 38.7°C (100.9° and 101.7°F). Two degrees or so above normal is indicative of ill-health. (See also fever; hypothermia; thermometer.)

temperature

A cord-like structure of tough connective tissue which attaches muscle to the bones of the skeleton. Tendons have their own nerves and blood vessels running through them. If torn by injury, tendons can be repaired by suturing with non-absorbent materials such as silk or stainless steel. Inflammation of the sheath which encloses the tendon occurs occasionally due usually to a bacterial infection or rheumatism.

tendon

The male reproductive glands, also known as the testicles or gonads, which produce spermatozoa for reproduction. They also manufacture the hormone testosterone. Each weighs an average of between 7 and 8g (¼ and ⅓oz).

testes

testes	There are two testes in the dog; they are oval in shape and contained by the scrotum. They are developed in the abdomen and descend into the scrotum during infancy. For show purposes dogs should have both testes descended into the scrotum. (See also orchidectomy; orchitis.)

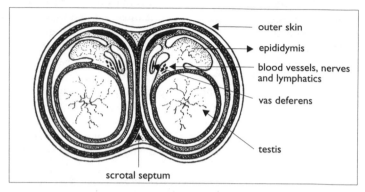

40 Section of testes and scrotum

testicles	See testes.
testosterone	The main male sex hormone secreted by the testes. It is responsible for the development of most male characteristics, including the ability to produce spermatozoa and sexual drive. Injected synthetically it is of minimal use in correcting infertility although low dosage for two or three days will increase libido.
tetanus	A disease, known as lockjaw, caused by an organism which infects the tissues through a wound, especially a deep puncture. It can be lethal, but fortunately it is relatively rare in the canine world. Antitoxins can be injected if a wounded dog is considered vulnerable to the disease. However, it is necessary to give anti-toxin before onset of the attack and, for this reason as well as others, all suspect wounds should be seen by a veterinarian. Later treatment consists mainly of the administration of muscle relax-ants (such as promazine) and other agents such as antibiotics and glucose saline. Careful nursing is also essential to the dog's chances of recovery.

Symptoms of tetanus include extreme muscular stiffness, staring eyes and drawn back ears and facial muscles. The spinal column may also twist or arch. |
tetracycline	An antibiotic with wide-ranging action against bacteria. It should not be given in late pregnancy or to growing dogs since it may affect the teeth. (See also antibiotics.)
thalamus	See brain.
thermometer	An instrument for measuring temperature. The most common type is of glass containing mercury which expands as temperature

increases, flowing up the internal tube and corresponding to predetermined graduations. The thermometer is very carefully inserted into the dog's rectum to take its body temperature. (See also fever; hypothermia; temperature.)

thermometer

(Vitamin B_1). See nutrition.

thiamin

The upper portion of the pelvic limb. The muscles of the thigh surround the femur, or thigh bone, and act mainly on the knee joint.

thigh

A short-acting anaesthetic drug. It is usually used for minor operations since its action lasts for only about five to fifteen minutes. If injected rapidly the duration of activity is at its shortest; if slowly it acts longer.

thiopentone sodium

Abnormal thirst can be a symptom of various diseases. While salty food or exercise in hot weather may account for a temporary increase in water consumption, excessive thirst under normal conditions can be indicative of such disorders as diabetes, nephritis, pyometra and Cushing's disease. A feverish dog is usually thirsty.

    It can also be the result of psychological trauma (stress), when veterinary treatment may be needed to restore the dog's drinking habits to normal.

thirst

A surgical operation comprising an incision in the chest wall. It may be performed in order to drain pus or fluid from the thoracic cavity in disease or as an exploratory operation when, for example, the presence of a foreign body or tumour in the respiratory system is suspected. Corrective surgery can then be carried out at the same time. As an emergency measure a thoracotomy may be performed by a veterinarian if the pulse ceases and after external heart massage has been unsuccessfully attempted.

thoracotomy

See chest.

thorax

A form of communication behaviour usually seen in the early stages of aggression prior to conflict. It may be accompanied (and sometimes replaced) by fear. A threatening dog does not always attack, particularly if its rival shows signs of submission, thus appeasing the aggressor. Even so, threat may develop into conflict regardless of the rival's attitudes and should be taken as a serious warning. The purpose of threat behaviour is to keep other dogs (and perhaps trespassing humans) at a distance without risking injury by conflict. Signs of threat include baring of teeth and wrinkling of nose with ears erect and forward. If ears are drawn back and mouth corners lengthen, fear accompanies the threat. Sudden shortening of mouth corners and ears pricking forward shows the threat is developing into a readiness to bite. (See also aggressiveness; behaviour; communication.)

threat

See pharynx.

throat

thrombocyte	See platelets.
thrombocytopaenia	Abnormal decrease in the number of platelets in the blood. While this condition can be caused directly by reduced production of platelets by the bone marrow, it is far more commonly a secondary disorder to other diseases, including rheumatoid arthritis, lupus erythematosus and some forms of anaemia. Diagnosis is made with the aid of laboratory tests after such symptoms as haematuria, nose-bleeding and haemorrhage from the mucous membranes and gums. In such cases as immune-mediated thrombocytopaenia, long term drug treatment to stabilise the condition and control the tendency to haemorrhage may be necessary. Platelets may also be destroyed in the blood by allergies, spleen disorders, thrombosis in the lungs or extensive burns.
thrombokinase	See thromboplastin.
thromboplastin	A biological activator, also known as thrombokinase, which converts prothrombin into active thrombin with the aid of calcium salts during the blood coagulation process.
thrombosis	The formation of a solid mass of blood in a vessel which causes partial or complete obstruction of circulation in the region. If a vessel wall is unhealthy or damaged a clot can form, increasing in size until blockage occurs. This clot obstruction can form virtually anywhere in the circulatory system, in veins or arteries. It can arise in heart, lungs, liver, uterus or mammary glands, for example, and in the brain it can cause a stroke. Thrombosis can also develop from phlebitis or tuberculosis and can occur as a result of road accidents, infections or post-operatively. Anticoagulant drugs, and occasionally surgery, are the regular forms of treatment. (See also coagulation.)
thrombus	The clot of blood which forms pathologically in a blood vessel. It is composed largely of fibrin, platelets and blood cells.
thymus	This lobulated lymphatic gland is situated in the thoracic cavity close to heart and lungs, and weighs about 50g (1¾oz) in the average-sized adult dog. It does vary in size, however, and is largest between birth and puberty, gradually shrinking in later life. Knowledge of its function is limited but it is thought to despatch lymphocytes to peripheral lymphoid tissue in early life and in some way primes lymphocytes to respond to stimulation by antigens. Its own stimulus for production may originate in the bone marrow. In lymphatic leukaemia there may be a tumour of the thymus and in myasthenia gravis removal of the thymus can sometimes effect a cure.
thyroid	A double-lobed gland situated in the neck and attached to the trachea. This gland influences metabolism and is essential for

normal growth. A deficient production of its hormone thyroxine causes hypothyroidism (myxoedema). Excessive production causes hyperthyroidism.

thyroid

The principal hormone secreted by the thyroid gland. Thyroxine is needed for reproduction and is involved in the stimulation of lactation. Its secretion is regulated by the activity of the pituitary gland so that if either the thyroid or pituitary is unhealthy, the other's activity may also be affected.

thyroxine

The hind leg bone which, with the fibula, is situated between the stifle (or knee) and hock (or ankle). It is larger than the fibula and flattened at the top to form the stifle joint with the femur. Its lower end is grooved to fit with one of the tarsal bones to form the hock joint.

tibia

See parasites.

tick

The fabric of the body. All tissue is made up of groups of cells with a common function and there are four basic types. Muscular tissue has the ability to contract and is associated with movement. Epithelial tissue forms the covering of the body and lines passages and internal cavities. Nervous tissue cells and fibres carry messages and stimuli within the body. Connective tissue binds all other forms of tissue together, acts as a supporting medium and carries nutrients to, and waste products from, the various cells of the body.

tissue

See claw; paw.

toe

Small, round-ended scissors for trimming the hair which grows between the pads of the feet. (See also grooming.)

toe scissors

The tongue is composed mainly of skeletal muscle fibres and covered with a specialised mucous membrane. It is long, thin, very mobile and normally pink in colour. It protrudes considerably when the dog is panting and is important in temperature regulation.

tongue

The tongue has extensive blood and nerve supplies and is roughened on the upper surface by several forms of papillae, most of which contain taste buds. Anchoring the tongue to the floor of the mouth is the frenulum, a thick fold of mucous membrane with muscles which help to extend and withdraw the tongue as required. (See drawing.)

The tongue is not only used in digestion to mix and direct food in the mouth on the next stage of its journey into the pharynx, but is also a delicate sensory organ for the senses of taste and touch. It is also used for lapping when drinking and for licking when the dog cleans itself.

The tongue should be examined periodically for signs of inflammation, discoloration, ulceration, and the presence of tumours or such foreign bodies as pins, fish-hooks, etc. (See also glossitis; taste.)

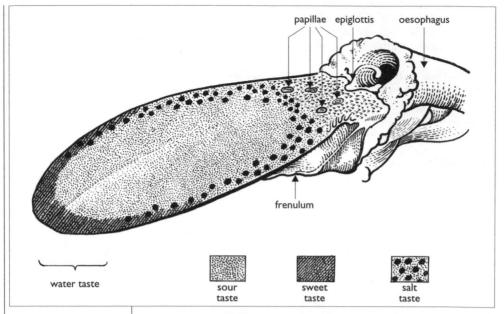

papillae epiglottis   oesophagus

frenulum

water taste

sour
taste

sweet
taste

salt
taste

41 The canine tongue showing areas of taste

tonsillitis	Inflammation of the tonsils. Although the tonsils cannot easily be seen when healthy, they become enlarged and painful during an attack of tonsillitis and the dog may cough and retch as a result. The condition is usually due to an infection which requires treatment with suitable antibiotics, but it can also be a symptom of viral hepatitis.
tonsils	Lymph nodes covered with a mucous membrane and situated in a depression, one on either side of the pharynx. Their purpose is to act as filter for the lymph passing through them from the mouth and to remove micro-organisms from it.
torsion	Twisting – a condition which may affect the stomach, intestines or uterus, for example. In tetanus, torsion of the spinal column may occur. In most cases of torsion surgery is necessary with some urgency since the blood supply may be cut off from the twisted portion of the affected organ. (See also stomach torsion; uterine torsion.)
touch	The sense of touch is achieved by the round-bodied nerve endings in the skin known as tactile corpuscles. The nerves which detect the sensations of pain and temperature extremes of both heat and cold end in fragile tree-like structures. Pressure can also be sensed by the touch mechanism so that force, weight and resistance can be evaluated. Impulses from the nerve endings or receptors are transmitted to the brain by way of the spinal cord. Tactile hairs on the muzzle also sense touch through nerve endings which are positioned around the hair follicles. (See also nervous system.)

An appliance used in emergency to arrest haemorrhage by compression. It usually consists of a bandage or other material wound round an affected limb and tightened and periodically loosened by means of a stick or pencil twisted in the material. It acts by constricting the arteries supplying blood to the wound and should be used only in cases where severe haemorrhage is out of control or where limbs have been severed. It is applied a few inches above the wound and adjusted so that the pressure is only just sufficient to stop the bleeding. It should be slackened off every five or ten minutes and should not be left on for more than fifteen minutes or gangrene of the lower portion of the limb is likely. If it is necessary to re-apply the tourniquet it should be done a little closer to the wound to allow the compressed tissues at the original site to recover. Tourniquets should be used only when other methods, such as pressure exerted by the fingers above a wound if an artery is cut and below if a vein is severed, have failed to stop the flow of blood. In such emergencies a veterinarian should be summoned immediately. (See also accidents; haemorrhage; wounds.) | **tourniquet**

Poisoning of the blood caused by the absorption of toxins released by organisms during infection (or from bites or stings). | **toxaemia**

Toxaemia can occur as an infection worsens, such as that from an abscess, for example. The symptoms of some diseases, such as tetanus, are produced entirely from the effects of the toxins rather than from the organism itself.

Symptoms of this often dangerous condition include a fever, rises in temperature and pulse-rate, quickened respiration, a general depression and loss of interest in food. Treatment consists mainly of combating the original infection, usually with the aid of antibiotics. Dextrose and physiological saline may be infused as supportive therapy.

Poisonous substances of animal origin which are usually released by bacteria or by the deterioration of waste products which, for some reason such as kidney failure, are not excreted. They can also be found in poisonous bites or stings from insects, snakes, etc. | **toxins**

Infection with a specific roundworm, *Toxocara canis*. Anthelmintics are used in treatment, including piperazine which is contained in many proprietary worming agents. (See also parasites.) | **toxocariasis**

A disease which primarily infects cats but can also be contracted by dogs, along with many other carnivores. Hunting cats may ingest mice, rats or other meat containing the infecting parasite (which can also live on ticks and lice). Dogs eating grass, infected meat or other refuse may contract them. It appears that antibodies against the disease are built up in the body. (It has been suggested that up to half the dogs in the USA, for example, have toxoplasma antibodies.) | **toxoplasmosis**

Symptoms of the disease may not be present or, if they are, they vary considerably including respiratory difficulties and diarrhoea. Sulphonamides (such as sulfadiazine) are a form of treatment.

toxoplasmosis

Prevention lies mainly in not feeding raw meat and controlling the activities of such intermediate hosts as flies, cockroaches and other faeces-eating creatures which may pass it on, and, if a cat is present in the family discourage it from hunting mice and rats and hygienically dispose of its faeces.

toys

It is very useful for a puppy to have toys since they help to develop its learning patterns, as well as preventing boredom and deflecting its attention from other objects around the house. However, they should be chosen with care. An old leather belt is fine for the puppy to chew, but not if it still contains sharp-pointed buckles, pins or studs. Old shoes may be interesting providing eyelets and shoelaces are removed. When the puppy grows and much of the chewing stage is over rubber rings and other specially-designed canine toys can be added, but until then only materials which are safely ingested should be given. Tennis balls are too large and too round for much to be chewed from them, so they make useful toys. Children's toys are very unsuitable, and potentially dangerous for dogs and puppies and should always be kept out of an animal's reach. (See also ball; foreign bodies; play.)

trace elements

See nutrition.

trachea

The air passage or windpipe which runs down from the larynx into the thorax to a point where it branches into the left and right bronchi. It is made up of about thirty-five rings of cartilage with muscle, ligaments and connective tissue.

The trachea may be injured in attacks from other dogs, road accidents, and encounters with shattered glass or barbed wire. Pain will be experienced and respiration will be noisy as well as troublesome. Frothy haemorrhage may be evident. When dressing a tracheal wound it is essential to ensure that no liquid enters the air passage.

If foreign bodies lodge in the trachea general anaesthesia is needed before surgical removal is attempted. Although collapse of the trachea is generally unlikely is does occur occasionally, especially in toy breeds. In these cases breathing difficulties and distress are usual symptoms.

A veterinarian should be asked to examine urgently all tracheal wounds or obstruction.

tracheotomy

An emergency operation performed to open the trachea and allow the entry of air during obstruction.

training

Carried out with firmness, patience, kindness and understanding of the dog's capabilities and limitations, training strengthens the bond between dog and owner.

A training programme commences with house training a puppy. While puppies have little control over themselves, most are anxious to please. They need to urinate soon after they wake from a sleep, for example, and should be hurried outside where they perform naturally. Praising the puppy at this time makes it quickly associate the sequence with rewarding words while, if it has an accident inside the house, growling, admonishing words have the reverse effect. It is never necessary to smack a puppy to house train it. If it persistently urinates indoors the admonition can be accompanied by a tap on the body (*not* the head) with a lightly-rolled newspaper. The noise reinforces the action. Scolding will, perhaps surprisingly, be rarely needed if the praise is sufficient and the owner's alertness in getting the pup to the garden is adequate. Puppies also need to defecate after a meal and should be accompanied into the garden for a while when food is finished. Be sure to praise when the act is achieved.

All dogs should be trained with a collar and lead. The so-called 'choke' chain, while suitable in extreme cases for obstinate individuals of the heavier active breeds (such as German shepherds, rottweilers, etc), is generally not advisable. It consists of a metal chain with a ring at one end through which the chain is dropped. The chain is hung round the dog's neck and the ring attached to a stout lead. When the dog pulls forward the 'noose' becomes tighter, slackening when it walks with the lead slack. Most dogs dislike the experience and, since training should be a pleasurable activity for the dog, a leather collar and lead are better. At the subsequent stage of training, you should be able to trust your dog to walk to heel and to be obedient enough to walk without a lead, although all dogs should be led when on roads (or crossing them) or when traffic is around.

Puppies should be trained to walk on the left side of their owners on a lead. The collar should not be uncomfortably tight and the lead should be long enough to allow some freedom. Patience is especially important – some dogs take to lead training more slowly than others. Persevere with firm, gentle, consistent tugs on the lead, returning the puppy to heel when it becomes too unruly and starts to pull. Teach it to sit at heel (praising it liberally on each triumphant occasion) and to move off at command. Make sure that the commands you use are consistent and that other members of the family are aware of them so that, after training has progressed, they will use the same words in a similar situation. It is best if one person trains a dog since the animal will learn voice tones which may vary from one human to another. Training sessions should not be so long that the dog tires or becomes bored; they should be fun for the dog *and* for its owner.

Following the basics of lead training a dog will be ready to respond to recognised commands when off the lead. When this stage is reached, take the student to a quiet place, away from noisy traffic and such distractions as other dogs to play with and people walking back and forth. By regular repetition of the words it has already learnt the dog will respond when free, leaving the way open for an opportunity to teach it to 'stay', 'fetch', 'come' and 'leave'. Once a word is learned, clear repetition by a patient owner produces the best results. Most dogs are anxious to please an owner they trust, respect and regard with affection.

training

Every dog should be taught at least to come when it is called, to sit and to walk to heel. These educational assets may help to save its life one day. Most dogs are more than capable of additional learning and, while some respond faster and more efficiently than others, there is no reason why a more detailed training programme could not be implemented once the dog has become proficient in basic training. Teach the dog one word or command at a time. When the word and the action are instantly coupled, the next command for another action can be taught. Do not forget to refresh the dog's memory from time to time on its earlier lessons.

A dog should never learn its training through fear – it becomes unhappy and its response unreliable; training sessions which are fearfully anticipated eventually damage the dog's health. The best time to train a dog is between six and twelve months of age. (See also behaviour; learning; obedience.)

tranquillisers

Drugs which calm the dog rather than sending it to sleep. They are very useful for the nervous or aggressive animal requiring extensive or detailed examination or subjected to certain necessary activities (such as travel, firework noise, thunderstorms etc) which are regularly found disturbing.

Diazepam and acetylpromazine maleate are examples used in veterinary medicine.

transfusions and infusions

A transfusion is the transfer of whole blood or plasma from a donor to a recipient. Infusions are other fluids, mostly given intravenously, which are prepared under laboratory conditions as physiological solutions. Commonly-used examples of infusions are normal saline (0.85 per cent sodium chloride in sterile water), dextrose-saline (normal saline with 5 per cent dextrose included) or electrolyte solutions (eg Ringer's solution).

Transfusions are given in such situations as massive haemorrhage, where blood loss must be replaced, or where blood cells are destroyed by disease. When a transfusion is planned a donor of similar blood group to that of the recipient is needed and laboratory tests (cross-matching) are carried out to confirm. If groups are incompatible between donor and recipient antibodies are formed and in about ten days the transfused blood cells begin to be destroyed in the recipient's body, causing a reaction. This reaction can also occur if a second transfusion is called for, with similar cell destruction and a serious effect on various organs. Symptoms of such a reaction include fever, muscular tremors, incontinence and shock. Treatment with soluble corticosteroids, oxygen and rest are then needed.

Infusions are administered to maintain or correct fluid volume in the body. Conditions where fluid loss occurs (dehydration) include prolonged diarrhoea, vomiting or where fluid intake is less than that excreted. (When body fluids equivalent to about 6 per cent of body weight are lost and not replaced, dehydration is serious.)

Transfusions or infusions may be prescribed as supportive therapy, eg in some cases of toxaemia. A local anaesthetic should

be used at the site where the needle enters the vein. (See also *transfusions and infusions*
blood group.)

transport

When a dog is being transported it needs water and, if travelling
for lengthy periods, food as well. It may also require the administration of a tranquilliser if it is particularly nervous or if the
voyage is likely to be disturbing through excessive noise, etc.

Whether travelling by air, sea, rail or road, a dog in transit also
requires special care to be taken in its confinement. Any crate or
container must be adequately ventilated and large enough to give
the dog room to move around and to stand up fully. It should
also be clearly and correctly labelled. The shortest possible route
should be chosen and collection at the dog's destination arranged
before arrival.

Dogs regularly transported by car (eg to shows, etc) are best in
an estate car with a dog guard fixed behind the rear seats or in
special travelling cages of a suitable size to allow the dog room
to stand and lie down comfortably. In this way the dog cannot
interfere with the driver's concentration and cannot fall off seats,
risking injury, in the event of sudden braking or an accident.
Dogs should never be left in cars in direct sunlight or in hot
weather.

Before arranging the transport of an unaccompanied dog apply
to the appropriate authority (eg railway, airline, shipping line,
etc) for regulations concerning the transport of live dogs. (See
also car sickness; heat stroke; importing/exporting.)

trauma

A wound or injury to the body, or emotional stress. Surgical trauma
is a term often applied to post-operative shock or stress.

travelling

See transport.

travel sickness

See car sickness.

tremor

A small spasmodic muscle contraction. Tremors usually signify
a disease of the nervous system or an emotional disturbance.
Nervous animals may produce tremors in the form of shivering.
Head tremors are a symptom of brain lesions and body tremors can
indicate damage to brain and/or spinal cord. Tremors may also
occur in rabies and kidney failure and are a symptom of chorea.
(See also shivering; spasm.)

trichiasis

Inward-growing eyelashes which brush the eye as the eyelids
flicker, causing pain and inflammation. Surgical treatment is
usually necessary to correct the condition.

trichinosis

A disease caused by infestation of the muscles by a form of small
roundworm. This parasite can be ingested from raw or under-
cooked meat. The condition is rare and most frequently affects sled
dogs in polar regions where raw seal or walrus meat may be
included in the diet. Pigs, however, can contract the disease and

trichinosis	any dog may receive the roundworm after eating uncooked, infected pork. (See also parasites.)
trichuriasis	A parasite infestation with a species of whipworm. Infective eggs ingested by the victim hatch out in the small intestine causing emaciation, flatulence and abdominal pain. Oral mebendazole for five days is a common cure after detection of eggs in faeces. (See also parasites.)
tricks	While most dogs can be trained to perform tricks, perhaps the best outlet for the canine intelligence is in training for more useful pursuits which provide enjoyable exercise and perhaps achievement, such as field trials or obedience programmes. Some tricks can be harmful to the dog and others can be the source of stress if the dog does not enjoy its performance. (See also training.)
trypanosomiasis	A disease caused by a single-celled blood parasite which occurs in tropical climates, including India, Central and South America and Africa. Specific drugs are available to treat such symptoms as ascites, anaemia, fever, weight loss and heart failure.
trypsin	An enzyme secreted by the pancreas and important in digestion for its role in the breaking down of proteins into amino acids. It becomes active only when in the presence of food (or it would destroy the protein of the pancreas itself) and is triggered into action by an intestinal juice, an activator called enterokinase.
tuberculosis	A chronic contagious disease which can be passed on from man or other animals (or from infected uncooked meat) to the dog. It is fortunately much less common now than it was some fifty years ago in the UK and USA. Preventive measures include a sound diet, hygiene and, in kennels, good ventilation. The disease is characterised by the spread of tubercles – small, soft nodules which invade the body tissues, affecting most organs including commonly the lungs, pleura, liver, intestines, etc. Often it is difficult to detect the disease until in advanced stages though, if it is suspected, laboratory tests can be performed to confirm the diagnosis. Symptoms in the early days can be vague, usually including a dry cough, some nasal discharge and increasingly distressed breathing in respiratory tuberculosis and alternating diarrhoea and constipation in abdominal tuberculosis. Weakness, loss of condition and tiredness following exercise are symptoms common to most forms. A variety of drugs is active against tuberculosis and careful nursing with the elimination of all forms of stress helps to provide the animal with a good chance of recovery. The patient should be isolated and barrier nursed to prevent spread of the disease, particularly to human contacts.
tumours	An abnormal growth. Tumours can be malignant or benign and vary considerably in type, rate of growth, etc. Malignant forms are mostly faster growing, invading and destroying normal healthy

tissue and, by means of individual cells detaching from the primary growth and circulating in the blood or lymph, can spread throughout the body and produce secondary tumours in other organs. In many cases entire organs need to be removed (if this is possible) by surgery. This should, of course, be done before secondary growths occur.

Benign tumours may also be removed surgically if necessary but do not hold the same threat to the dog's life. They remain at one site and are self-contained although they may increase in size or threaten the activity of an organ if at a critical site.

Virtually all areas and tissues of the body are vulnerable to the development of tumours, perhaps the most common of which are mammary tumours in the bitch. Deformed or 'rogue' cells form (usually for undiscovered reasons) and grow out of control by the body's normal growth-and-repair system. Any tumour should be examined by a veterinarian as soon as it appears and regular examination by the dog's owner does much to prevent the spread of tumours since early treatment often effects a cure.

See tremor.

tumours

twitching

U

ulcer

An open sore resulting from destruction of epithelial tissue or mucous membrane, usually due to prolonged infection. Ulcers are quick to spread and slow to heal, being resistant to treatment when established. They occur most frequently in the mouth (accompanied by foul-smelling breath and salivation), on the surface of mammary tumours in the bitch, or on various parts of the body. A sick animal which lies for lengthy periods on a flat surface is especially vulnerable to ulcers in the form of 'bedsores' and these are best prevented by regular turning of the patient and gentle massage of limbs and body. Rodent ulcers, which are slow-growing, low-malignancy ulcerating tumours of the skin, also sometimes affect dogs and in tuberculosis there may be ulcers on the skin. Corneal ulcers can be especially painful and can threaten the dog's sight.

Early treatment of all forms of ulcer is important and a veterinarian should be consulted at the first signs. Ulcers spread by necrosis of the edges of the sore and usually suppurate, being produced sometimes from neglected wounds (or even the application of an excessively strong antiseptic to a wound) or when a dog is 'run down' or out of condition due to chronic disease. Toxaemia can be an added complication of neglected ulcers.

Surfaces may be treated with acriflavine or gentian violet but surgery may be necessary in severe cases to separate dead cells from remaining healthy tissue.

ulcerative colitis

Inflammation of the colon which chronically causes ulceration. Causes of the disease include bad diet, infection, consumption of refuse, stress, etc. Although antibiotics may be of some use and steroids ease the problem, it is often incurable and peritonitis may result from the ulcers penetrating the intestinal wall. (See also colitis.)

ulna

This bone and the radius comprise the forearm. The ulna is attached to the radius by muscle tissue and can move around it. Together with the radius the ulna joins the humerus at its upper end to form the elbow joint. The ulna is the longest bone in the dog's body.

umbilical cord

The communication line between the umbilical region of the foetus and the placenta. The foetal blood returns to the placenta via the umbilical cord while the blood and nutrients from the dam enter the placenta from the uterine wall. The umbilical cord is severed at birth, usually by the dam biting through it, and the small remaining portion close to the puppy's abdomen withers away as it is no longer required. (See also whelping.)

umbilical hernia

See hernia.

umbilicus

The navel; a scar at the site of the umbilical ring where the umbilical cord joined the foetus prior to whelping.

Primary causes are generally brain or skull injuries, poisoning (usually by narcotics or other substances affecting the nervous system) or diseases such as epilepsy, cerebral haemorrhage from a stroke and extreme stress, all of which directly affect the nervous system. Secondary causes, when loss of consciousness is the result of an injury or disease which first affects other physiological systems prior to involvement of the nervous system, include diabetic coma, asphyxia, eclampsia, uraemia, heat stroke, heart failure and electric shock. Shock itself can also produce unconsciousness.

In many cases the cause of unconsciousness is obvious and immediate steps must be taken to provide the correct treatment. In other situations the reasons may not be so apparent and the patient must be thoroughly examined by a veterinarian to determine the cause and prescribe appropriate treatment – also with urgency, since unconsciousness is usually serious. Even if recovery to normal consciousness is rapid the patient should be checked over to see if any damage has resulted.

In examination of an unconscious dog a note should be taken of any accompanying symptoms such as convulsions, increased or shallow respiration, pulse-rate, dilated or contracted eye pupils, breath odour and incontinence. (See also coma.)

Many thousands of dogs become unwanted each year. The reasons are clear and simple: an endearing puppy, bought perhaps as a Christmas present, becomes bigger and more boisterous than the owners thought, it makes messes, chews furniture and tears up carpets, shoes and curtains through boredom or lack of training. The owners decide they cannot keep it and then either try to have it destroyed (or even cruelly release it on a major road to roam or be killed) or pass the responsibility for it to a rescue home. Sometimes they give it away, untrained, to another unprepared unsuspecting person and the cycle of misery for the dog begins again. The faults mentioned above rarely lie with the dogs but with owners who are totally unprepared for the responsibility of keeping them.

An international survey carried out several years ago showed that of a dog population in the UK of around 6.2 million, about 117,000 fell into the unwanted category. Out of these some 11,000 are put to sleep because a good home could not be found for them. Most animal welfare organisations, but not all, take great care about new homes for rescued dogs, in the hope of avoiding a repeat of the poor dog's previous home. Most are neutered and microchipped before rehoming. In the USA, with a canine population around 33 million, about 5 million are unwanted and destroyed each year. These horrifying figures could be drastically reduced by the spaying of bitches which are likely to suffer unwanted pregnancies. Neutering males also helps to reduce substantially the numbers of unwanted dogs. By far the largest percentage of straying dogs taken into care are males, probably having sired many in a new generation of unwanted dogs. The number of unwanted dogs could also be minimised by potential owners giving more forethought to the problems involved in providing for a dog's welfare.

unconsciousness

unwanted dogs

unwanted dogs

For anyone choosing a dog from the unwanted masses, the rewards can often be substantial. A local veterinarian or dog rescue organisation can put prospective owners in touch with a wide choice of these unfortunate animals.

Owners who find they have an unwanted dog, perhaps through an accidental misalliance or a change in domestic circumstances, should be responsible enough to ensure that it finds a good alternative home by all possible means. Contact the breeder if it is a pedigree dog, a chat with a veterinarian and placing local advertisements can all prove useful. An interview with potential new owners and a view of the dog's new home are also advisable. (See also Battersea Dogs' Home; choosing a dog; NCDL.)

uraemia

A serious disease signified by excessive amounts of urea in the blood. While urea is not very poisonous in itself, excessive amounts in the bloodstream indicate the presence of other waste products (such as guanidine and other related compounds) which are toxic. The condition is therefore indicative of kidney disorders, such as nephritis and failure of the kidney to filter off these waste materials. Measurement of urea levels in the blood is relatively simple in laboratory tests but detection of other poisonous substances is extremely difficult. Uraemia occurs in terminal stages of kidney failure but can be cured in less serious cases. Ruptures and obstructions in various parts of the urinary system may account for elevated blood urea, in which case surgery may be necessary.

Symptoms of uraemia include loss of appetite, foul breath with a slight smell of ammonia, a discoloured ulcerated tongue and mucous membranes of the mouth, 'coffee-ground' vomiting and sometimes diarrhoea. Dehydration often occurs with electrolyte imbalance (which also requires urgent administration of appropriate fluids by a veterinarian) and in severe cases convulsions and coma will result. Lungs can become clogged with fluid containing waste protein, and shock may also complicate the condition.

Veterinary treatment includes fluid replacement and treatment for the affected kidney so that it begins to function correctly again. Protein intake must be reduced in recovery to allow the kidneys to cope with the filtration of waste. Diet should include palatable, high quality food and probably additional water soluble vitamins as a form of supplement.

urban dogs

Canine residents of an urban environment need special consideration as they are subject to stresses which are not normally associated with the country dog. A city dog requires as much exercise as its rural counterpart and, wherever possible, enjoys it much better in parklands or woods, rather than on city streets amidst petrol fumes and noise. The lungs of the city-dwelling dog are much more liable to attack by chemicals found in polluted air and some respiratory diseases are therefore more prevalent. In the confines of concentrated populations, disease can also spread more quickly, making immunisation against such diseases as parvo virus, distemper and leptospirosis doubly important.

Suitability to an urban environment should be considered when choosing a dog. Some breeds, such as working collies, gundogs, etc often do less well in a city than in the country unless their natural instincts can be fulfilled. Guard dogs, such as Dobermanns, German shepherds, rottweilers, need special care when exercised in a community. Strict obedience training, discipline and control training are essential for naturally aggressive animals in a crowded area.

Strays and dogs off the lead in streets are hazardous to others, possibly causing, or being harmed in, street accidents, as well as presenting a potential health problem during epidemics.

Some breeds can be just as happy in a city as in the country, provided their owners understand their needs, have consideration for the problems which a city environment presents to dogs and those associated with them in other parts of the community, and fully accept responsibility in terms of food, exercise, shelter, comfort and sound veterinary care. (See also legal and moral responsibilities.)

urban dogs

A waste product from the breakdown of proteins. It is normally mostly excreted in the urine. Levels can be evaluated by laboratory tests to provide evidence of kidney function or malfunction. (See also uraemia.)

urea

The ureters are fibromuscular tubes lined by mucous membrane which carry urine from the kidneys to the bladder, entering at the neck of the bladder. Each has a diameter of between 0.6 and 0.9cm (¼ and ⅓in) and a length around 40cm (16in) in the average-sized dog, the right being a little longer than the left. They are prone to obstruction by calculi, to inflammation and occasionally rupture. Signs of damage or infection include abdominal pain, shock, haematuria and subsequently progressive uraemia and toxaemia. Abscesses may also develop and peritonitis is a probability without treatment.

ureter

The urethra is the canal which brings urine from the bladder to the body's exterior. In the male it also carries seminal fluid and is about 25cm (10in) long in the average dog, although this is subject to considerable variation. The female urethra also originates at the bladder and extends to the genital tract.

urethra

Inflammation of the urethra. It is usually a complication of cystitis as the infection spreads down from the bladder. It is symptomised by painful, prolonged passing of urine with simultaneous obvious distress and the urine either dribbling or being passed in short, sharp emissions. Obstruction of the urethra produces similar symptoms although urine may not be passed at all and an enlarged bladder can be felt against the abdomen.

urethritis

An inability to retain or control the passage of urine. The action of passing urine is effected by means of a complicated nervous system process like a series of circuits. Nervous tissue lesions

urinary incontinence

urinary incontinence (causing intermittent 'breaks in the circuit') may consequently be a reason for urinary incontinence. Fear is another. Nephritis, chronic inflammation and obstruction of the urethra or ureter can be others, producing straining and dribbling when attempts are made to pass urine. Aged dogs may be incontinent due to kidney deterioration (or calculus obstruction), spayed bitches because of a hormone imbalance and male dogs because of an enlarged prostate. Tumours of the bladder and severe cystitis can also produce urinary incontinence. A dog suffering from this condition has increased vulnerability to urinary infections and cystitis, urethritis and nephritis may therefore be less of a cause than an effect. It should be considered seriously and a thorough examination of the incontinent dog made by a veterinarian for an accurate diagnosis of the underlying reasons and appropriate treatment.

urinary retention Retention of urine can be caused by an obstruction, due either to damage or to calculi or tumours in the urinary system. There is usually pain and the bladder is distended with the retained urine. The dog strains to pass urine with no effect and shows signs of distress. The situation should be considered as an emergency and a veterinarian contacted immediately. If untreated the bladder may rupture and cause peritonitis, which can be fatal.

urinary system The urinary system, which comprises kidneys, ureters, bladder and urethra, filters waste products from the blood and passes them out in the form of urine for eventual excretion.

The kidneys act as regulators of the fluid balance of the blood as well as filtering waste. The ureters are connected one to each of the two kidneys and are the transport tubes which take the urine to the bladder where it is collected until expulsion is required through the urethra to the outside of the body.

urination The act of passing urine. The dog's bladder should normally be emptied about twice a day. Puppies, of course, pass urine more frequently and dogs with damage to or inflammation of part of the urinary system also wish to urinate more often. In puppies the sphincter which acts as a valve at the neck of the bladder functions automatically when the bladder is full but in adult dogs it is controlled by will. Control, however, can break down when the bladder becomes too full. Bladder contraction occurs which causes the passing of urine from the bladder down the urethra. (See also cystitis.)

urine Waste products from the body dissolved in water. Urine is excreted by the kidneys and its contents vary substantially according to diet and state of health. In sickness some toxins are filtered out by the kidneys and excreted in the urine. Uric acid is normally present from a carnivorous diet, phosphoric acid may also be included, along with calcium oxalate, hippuric acid, calcium carbonate and various phosphates. Albumin may be evident in kidney damage while pus is indicative of an infection in the urinary system, and sugar of diabetes. Bile in the urine can be a symptom of an obstructed bile-duct, as bile is then reabsorbed and filtered out by the kidneys.

Since the contents, colour and appearance of urine can be a guide to a variety of conditions and diseases, laboratory examination of it can consequently be a useful aid to diagnosis. Much, for example, can be gleaned from the colour, before resorting to chemical tests. The normal urine is straw-coloured (yellow to amber) and while particularly pale urine is often due to excessive fluid intakes (or perhaps a pathological thirst), it can sometimes point to the existence of diabetes, pyometra or nephritis. A dark orange colour shows that the urine is concentrated, which happens when fluid intake is reduced in dehydration and feverish conditions. Cloudy urine indicates the presence of an abundance of white blood cells which gather to combat infection of the urinary tract. If the urine is reddish, blood may be present due to damage within the urinary system (haematuria), and greenish urine denotes excessive bilirubin, a product of the liver.

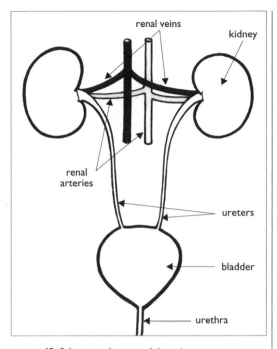

42 Schematic diagram of the urinary system

Collection of urine samples for laboratory examination should be done as hygenically as possible. Using a clean (preferably sterile) container with a wide neck (a deep saucer is useful for a bitch and a thoroughly cleansed yoghurt or ice-cream container or similar plastic receptacle for a dog), collect a 'mid-stream' specimen. This means that when the animal shows signs of urination you allow the flow to start before slipping the container into the stream of urine. This approach has a double advantage: the dog is unlikely to stop until finished once it has started and the collected specimen will also be cleaner, being less contaminated by the external genitalia. The collected specimen can be transferred to a more convenient container, but one which is also thoroughly cleansed.

urine

See reproduction; urinary system.

urogenital system

urolithiasis

A condition in which calculi are formed in the urinary system. Sometimes the calculi, generally composed of phosphate deposits, are large enough to cause obstruction; in other instances they are small and gravel-like, causing damage with associated urinary tract infection. They are most often found in the bladder and/or urethra. Although uncommon, excessive dietary magnesium is thought to be a cause of the disease. A virus infection is another.

If the stones cannot be passed or dispersed with the aid of drugs, surgical removal is often necessary.

urticaria

A non-specific condition of the skin, characterised by the appearance of red weals on the skin surface. It can arise following insect stings, exposure to some plants, as the result of an allergy or merely because the dog repeatedly scratches a skin area. It is by no means common to all dogs (some individuals seem predisposed to it) and antihistamines are generally used to cure it. It should be treated before the skin breaks or antibiotics may be needed to deal with almost inevitable infection. (See also allergy.)

uterine inertia

A complication of whelping where labour commences but ceases again, and the bitch settles down. Labour may also fail to start although signs of impending whelping are present. It can be due to muscular weakness with a resulting inability to produce contractions (elderly bitches are particularly vulnerable, as are bitches which have produced many previous litters, and pampered toy breeds). Lack of exercise in pregnancy can be another reason for the condition, which requires immediate veterinary attention. Intramuscular injections of, for example, meperidine hydrochloride may help to start contractions in nervous bitches and other drugs can be used to stimulate labour in other cases. If labour cannot be started by the use of drugs a caesarian section is usually necessary. (See also dystokia.)

uterine sepsis

See metritis; pyometra.

uterine torsion

This is relatively rare in the dog and is a complication of whelping where the uterus becomes twisted. It is symptomised by feeble activity prior to whelping, intermittent pain and restlessness. A caesarian section may be needed and veterinary examination with some urgency is called for.

uterus

The hollow muscular organ in the abdomen of the bitch in which the pups develop. It is Y-shaped with two 'horns', a body and a neck or cervix which leads to the vagina. The horns open into the Fallopian tubes leading to the ovaries. After conception the fertilised ovum attaches itself to the internal wall of the uterus which, at that point, provides a connection with the source of nourishment from the dam to the foetus.

There are two layers to the uterus and the entire organ is covered with a coat of peritoneum. The endometrium (in which the ovum becomes embedded) is a mucous membrane lining outer muscular tissue known as myometrium. It is thicker than the myometrium.

The uterus changes shape and position during pregnancy and rarely returns to its exact original form after whelping.

V

See immunisation.

vaccination

A preparation containing a weakened or inactive causative micro-organism of a disease which is injected into the body to stimulate the production of antibodies in defence of future invasion by the actual disease. Sometimes associated or related strains of the organism are used if antibody production can be stimulated in the same way. Weakening of bacteria is often attained by their passage through other species and inactivation of live viruses may be achieved by subjection to ultraviolet rays or by treatment with phenol. Some vaccines produce immunity for limited periods only and repeated dosing during life is needed to keep antibodies alert. Correct storage of vaccines is important; otherwise a loss of efficacy is likely.

vaccine

The vagina of the bitch lies entirely in the pelvis and is the muscular canal in which the male spermatozoa are deposited during mating and the passage by which the pups enter the world. It has a mucous membrane lining and is highly dilatable. It connects with the uterus via the cervix and extends to the external urethral orifice, being about 10 to 14cm (4 to 5½in) in length in the average bitch and around 1.5cm (½in) in diameter when undilated.

vagina

The vagus nerve is the tenth cranial nerve supplying the larynx and organs of the thorax and abdomen and is associated with secretion and movement. The origin of the name is derived from the word 'vagabond' (a wanderer) and the nerve is so-called because its branches 'wander' throughout the trunk. It is also known as the pneumogastric nerve and is a major component of the autonomic nervous system.

vagus

There are various valves in the body including in the heart and surrounding blood vessels where the bicuspid, tricuspid, aortic and mitral valves, for example, are located. They are also present in some veins, especially of the limbs, and consist of a pair of cusps or flaps of endothelium supported by connective tissue which open in the direction of the heart to ensure that blood progresses in one direction only. They are sometimes subject to malfunction or defects (some of which may be of a hereditary nature). Some such problems give little cause for alarm while others can be clinically significant requiring treatment.

valves

Varicose distension of the veins of a testis. Generally it is not serious unless pain is caused, in which case surgical removal of the affected veins may be prescribed.

variocele

There are in fact two vascular systems: one deals with blood and the other circulates lymph. They are both systems of tubes and the blood vascular system, with the heart at its centre, keeps the blood

vascular system

vascular system

circulating throughout the body while the lymphatic system circulates lymph and eventually joins the blood vascular system.

'Vascular' means 'pertaining to vessels' and the tube system of the blood vascular (or circulatory) system comprises blood vessels – a complex network of arteries (carrying oxygenated blood from the heart after oxygenation in the lungs) and veins (returning de-oxygenated blood after the oxygen has been burnt off in the tissues in a reaction to produce energy).

Arteries and veins have many branches as they proceed throughout the head, body, limbs and all internal organs and gradually they diminish in size as they reach extremities. Arteries become smaller (known as arterioles) and veins also reduce in diameter (as venules) until both form a fine network of capillaries – minute vessels in which, due to their thin walls, exchange of fluids or gases takes place in tissues and organs.

Some veins branch into complex tributaries of capillaries which meet others for the transfer of substances absorbed in one area to another close by without the need for additional extensive circulation. These are known as portal systems and are evident in the abdomen where blood from stomach, intestines, spleen and pancreas enters the liver via the portal vein which then divides into a plexus of capillaries where excess nutrients are removed and stored in the liver for future use. The blood passes on into veins which join up into larger hepatic veins.

The heart is divided into left and right sides and each side has an atrium or auricle and a ventricle. The right side handles de-oxygenated blood returned from the body by the superior and inferior vena cavae, while the left side pumps only oxygenated blood entering from the lungs via the pulmonary veins (the only veins to handle oxygenated blood).

Blood enters the right atrium of the heart which contracts, forcing it into the right ventricle. In the right ventricle the blood is driven into the pulmonary artery (the only artery to carry de-oxygenated blood) which divides into right and left carrying blood to the lungs for a fresh supply of oxygen. The left ventricle drives blood into the aorta for distribution to all parts of the body. (See also blood; lymphatic system.)

vas deferens

Also known as the ductus deferens, this is part of the spermatic cord which links the epididymis of the testes to the urethra of the male. The spermatozoa pass along this route during mating.

vasectomy

A surgical operation which involves severing the vas deferens to sterilise the male dog. Libido is not decreased by the operation but conception cannot take place. It is a less drastic operation than castration. Post-operatively the dog may not be sterile for up to three weeks.

vasoconstriction

A reduction of blood flow due to constriction of blood vessels. Sometimes drugs are given for this purpose and it can also happen naturally – in the skin during cold weather, for example, to

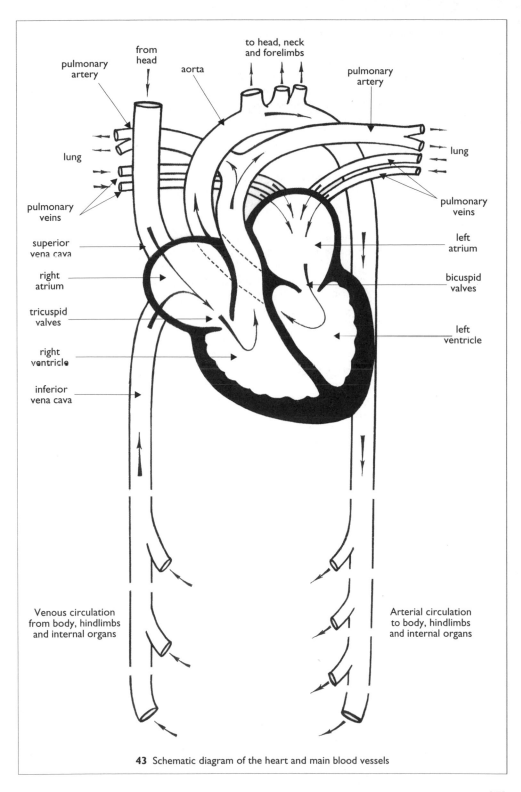

43 Schematic diagram of the heart and main blood vessels

vasoconstriction	conserve body heat, or due to extreme excitement causing a rise in blood pressure.
vasodilation	The dilation of blood vessels due either to the administration of a specific drug intended for this purpose or, for example, during inflammation where the increased blood flow which results produces heat in the inflamed area.
vasopressin	A hormone produced by the posterior lobe of the pituitary gland. It acts as an antidiuretic, is sometimes administered in severe pancreatitis to improve pancreatic microcirculation and may also be utilised as a response test in the diagnosis of diabetes.
vector	An insect or other organism which is able to transmit a disease from one host to another, usually by carrying fungal spores, living bacteria or viruses. Flies are a common example.
vegetables	Some vegetables can be of nutritional value to dogs while others are of little use. Generally, the seed vegetables such as peas and beans can be added to food, and carrots and potatoes are acceptable if thoroughly cooked. (See also diet.)
vein	A vessel of the blood vascular system. Veins generally carry deoxygenated blood back to the lungs (via the heart) for re-oxygenation. The exceptions to this rule are the pulmonary veins close to the heart which take the re-oxygenated blood from the lungs to the heart. Veins follow a similar route round the body to the arteries and the pressure in them (unlike that of the arteries) is low due to the absence of a pulse, and dependence for circulation on muscular movements of the thorax. Those veins which are furthest away from the heart mostly contain valves to prevent backflow of blood. (See also vascular system.)
vena cavae	There are two vena cavae – blood vessels supplying the heart with blood from the body on its way to the lungs for re-oxygenation. These are the superior vena cava situated at the top of the right auricle of the heart and the inferior vena cava entering the auricle from below. They both unite as they enter the heart though 'pouring' from different directions. They are major veins of the vascular system.
venepuncture	The puncture of a vein with a needle. This is usually done to obtain a sample of blood and the vein most commonly used is the radial vein of the forelimb. The fur on the area is shaved and the site swabbed with antiseptic. A sterile needle attached to a sterile syringe is pushed slowly into the vein and the blood flows into the syringe in a trickle; the syringe plunger is drawn out sucking the blood after it. When sufficient sample for laboratory testing is obtained the needle is withdrawn, the site swabbed again with antiseptic; the dog should have no ill-effects.

Any building which houses dogs should be well ventilated but without draughts. There is a wide variety of methods for ventilating kennel accommodation. One example is the provision of low inlets for fresh air with high outlets for polluted or stale air. Wall air-bricks and roof vents are alternatives, usually to supplement windows. Extractor fans also assist in the removal of stale air and these can be sited in windows at relatively low cost. Fresh air inlets should be carefully sited and, if necessary, shielded to ensure that all potential draughts are eliminated. (See also kennel.)
ventilation

The left and right ventricles form two of the four chambers of the heart. (See also heart; vascular system.)
ventricle

See anthelmintic.
vermicide

A drug which expels worms from the intestines. (See also anthelmintic; worming procedures.)
vermifuge

The vertebrae are the bones which make up the spinal column. They vary in size and shape according to region. There are five regions from skull to end of tail: neck (cervical), chest (thoracic), back (lumbar), lower back (sacral) and tail (coccygeal). There are approximately 50 vertebrae in all – 7 cervical, 13 thoracic, 7 lumbar, 3 sacral and varying numbers of coccygeal depending on length of tail but usually around 20. (See also spine.)
vertebrae

A book which is published by the Pharmaceutical Press, London WC1 on recommended dosages, use and action of drugs, vaccines, etc for veterinary use.
veterinary codex

A scheme for the recruitment, training and registration of veterinary nurses is operated by the Royal College of Veterinary Surgeons. Standards of the veterinary nursing profession are also promoted by the British Veterinary Nursing Association. Qualification takes around two years (four for a Degree course) where the student gathers a portfolio through practical and theoretical studies under supervision, continual assessment, and preliminary and final examinations. A qualified veterinary nurse will work with veterinarians in small animal practices or veterinary hospitals. A subsequent specialised course can be undertaken for equine nursing.
veterinary nursing

Veterinary nurses are important members of the veterinary team, particularly in running clinics for dental hygiene as well as for geriatric and obese small animals. They care for hospitalised animals, give advice on animal husbandry, assist the veterinarian in a variety of tasks and can carry out medical treatment or minor surgery to a pet at the direction of a veterinarian who need not necessarily be present. This does not include diagnosis or any procedure that involves entering a body cavity.

Training outside the UK can be a different process and in North America differs in various States. Overseas trained nurses seeking work in England must undergo detailed assessment of previous training and may require a further qualification or portfolio. (See Useful Addresses.)

Preliminary and final examinations are held annually under the auspices of the Royal College of Veterinary Surgeons. Trainees must be at least seventeen years of age when commencing training. (See Useful Addresses.)

villi Fine, velvety protrusions which project from the mucous lining of the small intestine. Their purpose is to absorb nutrients. Each minute villus contains a network of blood capillaries and a central lymphatic duct. Nutrients from digested food are absorbed by the villi cells, with digested proteins and carbohydrates (as amino acids and sugars respectively) passing into the capillaries for transport to the liver via the portal vein. Fats, in the form of fatty acids, are also absorbed but are carried by the lymphatic duct in the villus to arrive eventually in the bloodstream. So numerous are the villi within the small intestine that in the average-sized dog the surface area available for absorption can equal that of the floor of a small room.

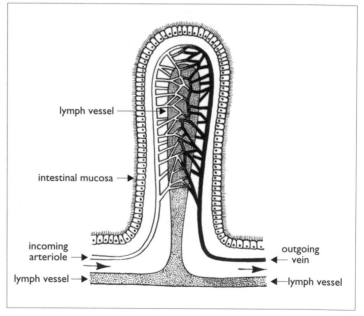

44 Section through the villus

virus An infective agent which is the smallest-known micro-organism. Much has still to be discovered about the viruses and classification of them changes frequently. Mutations and changes in characteristics are common.

Viruses vary in size but generally cannot be seen without the aid of an electron microscope. They are totally parasitic and can only reproduce in vulnerable living cells, weakening them by diverting their functions to their own needs and invading neighbouring cells as they multiply. They can be transmitted from one animal to another and are resistant to antibiotic treatment (though these drugs are sometimes prescribed to deal with secondary infections arising during the course of virus-based diseases). Their presence stimulates antibody production within the infected animal, though some viruses are often lethal. Some produce toxins, others have an affinity for mucus and some are transmitted by certain insects. Immunisation is available against some forms of virus. *virus*

Virus diseases include forms of pneumonia, influenza and other respiratory diseases, hepatitis, herpes, parvo virus, distemper, rabies and various intestinal disorders. Warts can also be caused by a virus.

A term referring to the internal organs of the body lying in large cavities, ie abdominal and thoracic viscera. **viscera**

The faculty of seeing is accomplished by the conversion of light rays passing through the eye into nerve impulses which are sent to the brain for interpretation. **vision**

Light rays pass through the cornea and the aqueous humour in the front chamber of the eye and by means of the pupil (an aperture in the iris) are concentrated on the clear lens. The lens focuses them through the vitreous humour in the posterior chamber onto the reception centre of the eye, the retina, where a sorting process is carried out and the conversion of the light rays to nerve impulses is effected. These impulses then pass to the brain along the optic nerve.

The exact visual capabilities of the dog, together with those of other animals, are difficult to determine, though it is clear that in some breeds sight is less developed (or less relied upon) than, for example, the sense of smell. It is believed that dogs are colour-blind and only see in black and white. (See also blindness; eye.)

Various vitamin deficiencies can be instrumental in causing ill-health. Vitamin supplements, however, are rarely necessary for the healthy dog and care should be taken with their use when a dog is sick since over-dosage can in some cases be just as harmful as a deficiency. A sound diet contains all that is needed in vitamin nutrition under normal circumstances. (See also diet; nutrition.) **vitamin deficiency**

See nutrition. **vitamins**

The jelly-like refracting medium which fills the posterior chamber of the eye between the lens and the retina. It assists in focusing light rays onto the retina and also keeps the retina in position. If through injury it leaks from the eye the retina loses its position and falls forward so that sight is impaired. **vitreous humour**

The vocal folds or cords are situated in the larynx and are formed by the mucous membrane of the larynx covering the vocal ligaments which are attached to slightly separated cartilages. The space **vocal folds**

vocal folds	between the folds and the cartilage is subject to the varying force of air passing through the larynx and the folds vibrate to produce a sound. (See also larynx; voice.)
voice	Sound produced by mechanisms in the larynx; the sound variation and pitch can be altered at will by muscular action on the larynx. A dog's voice is used to express a wide range of emotions and to communicate. It is used in greeting, excitement, happiness, fear and pain. It is used as a warning, as a specifically pitched bark or growl, for example. An owner can tell much from a dog's vocal expression and learns the sounds which are characteristic only of the one dog. Each dog is an individual and each voice is perceptibly different from that of another dog. (See also bark; howl.)
vomiting	Ejection of the stomach contents through the mouth. It is a symptom of various disorders from gastritis to obstruction and repeated vomiting should always be taken seriously. A veterinarian should be consulted since early diagnosis and correct treatment are important to counteract the dangerous dehydration which results. The symptom is frequently accompanied by diarrhoea (which increases the rate of dehydration), particularly in intestinal disorders or stress-related conditions. Vomiting is a complex muscular action involving muscles of abdomen, chest and larynx. Prior to vomiting a dog appears restless and uneasy, crouching low and usually seeking a place to hide. The action commences with visible contractions, or heaving, of abdominal muscles and after a few moments either stomach contents or a frothy vomit are ejected. If the act is not repeated the dog may merely have overeaten or taken something disagreeable but it should be carefully watched for other symptoms and/or more vomiting. Dogs can make themselves vomit by eating couch grass; however, eating grass does not necessarily produce vomiting and grass is sometimes taken for what appears to be medicinal purposes.
von Willebrand's disease	A hereditary blood disease in which there is a deficiency of Factor VIII, one of the components of the blood-clotting mechanism. The disease produces haemorrhage internally and subcutaneously in varying degrees of severity. It may occur after surgery and is treated by the infusion of plasma or blood containing concentrates of the missing factor. Some German shepherd strains are notably vulnerable.
vulva	The external lips of the genitalia of the bitch.

A sick dog should be kept warm as often body heat is burned up by the illness. In first aid (except in cases of heat stroke), particularly following accidents, keeping the patient warm and quiet is frequently beneficial; and warmth and draught-free fresh air make a good environmental combination for convalescent dogs. Puppies especially require warmth and a temperature of 21° to 24°C (70° to 75°F) is advisable around the whelping box.

Infrared lamps are a useful source of warmth when needed, such as after whelping, but are best suspended over the bed, never lower or closer than 75cm (30in) from the dog. Hot-water bottles should be thoroughly wrapped and out of contact with the dog. Skin can easily be scorched quite seriously by uncovered hot-water bottles and often the scorching remains undetected under the dog's coat until it worsens.

warmth

Small tumours which are caused by a virus. They can appear virtually anywhere on the dog's anatomy though they are perhaps most frequently found on the face or head. They do not usually continue to increase in size and often disappear of their own accord. They may cause little trouble unless they occur, for example, on an eyelid or other mobile or exposed part of the skin.

Some warts, affecting the mucous membrane lining of the mouth, appear in a disease known as oral papillomatosis, found most frequently in young rather than old dogs. These warts resemble small, pinkish-white cauliflowers and often disappear in two or three months without recurrence. Treatment may, however, be required as they have a tendency to ulcerate and can also be transmitted to other dogs. Sometimes a wart vaccine can be administered if the condition is serious or extensive.

warts

Gradual and substantial loss of weight. Wasting can be due to starvation or neglected diet or to disease such as tuberculosis, liver disease, chronic infection, etc. Any loss of weight which is noticeable should be referred to a veterinarian without delay. (See also atrophy.)

wasting

Second only to oxygen as the most essential element of life. A dog should always have access to clean, cool water which should be changed regularly to ensure freshness. If dry foods are offered, water will be taken more frequently. The quantity which a dog drinks in any one period depends on such factors as climate, temperature, daily activities, diet, etc. (See also diet; feeding; nutrition; thirst.)

water

Generally, if a dog is sick it is likely to be weak. If there are no apparent symptoms other than weakness, observe the dog carefully and make the following checks: does weakness appear at any specific time, ie after meals, during or after exercise; is appetite less or more than usual; is there any coughing or other respiratory change;

weakness

weakness

has the dog vomited recently; is there any diarrhoea; is the dog nervous, excited or apathetic; is the weakness general or does it only occur at intervals?

The dog should be examined by a veterinarian who will probably arrange for laboratory tests to eliminate or confirm diagnosis. It may be due, for example, to a heart condition, hypoglycaemia, a neuro-muscular disease, malnutrition or a malfunctioning adrenal gland.

weaning

Puppies' conversion from their dam's milk to nutrition from an outside source. The puppy can begin the weaning process at about three to four weeks of age when it is offered soft, wet foods which it soon learns to lap from a saucer or dish. Its digestive system takes a little time to become used to these changes and the dam's milk continues to be a major source of nutrition for the puppy until it is around five to six weeks of age; then more solid food, given four times a day, can be introduced to its diet. (See also diet; nutrition; puppies, care of.)

weight loss

See wasting.

Weil's disease

See leptospirosis.

whelping

The birth of puppies. Preparations for whelping include provision of a quiet, comfortable, draught-free place where the bitch can retire to have her puppies without disturbance. She may have them in her own basket if there is room or she may find her own place if not encouraged to make use of the bed provided for her. Some breeders make 'whelping boxes' with high sides to keep out the draughts and open fronts for ease of access. Specially-made heating pads can be fitted or infrared lamps suspended (more than 75cm (30in) above) to keep the family warm in chilly weather. The environmental temperature should, in any case, be 24° to 30°C (75° to 85°F) when the pups are born. (This can be reduced gradually to between 21° and 24°C (70° and 75°F) when the pups are about six days old.)

The bitch has a gestation period of about sixty-three days and around the fortieth day the quality of her diet should have been improved (see below). She should also have been checked over by a veterinarian so that she is in optimum condition for the delivery.

About one or two days prior to delivery her temperature will be lowered to below 38°C (100°F). As she comes close to delivery, labour pains begin with slight straining increasing to about three or four strains every three minutes or so. The water bag, about the size of a squash ball, appears outside the vagina and breaks to release the water which has cushioned the puppies. There will be much licking and cleaning up by the bitch and the first puppy should appear head first soon afterwards. If it has not done so within about an hour and a half a veterinarian should be contacted as there may be complications.

Most births happen quite naturally and while the bitch's owner or another close friend should be in attendance, encouraging her

Whelping Calendar   S – Served   W – Whelp

S Jan.	W Mar.	S Feb.	W Apr.	S Mar.	W May	S Apr.	W June	S May	W July	S June	W Aug.	S July	W Sep.	S Aug.	W Oct.	S Sep.	W Nov.	S Oct.	W Dec.	S Nov.	W Jan.	S Dec.	W Feb.
1	5	1	5	1	3	1	3	1	3	1	3	1	2	1	3	1	3	1	3	1	3	1	2
2	6	2	6	2	4	2	4	2	4	2	4	2	3	2	4	2	4	2	4	2	4	2	3
3	7	3	7	3	5	3	5	3	5	3	5	3	4	3	5	3	5	3	5	3	5	3	4
4	8	4	8	4	6	4	6	4	6	4	6	4	5	4	6	4	6	4	6	4	6	4	5
5	9	5	9	5	7	5	7	5	7	5	7	5	6	5	7	5	7	5	7	5	7	5	6
6	10	6	10	6	8	6	8	6	8	6	8	6	7	6	8	6	8	6	8	6	8	6	7
7	11	7	11	7	9	7	9	7	9	7	9	7	8	7	9	7	9	7	9	7	9	7	8
8	12	8	12	8	10	8	10	8	10	8	10	8	9	8	10	8	10	8	10	8	10	8	9
9	13	9	13	9	11	9	11	9	11	9	11	9	10	9	11	9	11	9	11	9	11	9	10
10	14	10	14	10	12	10	12	10	12	10	12	10	11	10	12	10	12	10	12	10	12	10	11
11	15	11	15	11	13	11	13	11	13	11	13	11	12	11	13	11	13	11	13	11	13	11	12
12	16	12	16	12	14	12	14	12	14	12	14	12	13	12	14	12	14	12	14	12	14	12	13
13	17	13	17	13	15	13	15	13	15	13	15	13	14	13	15	13	15	13	15	13	15	13	14
14	18	14	18	14	16	14	16	14	16	14	16	14	15	14	16	14	16	14	16	14	16	14	15
15	19	15	19	15	17	15	17	15	17	15	17	15	16	15	17	15	17	15	17	15	17	15	16
16	20	16	20	16	18	16	18	16	18	16	18	16	17	16	18	16	18	16	18	16	18	16	17
17	21	17	21	17	19	17	19	17	19	17	19	17	18	17	19	17	19	17	19	17	19	17	18
18	22	18	22	18	20	18	20	18	20	18	20	18	19	18	20	18	20	18	20	18	20	18	19
19	23	19	23	19	21	19	21	19	21	19	21	19	20	19	21	19	21	19	21	19	21	19	20
20	24	20	24	20	22	20	22	20	22	20	22	20	21	20	22	20	22	20	22	20	22	20	21
21	25	21	25	21	23	21	23	21	23	21	23	21	22	21	23	21	23	21	23	21	23	21	22
22	26	22	26	22	24	22	24	22	24	22	24	22	23	22	24	22	24	22	24	22	24	22	23
23	27	23	27	23	25	23	25	23	25	23	25	23	24	23	25	23	25	23	25	23	25	23	24
24	28	24	28	24	26	24	26	24	26	24	26	24	25	24	26	24	26	24	26	24	26	24	25
25	29	25	29	25	27	25	27	25	27	25	27	25	26	25	27	25	27	25	27	25	27	25	26
26	30	26	30	26	28	26	28	26	28	26	28	26	27	26	28	26	28	26	28	26	28	26	27
27	31	27	1	27	29	27	29	27	29	27	29	27	28	27	29	27	29	27	29	27	29	27	28
28	1	28	2	28	30	28	30	28	30	28	30	28	29	28	30	28	30	28	30	28	30	28	1
29	2	29	3	29	31	29	1	29	31	29	31	29	30	29	31	29	1	29	31	29	31	29	2
30	3			30	1	30	2	30	1	30	1	30	1	30	1	30	2	30	1	30	1	30	3
31	4			31	2			31	2			31	2	31	2			31	2			31	4
	Apr.		May		June		July		Aug.		Sep.		Oct.		Nov.		Dec.		Jan.		Feb.		Mar.

45 Whelping calendar

with gentle, reassuring words and an occasional stroke of the abdomen to help contractions if required, she will usually carry out the entire whelping without any other assistance. She certainly does not want a procession of people (or other dogs) peering at her to see how she is doing. She needs peace and quiet.

The puppy will arrive in a membrane or bag, gently protruding from the vulva and being eased into the world by contractions of the bitch's abdominal muscles. The puppy is born blind with its umbilical cord attached to the placenta and the bitch will bite through both membrane and cord to free it. She then sets about nuzzling and licking her offspring to stimulate its first intake of breath and to clean it up. If she is very young and inexperienced she may neglect this operation and the person in attendance must break the membrane to allow the pup to breathe and cut the cord (after tying a clean piece of cotton tape tightly round the cord about two inches from the pup's abdomen and cutting on the far side). If artificial inflation of the lungs becomes necessary it can usually be achieved with the help of a cardboard toilet roll tube placed over the pup's muzzle and gently blown into. The pup should also be rotated clockwise.

The placenta is expelled after the puppy, usually during the next contraction. A mental note should be made of its arrival as there should be one placenta passed for each pup; if one is missing it has been retained and unless an injection is given later by the veterinarian infection may occur (see below). The bitch may eat the placenta and should not be discouraged from doing so. It is thought that the placenta is not only nutritious but that it may also contain hormones, which helps to clear the uterus.

There may be short or lengthy intervals between the birth of each pup and the bitch needs to rest and sleep during them. Generally, though, there is about fifteen to twenty minutes between. After whelping is complete the bitch should be encouraged to drink a little milk with a teaspoonful or so of honey or glucose mixed in and then left with her family to rest. No strangers should be allowed near her family for at least two days – longer if she shows signs of resentment. In all contact with bitch and pups the utmost cleanliness must always be observed.

A veterinarian should examine the bitch after whelping and a long-acting antibiotic, such as ampicillin, and oxytocin may be given by injection to prevent infection. Many bitches retain uterine debris so this procedure is of importance.

The bitch has had a substantial shock to her system through whelping and attention should be given to building her up when the puppies have been born. A nutritious diet is needed (see below).

Puppies vary considerably in birth weight, depending on breed. Weights at birth range broadly from about 100g (3½oz) for a toy poodle and about 250g (9oz) for a medium-sized breed such as a fox terrier, up to around 600g (1¼lb) for a St Bernard and 700g (1½lb) for a great dane.

If puppies are born prematurely, if there is a particularly large litter or if the bitch has mastitis, for example, it may be necessary to hand feed the pups. Cow's milk can be used with an egg yolk and a drop or two of cod-liver oil added to compensate. The pups, if premature, can be fed with the aid of a small-diameter rubber tube and syringe. A measured amount of milk mixture is drawn into the syringe and the tube attached to the nozzle. The other end of the tube is inserted gently into the throat of the puppy from where it will be swallowed. It is essential that it is swallowed or the tube may inadvertently enter the trachea and the lungs fill with liquid, killing the pup. Observe the disappearance of the tube which can be related to the length of the puppy's neck to see just how far it is situated down the oesophagus. When in place gently depress the plunger of the syringe, expelling the warm liquid down the tube and slowly withdraw the tube when finished. About 1 to 2ml should be given at each feed (repeated every hour) to a pup weighing from 300 to 700g (10½oz to 1½1b). Afterwards the pup must be encouraged to urinate and defecate by gentle massage of the vulva or anus with a pad of warm lint or cotton wool.

Eventually the puppies may be encouraged to suck from the teat of a baby's feeding bottle which eliminates the need for syringe and tubing and saves both time and trouble. (See also breeding; puppies, care of.)

Whelping bitches – a typical dietary routine

1 Around the fortieth day of gestation (about twenty-three days before whelping) start giving extra milk, high quality food, vitamin A and D supplements, together with favourite meals.
2 Immediately after whelping is complete and the bitch has cleaned up, offer a drink of milk and water with a tablespoonful or two of glucose or honey added.
3 For at least twenty-four hours after whelping feed a liquid diet including, for example, beef broth, or a mixture of milk, water and honey or glucose. Feed about five times in the twenty-four hour period.
4 If temperature is normal on the second day, alternate the liquid diet with light foods such as scrambled egg and brown bread, boiled bone-free fish or lightly cooked minced beef.
5 Feed meals including fresh raw (good quality) beef from a butcher. This, with regular drinks of cold water, will help the milk supply and give strength. Eggs are a good supplement (raw or scrambled).
6 Reduce fluid in meals after the pups are weaned and reinforce the diet of the bitch with fresh meat, eggs, a good quality dog biscuit meal (brown bread or cereals are alternatives to biscuit meal), etc.

whiskers Stiff tactile hairs which protrude from the dog's muzzle. They are arranged roughly in four rows along the lips. They are associated with the sense of touch and provide the dog with information concerning, for example, the width of an entrance in relation to its head.

white cell	See leucocyte.
worming procedures	Puppies should be wormed at about three to four weeks of age, and again at two months and three months. Thereafter worming should be carried out at four to six monthly intervals. Watch the dog's faeces (and the hair around the anus where worm traces can be seen) for any signs of internal parasites so that worming can be done quickly. Proprietary worming tablets are available with dosage according to weight of dog marked on the packaging. These are normally quite palatable and can be easily fed by hand or mixed with the dog's food. While some tablets are active collectively against roundworms and hookworms, a specific medicament will generally be needed to eliminate tapeworms. If in doubt contact a veterinarian who will doubtless have the anthelmintics in stock.
Bitches should be dosed before mating and after whelping. Sick dogs should not be dosed without clearance from a veterinarian. (See also anthelmintics; parasites.)
worms	See parasites.
worry	See stress.
wounds	These may be caused by many different means including dog fights, road accidents, walking on broken glass, falls, bites, attacks by other creatures and tearing, for example, on barbed wire or nails. Wounds can be extensive, deep and penetrating or small and superficial. They all have one common aspect – they can all be dangerous and should all be taken seriously. Sometimes small untreated wounds can be as lethal as wide gashes and a puncture may be deep enough to damage an internal organ and cause additional complications. Most wounds require urgent treatment, many need the professional experience of a veterinarian to insert sutures, check for internal damage, set bone fractures which are often associated with a wound and to administer special drugs such as antibiotics to combat (and forestall) any infection.
Anticipating and preventing infection is of vital importance in the treatment of all wounds. Maximum cleanliness should be observed in cleaning wounds during first aid and in the promotion of healing and recovery. Any haemorrhage must also be arrested and treated and, since most wounded dogs can suffer shock, this too requires urgent veterinary attention. While some wounds do not need bandaging, others, such as those affecting the feet, will require protection during the healing process and to keep out dirt and infection. Wounds left for some six hours without proper treatment will be invaded by bacteria and by twelve hours infection will be substantial.
Small, superficial wounds which do not need suturing should be carefully cleansed with a warm saline solution (see entry) after surrounding hair has been gently clipped away. (To ensure that no cut hairs fall into the wound cover it temporarily with gauze soaked in warm water while clipping.) Do not put disinfectant or iodine

into a wound. Do check twice a day to see that the wound is pink and clean and not suppurating or becoming inflamed in and around the injured area. Chest or abdominal wounds may require the application of a warm saline-soaked bandage as a support during first aid.

In the surgery, wounds may be washed with a local anaesthetic solution and pain-relieving drugs given to make the patient comfortable prior to examination. After irrigation to remove debris and other contaminants, antibiotics or sulpha drugs will be administered and dressings may be applied to protect, absorb or compress (to prevent haematomas). Drainage tubes may be inserted if necessary and swabs taken for culture of bacteria in the laboratory and sensitivity testing.

Wounds may involve punctures, lacerations (tears), incisions (cuts) or abrasions. Puncture wounds which can, for example, be caused by savage bites, can produce extensive underlying injury and may need to be opened under a general anaesthetic in order to conduct a thorough examination. They are also very easily infected. (See also accidents; bandage; 'Elizabethan' collar; haemorrhage; shock; tourniquet.)

wounds

xiphoid	Sword-shaped. The xiphoid process is the last bone segment in the sternum which is extended by the xiphoid cartilage.
x-ray	See radiography.
yawning	A manifestation of tiredness, boredom or embarrassment and also occurs often on waking up. While in some species yawning is recognised as a low intensity threat, this is not so of dogs.
	Yawning can also be part of an amicable social behaviour pattern and some pack dogs collectively participate in ritualised yawning on emerging from rest. A dog will sometimes wag its tail and yawn simultaneously in a pleased greeting as it lazily emerges from sleep and sees a friendly face. Human yawning also appears to be as contagious to canine members of a family as it is to other humans.
zinc	See nutrition.
zoonoses	Diseases which are communicable between animal and man. They include actinomycosis, hydatid, leptospirosis, rabies, ringworm, toxocariasis, toxoplasmosis, tuberculosis (see under each entry) and parasitic worms such as tapeworms and some species of roundworm. (See also parasites.)
zygomatic arch	This is a heavy bridge of bone projecting forward along the face in front of the ear. It affords protection for the eye, and provides anchorage for facial muscles and articulation for the mandible.
zygote	The cell resulting from fertilisation of the ovum by a sperm. This subsequently grows by division.

USEFUL ADDRESSES

American Boarding Kennels Association, 4575 Galley Road, Suite 400A, Colorado Springs, CO 80915, USA. Telephone (719) 591 1113

American College of Veterinary Behavior, Dr Bonnie Beaver (President), Department of Animal Medicine and Surgery, CVM, Texas A&M University, College Station TX 77843, USA. Telephone (409) 845 2351, fax (409) 845 6978

American Holistic Veterinary Medical Association, 2214 Old Emmorton Road, Bel Air, MD 21014, USA. Telephone (410) 569 0795, fax (410) 569 2346

American Humane Association, 63 Inverness Drive East, Englewood, CO 80112, USA. Telephone (303) 792 9900, fax (303) 793 5333

American Kennel Club, 260 Madison Avenue, New York, NY 10016, USA (Registration of American pedigree dogs, information on shows, breeds, standards and activities in the USA. The AKC also has a useful library. Telephone (212) 696 8245, fax (212) 696 8281, e-mail library@akc.org

Battersea Dogs' Home, 4 Battersea Park Road, London SW8 4AA, UK. Telephone 020 7622 3626, fax 020 7622 6451, website www.dogshome.org

The Blue Cross, Shilton Road, Burford, Oxfordshire OX18 4PF, UK. Telephone 01993 822651, fax 01993 823083, website www.bluecross.co.uk

British Small Animal Veterinary Association (BSAVA), Woodrow House, 1 Telford Way, Waterwells Business Park, Quedgeley, Gloucestershire GL2 4AB, UK. Telephone 01452 726700, fax 01452 726701, website www.bsava.com

British Veterinary Nursing Association, Level 15, Terminus House, Terminus Street, Harlow, Essex CM20 1XA, UK. Telephone 01279 450567, fax 01279 420866, e-mail bvna@bvna.co.uk

Department for Environment, Food and Rural Affairs (DEFRA), 1a Page Street, London SW1, UK. Telephone 0207 904 6222, fax 020 7904 6834, website www.defra.gsi.gov.uk

International Association for Veterinary Homeopathy, c/o Dr Andreas Schmidt, General Secretary, Sonnhaldenstr. 18, CH-8370 Sirnach, Switzerland. Telephone (73) 26 14 24, fax (73) 26 58 14. In USA, Susan G Wynn DVM, National Secretary, e-mail swynn@emory.edu

International Veterinary Acupuncture Society, PO Box 1478, Longmont, CO 80502 1478, USA. Telephone (303) 682 1167, fax (303) 682 1168

The Kennel Club, 1–5 Clarges Street, Piccadilly, London W1J 8AB, UK. Telephone 0870 6066750, fax 020 7518 1058, e-mail info@the-kennel-club.org.uk, website www.the-kennel-club.org.uk

NCDL (National Canine Defence League), 17 Wakley Street, London EC1V 7RQ, UK. Telephone 020 7837 0006, fax 020 7833 2701, website www.ncdl.org.uk

PDSA (People's Dispensary for Sick Animals), Whitechapel Way, Priorslee, Telford, Shropshire TF2 9PQ, UK. Telephone 0800 917 2509, website www.pdsa.org.uk

Pet Travel Scheme (PETS), DEFRA, Area 201, La Page Street, London SW1P 4PQ, UK. Telephone 0870 2411710, fax 020 7904 6834, e-mail pets.helpline@defra.gsi.gov.uk

Royal College of Veterinary Surgeons, Belgravia House, 62–64 Horseferry Road, London SW1P 2AF, UK. Telephone 020 7222 2001, fax 020 7222 2004, website www.rcvs.org.uk

RSPCA (Royal Society for the Prevention of Cruelty to Animals), Wilberforce Way, Southwater, Horsham, West Sussex RH13 9RS, UK. Telephone 0870 010 1181, fax 0870 753 0048, website www.rspca.org.uk

Universities' Federation for Animal Welfare (UFAW), The Old School, Brewhouse Hill, Wheathampstead, Hertfordshire AL4 8AN, UK. Telephone 01582 831818, fax 01582 831414, e-mail ufaw@ufaw.org.uk, website ufaw.org.uk

FURTHER READING

Black's Veterinary Dictionary (A & C Black)

Canine Behaviour, Bonnie V Beaver (W B Saunders, USA)

Canine Clinical Parasitology, J R Georgi & M B Georgi (Lea & Febiger, USA)

Clinical Behavioral Medicine for Small Animals, Karen Overall (Mosby, USA)

Clinical Nutrition of the Dog and Cat, J W Simpson, R S Anderson, P J Markwell (Blackwell Scientific Publications)

Common Diseases of Companion Animals, Alleice Summers (Mosby, USA)

Complementary and Alternative Veterinary Medicine – Principles and Practice, ed Allen M Schoen and Susan G Wynn (Mosby, USA)

Dictionary of Veterinary Nursing, Lane & Guthrie (Butterworth Heinemann)

Dog & Cat Nutrition, ed A T B Edney (Pergamon Press, 1982)

Handbook of Veterinary Procedures and Emergency Treatment, Kirk & Bistner (W B Saunders, USA)

Infectious Disease of the Dog and Cat 2nd edition, Greene (Saunders & Co, 1998)

Manual of Companion Animal Nutrition & Feeding, ed Noel Kelly & Josephine Wills (BSAVA)

Manual of Veterinary Care, ed G Simpson (BSAVA)

Merck Veterinary Manual (Merck & Company, USA)

Miller's Anatomy of the Dog, Evans & Christensen (W B Saunders, USA)

Practical Animal Handling, A Edney (Pergamon Press)

Textbook of Small Animal Medicine, ed John Dunn (W B Saunders, USA)

The Book of the Bitch, J M Evans & Kay White (Henston)

Veterinary Nursing (formerly *Jones Animal Nursing*), ed D R Lane & B Cooper (Pergamon Press)